HIGHROAD GUIDE
—— TO THE ——
NORTH CAROLINA
MOUNTAINS

BY LYNDA McDANIEL

LONGSTREET
ATLANTA, GEORGIA

Published by
LONGSTREET PRESS, INC.
a subsidiary of Cox Newspapers,
a subsidiary of Cox Enterprises, Inc.
2140 Newmarket Parkway
Suite 122
Marietta, Georgia 30067

Printed by RR Donnelley & Sons, Harrisonburg, VA

1st printing 1998

Library of Congress Catalog Number 97-76535

ISBN: 1-56352-463-5

Book editing, design, and cartography
by Lenz Design & Communications, Inc., Decatur, Georgia

Cover illustration by Granville Perkins, *Picturesque America*, 1872

Cover design by Richard J. Lenz, Decatur, Georgia

Illustrations by Danny Woodard, Loganville, Georgia

Photos courtesy of the North Carolina Department of Tourism

For a long time my chief interest was not in human neighbors, but in the mountains themselves—in that mysterious beckoning hinterland which rose right back of my chimney and spread upward, outward, almost to three cardinal points of the compass, mile after mile, hour after hour of lusty climbing—an Eden still unpeopled and unspoiled.

—Horace Kephart

Contents

North Carolina

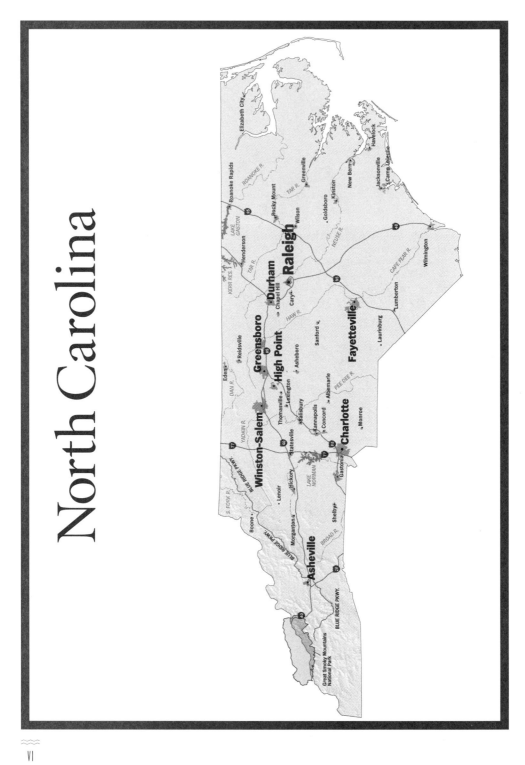

FIG #	MAP NAME	PAGE #

How Your Highroad Guide Is Organized

The Highroad Guide to North Carolina *is organized into seven different sections.*

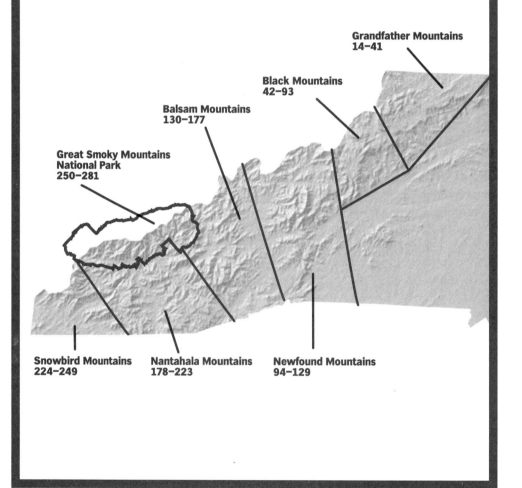

Grandfather Mountains
14–41

Black Mountains
42–93

Balsam Mountains
130–177

Great Smoky Mountains
National Park
250–281

Snowbird Mountains
224–249

Nantahala Mountains
178–223

Newfound Mountains
94–129

How to Use
Your Highroad Guide

The *Highroad Guide to the North Carolina Mountains* includes a wealth of detailed information about the best of what the North Carolina mountains have to offer, including hiking, camping, fishing, canoeing, mountain biking, and horseback riding. The *Highroad Guide* also presents information on the natural history of the mountains, plus interesting facts about North Carolina's flora and fauna, giving the reader a starting point to learn more about what makes the mountains so special.

This book is divided into six major sections using North Carolina's main mountain ranges, plus two additional sections. One is an introduction to the natural history of the mountains and the other details long trails. North Carolina's major mountain ranges include the Grandfather, Black, Newfound, Balsam, Nantahala, Snowbird, and Great Smoky mountains.

The maps in the book are keyed by figure number and referenced in the text. These maps are intended to help orient both the casual and expert mountains enthusiast. Below is a legend to explain symbols used on the maps. Remember, hiking trails frequently change as they fall into disuse or new trails are created. Serious hikers may want to purchase additional maps from the US Geological Service before they set out on a long hike. Sources are listed on the maps, in the text, and in the appendix.

A word of caution: the mountains can be dangerous. Weather can change suddenly, rocks can be slippery, and wild animals can act in unexpected ways. Use common sense when in the mountains so all your memories will be happy ones.

Legend

Amphitheater	Bathroom	Misc. Special Areas
Parking	Wheelchair Accessible	Physiographic Region/ Misc. Boundary
Telephone	First Aid Station	Appalachian Trail
Information	Picnic Shelter	Regular Trail
Picnicking	Horse Trail	State Boundary
Dumping Station	Horse Stable	
Swimming	Shower	Town or City
Fishing	Biking	11 Primary State Road
Interpretive Trail	Comfort/Rest Station	239 Secondary State Road
Camping	Park Boundary	1396 Forest Road

Preface

If, like those amphibians so long ago, we emerged from the sea and traveled west across North Carolina, we would find all along the way remnants of its ancient mountains, though they lie hundreds of miles to the west. Sand and pebbles and stone eroded thousands of years ago have been carried down the steep mountain slopes by water and wind racing toward the sea, covering the soft Coastal Plain and the wide Piedmont province.

Not until the town of Hickory do we first catch sight of these mountains. Just around a curve in the road, they suddenly reshape the horizon and, for a moment, make our breath catch. They are beautiful, majestic, glorious, and for the lucky ones, home. Magically, once they are in sight, we seem to coast toward them, even though the journey courses uphill the rest of the way.

The mountains of North Carolina are a complex compilation, no easy lines of parallel ridges or ranges. Geographers help us understand the lay of this up-and-down land, while geologists teach us distinctions between the myriad rocks and formations. Both disciplines refer to this region as part of the Blue Ridge province, but for the purposes of our book, we created divisions based on geographic considerations: the way the mountains lie, how people travel within these natural boundaries, and where sites and communities are clustered. Each section is named for a range dominant within its boundaries, whether because, as in the Black Mountains section, those mountains tower above the rest, or, as in the Snowbird Mountains section, because that name has become synonymous with the area.

Finally, as much as this book is about geology, flora, and fauna—the sciences—it is also about the experience of living and visiting here, about appreciating and looking at all the wonderful things found in the North Carolina mountains. Which is, in part, why our hearts do funny turns when we see them on the horizon. We know that within their ancient boundaries flourishes one of the most diverse ecosystems in the United States, resplendent with exquisite flowers, towering old growth trees, clear waters home to abundant fish and amphibians, a lush understory harboring mammals and reptiles, and a dense canopy offering shelter to migrating and resident birds. This book is your introduction and invitation to explore and appreciate, conserve and enjoy these wonders in the mountains of North Carolina.

—Lynda McDaniel

Acknowledgments

A book of this scope requires the help of many people and resources. I am particularly grateful for the research and editorial assistance of Paige Blomgren, Bob Gale, Carrie A. A. Frye, Peter Gregutt, Clare Hanrahan, and Ashley Felkel. My thanks, too, go out to Sylvia Mann, Tracey Turner, J. P. McCann, Laura Elliott, Glenn Taylor, Richard Bruce, Kevin Moorhead, Jerry West, Ernest Klatt, and Ina Parr and her coworkers at the Blue Ridge Parkway for their assistance. I am indebted to Dr. Hal Mahan, who wrote the introduction, and his wife, Laura, for their guidance and friendship. To ensure accuracy, I called on the expertise of several people, especially Dr. J. W. Miller, head of environmental sciences at the University of North Carolina at Asheville. Bob and Gussie Gray and Al Sommerville, volunteers with the Blue Ridge Parkway; Nancy Gray at the Great Smoky Mountains National Park; Burt Kornegay of Slickrock Expeditions; and Dwayne Stutzman, Mountain Region trails specialist, also served as patient and careful proofers. A special thanks to the staff at Asheville's Pack Memorial Library, especially those working the North Carolina Desk, where they dig and search until they find just the right fact, map, or article. I also want to express my gratitude for the fine, historic work of the WPA and the CCC, without whom

The North Carolina mountains have many beautiful features, including many spectacular waterfalls. Above, Linville Falls in Linville Gorge in the Black Mountains.

we would not have so many wonderful places to write about. Finally, there are many friends who loaned books and offered support: Glenda and Phillip Herman, Virginia McCullough, Nancy Byer, and, as always, Don McNair.

North Carolina Physiographic Regions

North Carolina has three distinct physiographic regions.

Coastal Plain

Piedmont

Blue Ridge

The Natural History of the North Carolina Mountains

By Dr. Hal Mahan, Adjunct Professor of Biology, University of North Carolina at Asheville

The overriding influence on the natural history of the southern Appalachians is its long and complex geological past. Estimated to be 500 million years old, these are some of the oldest mountains in the world. They are ten times older than the Rockies, Sierras, and the Andes. Moreover, the basement rock here is more than 1 billion years old. Written within the formations comprising our mountains is a history of geologic events that indicates an astonishing series of continents clashing and splitting apart, of major periods of mountain building and erosion, and the creation and subsequent filling-in of valleys.

[*Above*: The Blue Ridge mountains on a frosty morning]

1

Geologic Time Scale

Era	System & Period	Series & Epoch	Some Distinctive Features	Years Before Present
CENOZOIC	**Quaternary**	Recent	Modern man.	11,000
		Pleistocene	Early man; northern glaciation.	1/2 to 2 million
	Tertiary	Pliocene	Large carnivores.	13 ± 1 million
		Miocene	First abundant grazing mammals.	25 ± 1 million
		Oligocene	Large running mammals.	36 ± 2 million
		Eocene	Many modern types of mammals.	58 ± 2 million
		Paleocene	First placental mammals.	63 ± 2 million
MESOZOIC	**Cretaceous**		First flowering plants; climax of dinosaurs and ammonites, followed by Cretaceous-Tertiary extinction.	135 ± 5 million
	Jurassic		First birds, first mammals; dinosaurs and ammonites abundant.	181 ± 5 million
	Triassic		First dinosaurs. Abundant cycads and conifers.	230 ± 10 million
PALEOZOIC	**Permian**		Extinction of most kinds of marine animals, including trilobites. Southern glaciation.	280 ± 10 million
	Carboniferous	Pennsylvanian	Great coal forests, conifers. First reptiles.	310 ± 10 million
		Mississippian	Sharks and amphibians abundant. Large and numerous scale trees and seed ferns.	345 ± 10 million
	Devonian		First amphibians and ammonites; Fishes abundant.	405 ± 10 million
	Silurian		First terrestrial plants and animals.	425 ± 10 million
	Ordovician		First fishes; invertebrates dominant.	500 ± 10 million
	Cambrian		First abundant record of marine life; trilobites dominant.	600 ± 50 million
	Precambrian		Fossils extremely rare, consisting of primitive aquatic plants. Evidence of glaciation. Oldest dated algae, over 2,600 million years; oldest dated meteorites 4,500 million years.	

These mountain-building events took place between 500 and 250 million years ago [Fig. 2A]. Most modern geologists believe that parts of the continent then made of Europe and Africa collided with the east coast of the North American continent, and then separated from it, two different times. When the two continents separated the second time, the Atlantic Ocean was formed.

The second collision, approximately 290 million years ago (during the Permian period), was the event that produced the beginning of today's mountain topography. It was this collision, lasting for another 50 million years, that caused faulting and folding, resulting in an upheaval of mountainous terrain from Maine to Georgia. Here in the southern Appalachians this terrain has the appearance of accordionlike folds that parallel each other in a southwest to northeast direction for hundreds of miles. Millions of years of erosion have produced the soft peaks and rounded hills that we see today.

Interestingly, when the continents collided, older rock material was shoved up and over younger material. These older surface rocks are primarily composed of layered metamorphic rocks (compact and crystalline rock created by pressure, heat, and water) called gneiss and schist. These rocks were formed from the compression of other rocks, such as granite, basalt, and sandstone.

The southern Appalachians contain great mineral wealth. Rocks are made of minerals, and nowhere on this continent is there a greater variety of minerals, including many of great economic value such as mica and feldspar. Mineralogists who have studied the southern Appalachians have identified more than 300 different minerals there, including precious metals such as gold and silver, as well as garnets, sapphires, rubies, and emeralds. The first mineral to be mined, though, was mica. In earlier times, large sheets of it were used in stoves and as window coverings.

The Blue Ridge Province

All of the mountainous terrain of North Carolina lies within a physiographic zone that geologists describe as the Blue Ridge province—a mountainous range approximately 200 miles long by 15 to 50 miles wide in North Carolina. These mountains include 43 peaks that exceed 6,000 feet in elevation and with 82 peaks between 5,000 and 6,000 feet. To the west the Great Smoky Mountains [Fig. 43] make up the most massive peaks, mostly over 6,000 feet high. To the east the Black Mountains [Fig. 10] have at least 12 peaks over 6,000 feet in elevation, including eastern North America's highest peak, Mount Mitchell [Fig. 17] at 6,684 feet above sea level. Within this physiographic region, too, are the Pisgah Mountains [Fig. 26], the Newfound Mountains [Fig. 18], the Balsams [Fig. 22], the Cowee Mountains [Fig. 32], the Nantahalas [Fig. 29], and the Snowbirds [Fig. 37], and the Valley River Mountains [Fig. 32]. The mountains occur in a region of the state commonly referred to as Western North Carolina.

The climate of the Blue Ridge belt varies with elevation. The prevailing winds are from the northwest, and as one travels upward in elevation on the windward sides, the temperature, in general, decreases at 5.5 degrees Fahrenheit per 1,000 feet up to 4,000 feet. Above 4,000 feet, the temperature decreases 3.2 degrees Fahrenheit per 1,000 feet. Coming down the leeward side, however, there is a uniform rise in temperature of 5.5 degrees Fahrenheit per 1,000 feet. Overall, the climate in the Blue Ridge province is relatively mild, with average July temperatures ranging from 59 degrees Fahrenheit at Mount Mitchell to 73.8 degrees Fahrenheit in Asheville.

The Blue Ridge province is blessed with abundant rainfall, but it varies greatly with altitude. In the higher mountains above 5,000 feet, it may be as much as 80 inches per year, while Asheville, at 2,000 feet, receives only 37 inches per year. On average, the annual precipitation for the entire mountain region ranges from 44 to 58 inches, and, in general, it is uniform throughout the year.

Habitats, Niches, and Life Zones

For all of these reasons, the southern Appalachians are rich in natural places for plants and animals, what ecologists call their habitat. What each species does in such habitats (such as act as predators) is called its niche. The total geographic area where plants and animals live is designated as their range, and the characteristics of the total place where they occur, including the climate, is referred to as their life zone, or biome.

A traveler who moved in a straight line northward from southern Florida to the extreme north of Canada would pass through a variety of life zones. These zones would include semitropical forests, southern pine forests, oak-hickory forests, northern pine-hardwood forests, beech-maple forests, spruce-pine-birch forests, spruce-fir forests, and, finally, in the subarctic region, muskeg or tundra shrub-grasslands.

Instead of traveling north to visit colder life zones, a visitor can experience many of these life zones in Western North Carolina by traveling altitudinally: up the mountains, from the mixed pine-hardwood forests below an elevation of 2,000 feet to red spruce–Fraser fir forests and near tundralike places called balds at elevations above 5,000 feet. From a biological standpoint, then, traveling up the mountains to more than 6,000 feet is equal to traveling a distance of 1,000 miles north, almost to the Arctic.

In and around Asheville, one would find mostly mixed pine and hardwood forests. At higher elevations, one would encounter different forest assemblages along the mountain ridges and slopes and, if rivers were encountered, still different plant assemblages. At an elevation of approximately 3,000 feet, one would find stands of pines, and upward 1,000 feet more, one would enter hemlock and heath communities. Above 4,000 feet, within a northern type of hardwood-forest life zone, one would discover habitats that are restricted to the Appalachian Mountains: cove forests and areas that ecologists have named boulderfields. Both are unique. From a canopy standpoint, cove forests are the richest woodlands in the country, containing more than 30 species of trees that uniformly reach the sunlight.

In mature forests throughout the world, stratification occurs, that is, plants survive at different levels in the forest. Dominant plants form the canopy. The subtending vegetation must be able to reproduce and thrive in the shade of these dominant species. This arrangement leads to a layered effect or stratification: mostly mosses, ferns, and other herbaceous plants occur as ground cover; above these, shrubs and small young trees reach for the canopy; and finally, the ultimate mature trees form the forest's top layer.

One who traveled to the northern area of a midwestern state such as Michigan would find a type of plant community called a beech-maple forest where only two species dominate the canopy: American beech (*Fagus grandifolia*) and sugar maple (*Acer saccharum*). In the southern Appalachians, however, occurs a plant community known as a cove hardwood forest, where a great diversity of tree species comprise the canopy. Cove forests are usually dominated by Canada hemlock (*Tsuga canadensis*), yellow buckeye (*Aesculus flava*), American basswood (*Tilia americana*), sugar maple (*Acer saccharum*), sweet birch (*Betula lenta*), tulip poplar (*Liriodendron tulipifera*), cucumbertree (*Magnolia acuminata*), white ash (*Fraxinus americana*), American beech (*Fagus grandifolia*), and a small tree found only in the southern Appalachians, the Carolina silverbell (*Halesia carolina*). Cove forest communities might support as many as 30 species of canopy trees with a great variety of shrubs and wildflowers in the understory, making it the most diverse forest type in all of North America.

The Mystery of Balds and Boulderfields

Boulderfields, too, are most unusual natural places. They consist of many acres of jumbled boulders, mostly moss-covered and with a rich assemblage of wildflowers in late spring and early summer under such mid-altitude trees as yellowwood (*Cladrastris kentukea*), American basswood, and yellow birch. Currants and gooseberries are common shrubs found in these areas. Usually boulderfields occur above 3,200 feet elevation, and they almost always are found in steep, north-facing coves. Although it is not known exactly how they formed, boulders undoubtedly were created from bedrock during the last ice age, approximately 10,000 to 20,000 years ago. Even though the northern glaciers never reached the southern Appalachians, it is believed that the freezing and thawing and resulting fracturing and uplifting of bedrock during the ice age were primarily responsible for producing the boulderfields.

The most mysterious habitats in the southern Appalachians, though, are those known as balds. Balds are defined as high-altitude open areas devoid of trees, occurring as either shrub-dominated areas or tundralike grasslands at or near the summits of our highest mountains at the edges of Canadian-zone spruce-fir forests. Shrub balds, which usually consist of nearly impenetrable rhododendrons (*Rhododrendron maximum* or *R. carolinianum* at lower elevations and *R. catawbiense* at higher elevations) and mountain laurel (*Kalmia latifolia*), are sometimes known as heath balds, referring to the family of plants to which these shrubs belong. The grass balds appear to be grasslands overall with a few clumps of shrubs or stunted trees such as mountain-ash (*Sorbus americana*) and willows (*Salix* spp.).

No one seems to know how balds were formed or why they persist. Most natural areas evolve their vegetational composition over time, a process called succession, leading to the ultimate climax community, which would theoretically persist for a long time. At lower elevations in the southern Appalachians, the climax forest would be cove, oak-hickory, or pine forest; at the top of Mount Mitchell, the climax forest is spruce-fir. Yet, on many of the Appalachians' higher peaks are these open, heathlike or grassy bald areas that have not been invaded by the surrounding forest species and have apparently persisted in this state for thousands of years.

Although ecologists have offered many theories for the persistence of balds, no one theory has been universally accepted. Some speculate they could be the result of intermittent fire caused by lightning. Historically, early settlers used balds for grazing cows and sheep, an activity that limited plant succession. Native Americans may have done the same for their domesticated stock. Balds, however, still exist, and probably have not changed significantly for at least hundreds of years.

Mountain Bogs

One of the rarest habitats in the Appalachian Mountains is an area called a mountain bog. In many respects, mountain bogs resemble lowland bogs but are hundreds of miles north. Like all bogs, they are waterlogged areas covered with unique plants, primarily sphagnum moss (also known as peat moss, *Sphagnum* spp.), bog laurel (*Kalmia carolina*), golden club (*Orontium aquaticum*), swamp pink (*Helonias bullata*), cinnamon fern (*Osmuda cinnamomea*), and a variety of insectivorous plants such as sundew (*Droscera rotundifolia*) and pitcher plants (*Sarracenia* spp.). The latter two trap and digest insects and are among the most unusual plants in the world. Interestingly, some pitcher plants contain living insects called midges. The midge larvae swim and develop in the "pitcher" part of the plant that holds open water.

A bog may develop on any flat area with poor drainage. This causes decaying vegetation to accumulate, resulting in very acidic conditions that only a few species of plants can tolerate. Indigenous bog animals are rare, although bogs may be visited by a variety of birds including northern warblers, as well as raccoons (*Procyon lotor*) and white-tailed deer (*Odocoileus virginianus*). Threatened or endangered bog animals include the bog turtle (*Clemmys muhlenbergii*), bog lemming (*Synaptomys cooperi*), and water shrew (*Sorex palustris*). In fact, more than 90 species of bog plants and animals are considered rare, threatened, or endangered in North Carolina by state and federal agencies, and only 10 percent of the original southern Appalachian bogs remain, covering probably fewer than 500 acres.

A Biological Paradise

During the glacial period of 10,000 to 20,000 years ago, much of the northern part of North America was covered by a layer of ice as much as 2 miles thick. These glaciers did not reach the southern Appalachians, and this area became a haven for plant and animal species whose northern habitats were inundated by ice. Partly as a result and partly because of the great age of the mountains and the wide range of temperatures, there is a complex assemblage of plants and animals, including endemics and northern and southern species finding common ground here in the mountains.

The combination of the great age of the mountains, the absence of inundation by the northern glaciers, the high-elevation habitats, and the temperate climate results in a high diversity of flowering plants, plus the occurrence of many plants that are endemic and others that are northern plants occurring far south of their main range. Of the nearly 3,000 species of higher plants found in North Carolina, approximately 1,400 occur in the mountains. In addition, there are around 350 species of mosses and moss-allies and over 2,000 species of fungi.

Due to their abundance and variety, wildflowers of the Blue Ridge province are of particular interest to naturalists. From March through September, depending on your elevation, you can be treated to a spectacular display beginning on the forest floor and ending in roadside fields and openings throughout the summer. If you miss the peak of woodland wildflowers in April in Asheville, just travel upward a few thousand feet and see some of the same species blooming much later in the higher elevations.

Wildflower aficionados will want to search out southern Appalachian endemics such as galax (*Galax urceolata*), Michaux's saxifrage (*Saxifraga michauxii*), mountain wood shamrock (*Oxalis montana*), Vasey's trillium (*Trillium vaseyi*), mountain St. John's wort (*Hypericum graveolens*), and mountain krigia (*Krigia montana*). Luckily, there are a number of excellent wildflower field guides, including some specific to the Blue Ridge Parkway [Figs. 4,11,19,23,30] and the Great Smoky Mountains National Park [Fig. 44], which can help you in your search.

In addition to luxuriant plant growth resulting from a complex geologic past and suitable climate, the North Carolina mountains have always had an interesting, and in some cases unique, assemblage of animals. In historic times, now extirpated mammal species such as "mountain" bison (*Bison bison*), gray wolves (*Canis lupus*), and elk (*Cervus elaphus*) roamed here. But these species were quickly eliminated by the early European settlers.

Before the Civil War, few studies of animals, including the mammals, were made in the Appalachians. Within five years after the Civil War, however, a number of zoologists visited the area to do survey work. These included Edward Drinker Cope (he was famous for his work in paleozoology), William Brewster after whom the hybrid Brewster's warbler (*Vermivora pinus x V. chrysoptera*) is named, and John Simpson Cairns, a local ornithologist who accidentally shot and killed himself while collecting birds north of Balsam Gap. By the turn of the century, though, increasing numbers of zoologists had thoroughly explored the North Carolina mountainous area and produced a rich literature on its animals.

As with plants, animal populations vary according to elevation and the resulting climatic conditions. Red squirrels (*Tamiascirus hudsonicus*) and red-backed voles (*Clethrionomys gapperi*), for example, generally occur in the higher elevation red spruce-Fraser fir forests. At these higher elevations where there are rocky outcrops (talus slopes, for example), the eastern spotted skunk (*Spilogale putorius*) and long-tailed shrew (*Sorex dispar*) occur. At high elevations, too, one may find isolated populations of the northern flying squirrel (*Glaucomys sabrinus*) and rare water shrew (*Sorex palustris*), found only on Roan Mountain [Fig. 15], with small populations in the Great Smoky Mountains and near Mount Mitchell on Bald Knob.

On the balds, eastern voles (*Scalopus aquaticus*), meadow jumping mice (*Zapus hudsonius*), and least weasels (*Mustela nivalis*) occur, but at the lower elevation cove forests, different mammals are found: eastern chipmunks (*Tamias striatus*), gray squirrels (*Sciurus carolinensis*), black bears (*Ursus americanus*), and white-footed mice (*Peromyscus leucopus*). Still lower down the mountains in the oak-hickory woodlands are eastern cottontails (*Sylvilagus floridanus*), striped skunks (*Mephitis mephitis*), and Virginia opossums (*Didelphus virginiana*).

GALAX

(*Galax rotundifolia*) Also called "coltsfoot," galax is widespread in the mountains. It is evergreen but may turn purple or bronze in winter, and it is often used as a holiday decoration.

Several mammal species occur within more than one life zone: eastern chipmunks, gray squirrels, white-tailed deer, black bears, and raccoons occur in both cove and oak-hickory forestlands. Along nearly any roadway occur woodchucks—*Marmota monax*, sometimes called groundhogs—which were rare during colonial times, but, like opossums and deer, have greatly increased in numbers as the forested land has been opened.

Although a rarity in these mountains, wherever caves occur, a variety of bats can be expected. Some species that occur here belong to one genus, myotis: the little brown myotis (*Myotis lucifugus*), Keen's myotis (*Myotis keenii*), and the small-footed myotis (*Myotis leibii*). The Indiana myotis (*Myotis sodalis*) and Townsend's big-eared bat (*Plecotus townsendii*), like a number of our native species, are listed as threatened or endangered.

Although several of North Carolina's mammal species have been extirpated or nearly lost primarily because of habitat change and other factors, there are still approximately 67 fur-bearing species that occur in Western North Carolina.

Like mammals, birds are distributed in an altitudinal fashion. Northern saw-whet owls (*Aegolius acadicus*), common ravens (*Corvus corax*), and golden eagles (*Aquila chrysaetos*) inhabit Mount Mitchell State Park, elevation 6.684 feet. Wood thrushes (*Hylocichla mustelina*), northern cardinals (*Cardinalis cardinalis*), and the tufted titmouse (*Parus bicolor*) are common in Asheville, elevation 2,000 feet. Some overlap exists between the highest elevations and the cove forests, where such typically northern species of birds such as the dark-eyed junco (*Junco hyemalis*) and winter wren (*Troglodytes troglodytes*) overlap with the lower-elevation Carolina chickadee (*Parus carolinensis*) and red-eyed vireo (*Vireo olivaceus*). Several species of birds are extinct, including the passenger pigeon (*Ectopistes migratorius*), which occurred here in the millions but was lost primarily due to overhunting and decline of the birds' habitat.

Fish, amphibians, and reptiles, however, are much more tightly confined to restrictive habitats. There are 86 species of fish that occur in the western portion of North Carolina. Cold water with high oxygen content is required by trout, warmer water for bass. Because of colder temperatures, excellent populations of trout but relatively few bass inhabit North Carolina's mountain waters.

Yet the great variety of both game and nongame fish are of great interest to naturalists. Species that are largely restricted to Western North Carolina include the mountain brook lamprey (*Ichthysomyzon greeleyi*) and the American brook lamprey (*Lampetra appendix*); several minnows, including the central stoneroller (*Campostoma anomalum*); the blotched and potfin chub, (*Hybopsis insignis* and *H. monacha*); several species of shiners (*Notropis* spp.); as well as two species of dace, the blacknose (*Rhinichthys atrataulus*) and the longnose (*R. cataractal*). Several species of redhorse (*Moxostoma* spp.) and three genera of catfish (*Pylodictis*, *Noturus*, and *Ictalurus*) also occur in the region's warmer waters. Among the smaller panfish that are found here are the rock bass (*Ambloplites repestris*), the green sunfish (*Lepomis cyanellus*), the redbreast sunfish, (*L. auritus*), the bluegill (*L. macrochirus*), the pumpkinseed (*L. gibbosus*), and the redear sunfish (*L. microlophus*). A few mountain localities have the yellow perch (*Perca flavescens*). The small and colorful darters (*Percina* spp.) number over a dozen species in the Blue Ridge. Even walleyes (*Stizostedion vitreum*), saugers (*S. canadense*), and the freshwater drum (*Aplodinotus grunniens*) occur in a few fairly restricted localities, and there are at least three species of sculpins (*Cottus* spp.) found in the area.

Reptiles, unlike most mountain fish, require a relatively warm environment and therefore are rare at higher elevations. Yet Western North Carolina has 11 species of turtles, 9 different lizards, and 23 species of snakes. Only the copperhead (*Agkistroden contortrix*) and timber rattlesnake (*Crotalus horridus*) are poisonous; the copperhead, 24 to 45 inches in length, is the most common, living at elevations of up to nearly 3,000 feet in the mountains.

There is a wide variety of amphibians in Western North Carolina.

RED SALAMANDER
(Pseudotriton ruber)

Of these, over 50 different kinds of salamanders and related species and 14 species of frogs and toads occur in mountainous part of the state. Salamanders are more varied in Western North Carolina than any place in the world, and scientists from all over the world study them.

In addition to the great variety of salamanders, a variety of invertebrates, both aquatic and terrestrial, occur in the Blue Ridge province. Several hundred species of spiders are represented, as are a variety of crayfish and mollusks. The latter have over 100 terrestrial forms (snails); fewer are found in the mountain streams and stream impoundments. Throughout the western Appalachians there are approximately 23 freshwater clam varieties. Interestingly, 20 of these are fairly restricted to the Tennessee River system in North Carolina.

These bivalve mollusks have a very long life span, some having been known to live from 30 to 130 years. The ages of clams, like trees, can be determined from annular growth rings. Such growth patterns also reflect water quality and even the presence of heavy metals and other pollutants in our freshwater habitats. In addition to pollutants, though, the impoundment of many freshwater streams, resulting in deeper, cooler water, has had a deleterious effect on several mollusk species that prefer shallow riffle areas. The same habitat interference has undoubtedly decreased the number of native crayfish in several localities. Yet, there is still a good number of both mollusk and crayfish species in Blue Ridge waters.

These mountains also have a great variety of insects and, luckily for hikers and outdoor enthusiasts, few that bite. Most noticeable along woodland trails are assorted species of butterflies. The large and colorful Eastern tiger swallowtails (*Papilio glaucus*) are found everywhere in woodland settings but mostly along roadways, trails, and other forest openings. In the fall the North Carolina mountains are visited by thousands of migrating monarch butterflies (*Danaus plexippus*), passing through on their 2,000-mile trek to central Mexico where they overwinter. An autumn field, especially one containing goldenrod (*Solidago* spp.) and asters (*Aster* spp.), is an ideal place to view monarch butterflies. A well-known viewing spot during their fall migration is the Cherry Cove Overlook south of Mount Pisgah on the Blue Ridge Parkway. Thousands of migrating monarchs are sometimes seen there making their way through the mountain ridges.

Naturalists in North Carolina

The natural history of the North Carolina mountains—their geology, rocks and minerals, plants and animals—is not only varied but represents a storehouse of natural treasures to be savored by all those who enjoy the outdoors and are interested in learning about it. When the first naturalists visited the North Carolina mountains, they stood in awe. Never had they witnessed such variety in plants and animals. Never had they seen so great a variety of topographical features and complicated geological formations in such a relatively small geographic area. These early explorers of the southern Appalachians made vast collections of animals, plants, rocks, and minerals, many rare and unique to Western North Carolina and some that had never before been discovered.

Among the first naturalists to study this rich collection of plants and animals was André Michaux, a Frenchman whom Thomas Jefferson described as the best-trained naturalist to enter the American continent. In the late 1700s, he and his son, François (who later became equally respected for his botanical expertise), traveled throughout the Carolinas.

In the mountains, they discovered a new plant, *Shortia galacifolia*, which grows nowhere but in the Appalachians. *Shortia*, also known as oconee bells, resembles the much more common galax (*Galax urceolata*). Both plants have rounded, leathery, shiny leaves, but *Shortia* has much bigger and more beautiful bell-shaped flowers in the early spring. André Michaux collected only one specimen of this species, and not until much later was it found again in the wild. The specimen he collected was later discovered in a Paris museum by another famous Carolina mountain explorer, Asa Gray of Harvard University. Gray remains America's best-known botanist, largely because of his botanical textbook, *Gray's Manual of Botany*, still used in colleges today.

More important to American botany—especially for the Carolinas—was the work of John Bartram and his son, William. The latter's *Travels Through North and South Carolina* (Philadelphia, 1791) was the most complete published account of the natural history of the North Carolina mountains at that time. William Bartram may have been the first naturalist to explore and then describe in detail the plants and animals at the higher elevations.

Other early naturalists to visit this area, at least briefly, include John James Audubon; John Bachman, after whom the Bachman's warbler (*Vermivora bachmanii*) is named; and Peter Kalm, whose name is used for the genus of mountain laurel, *Kalmia*. Following these early naturalists into the mountains were John Fraser, for whom Fraser fir (*Abies fraseri*) is named; Moses Ashley Curtis in 1830 and 1854; Samuel Botsford Buckley in 1842; and Lewis Reeve Gibbs in the 1850s. Of even greater note was Elisha Mitchell, after whom the tallest peak east of the Mississippi was named. Mitchell was a scientist, educator, minister, and professor at the University of North Carolina at Chapel Hill with a keen interest in mountain geography and geology.

Today, naturalists working in Western North Carolina still find it a fascinating place because of the rich diversity of plants and animals. There are many reasons for this, including the region's unique geologic past, climate, and uninterrupted forests. A paucity of human development, when compared with other areas of the country, is an important consideration as well.

Conservation Issues

As with any area possessing natural beauty, however, the beautiful and species-rich North Carolina mountains have problems. In numerous cases humans inadvertently initiated chains of events that have had dire consequences on the natural world. The unintentional introduction in 1904 of a chestnut fungus (*Cryphonectria parasitica*) from China devastated the American chestnut (*Castanea dentata*) and eliminated this magnificent and once dominant tree from eastern North America. Estimated to comprise 40 percent of the temperate deciduous forests before the blight, the chestnut tree's annual mast crop was a very important food source for wildlife.

In recent times the introduction from Europe of two adelgid insects has wreaked havoc on fir and hemlock forests. As a result, in the last 20 years the pristine Fraser firs on Mount Mitchell have been mostly lost. In addition, airborne heavy metals from factories hundreds of miles distant have interfered with the physiology of many plants, and acid rain has hurt many forest species.

Man's effect on the environment may help some species while it hurts others. While it is true that cutting the forests has produced more deer—because deer like

North Carolina mountains are part of the Blue Ridge province of the eastern United States. Because of the Blue Ridge province's topography, there are many beautiful waterfalls to enjoy. This is Looking Glass Falls near Brevard, North Carolina.

openings—fragmenting the forests has had a devastating effect on songbirds. Recent analysis of 25-year studies of songbird populations, for example, indicate that 50 percent of such species as scarlet tanagers, as well as several species of thrushes, vireos, and warblers, have been lost in our northeastern states largely because we created huge openings in forest lands. In the case of songbirds, the effect is complicated. Some species, scientists now believe, simply cannot reproduce in open areas. Still more insidious is the fact that many songbirds are being decimated by the intrusion of a forest-edge bird, the brown-headed cowbird (*Molothrus ater*). This species has used openings made by humans to invade areas that were once deep in the forests. The cowbird parasitizes the nests of songbirds by laying its eggs in their nests. Cowbird young hatch first and dominate the other nestlings. Songbird parents will feed the cowbird young at the expense of their own young, often causing the complete failure of many songbirds' reproduction.

Even the acts of amateur gardeners sometimes have deleterious effects on wildlife. When pesticides are used in our gardens, we destroy not only the intended victims but a host of other useful insects as well, and, through food chains, destroy unintended victims such as songbirds and even predator species such as hawks and owls.

The greatest problem right now is setting aside habitats for wild creatures. Western North Carolina is fortunate in that its land and waterways have not been completely overdeveloped. But citizens must be ever vigilant. The North Carolina mountains, though, still hold exciting natural treasures. Readers should use this book to visit some of the high-altitude habitats mentioned. These mountains still have enough natural interest to engage naturalists for several lifetimes.

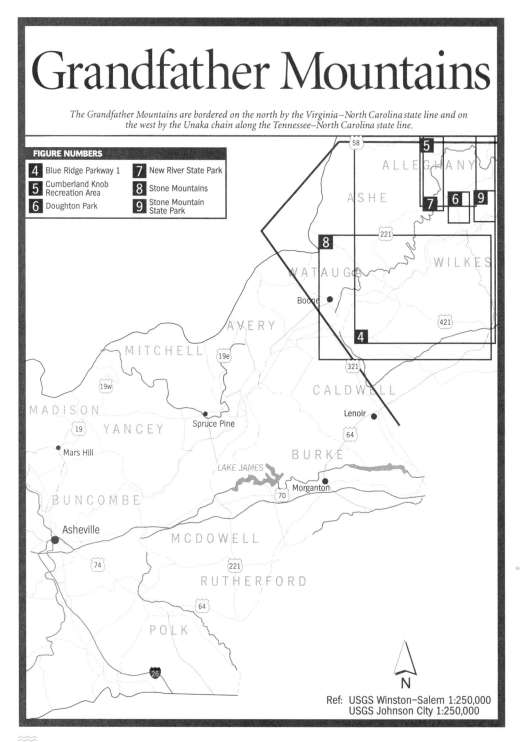

Grandfather Mountains

The Grandfather Mountains are bordered on the north by the Virginia–North Carolina state line and on the west by the Unaka chain along the Tennessee–North Carolina state line.

FIGURE NUMBERS

4 Blue Ridge Parkway 1		**7** New River State Park	
5 Cumberland Knob Recreation Area		**8** Stone Mountains	
6 Doughton Park		**9** Stone Mountain State Park	

Ref: USGS Winston–Salem 1:250,000
USGS Johnson City 1:250,000

The Grandfather Mountains

Much of the Grandfather Mountains section [Fig. 3] lies in the valley of the New River, North America's oldest river and one of the world's few north-flowing rivers. From its headwaters in Watauga County, the New River courses through a portion of the Blue Ridge province in North Carolina and Virginia where the terrain rises and falls from low ridges and mountains with elevations of only 1,200 to 3,000 feet. Within this section, however, dramatic change begins. The province starts to widen, gradually expanding from its narrow 15-mile width near the Virginia/North Carolina border to its 140-mile width along the borders with South Carolina and Georgia. As the province moves south, the modest peaks of the

[*Above*: Stone Mountain near Roaring Gap]

plateau become the highest points east of the Mississippi. Near Virginia, for example, elevations reach only 2,885 feet at the summit of Cumberland Knob [Fig. 5], but heading south along the Blue Ridge Parkway [Fig. 4], Bluff Mountain within Doughton Park [Fig. 6] rises to 3,800 feet and E. B. Jeffress Park [Fig. 4(4)] reaches almost 3,600 feet. Farther south, the Blue Ridge province reaches its highest point in the Black Mountains at Mount Mitchell, 6,684 feet.

Bordered on the north by the Virginia/North Carolina state line and on the west by the Unaka chain along the Tennessee/North Carolina state line, the Grandfather Mountains section extends south to an area near the town of Boone and east to Wilkes and Surrey counties. Cross ranges include the Grandfather Mountains (not to be confused with Grandfather Mountain in the Black Mountains section), Stone Mountains, and Beech Mountains. The Blue Ridge Parkway, which got its start near Cumberland Knob in 1937, snakes south from Virginia to Boone.

The complexity of the geology of the mountains in North Carolina is well illustrated in the curious patterns of the rivers. The New River, for example, and all the other Gulf-bound rivers in North Carolina's mountains make their way to the Mississippi through the Unaka chain that is generally 1,000 feet higher than the Eastern Continental Divide along the Blue Ridge crest. According to one theory, these rivers are able to defy gravity because they carved through the younger Unaka ranges faster than the Unakas were uplifted during periods of mountain making. The other major river in this section, the Yadkin River, also rises in Watauga County but runs its 203-mile course to the Atlantic by joining the Uwharrie River and later the Pee Dee River.

Other geologic wonders can be found in this section in three of the mountain region's five state parks. East of the Blue Ridge escarpment, the Stone Mountain monadnock rises an imposing 1,600 feet above the valley floor to an elevation of 2,305 feet. Mount Jefferson State Natural Area [Fig. 8(4)] and New River State Park [Fig. 7] feature numerous recreational activities.

Like most of North Carolina's mountainous regions, the Grandfather Mountains section hosts rich forests and abundant wildlife, but 10-foot-wide stumps along the forest floor tell a sadder story—the devastation of the once-glorious American chestnut (*Castanea dentata*) tree. At the turn of the century, the chestnut blight arrived in New York, making its way south over the next three decades. By the 1930s, the blight had infected almost 90 percent of the chestnut trees in Western North Carolina, eventually killing them all. As a result, the mountains were dramatically altered. Species dependent on the chestnut for food and housing were reduced, and new plant growth took over in areas once shaded by the mighty chestnut canopy. Oaks and hickories now dominate these forests, although young chestnut trees still sprout from the massive root systems unaffected by the blight. They grow as large as 4 inches in girth and bear nuts, but, regrettably, they, too, will eventually succumb. Genetic research and efforts to cross the American chestnut with the Chinese chest-

The loss of the chestnut tree to an exotic blight forever changed the ecosystem of the Appalachian Mountains. Providing food and shelter, the chestnut was an important tree to man and wildlife. The chestnut was a canopy species, rising to heights of more than 100 feet, and the tree ranged from southern Maine to central Mississippi. The annual mast crop, usually with the nuts from hickories and oaks, inundated the forest floor every fall, providing an easy bounty for Appalachian wildlife. A popular material for furniture, the chestnut's lumber is rot-resistant and was said to shelter a man "from cradle to grave." A blight imported on exotic plants in the early 1900s spread from New England to wipe out the chestnut. Today, saplings are found in the forest sprouting from rootstock, but the tree can't survive long before falling victim to the blight. Groups such as the American Chestnut Foundation continue to look for a "cure" and restore the chestnut to its former glory.

nut (*Castanea molissima*), which is resistant to the blight, continue, and some scientists report promising results from this hybridization.

The mountains formed natural barriers that meant isolation and hardship for generations of settlers until good roads made their way deep into the coves and valleys. One of the oldest roads through this section was the Old Buffalo Trail established by the heavy hooves of the buffalo that roamed the land. Later, the trail developed into Daniel Boone's Wilderness Road that led the way west into Kentucky.

For all this talk about isolation and hardship, there are benefits from the struggle. It drove these self-sufficient settlers to turn the abundant natural resources into tools and toys, clothes and coverlets, furniture and fiddles. Their desire to create things of beauty led settlers to put the finishing touches on these objects, and by the time the railroad carved its way into the mountains in the late nineteenth century, they had perfected their craftsmanship into what is now considered a prized American artform. Isolation also caused this area to be dubbed the "Lost Province," a phrase that makes some residents bristle. Looking back, though, it was this very remoteness, at least in part, that saved the area's pristine countryside from development, maintaining its natural beauty and earning the area a new—and coveted—moniker of "Unspoiled Province."

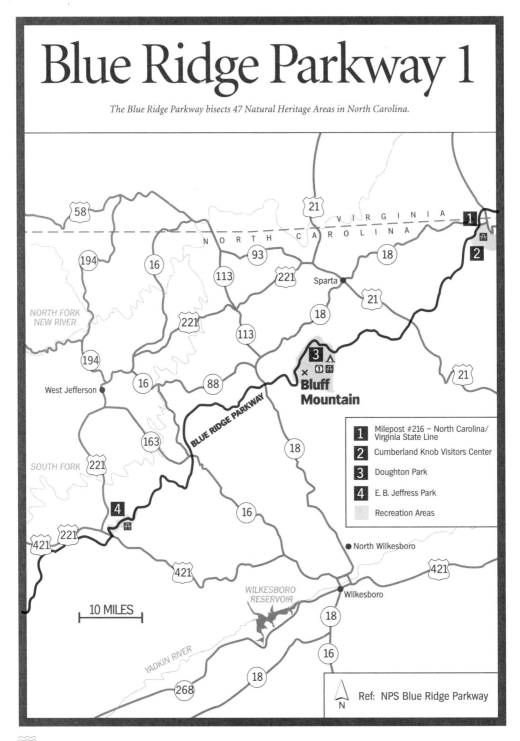

Blue Ridge Parkway 1

The Blue Ridge Parkway bisects 47 Natural Heritage Areas in North Carolina.

1 Milepost #216 – North Carolina/
Virginia State Line

2 Cumberland Knob Visitors Center

3 Doughton Park

4 E. B. Jeffress Park

Recreation Areas

Ref: NPS Blue Ridge Parkway

10 MILES

The Blue Ridge Parkway in the Grandfather Mountains

[Fig. 4, Fig. 3(4)] It could never happen today—469 miles of concrete coursing through mountainous wilderness, across two states, six congressional districts, 29 counties, 181 miles of national forests, and 11 miles of the Qualla Boundary Cherokee Indian Reservation. Today, red tape and paperwork would bury the project before the first shovel broke the ground.

But when plans for the Blue Ridge Parkway took shape, times were hard. It was the Great Depression, and people needed work. Although the idea for a road through the southern Appalachians had been around as long as the automobile, the Great Depression gave it new purpose. The National Industrial Recovery Act of 1933 ordered the Public Works Administration (PWA) to develop a program involving the construction, maintenance, and improvement of public highways and parkways. During that same year, President Franklin D. Roosevelt visited the Skyline Drive, a Civilian Conservation Corps (CCC) project in Virginia's Shenandoah National Park. When presented plans for a similar road connecting Shenandoah with the Great Smoky Mountains National Park, Roosevelt agreed. Later that year, Congress allocated $16.6 million for the project, and on September 11, 1935, officials broke ground on a 12-mile section at Cumberland Knob, just south of the Virginia/North Carolina border. The Blue Ridge Parkway was under way.

On June 30, 1936, an act of Congress placed the Parkway under the jurisdiction of the National Park Service of the U.S. Department of the Interior, ensuring its status as a resource of national merit under the National Park Service's mandate "to conserve the scenery and the natural and historic objects and the wildlife…and to provide for the enjoyment of the same in such manner and by such means as will leave them unimpaired for the enjoyment of future generations." Over the years, it has become increasingly apparent just how much care and dedication went into the project, fostered by a deep respect for the beauty of the land through which it was carved.

Work progressed in stretches and strips, as the necessary land had to be acquired from a variety of jurisdictions. Unlike national parks in the West where land could be "set aside" because it did not belong to anyone, much of the land in these mountains was privately owned. Careful negotiations and one-on-one consultations with landowners convinced them the Parkway would be an asset to the region and assured them they would receive a fair price for the land. The states of North Carolina and Virginia and the Resettlement Administration joined forces to assist those who were displaced. In addition to land purchases, the Parkway received some of its holdings from land transfers from the U.S. Forest Service and from three significant donations of private lands in North Carolina: Moses H. Cone Estate (1948), Julian Price Memorial Park (1949), and Linville Falls Recreation Area, purchased and donated by John D. Rockefeller Jr. (1952).

Road building also proceeded slowly because few maps of the land existed, often only sketch maps made by members of the Appalachian Trail Club. To find the best vistas, landscape architects and surveyors hiked the rugged terrain, asking local people their advice, weighing the advantages—scenic and monetary—of the myriad choices. Then, landscape architects met with engineers of the Bureau of Public Roads to determine the best sites for bridges and tunnels and the road itself.

At first, mountain residents thought of the Parkway as just another road that would help them get to market. The concept of the world's first recreational highway was difficult for these hard-working people to grasp. Yet they did benefit from the Parkway in a number of ways. By working closely with the landscape architects, local people learned about soil conservation, fire control, erosion prevention, and crop rotation, easing man's impact on the mountains in areas well beyond the Parkway's route. In addition, as part of the New Deal, contracts required contractors to hire labor from the rolls of the unemployed in the counties surrounding the Parkway. As much as 90 percent of the labor force came from local communities. Only when the terrain and scope of the project required unusual skills—stonemason artistry, for example, to build the distinctive stone bridges and retaining walls that have become Parkway trademarks—were talented Italian and Spanish stonemasons brought in. The Italians and Spaniards worked well together and developed friendly rivalries to see which group could build the finest bridges and walls in the shortest time at the lowest cost.

The project never faltered from its plan to make the least impact on the environment as possible, to blend the road with its environs carefully and deliberately. Unlike state and federal highways where drastic cuts expose the region's ancient geology, the Parkway reveals few of the folds and cracks, intrusions and veins along its route. Construction crews worked closely with the landscape architects to blast rough, natural-looking cuts in a deliberate attempt to blend with the environment. And by its very design, the Parkway often runs parallel to the geology rather than cutting across it.

Not only are habitats within the Parkway's boundaries protected from land development, but the construction of the Parkway actually helped create new habitats as it opened areas within closed, dry forests. These openings simulate gaps that would have been created by tree falls and fires, providing the proper "edge" habitat desired by some rare plant species. Several mountain bogs, for example, occur on Parkway lands and generally support a variety of rare plants.

It's hard to get lost on the Parkway, especially with hundreds of milepost markers along the route. The Parkway crosses into North Carolina at milepost 216.9 [Fig. 4(1)] and continues until its terminus at milepost 469 in the Qualla Boundary Cherokee Indian Reservation. The 250-mile section in North Carolina includes seven visitor centers and numerous smaller information centers offering literature and advice as well as five Parkway campgrounds; 25 tunnels; 72 hiking trails leading to geologic wonders such as waterfalls, gorges, and caves; and a wide variety of elevations ranging from 2,000 feet at the French Broad River to 6,053 feet at Richland Balsam. Approximately 1,250 vascular plant species are known to exist within Parkway boundaries, and of these, 106 plant species are either federally or state listed as endangered or threatened. In addition to nature's bounty, cultural remnants from days gone by—picturesque pioneer cabins, popular trading posts—also grace the landscape. For a detailed description of the length of the Blue Ridge Parkway, William G. Lord's *Blue Ridge Parkway Guide* offers fascinating lore and legend, facts and figures, along its 469-mile route.

A few nuts and bolts about the Parkway: Facilities are generally open May 1 through October. The exception is Linville Falls campground which remains open year-round. There are no showers at any Parkway campgrounds, although running water and restrooms are available. No swimming is allowed in any National Park Service waters. With the National Park Service's (NPS) Golden Age Passbook, available free to citizens 62 years of age and older, campground fees on the Parkway and at NPS campgrounds across the country are discounted by 50 percent; the card is also honored in national forest campgrounds.

A number of exits from the Parkway connect with state and federal highways: US 221 at Blowing Rock, Sandy Flats, Holly Mountain Road, Beacon Heights, and Linville Flats; and NC 226 at Gillespie Gap and Little Switzerland. The Parkway is open all year, but may close in sections if winter conditions become dangerous. Parkway information is available 24 hours a day by calling (800) 727-5928. Or for in-state visitors, (704) 298-0398.

BOG TURTLE
(*Clemmys muhlenbergi*)
This turtle grows to only 4 inches long.

Cumberland Knob
Recreation Area

The Blue Ridge Parkway started here in 1935 with a 12-mile stretch.

MEADOW CREEK

GRADY FORK CREEK

622

607

89

● McKnights Mill

BEAVER CREEK

T H E   G L A D E S

● Delhart

W. FORK CREEK

615

624

613

● Low Gap

V I R G I N I A
N. C A R O L I N A

● Edmonds

18

18

CRAB CREEK

1 2 3
CUMBERLAND
KNOB
RECREATION
AREA

89

GULLY CREEK

ROARING CREEK

1 Gully Creek Trail

2 Cumberland Knob Trail

3 Visitor Center

Cumberland Knob Recreation Area

Blue Ridge Parkway

N

RAMEY CREEK

Saddle Mountain

Ref: USGS Cumberland Knob 1:24,000

Cumberland Knob Recreation Area

[Fig. 4(2), Fig. 5, Fig. 3(5)] The world's first recreational highway, the Blue Ridge Parkway, started here in 1935 with a 12-mile stretch. Two years later, the first recreation area on the Parkway was built on this site, one of many projects carried out by the Civilian Conservation Corps. A pleasant 1,000-acre parcel, Cumberland Knob takes its name from the 2,885-foot mountain named after William Augustus, duke of Cumberland and son of King George III. Cumberland Knob Recreation Area includes a visitor contact station that stocks books and maps, picnic sites, and two hiking trails.

An easy, short walk along Cumberland Knob Trail [Fig. 5(2)] starts near the visitor center [Fig. 5(3)] and travels through woods filled with galax (*Galax aphylla*), flame azalea (*Rhododendron calendulaceum*), and rhododendron (*Rhododendron catawbiense* and *maximum*), as it gently winds toward the top, an elevation change of only 100 feet. A shelter with a rock fireplace and open areas at the top make excellent choices for leisurely picnics.

The Gully Creek Trail [Fig. 5(1)] is longer and moderately strenuous with an elevation change of 800 feet. The trail courses through a cove hardwood forest alongside Gully Creek, which flows over a series of cascades on its way through the 780-foot-deep ravine. The return trip leads hikers through patches of ferns and thickets of rhododendron and mountain laurel (*Kalmia latifolia*). Oak, pine, red maple (*Acer rubrum*), yellow-poplar (*Liriodendron tulipifera*), and serviceberry (*Amelanchier laevis*) shelter an understory of flowering dogwood (*Cornus florida*), smooth sumac (*Rhus glabra*), flame azalea, and sassafras (*Sassafras albidum*). The forest floor features abundant galax, houstonia (*Houstonia purpurea*), Venus' looking-glass (*Specularia perfoliata*), as well as prolific and pesky poison ivy (*Rhus radicans*).

Birds attracted to Cumberland Knob in late spring and summer are typical of those found in the middle elevations of the Blue Ridge province, such as downy woodpecker (*Dendrocopos pubsecens*), eastern wood peewee (*contopus virens*), eastern phoebe (*Sayornis phoebe*), great crested flycatcher (*Myiarchus crinitus*), white-breasted nuthatch (*Sitta carolinensis*), American goldfinch (*Spinus tristis*), and indigo bunting (*Passerina cyanea*). Also during late spring and summer, the trail along Gully Creek attracts blue-gray gnatcatchers (*Polioptila caerulea*), Carolina wrens (*Thryothorus ludovicianus*), catbirds (*Dumetella carolinensis*), red-eyed and solitary vireos (*Vireo olivaceus* and *V. solitarius*), hooded warblers (*Wilsonia citrina*), worm-eating warblers (*Helmitheros vermivorus*), and a few black-billed cuckoos (*Coccyzus erythropthalmus*). Even those who do not hike can find plenty of birding opportunities in the summer by keeping a watchful eye in the picnic and parking areas.

Directions: Blue Ridge Parkway milepost 217.5.

Activities: Hiking, picnicking.

Doughton Park

"The Bluffs" was renamed Doughton Park in 1961 to honor Robert Lee Doughton,
an avid Blue Ridge Parkway supporter and longtime U.S. congressman.

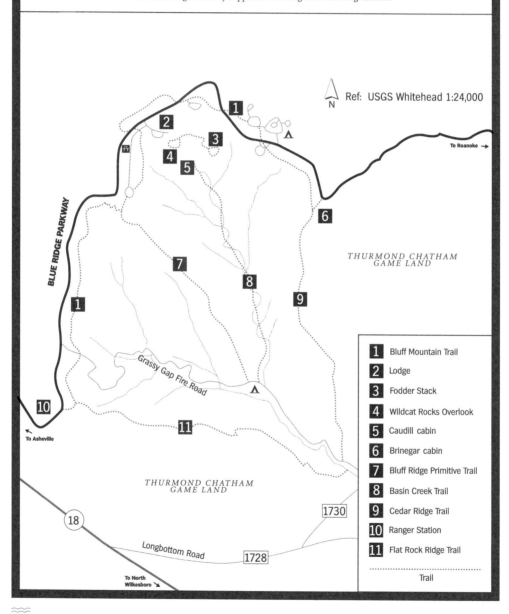

Ref: USGS Whitehead 1:24,000

N

To Roanoke →

THURMOND CHATHAM
GAME LAND

BLUE RIDGE PARKWAY

Grassy Gap Fire Road

To Asheville

THURMOND CHATHAM
GAME LAND

18

Longbottom Road

1730

1728

To North
Wilkesboro

1	Bluff Mountain Trail
2	Lodge
3	Fodder Stack
4	Wildcat Rocks Overlook
5	Caudill cabin
6	Brinegar cabin
7	Bluff Ridge Primitive Trail
8	Basin Creek Trail
9	Cedar Ridge Trail
10	Ranger Station
11	Flat Rock Ridge Trail

Trail

Facilities: Visitor center, restrooms, picnic area, water.

Dates: Open year-round; picnic area and visitor center open May–Oct.

Fees: None.

Closest town: Sparta, 18 miles.

For more information: Bluffs Ranger District, phone (910) 372-8568.

Elevation: Cumberland Knob, 2,885 feet.

Trail distance and configuration: Cumberland Knob Trail, 1 mile loop.

Degree of difficulty: Easy.

Surface and blaze: Forest floor.

Trail distance and configuration: Gully Creek Trail, 2-mile loop.

Degree of difficulty: Moderate.

Surface and blaze: Forest floor, creek crossings.

Doughton Park

[Fig. 6, Fig. 4(3), Fig. 3(6)] Originally called "The Bluffs" after the surrounding cliffs of the Blue Ridge escarpment, Doughton Park was renamed in 1961 to honor Robert Lee Doughton, an avid Parkway supporter and longtime U.S. congressman. One of the larger tracts along the Parkway, Doughton Park features more than 30 miles of hiking trails crossing and circling its 6,000 acres. A network of seven trails winds through pastures and meadows, along streams and ridges, and into coves and valleys that create distinctive habitats rich in wildlife.

Isolation was a way of life when the Brinegar family built their self-sufficient homestead here. They farmed the land from the 1880s until the 1930s, when the National Park Service acquired it for the Parkway. Today, the Brinegar cabin [Fig. 6(6)] is a popular destination within the park. Other families settled along Basin Creek and Cove Creek, although their numbers were never large. Martin Caudill's cabin [Fig. 6(5)], which is visible from several vantage points, was built in 1895 and is one of the few to survive a devastating flood in 1916.

Bluff Mountain Trail [Fig. 6(1)] is relatively level, though long at 15 miles round-trip, and offers many breathtaking vistas. There are shorter but more strenuous trails, such as Bluff Ridge Trail [Fig. 6(7)], Basin Creek Trail [Fig. 6(8)], and Flat Top Ridge Trail [Fig. 6(11)].

Large-toothed aspen (*Populus grandidentata*) (a rare sight in North Carolina, though the trees are common from Maine across to Minnesota), Carolina hemlock (*Tsuga caroliniana*), and Fraser magnolia (*Magnolia fraseri*) also grow here. In addition to the ubiquitous rhododendron and mountain laurel, witch-hazel (*Hamamelis virginiana*), sassafras, and dogwood make up the understory, with spring wildflowers such as violets, mayapple (*Podophyllum peltatum*), fire pink (*Silene virginica*), bluets (*Houstonia caerulea*), cinquefoil (*Potentilla*), and solomon's seal

(*Polygonatum biflorum*) blooming beneath their canopy. Blazing star (*Chamaelirium luteum*) thrives near the visitor station, and rhododendron tunnels along numerous trails are renowned for their intense and colorful blossoms in early to mid-June.

Three of the park's trails are recommended for bird-watching: Flat Rock Ridge Trail, Cedar Ridge Trail, and Grassy Gap Fire Road. Late-spring and summer birds include cedar waxwing (*Bombycilla cedrorum*), wood thrush (*Hylocichla mustelina*), gray catbird, solitary and red-eyed vireos, scarlet tanager (*Piranga olivacea*), and indigo bunting. Turkey vultures (*Cathartes aura*) and ravens (*Corvus corax*) soar along the ridges, making their nests in the rocky cliffs along the Cedar Ridge Trail. Other wildlife includes the white-tailed deer (*Odocoileus virginia*), wild turkey (*Meleagris gallopavo*), and seldom-seen bobcat (Felis rufus) and black bear (*Ursus americanus*). Thousands of monarch butterflies (*Danaus plexippus*) pass through here on their annual migrations to Mexico.

SCARLET TANAGER
(*Piranga olivacea*)

This bird has a distinctive "chick-kurr" call.

Basin Creek and Cove Creek offer approximately 5 miles of essentially wild trout fishing with some rainbow trout at the lower reaches. This area is classified as "special" by the National Park Service, which requires artificial lure on a single hook.

Directions: Blue Ridge Parkway between mileposts 238.5 and 244.7.

Activities: Hiking, cross-country skiing, fishing. Note: Park lies adjacent to Thurmond Chatham Game Land; check local hunting dates and regulations.

Facilities: Bluffs Coffee Shop, Bluffs Crafts and Gift Shop, Bluffs Lodge, Bluffs Gas Station, 107-site campground and 20-site RV area (no hook-ups), restrooms and water (no showers), 6-site backcountry camping area, picnic grounds.

Dates: Park is open year-round; facilities are open May–Oct.

Fees: A fee is charged for camping and lodge rooms.

Closest town: Sparta, 12 miles.

Trail distance and configuration: Pick up detailed trail information at Bluffs Gas Station. Most trails are well marked.

Elevation: Ranges from 1,425 feet on Basin Creek to 3,800 feet on Bluff Mountain.

For more information: Bluffs Lodge, Route 1, Box 266, Laurel Springs, NC 28644. Phone (910) 372-4499.

Mount Jefferson State Natural Area

[Fig. 8(4)] It measures only 541 acres, but Mount Jefferson State Natural Area has earned a reputation as a paradise for nature lovers. So much so that it was designated a National Natural Landmark by the National Park Service in 1975. Named after Thomas Jefferson and his father, Peter, who owned land in the area and surveyed the North Carolina/Virginia state line in 1749, the park features hiking and picnicking in the shadow of the mountain's summit.

Geologists know that the basement rock of Mount Jefferson is part of the Ashe Metamorphic Suite, rock deposited 800 million years ago as a mix of eroded land areas and volcanic debris in the floor of an ancient sea. What remains a mystery is why Mount Jefferson towers 1,600 feet above surrounding stream valleys. The black amphibolite, which gives Mount Jefferson its distinctive dark appearance, is usually found in lower elevations and is susceptible to erosion. Mount Jefferson's other dominant rocks—gneiss and schist—have a higher percentage of quartz, which makes them generally more resistant to erosion, but here they are thinner than usual, making them physically weaker and, therefore, more likely to erode. Except they haven't eroded—at least not as much the surrounding, softer, more sedimentary layers of an ancient plateau worn down by the two forks of the New River. This is but one of the conundrums geologists face as they study the complex geology of Western North Carolina.

Forest and plant life on 4,684-foot-high Mount Jefferson varies with altitude. A fine example of oak-chestnut forests lies above 4,000 feet on all but the north-facing slopes. Northern red oak (*Quercus rubra*) and white oak (*Quercus alba*) form the canopy over dogwood, mountain laurel, rhododendron, trillium, pink lady slipper (*Cypripedium acaule*), Dutchman's breeches (*Dicentra cucullaria*), and false lily-of-the-valley (*Maianthemum canadense*). At these higher elevations, the north-facing slope hosts the northern cove forest of yellow birch (*Betula alleghaniensis Britton*), basswood (*Tilia americana*), red maple, and yellow-poplar, with prairie willow, dog-hobble (*Viburnum alnifolium*), bluebeard lily, and mountain pepperbush. Trees here are subjected to ice and wind and, as a result, appear stunted or pruned, often growing no higher than 20 feet. Below 4,000 feet, the forests are primarily chestnut-oak with hickories, mountain laurel, serviceberry, bush honeysuckle (*Diervilla lonicera*), and rhododendron.

Typical of the stratification of wildlife in Western North Carolina, higher eleva-tions are home to species usually found only in New England and Canada. The anomaly of northern species growing so far south is evident below Luther's Rock where large-toothed aspen, lettuce saxifrage (*Saxifraga micranthidifolia*), and the rare rusty cliff fern (*Woodsia ilvensis*) can be found.

Red-tailed hawks (*Buteo jamaicensis*) soar above the mountains where chestnut-sided warblers (*Dendroica pensylvanica*), black-throated blue warblers (*D. caerule-

scens), Canada warblers (*Wilsonia canadensis*), slate-colored juncos (*Junco hyemalis*), white-breasted nuthatches, and rose-breasted grosbeaks (*Pheucticus ludovicianus*) make their nests. Several species of woodland salamanders live in the higher elevations, although reptiles and amphibians are generally hard to find. Common mammals—raccoons (*Procyon lotor*), opossums (*Didelphis marsuialis*), red foxes (*Vulpes fulva*), eastern chipmunks (*Tamias striatus*)—thrive here as do shrews, moles, woodchucks (*Marmota monax*), white-tailed deer, and an occasional bobcat.

When Elisha Mitchell noted in his diary in 1827 that he had never seen anything so beautiful as the view from the summit of Mount Jefferson, few were hardy enough to make the trip for themselves. In the 1930s, the Works Progress Administration constructed a road to the top, but over the years its state of repair and disrepair varied. The park finally achieved state park status in 1956, thanks to strong community support and generous donations. And the site was named a state natural area in 1994. Overlooks from the park road and Mount Jefferson's summit offer panoramic views into three states—Mount Rogers and Whitetop Mountain in Virginia, Snake Mountain in Tennessee, and Mount Mitchell and Grandfather Mountain, among others, in North Carolina. You can also see Pond Mountain, which holds the distinction of lying in all three states.

WHITE OAK
(*Quercus alba*)
The leaves on a single oak tree may have different shapes, making identification a challenge. White oak leaves have deep or shallow clefts between lobes.

SUMMIT TRAIL

The Summit Trail, as its name implies, ascends .3 mile to the highest point on Mount Jefferson, where nearby overlooks provide spectacular views. The Rhododendron Trail, a moderate 1.1-mile loop trail that begins near the end of the Summit Trail, follows a horseshoe-shaped ridge southeast along the crest of the mountain to Luther Rock, which on clear days offers great views of the New River. According to local lore, the bluffs of black mica gneiss extending along the ridge below the trail served as stops along the Underground Railroad that led escaped slaves to freedom. The return portion of this loop trail descends to the southern slope of the mountain where trees sheltered from the cold northern winds grow tall. The trail passes through a virgin forest of large northern red oaks and the remains of American chestnuts. The Rhododendron Trail is also a self-guiding nature trail; interpretive pamphlets, available at the trailhead, teach about the natural environment, history, and legends of the area. Park rangers offer seasonal interpretive programs such as guided nature walks, talks, and demonstrations, and report that early June is the prettiest time to visit, when the purple blossoms of the Catawba rhododendron cover the mountaintop.

Directions: In Jefferson at the junction of NC 88 and US 221, travel south 2.3 miles on US 221 to Mount Jefferson State Park Road (SR 1152). Turn left at the large brown state-park sign. The park gate is 1.5 miles ahead.

Activities: Hiking.

Facilities: 26 picnic tables, 9 grills in a wooded site near the summit, drinking water, restrooms.

Dates: Open year-round.

Fees: None.

Closest town: Jefferson, 4 miles.

For more information: PO Box 48, Jefferson, NC 28640. Phone (910) 246-9653.

E. B. Jeffress Park Area

[Fig. 4(4)] [Fig. 8(6)] A small recreational area off the Blue Ridge Parkway, E. B. Jeffress Park serves to honor a man who played a big role in the development of the Parkway. Chairman of the North Carolina Highway Commission in 1934, Jeffress was not only a supporter of the Parkway but an outspoken—and successful—advocate against making the Parkway a toll road.

Set along the edge of the Blue Ridge Plateau, the park features two short hikes leading to interesting natural and man-made destinations. The Cascade Trail [Fig. 8(7)] follows Falls Creek to where the creek plunges over a bare-rock cliff face on its way to the Piedmont 2,000 feet below. The trail courses through forests of yellow-poplar, hickory, black cherry (*Prunus serotina*), witch-hazel, basswood, black locust

(*Robinia pseudoacacia*), and Fraser magnolia. Benches, rustic footbridges, and two overlooks, one at the top of the rushing water, the other at a lower perspective, add to the trail experience. The Cascades Trail also features signs identifying plant life evident here and throughout the region.

The understory is thick with legendary dog-hobble, said to grow so intertwined that it traps bear-hunting dogs more intent on sniffing than watching where they are going; once caught, or "hobbled," they fall easy prey to waiting bears. Other understory vegetation includes solomon's seal, flame azalea, mountain laurel, and rhododendron.

The park attracts a number of birds, especially the late-spring and summer eastern wood peewee, wood thrush (*Hylocichla mustelina*), hooded warbler, ovenbird (*Seiurus aurocapillus*), and rufous-sided towhee (*Pipilo erythrophthalmus*).

Directions: Blue Ridge Parkway at Cascades Trail Parking Lot, milepost 272.
Activities: Hiking, picnicking.
Facilities: Picnic tables, restrooms, water.
Dates: Open year-round.
Fees: None.
Closest town: Boone, 12 miles.
Elevation: 3,570 feet at trailhead.

CASCADE TRAIL

Trail distance and configuration: 1.2-mile loop from picnic area.
Degree of difficulty: Moderate.
Surface and blaze: Paved trail near restrooms, then forest floor; steep wooden steps near the waterfalls.

TOMPKINS KNOB TRAIL

Tompkins Knob Trail [Fig. 8(8)] travels through the forest to a clearing for two old log structures: Cool Spring Baptist Church, where itinerant preachers rallied people from miles around, and Jesse Brown's Cabin, the home where the preachers often stayed the night.

Trail distance and configuration: 1 mile round-trip from parking lot.
Degree of difficulty: Easy.
Surface and blaze: Forest floor, pine needles, meadow.

THE FRESCOES OF ASHE COUNTY

[Fig. 8(21)] Winter/spring. Sow/reap. Wax/wane. Cycles lived and relived, season after season in the mountains. These patterns affect not just the land but also those making their way on its rugged terrain. Such was the case for a languishing Episcopal parish and a talented artist, who together turned their hardships into renewal.

The rector of the remote mountain parish, the story goes, was introduced at a party to artist Ben Long, who had returned from years of studying fresco painting in Florence, Italy. Eager to practice his skills in his home state, Long spent several months unsuccessfully searching for a North Carolina church that would accept his donation of a religious fresco. Long repeated his offer to the rector, who is said to have exclaimed, "We'll take it," followed by, "What is a fresco?" Long and his students eventually painted five frescoes in the parish's two churches, Holy Trinity at Glendale Springs and St. Mary's in West Jefferson, both in Ashe County.

The powerful frescoes have attracted thousands of visitors from across the country. In turn, they have inspired another kind of transformation. The parish is thriving once again, and nearby villages are enjoying an economic revitalization as old homes are converted to well-appointed bed and breakfast inns and interesting shops and restaurants are established in the region.

Both churches are open 24 hours a day, seven days a week for prayer and meditation. The parish asks only for donations for the privilege of seeing these inspired works of art. Such is the mountain spirit.

Directions: Holy Trinity Church in Glendale Springs is 400 yards off the Blue Ridge Parkway, milepost 258. Directions to St. Mary's are available at Holy Trinity.

Dates: Open daily year-round.

Fees: None; donations requested.

Closest town: Glendale Springs.

For more information: Parish of the Holy Communion, PO Box 177, Glendale Springs, NC 28629. Phone (910) 982-3076.

RACCOON (Procyon lotor)
The raccoon often appears to wash its food, resulting in its Latin name, "lotor," meaning "a washer."

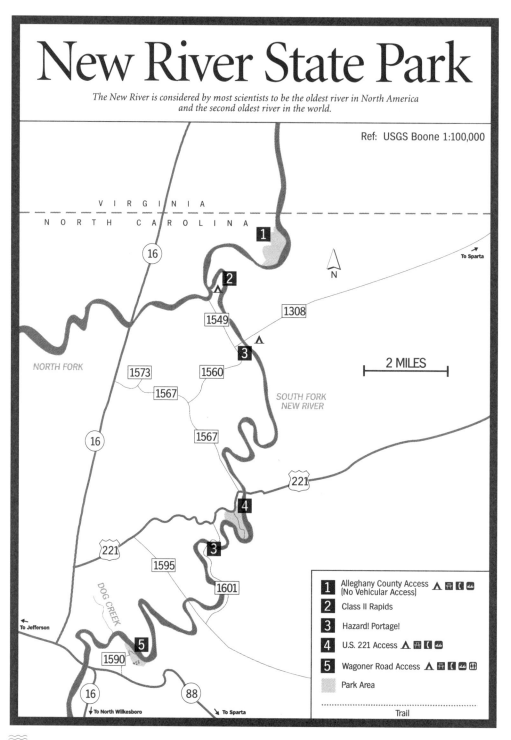

New River State Park

The New River is considered by most scientists to be the oldest river in North America and the second oldest river in the world.

Ref: USGS Boone 1:100,000

VIRGINIA

NORTH CAROLINA

To Sparta

N

16

1

2

1308

1549

3

2 MILES

NORTH FORK

1573

1560

1567

SOUTH FORK
NEW RIVER

16

1567

221

4

221

3

1595

DOG CREEK

1601

To Jefferson

5

1590

16

88

To North Wilkesboro

To Sparta

1	Alleghany County Access ⛺ ⛽ 🅲 🚻 (No Vehicular Access)
2	Class II Rapids
3	Hazard! Portage!
4	U.S. 221 Access ⛺ ⛽ 🅲 🚻
5	Wagoner Road Access ⛺ ⛽ 🅲 🚻 🚾
	Park Area
	Trail

New River State Park

[Fig. 7, Fig. 3(7)] Although it is not apparent from its name, the New River is considered by most scientists to be the oldest river in North America and the second oldest river in the world. Even before the Appalachian Mountains were formed, the New River ran almost the same path across the Blue Ridge Plateau it runs today. Since 1976, 26.5 miles of the New River have been protected as a National Wild and Scenic River System, which prohibits the construction of dams and reservoirs. This section of the New River (22 miles of the South Fork downstream to its confluence with the North Fork, and 4.5 miles of the main stem of the New River north to the North Carolina and Virginia line) and three designated parkland areas along its course make up the 1,460-acre New River State Park.

The New River's meandering course through the park has exposed rocks belonging to two major geologic units—biotite granitic gneiss of the Elk Park Plutonic Group, and gneiss and schist of the 800-million-year-old Ashe Metamorphic Suite. More than 1 billion years old, the Elk Park Plutonic Group formations represent some of the oldest rocks in the Appalachians.

While the New River's calm waters offer easy canoeing perfect for beginners, families, and groups, experienced paddlers also enjoy the unparalleled scenery and tranquillity. Along the way, river travelers experience such geological features as rapids, potholes, and floodplains. Paddlers along the South Fork of the New River can observe downfoldings of rocks, called the Ararat River Synclinorium, that formed a trough during the formation of the Appalachian Mountains. Also of note is a granite wall at the Alleghany County access area called The Bluffs. Rising 200 feet above river level, the ancient granitic wall is more than 1 billion years old.

Archeological investigations indicate the presence of humans in the New River area as early as 10,000 years ago. Precolonial Canawhay, Shawnee, Creek, and Cherokee Indians used the New River and the surrounding areas for migration, trade, and hunting. Later, European settlers used the land for farming, mining, and timber.

Despite its status as one of the most undeveloped Appalachian rivers, the New River area has suffered from major clearing and cutting. Most of the virgin forest is gone, and the woodlands are now composed of second- and third-growth trees. Where the soil is dry and shallow, oaks and hickories grow in abundance with maples, elms, Eastern redcedars (*Juniperus virginiana*), and pines. Along the banks of the New River's feeder streams, moist soil provides an ideal environment for American beech (*Fagus grandifolia*), blackgum (*Nyssa sylvatica*), yellow-poplar, black locust, and yellow birch trees. Beneath the forest canopy, dogwood, sourwood (*Oxydendrum arboreum*), sassafras, alder, huckleberry (*Gaylussacia baccata*), and hydrangea (*Hydrangea arborescens*) flourish. At least 14 species of rare, threatened, or endangered plants grow in the New River valley, including rattlesnake root, Carolina saxifrage, Carey's saxifrage, spreading avens, and purple sedge.

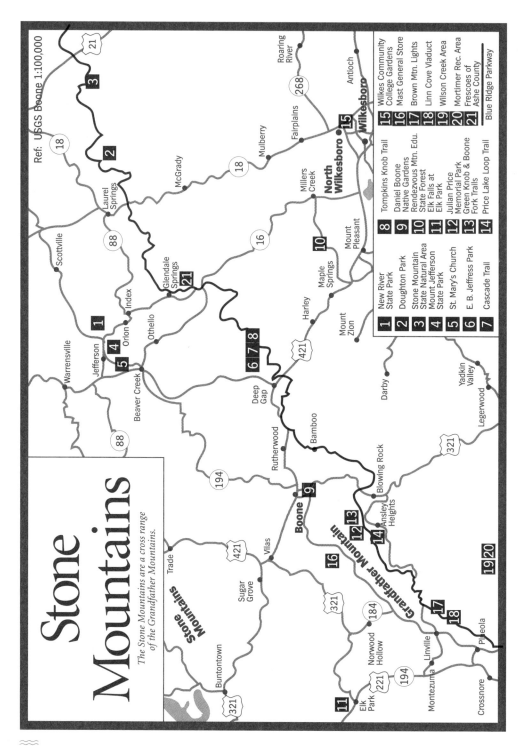

Stone Mountains

The Stone Mountains are a cross range of the Grandfather Mountains.

Ref: USGS Boone 1:100,000

1	New River State Park
2	Doughton Park
3	Stone Mountain State Natural Area
4	Mount Jefferson State Park
5	St. Mary's Church
6	E. B. Jeffress Park
7	Cascade Trail
8	Tompkins Knob Trail
9	Daniel Boone Native Gardens
10	Rendezvous Mtn. Edu. State Forest
11	Elk Falls at Elk Park
12	Julian Price Memorial Park
13	Green Knob & Boone Fork Trails
14	Price Lake Loop Trail
15	Wilkes Community College Gardens
16	Mast General Store
17	Brown Mtn. Lights
18	Linn Cove Viaduct
19	Wilson Creek Area
20	Mortimer Rec. Area
21	Frescoes of Ashe County
	Blue Ridge Parkway

Beavers (*Castor canadensis*) have recently been reintroduced to the New River area, and sightings of white-tailed deer, black bears, mink (*Mustela vison*), muskrats (*Ondatra zibethicus*), otters (*Lutra canadensis*), and raccoons are likely. A variety of lizards, turtles, salamanders, and nonpoisonous water snakes are common to the wetlands and river's edge, while smallmouth bass (*Micropterus dolomieui*) and rainbow trout (*Salmo gairdneri*) populate the river and its tributaries. In fact, locals claim that the New River offers some of the best bass fishing in the state. Most fishing is done by wading the shallow waters, as banks are either limited or privately owned.

For hikers, an easy, 1-mile, self-guiding nature trail at the Wagoner Road Access area [Fig. 7(5)] features 19 interpretive stations offering information about creek habitat, lichens, flowers, and trees. A new 1.5-mile hiking trail connects with the nature trail and courses through surrounding woodlands with a segment paralleling the river. Both trails are accessible from the Wagoner Road Access parking lot, picnic area, and campground.

Directions: New River State Park is located in Ashe and Alleghany counties. To reach the Wagoner Road access, from Jefferson take NC 88 southeast and turn north on SR 1590. The access is located 8 miles southeast of Jefferson, and the park office is located just beyond the entry gate. The US 221 access area is located 8 miles northeast of Jefferson, 1 mile upstream from the US 221 bridge at Scottville. The Alleghany access area is located 1 mile from the North Carolina/Virginia border, and may only be reached by canoe.

Activities: Canoeing, hiking, camping, picnicking. Park rangers lead programs on the natural and cultural history of the area.

Facilities: Park office, restrooms, drinking water, primitive camping, food and drink machines, trails, playgrounds. Park access areas include picnic areas.

Canoe launch: Canoeists may leave their vehicles and launch canoes at the Wagoner Road Access or at the US 221 Access. Canoes may also be launched from several bridges and roadways that cross the river. It is important to note that during heavy rains, the New River is subject to flooding. Canoeists should wear flotation devices and portage around all low-water bridges to avoid entrapment.

Camping: The 3 access areas at New River State Park provide canoe-in, or walk-in, primitive campgrounds. At the Wagoner Road Access, campers may park and carry their supplies to the campsite or canoe downstream to a take-out ramp at the campground. The US 221 Access has 9 primitive campsites. The Alleghany Access, which can only be accessed by canoe, has 8 sites. Campers must register with park staff or at a registration box.

Dates: Open year-round.

Fees: A fee is charged for camping.

For more information: New River State Park, PO Box 48, Jefferson, NC 28640. Phone (910) 982-2587.

Stone Mountain State Park

Stone Mountain State Park is North Carolina's largest state park with 13,500 acres.

Ref: USGS Boone 1:100,000

To Sparta

BLUE RIDGE PARKWAY 21

1

2

BULLHEAD CREEK

WIDOW'S CREEK

GARDEN CREEK

RICH MOUNTAIN CREEK

Roaring Gap

3

4

Stone Mountain

5

6

7

8

9

10

11

12

13

14

15

16

17

18

19

17

1 MILE

EAST PRONG / ROARING RIVER   1737

John P. Frank Parkway

BIG SANDY CREEK

21

N

1002

Traphill

To North Wilkesboro

To Elkin

1	Devil's Garden Overlook	**8**	Stone Mountain Trail	**15**	Park Office
2	Stone Mountain Overlook	**9**	Wolf Rock	**16**	Horse Trailer Parking
3	Widow's Creek Trail	**10**	Cedar Rock	**17**	Park Entrance
4	Widow's Creek Falls	**11**	Stone Mountain Falls Trail	**18**	Bridle Trail
5	View of Stone Mountain	**12**	Black Jack Ridge Trail	**19**	Lower Falls
6	Wolf Rock Trail	**13**	Middle Falls		Park Boundary
7	Cedar Rock Trail	**14**	Stone Mountain Falls		Trail

Stone Mountain State Park

[Fig. 3(9), Fig. 9] Just east of the Blue Ridge escarpment, a granite dome rises 600 feet above the valley floor to a height of 2,305 feet. In the morning sun, the smooth surface gleams in sharp contrast to the vegetation below. Geologists call it a monadnock, hikers call it massive, and rappellers dub it matchless.

The origins of Stone Mountain, the central focus and namesake of the 13,500-acre state park (North Carolina's largest) date back 500 million years when sandy, muddy sediments and volcanic lava and ash were deposited, buried, and compressed into rocks. Many upheavals during mountain-making periods followed, pushing these rocks closer to the surface in what geologists call the Alligator Back Formation. The granite that makes up Stone Mountain and its exposures—Wolf Mountain, Cedar Rock, Little Stone Mountain, Buzzard Rock, First Flat Rock, Hitching Rock—developed from magma cooling and crystallizing 400 million years ago. Almost 200 million years later, overlying rocks began eroding, with rivers carrying the resulting sediment eastward to the Atlantic. The pressure over the rock mass lessened, causing it to expand upward and creating lines of fractures and slabs of rock known as exfoliation sheets, which, as they erode, give the mountain its dome shape.

Twenty miles of hiking trails lead across and around the great dome and past natural rock shelters large enough to provide cover from a sudden rainstorm. Other geologic features along these trails include xenoliths and weather pits. Xenoliths, or "foreign rocks," are the remains of older rocks that were invaded by molten rock. When the hot, molten materials did not completely dissolve the surrounding rock, xenoliths formed. At Stone Mountain, they are composed primarily of biotite gneiss and amphibolite, which give a dark cast to the granite, similar to the rocks on Mount Jefferson west of the park.

Weather pits, which can give the granitic rock a distinctive pockmarked surface, form when certain minerals weather faster than others and water collects in the depressions; eventually the depressions enlarge and merge. Around these moist depressions, lichens and mosses are established and begin to spread. As they do, they not only loosen tiny rock particles but secrete a mild acid that aids in the chemical breakdown of rock, known as primary succession. Slowly, this process continues until eventually a thin layer of soil forms. Larger vegetation gradually finds a place to root, and over time, a very long time, reforestation occurs.

Stone Mountain has grown in popularity with rock climbers since 1965 when the first party reached the summit by way of the south face. Improvements such as strategically placed climbing bolts and hangers add to the mountain's attractiveness to climbers. Throughout the year, climbers can be observed near the base (which measures 4 miles in circumference) practicing on huge boulders before attempting one of the 13 ascent routes. Sporting colorful names such as Great White Way, The Great Arch, Mercury's Lead, Fantastic, No Alternative, and Grand Funk Railroad, the

A hiker enjoys the view from the summit of Stone Mountain at Stone Mountain Park. Stone Mountain is a granite dome that rises 600 feet above the surrounding forests. A variety of domes are visible in the 13,000-acre park, which are the exposed sections of a 25-square mile pluton or large igneous rock that was formed underground and eventually exposed due to erosion.

routes provide access to what many deem the best "friction climbing" in the South. (Friction climbing is a method of rock climbing that involves using the cracks and hollows discovered along the smooth surface for footholds.)

As the interconnecting hiking trails wind through the park, they pass through a number of habitats: dense woodlands, small streams, grassy meadows, mountaintop, and three waterfalls on Big Sandy Creek (Stone Mountain Falls [Fig. 9(14)], Middle Falls [Fig. 9(13)], and Lower Falls [Fig. 9(19)]). With so many habitats for both Piedmont and mountain species, Stone Mountain Park harbors abundant wildlife, earning it the designation of National Natural Landmark. Woodlands in the valley, with their yellow-poplar, hickory, birch, Fraser magnolia, and Eastern hemlock growths, are typical of the cove hardwood forest. Higher elevations feature chestnuts and scarlet oaks (*Quercus prinus* and *Q. coccinea*) with an understory of shrubs such as blueberry (*Vaccinium*) and mountain laurel. As the soil layer thins, the line between the rock and the trees becomes more pronounced with only lichen, mosses, and ferns clinging precipitously to the sheer, rocky surface.

Birds are plentiful in the park and include scarlet tanager, American woodcock

(*Philohela minor*), whip-poor-will (*Caprimulgus vociferus*), ruffed grouse (*Bonasa umbellus*), Eastern screech owl (*Otus asio*), wood duck, and wild turkey. Wild turkeys were once so abundant in Western North Carolina that, according to legend, the Cherokee would only allow their children to hunt the animals because the turkeys posed no threat. European settlers had an easy time of it as well, until the turn of the century when few turkeys remained due to years of unregulated hunting and habitat destruction. Restoration efforts by the North Carolina Wildlife Resources Commission have reversed this trend; wild turkey populations reached more than 30,000 statewide in 1992. Other interesting fauna roaming the park include an occasional sure-footed wild goat, white-tailed deer, box turtles (*Terrapene carolina*), and a number of salamanders.

Big Sandy Creek, Widows Creek, Garden Creek, and parts of Stone Mountain Creek are classified Wild Trout Waters. This classification refers generally to all waters that naturally support wild trout. Restrictions vary with each stream. Here the there are limits to the number of fish that can be taken, and only artificial lures with single hooks are allowed. Other designations such as Hatchery-Supported Trout Waters apply to waters such as the East Prong of Roaring River that are stocked throughout the fishing season. Regulations on Wild Trout Waters vary but include catch and release, fly-fishing only, artificial lures only, and natural bait allowance. A total of 17 miles of trout waters flow through the park.

Directions: From Sparta, travel south on US 21 approximately 10.5 miles south of the Blue Ridge Parkway to the junction with Traphill Road (SR 1002). Turn right and continue for 4.5 miles. At John P. Frank Parkway turn right; the park is 2.4 miles ahead. The visitor center is on the right.

Activities: Hiking, picnicking, camping, fishing, rock climbing. Note: The park is adjacent to the Thurmond Chatham Game Land; check local hunting dates and regulations.

Facilities: Picnic area with 3 picnic shelters (by reservation) and 71 tables and a grill; 37 campsites with table and grill; water nearby; restrooms; two primitive group camps; 6 backpack campsites.

Dates: Open year-round.

Fees: A fee is charged for campsites.

Closest town: Sparta, 12–14 miles.

For more information: 3042 Franks Parkway, Roaring Gap, NC 28668. Phone (910) 957-8185.

WILD TURKEY
(*Meleagris gallopavo*)
Turkeys can fly well for short distances but prefer to run.

Rendezvous Mountain Educational State Forest

[Fig. 8(10)] On land deeded to the state by Judge T. B. Finley in 1926, Rendezvous Mountain Educational State Forest serves as a 146-acre haven for the flora and fauna living within its woodlands. It opened to the public in 1984 as one of six educational forests in North Carolina.

Rendezvous Mountain takes its name from a legend dating back to the Revolutionary War. As local legend has it, Colonel Benjamin Cleveland rallied his militia of mountain patriots from its summit before leading them on to a decisive victory at the Battle of Kings Mountain (*See* Overmountain Trail, page 78). On an immense trumpet scaled to the size of its owner, himself an imposing 300 pounds, Cleveland blew long blasts facing north, south, east, and west, and then he watched as his men in the valleys below saddled their horses and galloped toward the mountain. It was said that the strength of the trumpet's blast was such that the sound echoed and reechoed until it finally broke on the Blowing Rock, some 30 miles west.

Rendezvous's small but commanding peak lies at the eastern edge of the Blue Ridge escarpment, in the foothills that separate the Blue Ridge Mountains from the gentle rolling hills of the Piedmont. Rendezvous rises to its narrow summit at the southeastern extremity of Judd Mountain, a larger mountain mass that forms a steep ridge between the Reddies River and the Lewis Fork Creek, both tributaries of the Yadkin River. This ridged rock formation, known to geologists as the Alligator Back Formation, was uplifted and thrust westward in mountain-making collisions more than 570 million years ago.

The same steep terrain that made the spot ideal for a military rendezvous also restricted timbering in the area. Undisturbed by man, a natural forest community of hardwoods flourished with oaks, yellow-poplars, red maples, hickories, and dogwoods, some now more than 200 years old and measuring 30 inches in diameter. Under this canopy, bloodroot (*Sanguinaria canadensis*), trillium, jack-in-the-pulpit, pink lady slipper, columbine (*Aquilegia canadensis*), and, more rarely, ginseng (*Panax quinquefolium*), bloom in early and late spring. Wild turkeys and ruffed grouse, many varieties of warblers, and indigo buntings make their home in the forest with the occasional white-tailed deer and black bear crashing through the brush.

A highlight of Rendezvous Mountain Educational State Forest is its Talking Tree Trail, where trees "tell" their own (recorded) stories, from their fears about forest fires to the history of their site. A Forest Demonstration Trail offers a scenic introduction to forestry practices. Ranger-conducted programs are also available to groups visiting the forest.

Directions: From Wilkesboro, travel west on US 421 to NC 16. Turn right and go 2.9 miles to Boone Trail (Old US 421). Turn left and travel 2.8 miles to Purlear Road

(SR 1346). Turn right and after 1.8 miles, turn left on Rendezvous Mountain Road and continue 1.3 miles to the forest entrance.

Activities: Hiking.

Facilities: Educational trails and exhibits, amphitheater, picnic shelter for 125, picnic tables and grills, restrooms.

Dates: Open mid-Mar.–mid-Nov. (Fri. before Thanksgiving).

Fees: None.

Closest town: Wilkesboro, 12 miles.

For more information: Rendezvous Mountain ESF, 1956 Rendezvous Mountain Road, Purlear, NC 28665. Phone (910) 667-5072.

Wilkes Community College Gardens

[Fig. 8(15)] From its cultivated roses to long stretches of native wildflowers, the gardens on the campus of Wilkes Community College provide a peaceful yet colorful respite from a busy world. A number of themed areas make up the gardens, such as the Native Garden, with its 1-mile walking trail through growths of native trees and wildflowers; the Japanese Garden; a 600-bush Rose Garden; and the Merle Watson Garden for the Senses.

In 1987, world-renowned musician Arthel "Doc" Watson founded the Merle Watson Garden for the Senses to honor his son and performing partner, Merle, who died two years before in a tragic accident. A benefit concert at the college to raise funds for the memorial garden has become an annual event known as Merlefest, a premiere outdoor concert performed by the biggest names in blue grass and folk music.

The Merle Watson Garden for the Senses has steadily grown over the past decade and is now close to completion. The emphasis on design and plant materials suitable for the visually impaired offers a tribute to Doc Watson, who lost his eyesight as a boy. Designed with gently sloping walkways, the garden hosts plants rich in fragrance and texture, Braille plant-identification signs, and a semirelief wall sculpture depicting animals and objects beginning with each letter of the alphabet.

Numerous varieties of native witch-hazel grace the garden. These deciduous shrubs are particularly beautiful in the spring when clusters of pure gold to deep yellow flowers bloom before leaves appear. Just to be different, one variety (*Hamamelis virginia*) blooms in the autumn with small, fragrant blossoms of crumpled, straplike petals that are creamy to bright yellow. Many of the plants are exotics and cultivars, from countries as far flung as Turkey, Iran, Japan, and Belgium.

Directions: In Wilkesboro at the intersection of US 421 and NC 268, travel west on NC 268 .5 mile to the campus of Wilkes Community College.

Dates: Open year-round.

For more information: Wilkes Community College Gardens, phone (910) 838-6100.

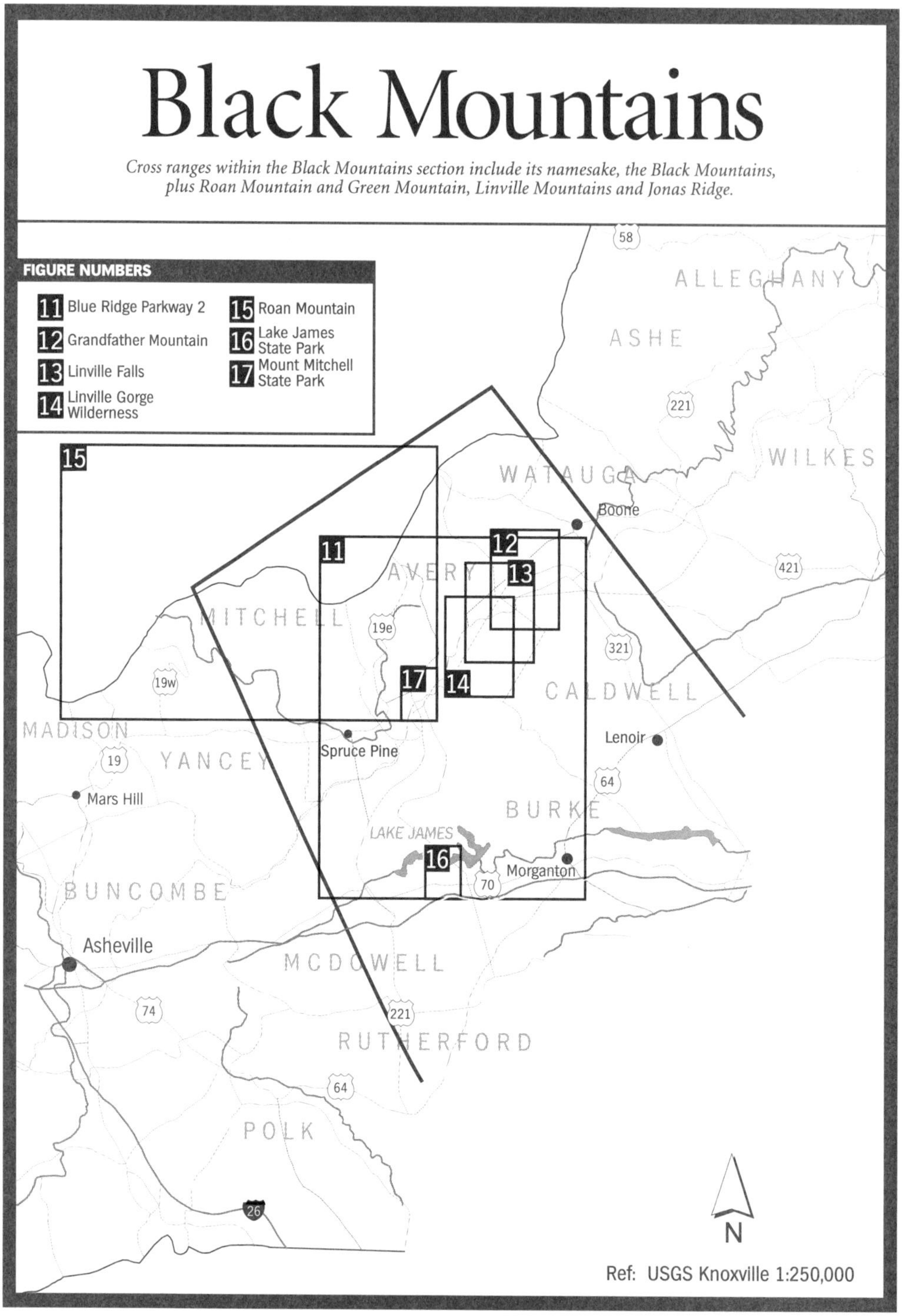

Black Mountains
Cross ranges within the Black Mountains section include its namesake, the Black Mountains, plus Roan Mountain and Green Mountain, Linville Mountains and Jonas Ridge.
FIGURE NUMBERS
11 Blue Ridge Parkway 2
12 Grandfather Mountain
13 Linville Falls
14 Linville Gorge Wilderness
15 Roan Mountain
16 Lake James State Park
17 Mount Mitchell State Park
58
ALLEGHANY
ASHE
221
WILKES
WATAUGA
Boone
421
AVERY
MITCHELL
19e
321
19w
CALDWELL
MADISON
Spruce Pine
Lenoir
19
YANCEY
64
Mars Hill
BURKE
LAKE JAMES
Morganton
70
BUNCOMBE
Asheville
MCDOWELL
74
221
RUTHERFORD
64
POLK
26
N
Ref: USGS Knoxville 1:250,000

The Black Mountains

In the Black Mountains [Fig. 10], the Blue Ridge Mountains reach their grandest scale, higher and more massive than anywhere along their Pennsylvania-to-Georgia expanse. This section of mountains covers an area extending from Boone in the north to Mount Mitchell in the south and bordered on the east by the Blue Ridge escarpment and on the west by the Unaka Mountains. The Blue Ridge Parkway [Fig. 11] courses down its heart, along its ridges, and in the shadow of its peaks. And while all of Western North Carolina is a natural wonderland, this section offers some of the most remarkable geological sites and botanical specimens in the eastern United States. The mountains of North Carolina can be confusing because many share the same name. Consider the Black Mountains. Three peaks in three different areas of the state bear that name. The town of Black Mountain is connected with

[*Above*: Hikers on Grandfather Mountain]

none of them. Moreover, the Black Mountains aren't black; early settlers called them "Black" because of the dark appearance of the fir trees that cover the mountains.

Many times, similar names were used because of the isolation the mountains created. The railroad did not open up the mountains until late in the nineteenth century. As a result, good maps were not available until the turn of the century, and even then, the mountain names selected for maps were usually names used by the local people. The same name continued to be used for different mountains and towns, and confusion persisted.

The Black Mountains, a single, relatively short, horseshoe-shaped ridge extending only 15 miles, are the chief cross range of this section but feature a dozen peaks towering more than 6,000 feet in elevation. Its peaks, often with colorful names such as Potato Hill, Cattail Peak, and Big Tom, include Mount Mitchell (*see* Mount Mitchell, page 89), which holds the distinction of being the highest peak east of the Mississippi with an elevation reaching 6,684 feet.

The mountainous topography affects many aspects of life in the Black Mountains. The height of the mountains changes the air temperature at the rate of approximately three degrees Fahrenheit for every thousand-foot elevation change. At the higher elevations of Mount Mitchell and Grandfather Mountain, habitats more common to New England and Canada support many boreal plants. The mountains also affect rainfall—conditions are wetter on the windward or westward side and considerably drier on the east. Mount Mitchell, for example, receives up to 80 inches of rain each year, twice what falls on Asheville just 25 miles south.

Rivers within this section are directed east and west by the Eastern Continental Divide. Atlantic-bound rivers include the Linville, Yadkin, Johns, and Catawba rivers. The New River is born here among the streams on Flat Top Mountain before heading ultimately to the Ohio River, Mississippi River, and Gulf of Mexico. Other western-flowing rivers include the North Toe, South Toe, Cane, and Nolichucky. The topography of the region affects the speed as well as the direction of the flow. Streams and rivers on the eastern rim travel steeper slopes, gaining speed and cutting rapidly into the underlying rock. Consequently, the eastern slopes have eroded faster than the more gentle slopes of the western side, which, at least in part, explains the dramatic escarpment on the eastern rim.

The topography affects rivers in yet another way. Occasionally the slower western-flowing rivers are "captured" by a more energetic eastern river. For example, as the swift Linville River flows east toward the Atlantic Ocean, it erodes the land upriver and cuts the gorge behind it deeper. As erosion moves upriver over millions of years, the Linville River may change the continental divide, capturing a slower western-flowing river and bringing it east.

In addition to boasting the highest peak east of the Mississippi, this section includes other noteworthy features: a United Nations Biosphere Reserve, snow-covered mountain peaks that support a thriving ski industry, multichambered caverns, and such varied habitats that in some areas migrating birds only have to travel up and down the mountain slope as the seasons change. The first piece of national forest purchased east of the Mississippi lies within this section, southeast of the site of the first state park in North Carolina and near one of the original wilderness areas in the United States that remains as pristine and unspoiled as when the Cherokee lived there. The natural integrity of the region is enhanced by several man-made wonders ranging from botanical gardens to such engineering feats as Lake James and the Linn Cove Viaduct [Fig. 11(4)]. Finally, the region is rich in minerals and gemstones. Mining has played a key role in the economy here, and as more people visit the area, gem mines have opened to families and individuals. While some may call them "touristy," they provide a unique opportunity to expose people young and old to the wonders within the earth's crust.

Brook Trout

Artists paint them. Scientists study them. And grown men, often taciturn about their feelings, write long, heartfelt essays about them. The brook trout (*Salvelinus fontinalis*) is the only trout native to Western North Carolina, living in isolated, high-altitude headwater streams and brooks. Though small in size, averaging 8 to no more than 12 inches, the brook trout holds great allure. To start with, it is beautiful. Its back and upper sides are typically colored olive green with mottled, dark-green wavy markings reaching the dorsal and caudal fins. Its lighter lower sides sport yellow spots and a few red spots surrounded by blue; orange lower fins feature black and white bands. The brook trout's habitat is beautiful, too. Tranquil and remote, pristine streams surrounded by rocks and boulders, hemlocks and rhododendron provide sanctuary from a hectic world. And, of course, the delicate flavor of the brook trout adds to its appeal.

"Brookies" or "speckles," as they are often called, originated in colder northern waters but traveled south with the advancing ice of the glacial age. Once the earth warmed again, they remained in the colder headwaters at elevations above 3,000 feet where the water temperature rarely exceeds 68 degrees Fahrenheit. They cannot survive in temperatures warmer than 75 degrees Fahrenheit. Brook trout prefer clear, stable streams and silt-free gravel for spawning—conditions that have been compromised by human intervention. Late in the nineteenth century, logging operations began the destruction of brook trout habitat when they built poor roads and rail lines that resulted in extensive erosion, siltation, and scouring. In an effort to replace the declining brook trout, Pacific-Coast rainbow and European brown trout were introduced to southern mountain waters early this century. Unfortunately, brook trout compete poorly against these larger, more aggressive fish and are forced to retreat into higher, more remote habitats. Exotic species coupled with acid rain and overfishing have contributed to the decline of the brook trout's range by approximately 75 percent.

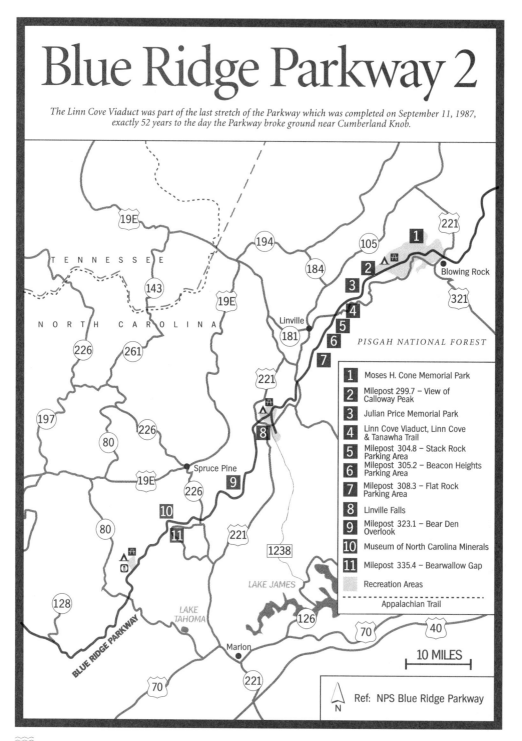

Blue Ridge Parkway 2

The Linn Cove Viaduct was part of the last stretch of the Parkway which was completed on September 11, 1987, exactly 52 years to the day the Parkway broke ground near Cumberland Knob.

1 Moses H. Cone Memorial Park

2 Milepost 299.7 – View of Calloway Peak

3 Julian Price Memorial Park

4 Linn Cove Viaduct, Linn Cove & Tanawha Trail

5 Milepost 304.8 – Stack Rock Parking Area

6 Milepost 305.2 – Beacon Heights Parking Area

7 Milepost 308.3 – Flat Rock Parking Area

8 Linville Falls

9 Milepost 323.1 – Bear Den Overlook

10 Museum of North Carolina Minerals

11 Milepost 335.4 – Bearwallow Gap

Recreation Areas

Appalachian Trail

10 MILES

Ref: NPS Blue Ridge Parkway

The Blue Ridge Parkway in the Black Mountains

[Fig. 11] Breathtaking vistas, waterfalls, hiking trails, trout lakes, nature museums, craft heritage trails, and tunnels are plentiful along this section of the Parkway. So full of wonders, in fact, it hosts four of the seven National Park Service Visitor Centers in North Carolina: Cone Memorial Park [Fig. 11(1)], Linn Cove [Fig. 11(4)], Linville Falls [Fig. 11(8)], and the Museum of North Carolina Minerals Visitor Center [Fig. 11(10)].

Many of the larger parks and trails along the Parkway are covered below, but all of the overlooks are worth a stop, too, such as the View of Calloway Peak at milepost 299.7 [Fig. 11(2)]. In addition to offering a peek at the highest point on Grandfather Mountain (Calloway Peak is Grandfather's nose), the overlook includes two "whaleback" rock outcrops. Geologists call them whalebacks because of the humpbacked shape that develops after centuries of erosion by water, ice, and wind.

At Stack Rock Parking Area, milepost 304.8 [Fig. 11(5)], a short walk along the Tanawha Trail leads to a view of Stack Rock, a natural formation that, as the name implies, appears to be a stack of large rocks. The Beacon Heights parking area, milepost 305.2, offers a short, leg-stretching walk through rhododendron (*Rhododendron catawbiense* and *maximum*), mountain laurel (*Kalmia latifolia*), hemlock (*Tsuga canadensis*), and a host of wildflowers such as teaberry (*Gaultheria procumens*), speckled wood lily (*Clintonia umbellulata*), and wild lily of the valley (*Convallaria montana*). The view from Beacon Heights [Fig. 11(6)] spans across the Linville Falls area, where distinctive Table Rock and Hawksbill Mountain stand out on the horizon.

The effect of strong winds is evident at the Flat Rock Parking Area, milepost 308.3 [Fig. 11(7)], elevation 3,948 feet. Trees here appear to be pruned, but that is actually the handiwork of whipping winds, some clocked at close to 100 miles per hour. The moderately easy, .7-mile, self-guiding loop trail features information describing the rich flora found along the Parkway and passes the Flat Rock, a quartzite outcropping interwoven with white quartz veins formed when still-molten quartz filled cracks between faster cooling rock. Farther south, Bear Den Overlook, milepost 323.1 [Fig. 11(9)], and Bearwallow Gap, milepost 335.4 [Fig. 11(11)], are just two Parkway stops recognizing an important mountain resident. As many as 100,000 black bears (*Ursus americanus*) once lived in North Carolina; today only 4,000 bears live throughout the state because of declining habitat and poaching. Black bears are very shy and nonaggressive, but they occasionally wander into populated areas in search of food. In case of an encounter, visitors are advised to stop and slowly back away.

While the entire length of the Blue Ridge Parkway is an engineering marvel, the five tunnels and renowned Linn Cove Viaduct [Fig. 11(4)] in this section are especially noteworthy. As a result of local concern for the environment and the Parkway's commitment to the protection of the ecology, construction took much longer than normal. The Linn Cove Viaduct was part of the last stretch of the Parkway to be completed on September 11, 1987, exactly 52 years to the day the Parkway broke ground near Cumberland Knob.

Elk Falls at Elk Park

[Fig. 8(11)] Elk Park draws its name from a settlement near the North Carolina/Tennessee line that dates back to 1885. The once-abundant elk (*Cervus elaphus*) were extirpated from North Carolina around 1800, but early settlers memorialized these glorious 1,000-pound beasts by naming many favorite places "Elk."

The Elk River flows through a broad valley leading to Elk Falls on a small tract of the Pisgah National Forest. Elk Falls can claim many superlatives: its 50-foot plunge surrounded by sheer cliffs makes it one of the most beautiful in the state, it features one of the largest and deepest pools in the state, and it is very easy to reach. A short, .25-mile trail leads downstream from the picnic area through a forest of hemlock and rhododendron along the Elk River. At the head of the falls, a flight of steps leads to the bottom where flat rocks make an ideal spot for sunbathers, picnickers, and swimmers taking a rest. Public trout-fishing areas are limited but offer good conditions. Elk Park is on the Mission Crossing Scenic Byway established by the NC Department of Transportation.

Directions: From NC 19E in Elk Park, turn onto NC 1303 and travel .3 mile to Elk River Road (SR 1305). Turn left and drive 3.9 miles (the last 1.5 miles gravel surface) to a small parking area and the picnic grounds.

Activities: Hiking, fishing, picnicking

Facilities: Picnic area with 12 tables an

Dates: Open year-round.

Fees: None.

Closest town: Elk Park, 4 miles.

ELK FALLS TRAIL

Trail distance and configuration: .5-mile round trip.

Elevation: 2,800 feet.

Degree of difficulty: Easy.

Surface and blaze: Forest floor and rock.

SPRING PEEPER
(Hyla crucifer)
This treefrog is identified
by an X on its back.

Ski Resorts in Western North Carolina

More than 1 billion years ago, intrusions of igneous and volcanic rocks flowed over and through the mountainous regions of the state. Near the modern towns of Linville and Beech Mountain in Avery County, the intruding rocks comprise more than 50 percent of an ancient terrain known as the Elk Park Plutonic Suite. Rich in granite, this area was less susceptible to the powers of erosion, leaving towering, snow-covered peaks ideal for skiing. Most years the climate cooperates, with mean temperatures more akin to Canada than the valleys below. Thousands of winter sport fans are served by four ski resorts in Avery and Watauga counties with expert, advanced, and beginner slopes, snowboarding, snow skating, and skating rinks. In addition, some resorts offer access to cross-country skiing trails. To take advantage of the mild summer temperatures, ski areas are also opening up to mountain bike competitions during the summer months.

At 5,505 feet, Beech Mountain is the highest ski area in eastern North America. Nearby Sugar Mountain reaches 5,300 feet, Hawksnest measures 4,819 feet, and Appalachian Ski Mountain peaks out at 4,000 feet. Vertical drops range from a dramatic 1,200 feet to 365 feet. (*See* Appendix F, page 302 for detailed listings of all ski areas in the state.)

Mast General Store

[Fig. 8(16)] Isolated by twisting roads in questionable condition, mountain settlers came to rely on general stores to keep them in touch and supplied. Since 1883, Mast General Store has played a key role in the community surrounding Valle Crucis, so named because three creeks converge there in the shape of a cross.

The store, which once had the reputation for carrying "everything from cradles to caskets," continues to serve both as a place to gather and a storehouse of clothing, footwear, outdoor gear, maps, and books. Nearby, an antique post office is still used by the valley's residents.

Because the valley remains much as it was in its early days, the state of North Carolina has recognized this area as its first Rural Historic District.

Directions: From Boone, take NC 105 south 5 miles. Turn right on SR 1112 (Camp Broadstone Road) into Valle Crucis on NC 194, one of 9 roads in Western North Carolina designated by the NC Department of Transportation as scenic byways.

Dates: Open year-round.

Closest town: Boone, 8 miles.

For more information: Mast General Store, Highway 194, Valle Crucis, NC 28691. Phone (704) 963-6511.

Daniel Boone Native Gardens

[Fig. 8(9)] The lore and legacy of the great frontiersman Daniel Boone lives on at Daniel Boone Native Gardens, located near his famed Wilderness Road. A wrought-iron gate at the entrance of the 6-acre gardens was a gift from Daniel Boone VI, a direct descendant of the legendary pioneer. The extensive collections of native plants grow much as they would have when the region was still wild. Informally landscaped with trails, ponds, and split-rail fences, the gardens feature North Carolina native plants (many marked for easy identification) such as spring's nodding trillium (*Trillium cernuum*), bloodroot (*Sanguinaria canadensis*), and yellow lady slipper (*Cypripedium calceolus*). A splash of color ushers in summer when the flame azalea (*Rhododendron calendulaceum*), rhododendron, butterfly weed (*Asclepias tuberosa*), and fiery red cardinal flower (*Lobelia cardinalis*) bloom. Goldenrod (*Solidago roanensis*, named for Roan Mountain where it was presumably first discovered) and aster (*Aster curtisii*) bloom from late summer into autumn, when the fall foliage extravaganza steals the show across the horizon. The gardens also serve as a haven for small mammals and birds native to or migrating through the Blue Ridge.

The Daniel Boone Native Gardens are adjacent to *Horn in the West*, an outdoor drama depicting Daniel Boone and the Mountain Men in their struggles toward independence and frontier settlement. Hickory Ridge Homestead, a living museum of early mountain life and culture, shares the grounds where costumed interpreters offer demonstrations in weaving, spinning, candlemaking, and other crafts.

Directions: In Boone at the intersection of NC 105 and US 321, continue north on NC 105 Extension for less than 1 mile to Horn Avenue. Turn left; parking area is ahead.

Facilities: Museum, theater, and gardens.

Dates: Open May–Oct.

Fees: There is a fee for admission.

Closest town: Boone, 1 mile.

For more information: Phone (704) 264-6390.

SUGAR MAPLE (Acer saccharum)
Sugar maple's sap is the source of maple syrup and sugar.

Moses H. Cone Memorial Park

[Fig. 11(1)] Moses H. Cone Memorial Park is an excellent example of Western North Carolina's bountiful natural resources. Twenty-five miles of carriage trails meander throughout the 3,517-acre estate, circling the 22-acre Bass Lake and the 16-acre Trout Lake and ascending two mountains before dropping down to the 20-room, Victorian, neo-Colonial manor house crowning Flat Top Mountain. Cone, the son of a German immigrant who built a thriving wholesale grocery business in the Northeast, ventured south after the Civil War, where he eventually earned a reputation as "the Denim King" with more than 30 textile plants bearing his name. When the railroad and improved roads opened the mountains at the turn of the nineteenth century, Cone acquired more than 3,500 acres ranging in terrain from Flat Top Mountain at 4,558 feet to 500 acres of rolling farmland, patches of meadowland, and virgin hardwood and evergreen forests. He oversaw the planting of apple orchards, imported sugar maples (*Acer saccharum*) from New England, and obtained advice from Gifford Pinchot, the pioneering forester (*see* Cradle of Forestry, page 150), on planting white pine forests and hemlock hedges. Bertha Cone, his widow, continued to live on the estate for almost four decades after Cone's death in 1908. The estate was donated to the National Park Service in 1950.

The Cones rejoiced in their land and its natural beauty. The well-maintained carriage trails, for example, which were designed to give Bertha joy, comfort, and seclusion as she explored her estate, today are havens for hikers, joggers, walkers, equestrians, and cross-country skiers. The Rich Mountain and Flat Top Mountain carriage trails ascend moderately from the Manor House, winding in and out of open land, across streams and meadows, affording spectacular views of rocky Grandfather Mountain. They wind through hardwood forests with thickets of Fraser magnolia (*Magnolia fraseri*), a small tree (up to 40 feet high) found at elevations between 2,000 and 4,000 feet, with pale, yellow flowers up to 12 inches in diameter. Wildflowers are abundant throughout the estate, including spring's painted trillium (*Trillium undulatum*), lousewort (*Pedicularis canadensis*), and wild geranium (*Geranium maculatum*), in addition to the ubiquitous rhododendron and mountain laurel.

While there is no fear of getting lost in The Maze, an area of trees designed by Gifford Pinchot and planted to form sharp switchbacks, this perplexing trail twists and turns through forests of pine, oak, and more magnolia. Pinchot's influence is again felt in the careful placement of the trees. Golden-crowned kinglets (*Regulus satrapa*) and blackburnian warblers (*Dendroica fusca*) can be heard singing high above in the white pines.

The Trout Lake Trail is an easy, 1-mile pathway teeming with wildlife. Set in an impressive hemlock-dominated cove forest with ancient conifers and thickets of rhododendron, Trout Lake offers a diversity of plants and birds common to the higher-elevation spruce-fir and northern hardwood forests. Bird species include

Moses H. Cone Memorial Park is close to excellent skiing opportunities during winter in nearby Blowing Rock, North Carolina.

solitary and red-eyed vireos (*Vireo solitarius* and *Vireo flavoviridis*), rose-breasted grosbeak (*Pheucticus ludovicianus*), Acadian flycatcher (*Empidonax virescens*), black-throated blue warbler (*Dendroica caerulescens*), and Canada warbler (*Wilsonia canadensis*).

The Manor House is now home to the Parkway Craft Center, a craft shop of the Southern Highland Craft Guild, exhibiting works by the finest craft artists from the nine Appalachian states. All mediums are represented, ranging from baskets and woodcarving to quilts and ironwork. The book shop carries trail maps, brochures, nature books, and guidebooks.

Moses H. Cone Memorial Park is only 2 miles outside the charming mountain village of Blowing Rock. At an elevation of 4,000 feet, Blowing Rock offers cool weather in the summer and outstanding skiing opportunities nearby in the winter. An array of interesting shops is complemented by cozy to elegant accommodations and some of the finest dining in the Southeast.

Directions: Blue Ridge Parkway between mileposts 292 and 295.

Activities: Hiking, fishing, horseback riding, cross-country skiing. Boating is not allowed. Trout Lake and Bass Lake are designated as Wild Trout Water, a designation for streams and lakes that sustain wild trout and are not hatchery supported. A variety of regulations apply depending on the site.

Facilities: Manor House craft shop, bookstore. Nearby stables on US 221 between the Parkway and Blowing Rock rent horses by the hour or day.

Dates: Park is open year-round. Manor house and visitor center are open Mar. 21–Jan. 6.

Fees: None.

Closest town: Blowing Rock, 2 miles.

▨ MOSES H. CONE TRAILS

Trail distance and configuration: 25 miles of carriage trails for hiking and horses (no bikes).

Elevations: Bass Lake, 3,560 feet, to Flat Top Mountain, 4,558 feet.

Degree of difficulty: Easy to moderate.

Surface and blaze: No blazes but most are signed at trailheads and junctions. Trail floors range from cinders and crushed gravel to sometimes-muddy forest floor. Benches can be found along some routes.

Julian Price Memorial Park

[Fig. 8(12), Fig. 11(3)] This 4,344-acre tract at the foot of Grandfather Mountain lies between the higher elevations of the Blue Ridge province and the middle-elevations of the Blue Ridge Plateau, giving rise to an abundance of wildlife species along its three trails. The park was donated to the National Park Service as a public recreation area by Jefferson Pilot Standard Life Insurance Company after the death of its president, Julian Price, who owned the land. The Price Lake Loop Trail circles the 47-acre, well-stocked lake where the work of muskrats (*Ondatra zibethicus*), otters (*Lutra canadensis*), and beavers (*Castor canadensis*) is evident. The beaver played an important role in the economy of the state well into the nineteenth century. Trapped nearly to extinction because of its valuable fur, the beaver has benefited from re-stocking programs. While opinions vary as to benefits of beavers, in areas like Julian Price Lake where their presence does not interfere with agriculture and roadways, their positive contributions far outweigh the negative. Beaver constructions can slow runoff from drainage, retard erosion, and provide habitats for other species, including endangered species, especially waterfowl and fish. Populations of wood duck (*Aix sponsa*), for example, grew significantly following increases in beaver populations.

The trail continues through oak forest with laurel and rhododendron and boggy, wetland areas. Wildflowers such as solomon's seal (*Polygonatum biflorum*) and mayapple (*Podophyllum peltatum*) can be easily spotted near the campground, where the Tanawha Trail (*see* Tanawha Trail, page 55) cuts through the park. A lengthy list of late-spring and summer birds includes cedar waxwing (*Bombycilla cedrorum*), chestnut-sided warbler (*Dendroica pensylvanica*), scarlet tanager (*Piranga olivacea*), and ovenbird (*Seiurus aurocapillus*). Waterfowl are not abundant here, but the lake can attract the great blue heron (*Ardea herodias*), green heron (*Butorides virescens*), and wood duck. During the cooler months when the lake is not frozen over, the common loon (*Gavia immer*), Canada goose (*Branta canadensis*), pied-billed grebe (*Podilymbus podiceps*), and green-winged teal (*Anas carolinensis*) have been sighted.

The lake's moist surroundings support interesting wildlife, such as a variety of fungi, including the jack-o'-lantern mushroom (*Omphalotus illudens*) that glows in the dark; the northern water snake (*Nerodia sipedon*), which is often mistaken for its venomous look-alike, the cottonmouth or water moccasin (which does not live within 100 miles of the lake); snapping turtles (*Chelydra serpentina*); bobcats (*Felis rufus*); and other nocturnal mammals such as seldom-seen foxes and more common raccoons (*Procyon lotor*).

Two other trails traverse the park [Fig. 8(13)]: the Green Knob Trail and Boone Fork Trail intersect with the park at the picnic area (*see* Boone Fork Loop Trail, page 54). In a relatively short distance, Green Knob Trail traverses many of the vegetation zones found along the Parkway: lakeside at Sims Pond; bottomland cove forest of old-growth hemlock, maple magnolia, birch, and beech; laurel thickets; and wildflower meadows and open pasture lands with vistas of the rugged Grandfather Mountain. Popular late-spring and summer birds include a wide variety of woodpeckers, eastern phoebe (*Sayornis phoebe*), red-breasted nuthatch (*Sitta canadensis*), wood thrush (*Hylocichla mustelina*), eastern kingbird (*Tyrannus tyrannus*), and as many as 10 warbler species.

Directions: On the Blue Ridge Parkway between mileposts 295.1 and 298.

Activities: Canoeing, hiking, fishing, camping. Boating not allowed.

Facilities: Canoe rentals daily (seasonally) near the parking lot for the Boone Fork Overlook; RV/tent campground with 198 sites that include a tent pad, picnic table, and grill; 6 restrooms (no showers) and water spigots are spread throughout the campground.

Dates: Park open year-round. Campground open May–Oct.

Fees: A fee is charged for camping.

Closest town: Blowing Rock, 4 miles.

PRICE LAKE LOOP TRAIL

Trail distance and configuration: 2.7-mile loop trail.

Elevation: 3,400 feet on Price Lake.

Degree of difficulty: Easy.

Surface and blaze: Forest floor, sometimes moist and boggy; lake trail includes paved sections suitable for handicapped access; no blaze.

GREEN KNOB TRAIL

Trail distance and configuration: 2.3 miles round-trip.

Elevation: 3,920 feet on Green Knob.

Degree of difficulty: Moderate.

Surface and blaze: Forest floor, meadow; no blaze.

BOONE FORK LOOP TRAIL

[Fig. 8(13)] Boone Fork Loop Trail offers a variety of changing terrain and waterways. Beginning on the outskirts of Price Lake near the picnic area in the campground, the trail extends beyond the park, passing through the sphagnum bogs of the Boone Fork wetlands and the banks of Bee Tree Creek. Once an ancient lake bed filled with rich alluvial deposits, this section is now home to diverse plant life including wild mustard (*Brassica*), bloodroot, dwarf iris (*Iris verna*), and red maple (*Acer rubrum*), also called swamp maple. Caves overlooking the area are thought to have sheltered Indians.

Water is seldom out of earshot, as much of the trail borders Boone Fork Creek or Bee Tree Creek, twisting back and forth over wooden bridges and stepping-stones. In a short stretch, Boone Fork transforms itself from a trickling stream into rushing whitewater, tumbling over boulders to form a series of small waterfalls. Sections offer catch-and-release fishing of native brook trout (*Salvelinus fontinalis*).

The land-based environment is equally diverse. In addition to a mountain meadow, the trail passes through second-growth hardwood forests of hemlock, spruce, and an occasional fir mingled with hickory, yellow-poplar (*Liriodendron tulipifera*), and several varieties of birch. Pads of pine needles underfoot give way to sections kept moist by dense thickets of rhododendron, mountain laurel, and flame azalea, which ignite with color in May or June. Beaver activity is evident along Boone Fork Creek, and bird watchers report that the first 700 yards of the right branch of the loop is best for viewing the American woodcock (*Philohela minor*) perform its courtship display from mid-March to April. Indigo bunting (*Passerina cyanea*), scarlet tanager, belted kingfisher (*Megaceryle alcyon*), and cedar waxwing, among others, are present from late spring through summer. The alder flycatcher (*Empidonax traillii*) nests here in the summer (although there are no alder trees), and sightings of broad-winged hawks (*Buteo platypterus*) occur frequently.

Directions: From the Blue Ridge Parkway, stop at the Julian Price Memorial Park picnic area at milepost 296.5. Cross the footbridge leading from the picnic area over Boone Fork Creek to the signed trailhead.

Closest town: Blowing Rock, 5 miles.

Trail distance and configuration: 4.9-mile loop.

Elevation: Boone Fork wetlands are 3,340 feet.

Degree of difficulty: Moderate.

Surface and blaze: Varied, including pine-needle pads, unpaved pathways, stepping-stones, and wooden bridges.

🌄 TANAWHA TRAIL

[Fig. 11(4)] The Tanawha Trail, like the magnificent Linn Cove Viaduct under which it passes, was built to foster appreciation for the natural world and protect the delicate balance of nature that sustains it. At a cost of $750,000, the walkways were carefully designed to protect fragile sections of the mountain-heath ecosystem. Wrapping around the southeastern ridge of Grandfather Mountain, this segment of the Mountains-to-Sea Trail (*see* Mountains-to-Sea Trail, page 287) winds through a variety of geologic features ranging from flat-topped boulders and natural rock gardens to rough outcroppings and cavelike crevices between boulders.

Tanawha, which appropriately is the Cherokee word for "fabulous hawk or eagle," offers soaring sights along its 13.5-mile course, none more beautiful than those on the segment from the Rough Ridge overlook (milepost 302.9) to the top of a rocky ridge. Long stretches of boardwalk and boulder-filled pathways lead past spectacular overlooks to the breathtaking summit. Striking panoramas of the Linn Cove Viaduct adjacent to Grandfather Mountain and the vast horizon punctuated by Hawksbill and Table Rock mountains are always in sight.

Portions of the trail descend into dark and sometimes waterlogged evergreen forests of hemlock and spruce. Others meander through thick patches of rhododendron and mountain laurel mixed with galax (*Galax aphylla*), witch-hazel (*Hamamelis virginiana*), Allegheny sand myrtle (*Leiophyllum buxifolium*), and turkey beard (*Xerophyllum asphodeloides*). Blueberry bushes (*Vaccinium*) splash red across the landscape in early fall. Poplar and mountain-ash (*Sorbus americana*) and undergrowth of jack-in-the-pulpit (*Arisaema triphyllum*), jewelweed (*Impatiens capensis*), and black cohosh (*Cimicifuga racemosa*) fill shady valleys. An isolated stand of large-toothed aspen at its southern limits and shelters of hardwoods such as oak, cherry, and maple contrast with open fields.

The various tree and bush populations support abundant bird life. Early portions of Tanawha are ideal for spotting the barred owl (*Strix varia*), golden-crowned kinglet, black-throated blue warbler, and rufous-sided towhee (*Pipilo erythrophthalmus*). Deeper forested areas harbor white-breasted nuthatch (*Sitta carolinensis*), rose-breasted grosbeak, solitary vireo, and overhead the raven (*Corvus corax*) and peregrine falcon (*Falco peregrinus*).

Meadows are alive in early spring with bluets (*Houstonia caerulea*), cinquefoil, violets, buttercups, and clusters of mayapple. Painted trillium border some pathways, and a variety of ferns thrive along the rocky terrain. An occasional population of umbrella leaf (*Diphylleia cymosa*) is also found here, an uncommon endemic of the southern Appalachians.

Tanawha Trail crosses four creeks, with watercourses ranging from gentle cascades to powerful shoots. Their banks nurture pink turtlehead (*Chelone yoni*), yellow coneflower (*Rudbeckia fulgida*), and scarlet Oswego tea (*Monarda didyma*). In its final section, the trail passes apple orchards, favorable environments for edible fungi such as morels (*Morchella esculenta*).

Directions: The trail runs alongside the Blue Ridge Parkway between mileposts 305.5 (1.5 miles south of Linn Cove Viaduct) and 297.1 (Julian Price Memorial Park campground). There are more than half a dozen parking areas with access to the trail between these points. The Beacon Heights parking area is .1 mile south of the junction of the Blue Ridge Parkway and US 221.

Closest town: Linville, 5 miles (start) or Blowing Rock, 6 miles (terminus).

Trail: 13.5 miles one-way. For easier hiking, it is recommended that this trail be hiked from south to north.

Elevation: Between 4,200 and 4,600 feet.

Degree of difficulty: Ranges from easy to strenuous, with the most challenging section just above Linn Cove Viaduct.

Surface and blaze: Dirt paths, forest floor, boardwalks, and wooden and stone stairs, plus a .15-mile, paved, handicapped-accessible section. All access points are signed with a feather logo.

Linn Cove Viaduct

[Fig. 11(4), Fig. 8(18), Fig. 12(6)] In 1967, all but 7.5 miles of the Blue Ridge Parkway were complete. What became known as the "missing link" would take another 20 years to construct. The delay? A grand mountain and a commitment to its protection. The rugged boundary of Grandfather Mountain stood where customary construction practices said a road should be. After much controversy, North Carolina's then-Governor Dan K. Moore challenged National Park Service landscape architects and Federal Highway Administration engineers to break with convention. They were charged with finding an alternative to blasting through the edge of one of the most ancient mountains in the world. The solution was an engineering feat that resulted in a breathtaking monument to the coexistence of man and nature.

Linn Cove Viaduct, wrapping around Grandfather Mountain, is the most famous feature of the Blue Ridge Parkway in North Carolina and is popular with professional and amateur photographers.

The construction process was an innovative one. The .25-mile-long viaduct was pieced together from above, segment by 8-foot, 50-ton segment, using a crane to virtually eliminate the damage that construction roads and heavy equipment would have imposed on the ground below. Only the drilling for the seven permanent piers that support the structure occurred on the ground, and, through the entire process, only the trees immediately under the viaduct were cut. The elevated bridge seemingly grew northward out of thin air, as each new segment was delivered to the edge of the existing segments, then hoisted over and down and secured into place. The latest computer casting technology was used to measure each uniquely shaped segment to within .0001 feet of accuracy, scientifically shaping the new man-made structure to the curves and contours of the age-old mountain. Finally, the concrete was tinted with iron oxide to make it less obtrusive against the pristine, quartzite summit.

The Linn Cove Viaduct was completed in 1983, and the rest of the 7.5-mile unfinished section of the Blue Ridge Parkway was in place by 1987. At an elevation of 4,100 feet, the viaduct coils like an S-shaped roller coaster track around the mountain's rocky perimeter, providing motorists with spectacular views through what feels like a soaring flight around the edge of the world.

Directions: At Blue Ridge Parkway milepost 304.6.

Closest town: Linville, 4 miles.

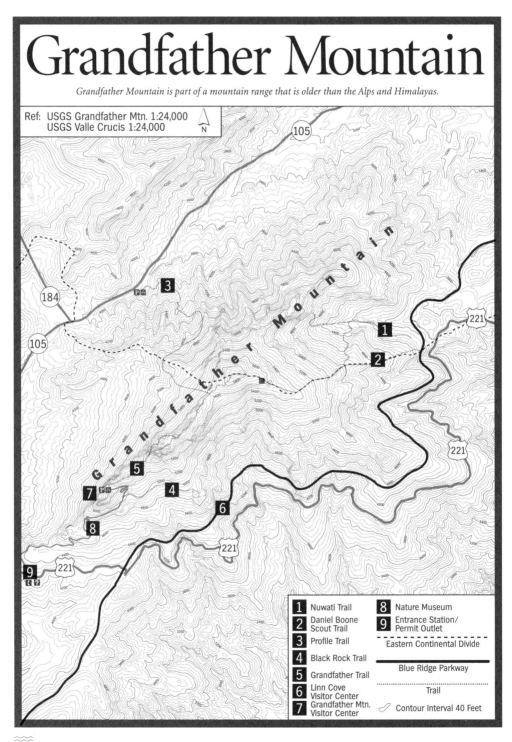

Grandfather Mountain

Grandfather Mountain is part of a mountain range that is older than the Alps and Himalayas.

Ref: USGS Grandfather Mtn. 1:24,000
USGS Valle Crucis 1:24,000

1	Nuwati Trail	8	Nature Museum
2	Daniel Boone Scout Trail	9	Entrance Station/ Permit Outlet
3	Profile Trail		Eastern Continental Divide
4	Black Rock Trail		Blue Ridge Parkway
5	Grandfather Trail		Trail
6	Linn Cove Visitor Center		Contour Interval 40 Feet
7	Grandfather Mtn. Visitor Center		

Grandfather Mountain

[Fig. 12] Looming rough and ornery from the Blue Ridge Parkway, Grandfather Mountain is a 4,000-acre reserve teeming with natural diversity. So much so, in fact, that in 1994 the United Nations designated the 4,000-acre park as a member of the international network of Biosphere Reserves. To meet strict biosphere criteria, Grandfather Mountain had to prove that it had global ecological significance, legal protection from development, a history of scientific study, and provisions for public education. Grandfather Mountain is the first privately owned biosphere out of 337 units in 85 countries.

More than a century ago naturalist Elisha Mitchell noted that the rocks here were unusual for the eastern Blue Ridge. Grandfather Mountain is at the heart of a geologic paradise known appropriately as the Grandfather Mountain Window, a region covering more than 800 square miles in northwestern North Carolina. Millions of years ago when these mountains were formed by the collision of two continental crusts, huge sheets of rock were pushed over each other. The Blue Ridge Thrust Sheet moved more than 60 miles to cover what is now Grandfather Mountain. Some scientists believe these mountains were once 10 times as high as they are today, but erosion over hundreds of millions of years has opened a "window" where younger rock shows through. This window, surrounded by mostly older rock, permits the study of a sequence of rocks ranging in age from old to young. Grand-father Mountain also holds the distinction over other southern mountain terrains as the most extensively bouldered.

Sixteen distinct habitat types can be found on Grandfather Mountain. Each supports a different balance of life, and together they support one of the most diverse groups of flora and fauna in the Southeast. In addition to a range of fir, spruce, and oak forests, Grandfather hosts the rich cove forest, acidic cove forest, and Canada hemlock forest. The montane calcareous cliff habitat features cliff communities with an open canopy and bare substrate resulting from its steepness and rockiness. The heath-bald habitat is distinguished by the absence or near absence of trees; any trees found here are stunted and not much taller than shrubs. The spray-cliff habitat has vertical to gently sloping rock faces, constantly wet from the spray of waterfalls, and the high- elevation rocky summit has substantial areas of bare rock.

The short drive from the preserve's entrance to the top passes through as many climate zones as a drive from North Carolina to Newfoundland, including temperature changes from 5 to 10 degrees Fahrenheit. Halfway up the mountain lies a complex of natural wonders such as Split Rock and Linville Bluffs and man-made wonders such as the seven wildlife habitats, the Visitor Center [Fig. 12(7)], and Nature Museum [Fig. 12(8)]. The habitats are home to more common species such as black bears, white-tailed deer, otters, and golden eagles (*Aquila chrysaetos*), as well as fauna such as panthers (*Felis concolor*) and bald eagles (*Haliaeetus leucocephala*) that

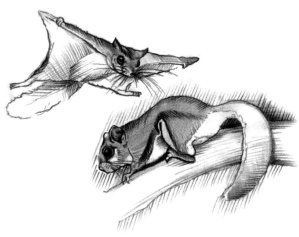

SOUTHERN FLYING SQUIRREL
(Glaucomys volans)
This squirrel doesn't fly but glides.

are now rare to the area. Together, however, these habitats provide a sense of the wildlife that roamed here 200 years ago when the Cherokee called the mountain *Tanawha,* or "Great Hawk." In keeping with its name, the mountain is populated with hawks and owls, including endangered species such as the northern saw-whet owl (*Aegolius acadicus*) and peregrine falcon. Grandfather Mountain is also a central rallying point for approximately 50 ravens, possibly the largest colony east of the Rockies and south of New England.

A contemporary, 11,000-square-foot Nature Museum hosts an auditorium presenting award-winning nature films and sophisticated weather stations open to the public, as well as the Nature Museum itself. The museum houses two dozen remarkably realistic displays of wildflowers, edible berries, mushrooms, minerals, birds, and some of the endangered species living in the biosphere. Grandfather hosts 11 globally imperiled species (species found in 20 or fewer places worldwide) such as the North Carolina Funnelweb tarantula, rock gnome lichen, bent avens, Blue Ridge goldenrod, spreading avens, Heller's blazing star, mountain bittercress, trailing wolfsbane (*Axonitum reclinatum*), Gray's lily (*Lilium grayi*), Carolina saxifrage, and manhart's sedge. A total of 42 rare and endangered species have been identified on the mountain (more than in all of the Great Smoky Mountain National Park), including North Carolina critically imperiled species (five or fewer occurrences) such as Virginia big-eared bat (*Plecotus townsendii virginianus*), Carolina northern flying squirrel (*Glaucomys sabrinus coloatus*), magnolia warbler (*Dendroica magnolia*), mountain bluet, rosefoot, and hemlock parsley. Grandfather Mountain is also distinguished as one of the Blue Ridge's best sites for salamanders with up to 16 species. The Yonahlossee salamander (*Plethodon yonahlossee*), for example, is unique to a small area leading to the edges of Virginia and Tennessee with Grandfather Mountain at the center. Such a diverse and lush ecosystem helps explain Grandfather's longtime attractiveness to naturalists and botanists. Asa Gray, André and François Michaux, Elisha Mitchell, and more recently John Muir have all rejoiced in the native bounty they found here (*see* Naturalists, page 230).

As the road winds toward the top, several points along the way are worth a stop, including the panoramic Cliffside Picnic Area and Scheer Bluff overlooking red spruce–hardwood forests to the mountains beyond. Almost 2 miles from the top, the Black Rock Parking Area offers a seemingly endless mountain vista, as well as the entrance to Black Rock Nature Trail and Bridge Trail.

TRAILS OF GRANDFATHER MOUNTAIN

Black Rock Nature Trail [Fig. 12(4)] is a 1.8-mile-long, easy-to-moderate walk through northern hardwood and spruce forests at elevations ranging from 4,700 feet to 5,040 feet. In spring and summer, bird watchers flock here to spot red-breasted nuthatches, winter wrens (*Troglodytes troglodytes*), and chestnut-sided warblers. Near the well-marked trailhead, interpretive pamphlets, stored in a box, are packed with interesting facts about the 35 stops along the trail. The American mountain-ash, yellow birch (*Betula lutea*), and sweet pepperbush (*Clethra acuminata*) are cited, as well as the nutritious and medicinal smooth rock tripe (*Umbilicaria mammulata*) growing along the Arch Rock.

At the Moss Garden, quartz veins, formed when still-molten quartz filled cracks between faster-cooling rock, are studied, and the role of small plants and mosses in soil formations is explored. Sand myrtle (*Leiophyllum buxifolium prostatum*) helps explain Grandfather Mountain's nickname, "An Island of the North in the South." This low-growing evergreen shrub, which thrives on the mountain's exposed rocky outcrops, is not usually found this far south. Many species found only in New England or Canada grow in the upper elevations of the Blue Ridge, remnants of early ice ages when cold-climate species grew throughout the Southeast. As temperatures warmed, the flora and fauna moved to these higher elevations to survive, and many remain there today. Finally, the trail leads to a spectacular view of Table Rock, Hawksbill Mountain, Linville Gorge, and Mount Mitchell, among others, before turning to retrace the path back to the parking lot.

The Bridge Trail is a moderate, .4-mile, switchback trail that leads to the famed Mile High Swinging Bridge, built in 1952 to span an 80-foot-deep ravine. It is reportedly the highest suspension footbridge in America. The route travels through massive rock formations that help form Grandfather's craggy Linville Peak and a cross-section of trees, shrubs, and wildflowers including examples of *Azaleea vaseyi*, a rare and endangered May-blooming shrub; Grandfather Mountain has the largest population of vaseyi in the world.

Some of the South's finest alpine hiking trails traverse Grandfather Mountain. When French explorer-botanist André Michaux arrived at the summit of Grandfather Mountain during the eighteenth century, he broke into song, certain he had reached the highest point in America. Although at 5,964 feet the mountain falls short of that distinction, it is still a spectacular sight. The 12-mile trail system is documented in the free *Backcountry Trail Guide* available with admission tickets or hiking permits. Within the nine-trail

EASTERN WHITE PINE
(Pinus strobus)

system, Grandfather Trail [Fig. 12(5)] is the most spectacular. It starts near the Swinging Bridge and eventually connects to Grandfather's three highest peaks. Its length of only 2.2 miles is deceiving—Grandfather Trail is rugged and difficult to navigate (requiring wooden ladders in places to traverse sheer cliff faces). It intersects with the Daniel Boone Scout [Fig. 12(2)] and Cragway trails, which in turn lead to the Tanawha Trail and the Blue Ridge Parkway.

Profile Trail [Fig. 12(3)], with a trailhead off Highway 105 near Banner Elk, offers a gradual ascent with numerous switchbacks to ease the climb up the mountain face along its 2.7-mile trek (one-way). Like all the trails on Grandfather Mountain, it eventually connects with the other trails. Along the way, Profile Trail passes through more ecological communities and climate zones than any other trail on the mountain.

Permits or admission tickets are required for hiking all trails (strictly enforced). All hikers should obtain a *Backcountry Trail Guide* when purchasing permits/tickets. Trails are carefully mapped and illustrated with information on length, degree of difficulty, and blaze color.

The dramatic geology has produced a number of waterfalls in the area. Streams on Grandfather's northern side feed into the Watauga River before they develop enough size to create waterfalls. Streams on the southern side, however, are able to build in size before tumbling down the Blue Ridge escarpment, which from the summit of Calloway Peak to the valley below is a drop of 5,000 feet, the greatest drainage relief found along the escarpment. In his book *North Carolina Waterfalls*, Kevin Adams offers detailed information on locating nine nearby waterfalls.

Directions: From the junction of US 221 and NC 105 in Linville, turn north on US 221 at the large Grandfather Mountain sign. Go 2.2 miles up the winding road to the entrance gate on the left. Or, from the Blue Ridge Parkway at milepost 305.3, take US 221 1 mile south to the entrance gate on the right.

Activities: Hiking, primitive backcountry camping in designated areas, picnicking. Fishing, hunting, mountain biking, and horseback riding are not allowed.

Facilities: Visitor center, nature museum, picnic areas.

Dates: Open year-round.

Fees: There is a fee for admission and for hiking permits. *Backcountry Trail Guide* is free with admission.

Closest town: Linville, 2.2 miles.

For more information: Grandfather Mountain, PO Box 129, Linville, NC 28646. Phone (800) 468-7325 or (704) 733-4337.

Wilson Creek Recreation Area

[Fig. 8(19)] The Wilson Creek Recreational Area stands as testimony to nature's unfailing ability to rejuvenate. Damaged by repeated logging, two fires, and two floods early in this century, Wilson Creek today boasts approximately 100 square miles of forested mountains and streams with more than a dozen hiking trails, a network of trout fishing streams, and several scenic waterfalls. Located in Pisgah National Forest northeast of Morganton, Wilson Creek is adjacent to other noteworthy sites such as Grandfather Mountain, Linville Gorge Wilderness Area, and Brown Mountain.

This area was once a Cherokee hunting ground and includes a portion of the Nickajack Trail, an important Native American pathway that extended from Hickory, North Carolina, to Chattanooga, Tennessee. Shortly after 1750, the European pioneers settled here and began logging the dense forests. Mortimer, the largest community, was the site of the Riddle Lumber Company sawmill and a small textile mill, which provided jobs for the community's 800 residents. Substantial logging took place between Wilson and Steel creeks, and the trees were hauled to the mill via a narrow-gauge railroad.

In 1916, a fire burned from Grandfather Mountain to Wilson Creek, and was immediately followed by a flood which destroyed the logging railroad. In 1925, a second fire swept through, this time from Upper Creek to the south. The railroad, which had been rebuilt, was lost once again. When a second flood hit the area, it washed away both the sawmill and the textile mill. Those economies never recovered, and few residents remain in the community today.

The Wilson Creek area now enjoys a new tourism economy based on its rich backcountry. More than 75 miles of hiking trails offer treks through a variety of habitats: creekside, ridgetop, rocky overlooks, woodland, and waterfalls. The trails course through yellow birch and sycamore trees growing in lowland sites in the Wilson Creek area and through oak, maple, and hickory stands in the highland forests. Mountain laurel and rhododendron grow in dense thickets throughout the region. One off-road vehicle trail has been designated along Wilson Ridge, far removed from the hiking trails.

Late-spring and summer birds include the wood thrush, catbird (*Dumetella carolinensis*), chestnut-sided warbler (*Dendroica pensylvanica*), ovenbird, and near Wilson Creek the least flycatcher (*Empidonax minimus*) and warbling vireo (*Vireo gilvus*). Wilson Creek is also known as a good site for watching the autumn hawk migrations. The area has been stocked with bear and wild turkey (*Meleagris gallopavo*) and supports a large white-tailed deer population, plus many squirrels and ruffed grouse (*Bonasa umbellus*). More than 100 miles of trout streams are designated as general, native, or trophy trout waters and have made Wilson Creek one of the best fishing destinations in the region.

As the river runs through the Wilson Creek Gorge, it tumbles and turns over rocks and boulders to form cascades, small falls, and pools ideal for kayaking and canoeing by experienced paddlers. There are numerous places, too, for the more leisurely water enthusiast. Popular mountain biking-trails include the 15-mile Wilson Ridge Trail and the 2.4-mile Woodruff Branch Trail; both are rated moderate. The mystery of the Brown Mountain Lights adds another enjoyable element to a trip into Wilson Creek (*see* Brown Mountain Lights, page 65).

(From top to bottom)
BROWN TROUT (Salmo trutta)
BROOK TROUT (Salvelinus fontinalus)
RAINBOW TROUT (Oncorhynchus mykiss)
The brook trout is the only fish of these three that is native to the Appalachians; the others are stocked.

Directions: To Mortimer Recreation Area: From Morganton, travel 10.5 miles north on NC 181 to Brown Mountain Beach Road (also referred to as Collettsville Road and SR 1405). Turn right and continue for 5 miles to SR 1328. Turn left and continue 4.5 miles. Cross the Wilson Creek bridge and bear to the right; turn left at the stop sign. The campground is 4.5 miles ahead.

Activities: Hiking, car camping, backcountry camping, off-road vehicle riding, trout fishing, kayaking/canoeing, mountain biking.

Facilities: Campground (with parking) at Mortimer Recreation Area. There is one developed campground, near the sparsely populated Mortimer community, as well as a picnic site, the Barkhouse Picnic Area, located on NC 181 near the western boundary of the Recreation Area.

Dates: Open year-round.

Fees: A fee is charged for camping at Mortimer; camping is free elsewhere.

Closest town: Linville, 2 miles; Morganton, 25 miles. Although the Wilson Creek recreation area northwest boundary lies on the east side of the Blue Ridge Parkway, only 2 miles from Linville, it is a difficult road to the campground.

For more information: U.S. Forest Service District Ranger, Route 1, Box 110A, Nebo, NC 28761. Phone (704) 652-2144.

BROWN MOUNTAIN LIGHTS

[Fig. 8(17)] Some say they are quick, bright flashes. Others insist they're a slow, hazy glow. According to Indian legend, they have haunted Brown Mountain since the 1200s. And local lore maintains that Thomas Alva Edison, inventor of the electric light bulb, was among those who admitted that they defy scientific explanation.

Nevertheless, plenty of explanations, scientific and otherwise, have been proposed for the strange Brown Mountain Lights that flicker and gleam from this spot in the Pisgah National Forest. Reflection from cars or a passing locomotive is a common theory. But those who dispute this theory say the lights were reported long before either modern invention existed. Since 1913, several studies of the lights have been commissioned. Researchers speculate that the luminous appearances could be due to St. Elmo's Fire (electrical discharge during thunderstorms), Andes Light (named for the radiant discharges seen over the crests of Chilean mountains), fox-fire (phosphorescent light emanating from fungus and decaying matter), or simply moonlight shining on fog. Thousands of people have reported seeing the lights, with sightings occurring in all seasons. While some believe they are a natural phenomenon, others subscribe to one of the folktales or myths centering on murder, loyalty, Indian battles, and lost love. But whether the cause is rooted in science or the supernatural, many agree that the lights are a part of the magic of the mountains.

Directions: The lights are reported to be visible from the overlook at Blue Ridge Parkway milepost 310.

Closest town: Linville, 8 miles.

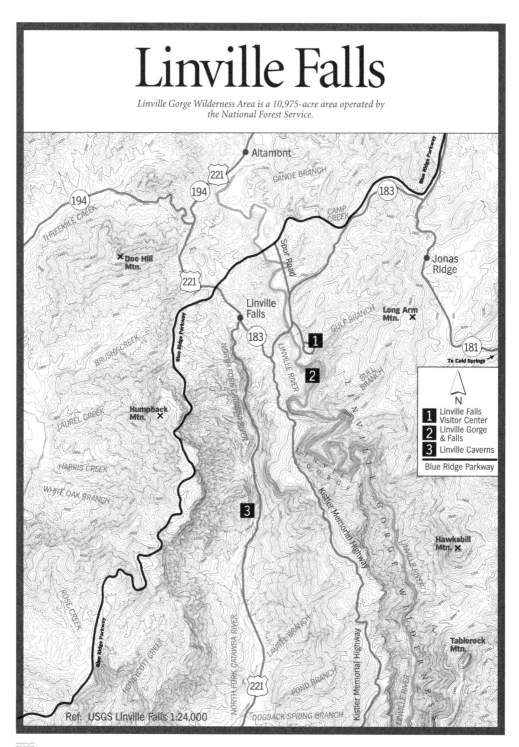

Linville Falls

Linville Gorge Wilderness Area is a 10,975-acre area operated by the National Forest Service.

N

1 Linville Falls Visitor Center
2 Linville Gorge & Falls
3 Linville Caverns

Blue Ridge Parkway

Ref: USGS Linville Falls 1:24,000

Linville Falls Recreation Area

[Fig. 13] In nature's ever-changing flow, Linville Falls has been steadily shifting upstream. Approximately 450 million years ago during ancient periods of continental collision, the earth's crust folded and faulted, thrusting older rock northwestward over younger rock. At the falls, a layer of billion-year-old Cranberry Gneiss (named for the North Carolina town Cranberry, not the color) graphically illustrates this ancient occurrence.

Over millions of years, the river plunged over the hard rock layer on top and scoured the softer beds below. As the undermined lip eroded, the falls moved upstream, creating the gorge. Geologists believe that millions of years ago the falls were as much as 12 miles farther downstream. Currently, hard quartzite rock extends down to the floor of the gorge, making further migration of the falls much slower.

Not all changes in the terrain date back to the days of dinosaurs. As recently as 1916 the Upper Falls and Lower Falls, which were then approximately the same height, were ravaged by floodwaters. A ledge on the Upper Falls broke off and lodged at the top of the Lower Falls, reducing the height of the Upper Falls and increasing the height of the Lower Falls. Plunging 90 feet to the gorge below, Lower Falls is now the highest falls on the river.

The Cherokee first called the river *Eeseeoh*, appropriately meaning "a river of many cliffs." The name changed to honor William Linville, who, with his son, John, explored and hunted in the gorge in the eighteenth century. Indians surprised and attacked them in 1766 as they slept by the river below the falls. William died, but typical of much of the lore of the region, accounts vary as to whether John survived. In 1952, John D. Rockefeller Jr. donated the land to the National Park Service with the stipulation that the tract be protected in its natural state.

STONEFLY NYMPH
(Family Perlidae)
The adult stonefly is found near mountain streams in late spring and summer. Nymphs, or naiads, take as long as three years to develop into adults and are important food for fish.

Linville Gorge

[Fig. 13] In the case of the Linville Gorge area, shared names can cause confusion and real problems. Two destinations—one a family fun site and another an isolated wilderness—have Linville in their names. Here's how it breaks down: geographically, Linville Gorge, one of the most scenic areas in the eastern United States, is formed by Linville Mountain on the west and Jonas Ridge on the east. As the Linville River flows from high atop Grandfather Mountain and drops into the Catawba Valley and the Piedmont below, it has cut one of the deepest and most rugged gorges east of the Mississippi River, 1,700 to 2,000 feet deep depending on your source. Two distinct natural areas surround Linville Gorge: Linville Falls Recreation Area just off the Blue Ridge Parkway and the Linville Gorge Wilderness Area. Linville Falls Recreation Area is operated by the National Park Service and offers several easy to moderate trails that lead to stunning views of the falls. Linville Gorge Wilderness Area, operated by the National Forest Service, is a 10,975-acre primitive environment far removed from the conveniences of civilization. Finally, the community of Linville Falls is a small village at the intersection of NC 183 and US 221, not to be confused with the town of Linville, 12 miles north on US 221.

TRAILS OF LINVILLE FALLS RECREATION AREA

[Fig. 13(1)] Four trails lead from the visitor center to different points along the river. Erwins View Trail (some books refer to it as the Linville Falls Trail, but signage reads Erwins View Trail) is a moderate hike that features four overlooks, each providing a different perspective on the geology and geography of the falls area. A number of heath gardens grow in this area along exposed, rocky sites where sandy soil supports sand myrtle, blueberry, the unusual turkey beard, and rare sweetleaf (*Symplocos tinctoria*). This trail is also remarkable for the virgin forest where sourwood (*Oxydendrum arboreum*) and Carolina hemlock (*Tsuga caroliniana*) thrive alongside oaks and white pine. The range of the Carolina hemlock is only 100 miles long by 20 miles wide in the southern Appalachians, with the largest stands found in the Linville Gorge area. Ledges and cracks in the steep rock faces become veritable hanging gardens during the blooming seasons of tenacious shrubs and trees such as Fraser magnolia, mountain laurel, swamp azalea, and three varieties of rhododendron.

From the visitor center, the Linville Gorge Trail descends into the gorge after .7 mile, climbing down steep trails and in one area a set of 27 wooden steps to negotiate the steep terrain. Massive rocks form the sheer gorge wall as the trail continues down toward the river, ending at a place adjacent to the Lower Falls. Along its route, the trail passes through tunnels of mountain laurel and past magnolia and rhododendron. This is an excellent hike that provides ample rewards to make up for the sometimes strenuous climb back up.

For a breathtaking view of the river before it tumbles over the Lower Falls into a deep pool below, take the Plunge Basin Trail (1 mile round-trip). At the stone overlook, the view of the Chimneys, which are chimney-like rock outcroppings located to the left of the waterfall, is also outstanding.

Duggers Creek Trail is an easy .5-mile stroll across a rushing creek with waterfalls and a ravine as beautiful as Linville Falls, albeit much smaller. This is a different type of interpretive trail. Rather than identifying trees and wildflowers, the signs offer thought-provoking quotes from leading naturalists such as John Muir

GOLDEN-CROWNED
KINGLET
(Regulus satrapa)
A restless, flirtting movement and a high, thin "ssst" identify the kinglet.

and Marjorie Rawlings. None of the trails at Linville Falls connect with trails in the Linville Gorge Wilderness Area. Maps are available at the headquarters building from May through October. Along the trails, the abundant white pines and hemlocks shelter red-breasted nuthatch, blackburnian warbler, and golden-crowned kinglet. In addition to species common to this region, least flycatchers (*Empidonax minimus*), red crossbills (*Loxia curvirostra*), and cerulean warblers (*Dendroica cerulea*) have been spotted in and around the trails. Green-backed heron, belted kingfisher, Acadian flycatcher, and Louisiana waterthrush (*Seiurus motacilla*) frequent the river where it flows more gently in an area visible behind the visitor center. While the roar of the falls is part of its appeal, it does drown out more delicate bird calls.

Directions: Exit Blue Ridge Parkway at milepost 316.3 and follow a paved 1.2-mile spur road to the visitor center.

Activities: Hiking, camping, fishing.

Facilities: Picnic area, camping sites with tables and grills, comfort stations (no showers), a small bookshop (open May 1–Oct.), information shelter.

Dates: Open year-round.

Fees: A fee is charged for camping.

Closest town: Linville Falls, 3 miles.

For more information: Leonard Adkins's book, *Walking the Blue Ridge*, covers these trails and many others along the Parkway in great detail.

Linville Gorge Wilderness

In 1952, John D. Rockefeller Jr. donated the Linville Gorge Wilderness land to the National Park Service with the stipulation that the tract be protected in its natural state.

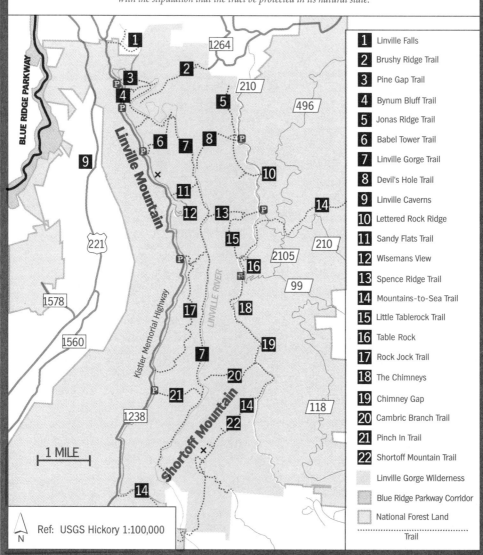

1 Linville Falls
2 Brushy Ridge Trail
3 Pine Gap Trail
4 Bynum Bluff Trail
5 Jonas Ridge Trail
6 Babel Tower Trail
7 Linville Gorge Trail
8 Devil's Hole Trail
9 Linville Caverns
10 Lettered Rock Ridge
11 Sandy Flats Trail
12 Wisemans View
13 Spence Ridge Trail
14 Mountains-to-Sea Trail
15 Little Tablerock Trail
16 Table Rock
17 Rock Jock Trail
18 The Chimneys
19 Chimney Gap
20 Cambric Branch Trail
21 Pinch In Trail
22 Shortoff Mountain Trail

Linville Gorge Wilderness
Blue Ridge Parkway Corridor
National Forest Land
.... Trail

Ref: USGS Hickory 1:100,000

1 MILE

N

Linville Gorge Wilderness Area

[Fig. 14] Linville Gorge was first designated a wilderness area in 1951, making it the first wild area established east of the Mississippi. With the signing of the Wilderness Act of 1964, the 7,575-acre tract became one of the original components of the National Wilderness Preservation System. In 1984, the North Carolina Wilderness Act increased its size to 10,975 acres. Pristine and unspoiled, the Linville Gorge Wilderness Area remains much as it was when the Cherokee lived here.

As with other wilderness areas, many human activities are prohibited, such as road building, timber harvesting, commercial enterprises, use of motorized vehicles, and bicycling. Trails are not blazed or marked, but the area is popular enough that many trails are easy to follow. Nevertheless, compass and maps are a necessity here, and permits are required for overnight camping. Day hiking does not require a permit.

Many overlooks along the Blue Ridge Parkway spotlight the peaks and unusual formations along the eastern rim of the gorge—the Chimneys [Fig. 14(18)], Sitting Bear Rock, Table Rock [Fig. 14(16)], Hawksbill, and Gingercake mountains—but here they become destinations. The interesting names of formations and trails are often based on Cherokee legend, such as Lettered Rock Ridge which refers to the letters or markings painted by the Cherokee on a rock at the turnoff point to the Table Rock, their mystic altar for sacred ceremonies. Several of these rock formations along Jonas Ridge provide opportunities for beginner, intermediate, and advanced rock climbing.

The area offers 39 miles of trails. The 11.5-mile Linville Gorge Trail [Fig. 14(7)], the longest trail in the wilderness, follows the river from below Brushy Ridge near the falls to the wilderness boundary near Shortoff Mountain and Lake James; elevation at its lowest point is 1,300 feet. Along the way the trail passes through hardwood forest, rhododendron and mountain laurel, wildflowers, huge rocks and boulders, cascades, and sheer, rugged cliffs where peregrine falcons have been spotted nesting. Once the steep inclines have been negotiated, there are long stretches of riverside hikes and secluded camping sites. Through-hikers should expect a strenuous hike lasting at least two days and must secure a permit for overnight stays between May 1 and October 31.

Seven connecting trails on the western rim and two on the eastern allow hikers to make shorter loop hikes. Devil's Hole Trail [Fig. 14(8)], for example, connects with Linville Gorge Trail; it can be accessed from the parking space off Gingercake Acres Road (SR 1265, which turns into FR 210). After an initial ascent, Devil's Hole Trail drops 1,160 feet in elevation on its way through a cove of rhododendron, hemlock, and oak. At 1.5 miles into the hike, after crossing a stream with rocky areas, the trail climbs a cliff top before descending to the river. Cautiously rock-hop or wade across the Linville River to connect with the Linville Gorge Trail, or backtrack for a total hike of 3 miles.

Shortoff Mountain Trail [Fig. 14(22)] is also part of the Mountains-to-Sea Trail [Fig. 14(14)] (see MST, page 287). Brushy Ridge Trail [Fig. 14(2)] is a moderate hike of 4 miles round-trip that will satisfy those looking for an isolated hike that does not connect with other trails in the wilderness. Access the trailhead off Old Gingercake Road or SR 1264. (Because trails in the wilderness are unblazed and unmarked, it is imperative that hikers use an official map with explicit instructions and a compass.)

The first mile of Brushy Ridge Trail uses an old forest road for easy hiking before descending toward excellent views of the gorge. A little farther down, along a rocky stretch, spectacular vistas of Hawksbill, Table Rock, and Babel Tower come into view. Canadian hemlock and Eastern hemlock line the dense, rocky trail; at the 2-mile point, backtrack to the trailhead.

Not surprisingly, the gorge is rich in wildlife. Old-growth forest of hickory, oak, maple, locust, and poplar with pockets of fir and Carolina hemlock, four species of rhododendron, orchids, wild indigo (*Baptisia tinctoria*), and yellowroot (*Xanthorrhiza simplicissima*) grow here, providing cover and food for the white-tailed deer, raccoons, skunks (*Mephitis mephitis*), and the occasional black bear. However, some areas at higher elevations dominated by massive rock formations of granite and quartzite are devoid of vegetation other than the most hardy lichens and mosses.

Sections of the river contain rainbow (*Oncorhynchus mykiss*) and brown trout (*Salmo trutta*), and butterflies and birds are numerous, as are lizards. Snakes are also found in the gorge, including timber rattlesnakes (*Crotalus horridus*) and copperheads (*Agkistrodon contortrix*), the only two poisonous snakes in the mountains of Western North Carolina. The wilderness area is a haven for many varieties of warblers, the pileated woodpecker (*Dryocopus pileatus*), Eastern phoebe (*Sayornis phoebe*), white-breasted nuthatch, cedar waxwing, scarlet tanager, and indigo bunting. Hawks and vultures soar above the gorge.

Directions: From the Blue Ridge Parkway milepost 317.5, travel south on US 221 to the junction with NC 183. Turn left and travel .07 mile to Kistler Memorial Highway (contrary to the sound of its name, this is a rough, gravel state road).

EASTERN HEMLOCK
(*Tsuga canadensis*)
Long-lived hemlocks develop slowly in the shade. Their bark was once a commercial source of tannin in the production of leather.

Activities: Hiking, camping, fishing, rock climbing.

Facilities: None.

Dates: Open year-round.

Fees: Free overnight permits are required on weekends and holidays May 1–Oct. 31; no more than 2 nights and 3 days are allowed during that period and no more than 10 in a group.

Closest town: Linville Falls, .7 mile from entrance at Kistler Memorial Highway.

For more information: U.S. Forest Service District Ranger, Route 1, Box 110A, Nebo, NC 28761. Phone (704) 652-2144.

TABLE ROCK

[Fig. 14(16)] The ancient quartzite of the Grandfather Mountain Window provides this area of North Carolina with some of the most diverse and exciting multipitch rock-climbing sites in the United States. And with its variety of overhangs, hand and foot holds, vertical walls, and low-angle slopes, Table Rock Mountain is considered by many climbers to be one of the best—especially for beginning and intermediate mountaineers. The Cherokee also revered the Table Rock, which served as a mystic alter for their sacred ceremonies.

Viewed from numerous overlooks along the Blue Ridge Parkway, the 3,909-foot summit appears to be as flat as the tabletop its name implies. But in fact, it is slightly tilted, and the surface, irregular rather than smooth, is a melding of huge boulders. The sandy, dry soil produced from quartzite erosion is not nutrient rich, but the hardy plants that take root at the rock's top, including Allegheny sand myrtle, mountain laurel, blueberry, pine, and various sedges, use it to brace themselves against the heavy gusts of wind that are an everyday part of cliff-dwelling life.

A short trail leading from the parking area to the summit snakes through several narrow passageways before breaking out onto a panoramic, 360-degree view. It's an ideal place for watching the hawk migration in September.

Directions: From I-40 take Exit 105. Follow signs to Highway 181 North. Turn left at the first Pisgah National Forest Table Rock Picnic Area sign and onto a maintained—though often rough—gravel road. Continue 16 miles, past the entrance to the North Carolina Outward Bound School base camp, to a parking and picnic area. The summit trail begins here.

Activities: Rock climbing, hiking.

Facilities: Restrooms.

Closest town: Morganton, approximately 12 miles.

Trail: Table Rock Summit Trail, 2.4 miles round-trip.

Elevation: 3,920 feet.

Degree of difficulty: Moderate.

Surface and blaze: Dirt path, unblazed.

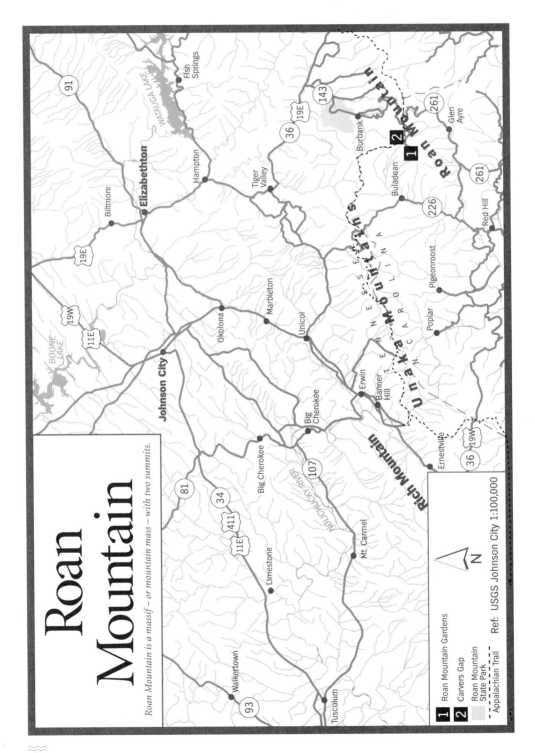

Roan Mountain

Roan Mountain is a massif – or mountain mass – with two summits.

1 Roan Mountain Gardens
2 Carvers Gap
Roan Mountain State Park
Appalachian Trail

Ref: USGS Johnson City 1:100,000

Roan Mountain and Roan Mountain State Park

[Fig. 15] Whether explored by car, on skis, through a vigorous hike, or on a leisurely ramble, Roan Mountain, with its caps of open grasslands, is thought by some to be the most beautiful mountain east of the Rockies.

The origins of its name also tell the story of the early pioneers here. Many of the English and Scottish settlers were unschooled and could not spell; their only book was the Bible. When they saw the mountain-ash tree, it reminded them of their European version, the Rowan tree. Over the years the name lost a syllable and became simply, "Roan."

One of the first to declare its beauty was Harvard botanist Asa Gray (*see* Naturalists, page 230), who studied the mountain's diverse plant life in 1841. André Michaux of France and plant collector John Fraser of Scotland also explored the mountain. All were attracted, as naturalists are today, to the region's unique treeless peaks, which are some of the largest expanses of grassy balds in the world, and to the wide representation of flora and fauna otherwise rarely found outside the mountains of eastern Canada.

Roan Mountain is actually a massif, or mountain mass, with two summits. It is part of a ridge known as the Roan Highlands, and is the highest peak in the Unaka Mountain Range. At its lower elevations, vegetation as southern as subtropical orchids can be found. But at the mountain's height, vestiges from the ice age remain, including wood sorrel (*Oxalis montana*), witch hobble (*Viburnum alnifolium*), and green alder (*Alnus crispa*), a species usually found in New England.

In June, Roan's open balds burst with the magenta-colored blooms of Catawba rhododendron, which John Fraser designated *Rhododendron catawbiense* on this mountain during his 1799 expedition. Each plant in the 600-acre spread of natural rhododendron "gardens" might produce as many as 100 flowers.

The Roan Mountain–Rhododendron National Recreation Trail is an easy, 1-mile loop trail through the rhododendron gardens near Carvers Gap [Fig. 15(2)] on the North Carolina/Tennessee state line. The trail is actually in the form of three loops, the first one paved and ideal for handicapped visitors. An interpretive trail, this loop features 16 stations keyed to information in a brochure about the northern climate species and rare plants found here, such as spreading avens, hair cap moss, and Allegheny sand myrtle. The trail courses deep into Canadian-zone forests of red spruce, mountain-ash, Fraser fir, and wild berry bushes. It connects with the lower loops, which are also gradual and easy, making this an excellent trail for families and the elderly. An observation deck affords spectacular vistas that extend, on a clear day, to the Black Mountains and Great Craggie Mountains. Scientists have not determined why the range's peaks don't support trees, but theories abound. (For more

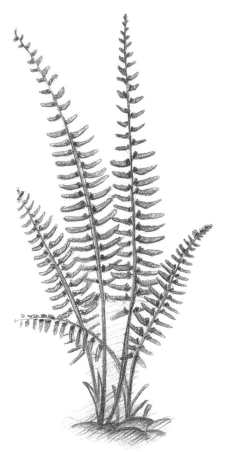

CHRISTMAS FERN
(Polystichum acrostichoides)

information on balds, see Introduction to the Natural History of the North Carolina Mountains, page 1.)

The combination of heath balds, Canadian-zone spruce-fir forests, and, at lower elevations, hardwood coves, supports more than 1,500 species of native plants, flowers, herbs, trees, shrubs, ferns, club mosses, lichens, and mushrooms. Bird scholar Fred W. Behrend named the snow bunting (*Plectrophenax nivalis*) when he discovered it wintering on the balds. The area is also home to one of southern Appalachia's greatest concentrations of threatened, endangered, or sensitive plant and wildlife species, with nearly 30 identified, including Gray's lily, saxifrages, sedges, the saw-whet owl, and the northern flying squirrel. In 1941, 7,000 acres of this naturally significant area were incorporated into the Pisgah National Forest and Cherokee National Forest.

Though most of Roan Mountain is in North Carolina, 2,156 acres in a Tennessee valley on the mountain's north slope make up Roan Mountain State Park, an amenity-filled base for exploring the entire region. Camping, picnicking, and educational programs such as wildflower tours and bird walks reach their height during the June rhododendron festivals. And with 100 inches of annual snowfall, this is also the only state park in the south to offer cross-country skiing. Hiking trails course through the park and national forests. They accommodate enthusiasts looking for an easy stroll as well as others interested in trekking a stretch of the Appalachian Trail (*see* Appalachian Trail, page 291) on what is thought to be one of its most scenic sections. Hiking maps are available at the park office.

Directions: From I-40, exit at Marion on US 226. Near Bakersville and Spruce Pine, US 226 intersects with NC 261. Travel on NC 261 to the North Carolina/Tennessee state line and follow the signs to Roan Gardens and Carvers Gap parking lots. To reach the Tennessee state park, continue on NC 261, which becomes TN 143 at the state line. The state park is 8 miles ahead at the bottom of the mountain.

Activities: Hiking, cross-country skiing. The state park recreational activities include swimming, horseshoes, badminton, volleyball, and table tennis.

Facilities: Campgrounds, cabins, restaurant, picnic tables and pavilions, restrooms, laundromat, playgrounds, heated pool, hiking/skiing trails.

Dates: Park: open year-round. Restaurant: open seasonally. Swimming pool and campground: 0pen Memorial Day–Labor Day.

Fees: A fee is charged for campsites and for cabins at state park.

Closest town: Bakersville, NC, or Roan Mountain, TN, approximately 25 miles.

For more information: Roan Mountain State Park, Rt. 1 Box 236, Roan Mountain, TN 37687. Phone (423) 772-3303 or (800) 250-8620.

Linville Caverns

[Fig. 13(3), Fig. 14(9)] Deep within the earth, a Franciscan monk watches as blind trout weave their way through underground streams. The "Monk" is one of many extraordinary stalactites and stalagmites at Linville Caverns. Centuries of chemical erosion slowly formed these caverns inside Humpback Mountain when carbon dioxide combined with water to make carbonic acid and began dissolving calcium carbonate in the rock along its course.

As the dripping water evaporated, hundreds of stalactites and stalagmites gradually formed. The natural process creates magical results: three levels of richly layered, undulating creations that resemble frozen waterfalls, draperies, natural bridges, and whatever else the imagination cares to conjure.

Linville Caverns were discovered by H. E. Colton and his local guide, Dave Franklin, in the 1880s. Mystified by what appeared to be fish swimming out of the mountain, they followed their curiosity deep within the mountain, traveling with the underground stream as it worked through passageways and rooms they reported to "look like the arch of some grand old cathedral" when illuminated by their torches. Legend has it that the caverns were a popular hiding place with soldiers from both sides of the Civil War and a workshop for a resourceful old man who made and mended soldiers' shoes.

Experienced guides lead visitors on the half-hour tour along a level path into the innermost recesses of the caverns where the steady 52-degree Fahrenheit temperature feels cool in the summer and mild in the winter. In addition to the formations, other natural wonders are born in this rarified environment. Thousands of daddy longlegs hibernate here in the even warmth of the caverns.

Directions: Located between Marion and Linville Falls on US 221, 4 miles south of the Linville Falls Exit on the Blue Ridge Parkway.

Facilities: Caverns, gift shop, restrooms.

Dates: Open year-round, hours are seasonal.

Fees: There is a fee for admission.

Closest town: Linville Falls, 3.5 miles north.

For more information: Phone (800) 419-0540 or (704) 756-4171.

Overmountain Victory National Historic Trail

[Fig. 21(1)] The mountains of North Carolina have long held a reputation for making life hard. Early settlers to this rugged New World soon encountered hardships, growing as strong and resourceful as the land beneath their feet. Later, in 1780, Lord Charles Cornwallis, British commander during the American Revolution, was severely tried by these mountains. The men the mountains shaped, men who lacked any formal military training, whom the British called mongrels, defeated his Royal troops at Kings Mountain, a battle that proved to be the beginning of the successful conclusion of the war.

The Overmountain Victory National Historic Trail, only one of two trails east of the Mississippi to earn that designation, follows the route of the Kings Mountain campaign, starting near Abingdon, Virginia, coursing through Tennessee and the high mountains of North Carolina to Kings Mountain National Military Park in South Carolina. Like the war itself, the formation of the 220-mile National Historic Trail took a cooperative effort by many groups, including the National Park Service, U.S. Forest Service, U.S. Army Corps of Engineers, Overmountain Victory Trail Association (OVTA), local governments, citizens' associations, historical societies, and the states through which it travels.

Once a year history buffs and reenactors converge for a 15-day trip back in time, walking the trail and reliving the battles. There are three routes designated as the Overmountain Victory Trail: the actual historic route, which today is often inaccessible; the route used by OVTA each year during their September 23 through October 7 reenactment; and the public motor route through Elk Park, down US 19E to Spruce Pine, along US 221 and US 226, intersecting the Blue Ridge Parkway at Gillespie Gap, where troops camped on the night of September 29, 1780, before heading south to victory on October 7.

The OVTA route used by the reenactors is popular with hikers year-round, though some areas may become overgrown. Areas of the trail that are easily accessible surround Sycamore Shoals State Historic Area in Elizabethton, Tennessee; Roan Mountain State Park in Roan Mountain, Tennessee; and the Museum of North Carolina Minerals near Spruce Pine, North Carolina. Look for the brown and white sign with the soldier and rifle logo at the trailheads.

Displays and brochures are available at the Museum of North Carolina Minerals in Gillespie Gap.

Museum of North Carolina Minerals

[Fig. 11(10)] In the dark and weathered rock outcrops along the Blue Ridge Parkway, mica glitters from dikes and sheets of coarsely crystalline pegmatite and granite, its silver flash giving just a hint of the geologic history of the region. The rock outcrops, made of gneiss, are a prominent feature in the Blue Ridge province of Western North Carolina, and the shiny white and gray pegmatite bodies are the source of many of the minerals and gems displayed in the Museum of North Carolina Minerals near Spruce Pine.

This unusual treasury opened in 1955 in the Spruce Pine Mining District, an area of the state so rich in minerals that many of the more than 300 known varieties of North Carolina minerals and rocks can be found there. Most of the displays in the museum date back to its opening and give an interesting perspective on earlier industrial uses for local minerals.

The museum displays large sheets of mica in shimmering and translucent layers. Once mined extensively in the area, mica was used for insulation in stoves, as window glass, and in the vacuum tubes of old radios, radar, and televisions. Now it is extracted as a by-product of feldspar and quartz mining and ground into a glittery powder with many uses.

Feldspar, found in large quantities in the earth's crust, and its weathering products including the clays kaolin and halloysite, have been of great econom-

BROAD-WINGED KATYDID
(Microcentrum rhombifolium)
Heard more often than seen,
these insects are named for their
shrill song.

ic benefit to the Spruce Pine area for more than half a century. Quartz is plentiful here also, found at its purest in the center of pegmatite rock and used in high-tech products such as fiber-optic cable and the heat-resistant tiles on NASA's space shuttles.

One museum display crackles with radioactive minerals and another glows with a luminous assortment of fluorescent rocks under blacklight. Museum visitors can learn about the unusual properties and uses of kyanite, uranium, thorium, olivine, tungsten, corundum, and other minerals.

Gemstones, of course, make the most dazzling displays. Gold, emerald, sapphire, ruby, amethyst, beryl, garnet, topaz, turquoise, tourmaline, opal, and quartz are part of the natural wealth of these ancient mountains.

The museum is a good stop for an educational interlude or a leg-stretching walk along a moderate, 5-mile section of the Overmountain Victory Trail (*see* Overmountain Victory Trail, page 78). A display in the museum and a trail marker at the museum entrance describe its revolutionary history.

The Mitchell County Chamber of Commerce maintains an office in the museum and is a good source of information on local attractions, including nearby gem mines where visitors can pan for semiprecious minerals.

Directions: Blue Ridge Parkway at Gillespie Gap, milepost 331.

Activities: Hiking.

Facilities: Visitor center, museum, restrooms.

Dates: Open year-round, hours are seasonal.

Fees: None.

Closest town: Spruce Pine, 5 miles.

For more information: Mitchell County Chamber of Commerce, phone (800) 227-3912. Museum of North Carolina Minerals phone (704) 765-2761.

PENLAND SCHOOL OF CRAFTS

[Fig. 21(2)] Many chapters from the story on mountain crafts could be written in Penland's picturesque valley. It was no different from other areas in the mountains—the land provided abundant natural resources, and it enforced a hardship and isolation that spawned crafts of necessity from the independent, self-reliant mountain residents. What made Penland different was the tenacity and dedication of Lucy Morgan.

In 1923, with only three looms and a strong will, Miss Lucy (as she came to be known) started what would become Penland School of Crafts which today is an internationally acclaimed school for contemporary craft instruction. She had two goals: revive handweaving and bolster the meager incomes in the region. The economic benefits of the Industrial Revolution had not yet made their way into southern Appalachia but the products had, all but wiping out the time-honored art of handweaving. Miss Lucy put that trend on hold when she established the Penland Weavers; soon additional crafts instruction in dyeing and spinning, pottery, and other traditional folk arts was added. Word spread, and the number of requests for instruction from other areas of the country grew, leading to the formation of Penland School of Crafts in 1929. Penland continues to promote individual and artistic growth in crafts (although today's focus is more contemporary than folk) in such disciplines as pottery, sculpture, drawing, glassblowing, metalworking, photography, printmaking, weaving, and woodworking. During one- and two-week sessions in June through August and two-month Concentration Sessions in spring and fall, instructors from across the United States and occasionally Europe foster a tradition begun more than 70 years ago.

Directions: From US 19E in Spruce Pine, drive west approximately 5 miles to

Penland Road. Turn right and drive .2 mile. Turn right again (still Penland Road) and drive 4 miles. Bear left onto Penland School Road and drive .7 mile to the Penland Gallery and Information Center.

Dates: Penland Gallery and Information Center: early Apr.–first weekend in Dec.

Closest town: Spruce Pine, 9 miles.

For more information: Penland School of Crafts, Penland, NC 28765-0037. Phone (704) 765-2359. Gallery phone (704) 765-6211.

NOLICHUCKY RIVER

Except for occasional background noise from the Clinchfield CSX railroad, the setting is one of isolated wilderness for the rafters, canoers, and kayakers who count the Nolichucky River among their favorites. Its Class III–V whitewater rapids course through one of the deepest gorges in the eastern United States, where steep crags shoot sharply up from the river's banks and keep the highway and other encroachments at a distance.

The Nolichucky is a natural-flow river, created at the confluence of the Toe and the Cane rivers, and it drains the entire Toe River Valley on its way to the Gulf of Mexico. The Nolichucky provides a 10-mile run down the 100-foot-wide passageway bordered by the Unaka Mountains on the north and the Bald Mountains to the south. Early spring, with its high water, is one of the more adventurous times to run the Nolichucky. Blooming dogwood (*Cornus florida*) and redbud (*Cercis canadensis*) can also make it one of the prettiest. Though the area's wildlife is less active and visible during daylight rafting hours, occasional white-tailed deer and snakes are seen.

Those willing to wade the heavy water also report excellent fishing of muskellunge (*Esox masquinongy*) and smallmouth bass (*Micropterus dolomieu*). The only signs of civilization the watercourse passes are the crumbling foundations and chimneys of what local river guides call the "Lost Cove Settlement," which, legend has it, was developed as a hideout during the Civil War.

The Nolichucky River should be considered off-limits for the novice paddler, although outfitters are available for tours and instruction (*see* Appendix C page 300).

Directions: From Spruce Pine, take NC 226 north past Red Hill, turn left on NC 197 north, go 11 miles to one of several access points along the river.

Activities: Rafting, canoeing, kayaking, fishing.

Closest town: Bakersville, approximately 14 miles.

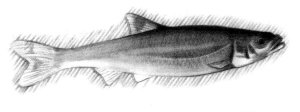

WARPAINT SHINER
(*Luxilus coccogenis*)
Deriving its name from its bright red cheeks, this shiner grows to 5 inches long.

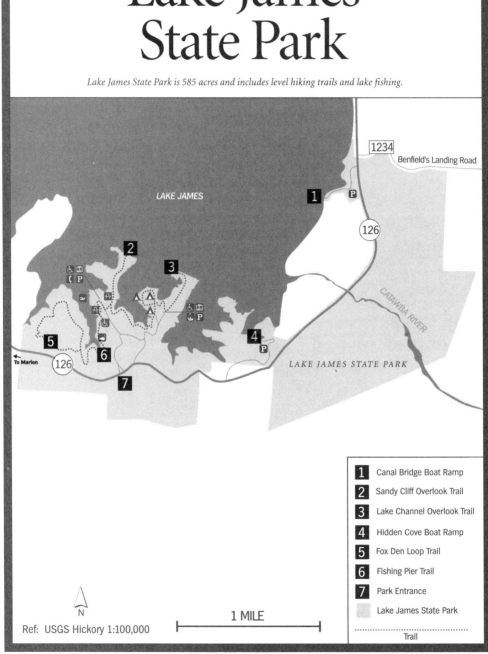

Lake James State Park

Lake James State Park is 585 acres and includes level hiking trails and lake fishing.

1234 Benfield's Landing Road

LAKE JAMES

126

CATAWBA RIVER

To Marion 126

LAKE JAMES STATE PARK

1	Canal Bridge Boat Ramp
2	Sandy Cliff Overlook Trail
3	Lake Channel Overlook Trail
4	Hidden Cove Boat Ramp
5	Fox Den Loop Trail
6	Fishing Pier Trail
7	Park Entrance
	Lake James State Park
	Trail

N

1 MILE

Ref: USGS Hickory 1:100,000

Lake James State Park

[Fig. 16] With long stretches of blue water surrounded by lush green foliage and a backdrop of dramatic mountain terrain, there are advantages to the lowlands, especially at Lake James State Park, where 585 acres include level hiking trails and lake fishing in the shadow of breathtaking mountain peaks.

Opened in June 1989, Lake James State Park lies on the south shore of a 6,510-acre impoundment on the Catawba River and its two tributaries, Paddy Creek and the Linville River. Formed between 1916 and 1923 as one of nine man-made lakes by Duke Power Company, Lake James is named for James B. Duke, founder of Duke Power Company.

The lake's 150 miles of wooded shoreline extends into coves and peninsulas that provide easy access to an assortment of water sports and fishing. The lakeshore behind the multipurpose park building, which houses the park office, concession stand, restrooms, and rinse-off showers, has been developed as a protected beach for swimming. In addition, skiing and all types of boating are permitted. Two boat ramps, Hidden Cove [Fig. 16(4)] and Canal Bridge [Fig. 16(1)], are within the park, and numerous privately operated launch sites and marinas circle the lake, some offering boats and motors for rent. Because of Lake James's numerous coves, canoeing here can be peaceful and private.

Submerged islands, rocky points, and plentiful coves make Lake James the site of annual fishing tournaments and friendly competitions. Record-breaking catches have been reported and verified as more than just another fishing story. Fish populations include three types of bass: largemouth (*Micropterus salmoides*), smallmouth (*Micropterus dolomieui*), and white (*Morone chrysops*). Walleye (*Stizostedion vitreum*) and bluegill (*Lepomis macrochirus*) are also popular catches at Lake James. While most choose boat fishing, casting sites include a small pier near the park office and one along the shore. During a quiet morning of fishing, a pair of Canada geese and flocks of wood ducks and other waterfowl can be seen only a few feet from the Lake Channel Overlook.

While some may call the hiking trails within the park easy, none would contest their spectacular views. Two gentle footpaths, the Lake Channel Overlook Trail [Fig. 16(3)] and Sandy Cliff Trail [Fig. 16(2)], wander in and out of the shoreline on their way toward wooded overlooks with benches. Along the way they provide spectacular vistas of the mountains in general and of the granite-faced Table Rock in particular, as well as the upper elevations of Linville Gorge. It can be windy along the lakeshore, something to keep in mind when planning a winter hiking trip. That wind, coupled with the water erosion, is responsible for the loss of as much as 1 foot of land per year on the lake's north side.

Both trails wind through the park's young pine-hardwood forests that support huge specimens of oak, hickory, poplar, pine, and some cedar. Dogwood trees are particularly evident during late April and early May when their white bracts are in full bloom. In this rugged section of the country these trails afford a pleasant opportunity to hikers who cannot walk great distances.

Wildflowers thrive in the moist, wooded conditions of the park. A full array of specimens bloom from early spring through fall, among them pink lady slipper (*Cypripendium acaule*), jack-in-the-pulpit, bloodroot, and a variety of violets. Blackberries (*Rubus argutus*) and dewberries (*Rubus fagellaris*) are also here for the picking in July.

Park rangers present nature programs twice a month including guided hikes, tree identification sessions, canoe trips, and wildflower walks.

Directions: From Marion travel east on US 70 approximately 5 miles to NC 126 in the community of Nebo. Turn left and travel 2.9 miles to park entrance on left.

Activities: Canoeing, fishing, boating, hiking, skiing, swimming.

Facilities: 2 boat ramps, 18 backpack campsites (300–1,500 yards from the parking lot) and 2 handicapped-accessible sites with grill, picnic tables, and nearby water. Seasonal canoe rentals. Picnic shelter, handicapped-accessible fishing pier, concession stand.

Dates: Open year-round; concession stand and canoe rentals are seasonal.

Fees: A fee is charged for camping, canoe rentals, and picnic shelter reservations.

Closest town: Marion, 8 miles.

For more information: Lake James State Park, PO Box 340, Nebo, NC 28761. Phone (704) 652-5047.

LAKE CHANNEL OVERLOOK TRAIL

Trail distance: 1.5 miles round-trip and Sandy Cliff Trail, 1.2 miles round-trip.
Elevation: 1,200 feet.
Degree of difficulty: Easy.
Surface and blaze: Mulched.

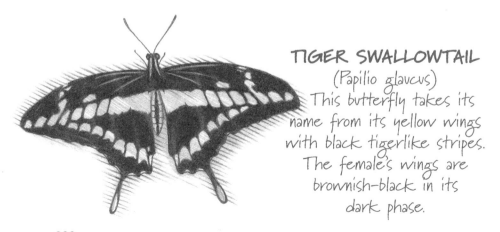

TIGER SWALLOWTAIL
(Papilio glaucus)
This butterfly takes its name from its yellow wings with black tigerlike stripes. The female's wings are brownish-black in its dark phase.

Crabtree Meadows

[Fig. 21(5)] Early European settlers called this area Blue Ridge Meadows and believed that the open expanses that adjoin hardwood forests were fire-cleared centuries ago by Indians. Today, the 250-acre site is a cool and peaceful recreation area of the National Park Service offering camping and picnicking, nature walks, and its premier attraction—Crabtree Falls [Fig. 21(6)].

Though the southern crab apple (*Malus angustifolia*) that give the area its current name no longer fill meadow orchards (it seems that many of these trees have died of old age without reseeding themselves), pink and red blossoms still dot the landscape in isolated patches in late spring, with small sour apples appearing in late summer. The mature forests that shelter the camping area include oaks, tulip trees, maples, Eastern hemlocks, and patches of Carolina hemlock. Habitat diversity provided by the forests, the abutting field, and the forest edge in between makes the recreation area a good spot for observing birds not often seen in other areas of the Parkway, including least flycatchers, black-billed cuckoos (*Coccyzus erythropthalmus*), and great crested flycatchers (*Myiarchus crinitus*).

Throughout the picnic area and into the forests, the spring wildflower display includes columbine (*Aquilegia canadensis*), yellow lady slipper, and dwarf iris. In June, speckled wood lily, goatsbeard (*Aruncus dioicus*), sundrop (*Oenothera fruticosa*), beard tongue (*Penstemon canescens*), and mountain laurel appear.

Perhaps the most dramatic natural offering at Crabtree Meadows is Crabtree Falls, Big Crabtree Creek's 70-foot cascade over a rock cliff, approximately 1 mile from the campground entrance. These falls are rare in that they do not have a basin or plunge pool at their base.

The loop trail to the falls descends into a mix of hickory, oak, hemlock, and birch and passes through a rhododendron thicket. More than 40 species of wildflowers color the undergrowth along the trail, and many join ferns in enjoying the cool water spray at the falls itself. Several species of salamanders find a home in damp leaf litter, wet-weather springs, and slippery rocks near the falls. The trail is also an excellent place to watch for Eastern wood pewee, Acadian flycatcher, scarlet tanager, wood thrush, and a variety of warblers. Barred owls are a possibility at night. Trail guides are available at the campground during summer months.

Directions: Blue Ridge Parkway milepost 338.9.

Activities: Hiking.

Facilities: Car campground with both tent and RV sites, picnic area, restaurant/ gift shop/camp store.

Dates: All facilities open May 1–Oct. 31.

Fees: A fee is charged for campsites.

Closest town: Burnsville or Marion, 20 miles.

For more information: Blue Ridge Parkway phone (704) 765-6082.

CRABTREE FALLS TRAIL

Trail: 2.5-mile loop.
Elevation: 3,500 feet.
Degree of difficulty: Moderate to strenuous.
Surface and blaze: Forest floor, rocky and waterlogged in places.

CAROLINA HEMLOCK RECREATION AREA

[Fig. 21(8)] Located on the east bank of the South Toe River, Carolina Hemlocks is a popular camping and day-use area at the base of the Black Mountain range near Burnsville. Rhododendron provides a dense canopy over the wooded picnic area hosting 12 tables, grills, and a shelter along the river. (Reservations for the shelter are required.) A nearby natural swimming hole with access along a sandy bank is a favorite spot in the summer. The South Toe, a hatchery-supported river, is also a favorite for fishing.

Two hiking trails start nearby—Colberts Ridge Trail follows the ridgeline to Deep Gap for 3.7 miles before connecting to the Black Mountain Crest Trail [Fig. 17(3)], a 12-mile hike featuring outstanding vistas. The Hemlock Nature Trail starts at the swimming area and follows the river for 1 mile. For horseback-riding enthusiasts, the Buncombe Horse Range Trail [Fig. 17(2)] is an 18-mile trek through the surrounding mountains; it also connects with trails in Mount Mitchell State Park.

Directions: Exit the Blue Ridge Parkway at milepost 344.2 and travel west on NC 80 for 5.3 miles. The recreation area is on the left.

Sports: Hiking, camping, picnicking, horseback riding, fishing.

Facilities: 31-site campground with picnic table, grill, and lantern post; flush toilets; sinks.

Fees: There is a charge for day use and camping.

Closest town: Burnsville, 10 miles.

For more information: Toecane Ranger District, PO Box 128, Burnsville, NC 28714. Phone (704) 682-6146.

EASTERN MOLE (Scalopus aquaticus) Spending most of its life underground, the mole feeds on earthworms and insect larvae in its passageway of tunnels 10 inches below the surface. It is identified by a pink snout, hairless tail, and furry body that grows to 6 inches.

Mountain Handicrafts in North Carolina

The landscape of Western North Carolina is defined by its ancient mountains, rising and falling in a sea of wavelike patterns across the horizon. They change with each season, renewed in spring by delicate pastels that gradually deepen to the dark green foliage of summer's cooling shade. Fall's spectacle follows as verdant peaks give way to a carnival of color, until winter once again exposes the rugged terrain, softened from time to time by blankets of deep, white snow.

It is one thing to admire the mountains and their seasons, but it is quite another to make a living off this uncompromising land. In the eighteenth century when Daniel Boone roamed these mountains, harsh frontier life demanded much from its Native Americans and European settlers. Isolated by the steep landscape, they relied on nature for their needs, turning rivercane into baskets, clay into vessels, and native hardwoods into instruments and furniture. In turn, they created a uniquely American art form.

A number of individuals and institutions have helped this mountain region achieve its reputation for craft excellence. Earlier this century, the Southern Highland Craft Guild, John C. Campbell Folk School, and Penland School (*see* stories, pages 116, 238, 80 respectively), to name only three, established settlement schools that fostered the bountiful native talent.

Today, HandMade in America, an Asheville-based nonprofit organization, continues this tradition. With the help of entrepreneurs, small businesses, associations, educators, regional institutions, and corporations, HandMade is implementing a 20-year strategic plan that establishes Western North Carolina as the geographic center for handmade objects in America. A bold stance, for sure, but crafts grow here as naturally as the rhododendron and flame azalea. In fact, today as many as 4,000 full- or part-time artisans working in the region contribute $122 million to the local economy—earning them the nickname "the invisible factory."

One of HandMade's more recent successes is *The Craft Heritage Trails of Western North Carolina*, a 120-page book that organizes this diverse area into seven trails and features 350 craft studios, art galleries, historic bed and breakfast inns, fine dining, and historical sites. The Blue Ridge Parkway serves as the connecting link for the 1,000 miles of trails. HandMade staff explored and enhanced what was already here in abundance—natural beauty and handicrafts. They combed the trails, negotiated with independent craft artists to open their studios, offered training sessions for all participating sites to ensure knowledgeable staff along the routes, and rigorously authenticated everything along the way as truly handmade in America. The program is so successful that other states and communities are calling on HandMade to share its strategies for garnering recognition and guaranteeing responsible development of native beauty and natural resources.

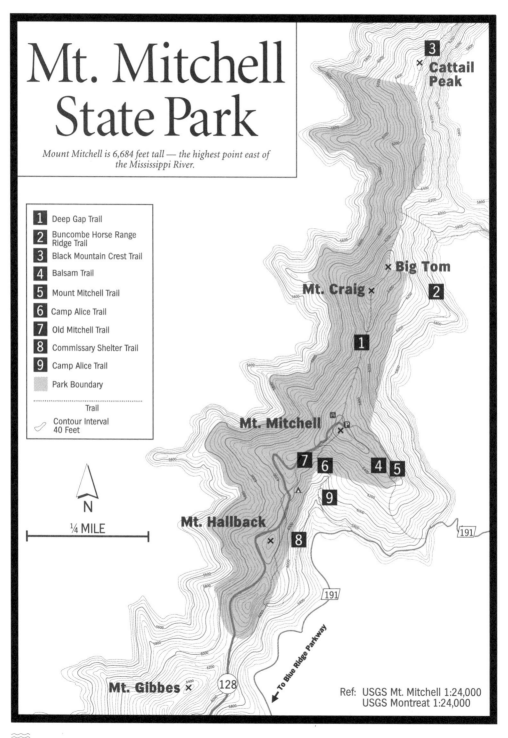

Mt. Mitchell State Park

Mount Mitchell is 6,684 feet tall — the highest point east of the Mississippi River.

1 Deep Gap Trail
2 Buncombe Horse Range Ridge Trail
3 Black Mountain Crest Trail
4 Balsam Trail
5 Mount Mitchell Trail
6 Camp Alice Trail
7 Old Mitchell Trail
8 Commissary Shelter Trail
9 Camp Alice Trail

Park Boundary

Trail

Contour Interval 40 Feet

N

¼ MILE

× Cattail Peak
× Big Tom
Mt. Craig ×
Mt. Mitchell ×
Mt. Hallback ×
Mt. Gibbes ×

191
128

To Blue Ridge Parkway

Ref: USGS Mt. Mitchell 1:24,000
USGS Montreat 1:24,000

Mount Mitchell/Mount Mitchell State Park

[Fig. 17] Already venerable when the Rockies were yet unformed, Mount Mitchell reigns as the highest point east of the Mississippi at 6,684 feet.

The underlying rocks, part of the Ashe Metamorphic Suite, were deposited in a Precambrian sea and intruded by iron- and magnesium-rich magma approximately 800 million years ago. Several hundred million years later, land collisions forced layers within the earth to fold and fault and form great mountain chains. The rocks buried in the process were metamorphosed by heat and pressure into gneiss and schist, while deposits of sand and clay were also transformed into primary minerals— quartz, feldspar, and biotite mica. Concentrations of these minerals with their light and dark variations give the mountain's rocks a layered look. Though the durable mountain is erosion-resistant, millions of years of weather and water have slowly worn down what was once a much higher peak, leaving a still-rugged and majestic Mount Mitchell.

In 1916, at a time when extensive logging threatened the region's virgin, old-growth forests, Governor Locke Craig led an effort that resulted in the establishment of Mount Mitchell as North Carolina's first state park. The 1,700-acre protected area that extends approximately 5 miles along the summit of the Black Mountains pre-served a piece of a unique ecosystem, where alpine forests exist in the South.

Mount Mitchell's peak is well known as a biological island, an isolated environ-ment that the retreating glaciers of the Pleistocene left behind. At its higher eleva-tions, the mountain receives 60 inches of annual snowfall and records average daily temperatures of 51 degrees. Certain subspecies of flora and fauna are found nowhere else, and some migrating birds, including wrens, Carolina chickadees (*Parus carolin-ensis*), and slate-colored juncos (*Junco hyemalis*), have only to travel up and down the mountain with the changing seasons.

The history of measuring and naming this ancient landmark is appropriately filled with tales of hardy and individualistic mountaineers. In 1787, when French botanist André Michaux came to gather cuttings of the range's more than 2,500 specimens of trees, shrubs, and other plants, he predicted that the highest peak in eastern North America would be found in the Black Mountain range. Elijah Mitchell, a science professor at the University of North Carolina and head of the North Carolina Geologic Survey, set out to prove just that in 1835, using bear trails, a mountain guide named Big Tom, a barometer, and mathematical formulas.

After several expeditions, Mitchell calculated the elevation of the range's highest peak at 6,672 feet, only 12 feet below its true height. When his former student and then-U.S. Senator Thomas Clingman disputed his claim in the 1850s, the elderly Mitchell returned to verify his measurements. Tragically, he fell from the rocks above a 40-foot waterfall, was knocked unconscious, and drowned. His body was buried atop the mountain that bears his name. Lower peaks nearby were christened Clingman's Peak and Big Tom.

Ninety-one species of birds, many more characteristic of New England and Canada than North Carolina, can be found here, including golden-crowned kinglets, red crossbills, and ruffed grouse (*Bonasa umbellus*). Twenty species, such as evening grosbeaks and purple finches (*Carpodacus purpureus*), are thought to spend the winter in the park. Hobblebush (*Viburnum alnifolim*), oxalis, oxeye daisy (*Heliopsis helianthoides*), purple-fringed orchis (*Habenaria fimbriata*), and other plants, herbs, and flowers typically found in boreal forests are plentiful. Several threatened and endangered species found only in spruce-fir forests in North Carolina and Tennessee, such as Rugel's ragwort (*Rugelia nudicaulis*), spreading avens, and Heller's blazing star, also exist here. In August, the mountaintop is covered with red raspberries (*Rubus idaeus*). It is legal to pick berries and other edibles along National Park Service trails, but only what can be picked from the trail for self-consumption.

Mount Mitchell's peak and its top slopes were once densely covered with Fraser fir and red spruce. Now, only trace stands of the original climax forest remain, surrounded by younger specimens of fir and spruce, a graveyard of dying trees and decomposing logs, and shrubs such as blueberry and mountain cranberry (*Vaccinium macrocarpon*). Major research has been conducted into the massive dying of the mountain's spruce-fir forests. Scientists have determined that a tiny sucking insect, the balsam woolly aphid, is killing the Fraser fir. There is some hope that younger trees may develop resistance to the aphid, or a natural enemy may be developed to combat the insect (*see* Devil's Courthouse Trail, page 164). Other factors, more mysterious and indeterminate, are killing the red spruce. Air pollution, causing acid rain and high ozone levels, is thought to compound the crisis, weakening the trees' ability to withstand natural stresses.

At lower elevations, oak, hickory, silky willow (*Salix sericea*), and mountain maple (*Acer spicatum*) are now predominant, with mountain-ash most abundant at even lower elevations. Wood sorrel and ferns cover much of the ground, where downed logs are home to mosses and mushrooms.

Numerous endangered and threatened animals are found in this diverse ecosystem, including northern flying squirrels, the predatory saw-whet owl, Weller's salamander (*Plethodon welleri*), and the long-tailed shrew (*Sorex dispar*). Bobcats are occasionally seen, along with gray foxes (*Urocyon cinereoargenteus*), black bears, and white-tailed deer. Short-tailed shrews (*Blarina brevicauda*), deer mice (*Peromyscus maniculatus*), and southern red-backed voles (*Clethrionomys gapperi*) thrive among rocks and fallen logs, and the cool, wet forest hosts one of the world's widest assortment of salamanders. Members of the Plethodontidae family (woodland or lungless salamanders) are most prolific.

The park's five hiking trails lead to or just below Mount Mitchell's summit, where an observation tower provides 70-mile views on clear days. A detailed map is available at the park office. In addition, the mountain features five waterfalls.

Directions: Turn north onto NC 128 at Blue Ridge Parkway milepost 355.4. The park gate is 2.4 miles ahead.

Activities: 18 miles of hiking through 5 trails.

Facilities: Concession stand, observation tower, museum, picnicking, restaurant, restrooms, and tent camping (9 sites).

Dates: Open year-round, hours are seasonal. Camping: May 1–Oct. 31. Concession stand and museum: Memorial Day weekend–Labor Day and weekends through late Oct. Restaurant: mid-May–late Oct.

Fees: A fee is charged for camping.

Closest town: Burnsville or Asheville, each approximately 30 miles.

For more information: Mount Mitchell State Park, Rt. 5 Box 700, Burnsville, NC 28714. Phone (704) 675-4611.

FRASER FIR

(Abies fraseri)
This species, which is found at high altitudes in the southern Appalachians, is recognized by its flat, blunt needles and cones that point upward.

RED SPRUCE

(Picea rubens)
This species is recognized by its sharply pointed, four-sided needles and cones which hang downward

OLD FORT HISTORIC MUSEUMS

[Fig. 21(14)] Sitting at the foot of the Blue Ridge escarpment, the town of Old Fort appropriately bills itself as the "Gateway to the Smokies." In fact, Old Fort has enjoyed gateway status for more than two centuries. In the eighteenth century, Old Fort was the westernmost outpost of the United States.

In keeping with its notable past, Old Fort hosts three historic museums, something of a record for a town with fewer than 1,000 people; all three museums are within an easy walk of one another in the heart of town. The Mountain Gateway Museum [Fig. 21(15)] features a collection of exhibits documenting pioneer life in and around the mountains. Displays of weaving and spinning natural fibers, herbal remedies, and local pottery flank the reconstructed log cabin on the second floor of the building constructed in 1936 by WPA workers. Outside, 200-year-old log cabins, a picnic pavilion, and an amphitheater hug the banks of Mills Creek, a tributary of the Catawba River.

A 12-minute video portrays the history of the area, including the massacre and expulsion of Native Americans who had made the mountains and valleys their home long before European settlers arrived. It seems fitting, then, that only two blocks away Grant's Indian Museum [Fig. 21(16)] houses the second largest collection of Native American artifacts in Western North Carolina. Arrowhead and gem exhibits; stuffed foxes and bobcats, white-tailed deer and bears; and Native American artwork and baskets are part of the eclectic and sometimes kitschy collection.

The town's 1890 Southern Railway depot now serves as a visitor center and railroad museum [Fig. 21(17)]. In a former waiting room and ticket office, displays of train whistles, bells, lanterns, signal lights, and photos help explain the dramatic impact the railroad made on the area. The depot sits adjacent to the town's trademark arrowhead monument.

Directions: From I-40, take Exit 73 to Catawba Avenue. The town center is less than .5 mile ahead at the junction with US 70.

Dates: Mountain Gateway Museum and Grant's Indian Museum are open daily. Railroad museum and visitor center, open Tues.–Sat.

Fees: Only Grant's Indian Museum charges an admission fee.

For more information: Mountain Gateway Museum, phone (704) 668-9259; Grant's Indian Museum, phone (704) 668-3143; visitor center and railroad museum, phone (704) 668-7223.

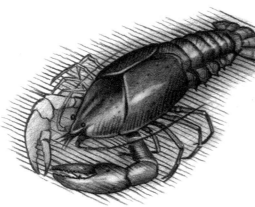

EASTERN CRAYFISH
(Cambarus bartonii)

Curtis Creek Area

[Fig. 21(9)] Rushing waters. Massive boulders. Towering hemlocks. Lush rhododendron. In addition to its pristine beauty, Curtis Creek Area holds the distinction of being the first national forest land purchased east of the Mississippi following the Weeks Act of 1911. This law, which was used to create new national forests, authorized the purchase of public lands in order to protect watersheds of navigable streams, especially in the east.

The roadway to the 8,100-acre tract in the Pisgah National Forest follows Curtis Creek as it flows from its headwaters farther north. A sign at the entrance offers a dedication to Chase P. Ambler (*see* Rattlesnake Lodge, page 107), a prominent pulmonary physician and outdoor enthusiast who was committed to the establishment of additional national forest lands. A small campground within the area hosts seven sites and three trails leading through hardwood forest to the ridges that surround Curtis Creek. These are backcountry trails that are not blazed and are sometimes difficult to follow. As a result, the lure of such isolation should be balanced with good maps and a compass. The trailheads for Hickory Branch Trail and Snooks Noose Trail are in or near the campground, while the third trail, Mackey Mountain Trail, starts where FR 482 meets FR 1188. The trails do not connect. Stretches of the creek north of US 70 are wide with a broad flood plain that make access easy for fishing. This section is hatchery supported. The section of the creek adjacent to FR 482, where the creek is smaller and flows faster, is classified as Wild Trout Water.

Directions: From I-40 take Exit 73 to Catawba Avenue. The junction of US 70 is less than .5 mile ahead. Turn right onto US 70 and travel 2 miles. Turn left at the Curtis Creek sign at NC 1227. Travel 5.1 miles (after 2.6 miles the pavement ends; after another 1.1 miles the road becomes FR 482).

Activities: Hiking, camping, fishing.

Facilities: 7 sites with picnic table and grill; pit toilets.

Dates: Open Apr.–Dec. 31.

Closest town: Old Fort, 7 miles.

CURTIS CREEK AREA TRAILS

Trail distance and configuration: Hickory Branch Trail, 4 miles round-trip; Snooks Noose Trail, 6 miles round-trip; Mackey Mountain Trail, 16 miles round-trip.

Elevation: 1,800 feet at the campground. Elevations rise sharply on either side of Curtis Creek.

Degree of difficulty: Moderate to strenuous.

Surface and blaze: Forest floor.

For more information: U.S. Forest Service District Ranger, Route 1, Box 110A, Nebo, NC 28761. Phone (704) 652-2144.

Newfound Mountains

The Newfound Mountains constitute the dominant range in this section with the Great Craggy and Green mountains running southeasterly through the upper portions.

FIGURE NUMBERS

19 Blue Ridge Parkway 3
20 Hot Springs Area
21 French Broad River

Ref: USGS Knoxville 1:250,000

The Newfound Mountains

The Newfound Mountains section [Fig. 18], with the city of Asheville at its heart, marked by the Tennessee/North Carolina border on the northwest, is an area lying between Mount Mitchell, Asheville, and the town of Chimney Rock. The Newfound Mountains constitute the dominant range in this section with the Great Craggy and Green mountains running southeasterly through the upper portions. Additional ranges include the Walnut Mountains, approximately 20 miles north of Asheville, and the Swannanoa Mountains, just east of the city. Elevations range from 6,085 feet at Craggy Dome to only 2,000 feet in the valley of the French Broad River.

The Great Craggy Mountains, known locally as the Craggies, run for approximately 15 miles from Asheville northeastward to where they join the Black Mountains, near Balsam Gap. Craggy Dome is the range's highest peak at 6,085 feet, and in

[*Above:* Writer Thomas Wolfe's home in Asheville]

RED-TAILED HAWK
(Buteo jamaicensis)
This hawk hunts for small animals from the air or from exposed perches.

general the peaks of this range make for excellent viewing of the autumn hawk migration. This annual fall translocation is remarkably predictable in its route, though, of course, the patterns of each species and the effects of weather systems do change. September through November is the time period for sighting the most hawks, although some early birds in August and stragglers in December can be spotted. Daily flights of thousands of broad-winged hawks (*Buteo platypterus*) may be seen in September. Ospreys (*Pandion haliaetus*) and bald eagles (*Haliaeetus leucocephala*) are also noted in September. Sharp-shinned hawks (*Accipiter striatus*) are prevalent in October, with red-tailed hawks (*Buteo lineatus*) gliding along the crest lines in late October and into November. Other species such as the northern goshawk (*Accipiter gentilis*) and golden eagle (*Aquila chrysaetos*) are likely to migrate through the region in November after the leaves have fallen.

The hawks take advantage of two features created by the topography of the region: thermals and updrafts. Columns of warm air rising from sun-warmed fields and cleared ground rise to form upward spiraling thermals. Hawks catch a ride on the thermal until it reaches its highest altitude, at which point the hawks strike out on their own, descending in a long, linear direction until they can connect with another thermal. Updrafts form as winds are deflected upward upon hitting the ridges, gorges, and slopes of the Blue Ridge terrain. Broad-winged hawks prefer thermals to updrafts, while eagles, sharp-shinned hawks, and red-tailed hawks enjoy the updrafts. Optimum times for watching the spectacle are 9 a.m. through 4 p.m., although the hawks are conspicuously absent an hour or two around noon. One theory proposes that at noon thermals have taken them so high that they are difficult to see.

In addition to the Great Craggy Mountains, numerous areas in Western North Carolina offer excellent opportunities for watching this annual migration. For more information, consult *Birds of the Blue Ridge Mountains,* by Marcus B. Simpson, an outstanding source on this and other ornithological issues.

Coursing through these valleys, the French Broad River, one of the world's few north-flowing rivers, forms the Asheville Basin, the largest intermountain basin in the Blue Ridge Province. This basin, which provides fairly level terrain for a network of interstates, highways, and railroads, was formed when the forces of erosion broadened and flattened the valley floor. The city of Asheville developed in the basin, growing from a small agricultural community 200 years ago into a bustling commercial and cultural center of Western North Carolina.

Interstates I-40 and I-26 converge in Asheville, and I-240 travels directly through the downtown. Unlike the subtle and more natural cuts of the Blue Ridge Parkway, these interstates feature dramatic slices through sections of mountains along their routes. For the student of geology, they offer laboratory-like specimens from an array of epochs. Consider the I-240 cut through Beaucatcher Mountain on the east side of Asheville. This $10 million project completed 20 years ago provides excellent views of rock types and structural features common to Western North Carolina. The rocks are part of the late Proterozoic Ashe Metamorphic Suite, a sequence composed of metamorphosed sedimentary and volcanic rock. The outcrop is dominated by biotite- and quartz-rich rock that formed and recrystallized during metamorphism. Foliation (the layering of leaf-shaped minerals such as micas in a metamorphic rock) is well developed here with many folds and in some places refolding; faults are also evident.

The North Carolina Department of Natural Resources Geologic Survey office in Asheville (phone 704-251-6208) distributes information on the geology and other natural resources along both I-40 and I-26. Sand and gravel production in North Carolina, for example, averages $20 million annually. In many cases, this industry is a direct result of sand and gravel deposited when fast-flowing mountain and upland streams decrease their velocity upon entering less rugged territory or, as in the Swannanoa River Valley, when the river connects with another stream in a broader, more gently sloping valley.

BIRDFOOT VIOLET

(*Viola pedata*)
This violet is identified by its bird's-foot shaped leaves.

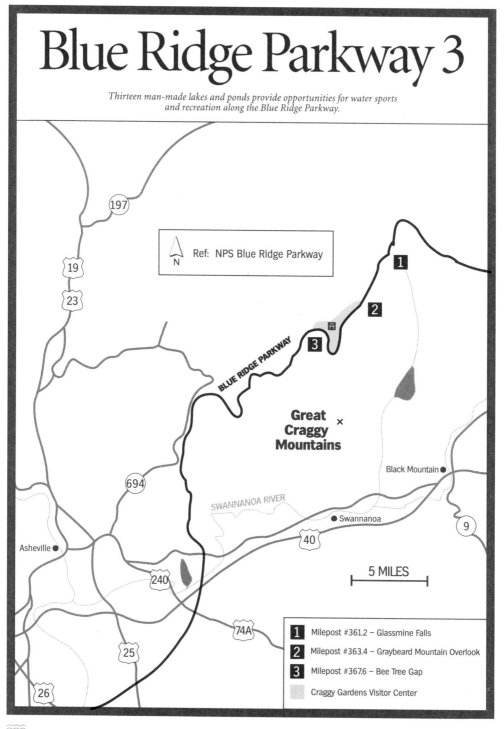

Blue Ridge Parkway 3

Thirteen man-made lakes and ponds provide opportunities for water sports and recreation along the Blue Ridge Parkway.

Ref: NPS Blue Ridge Parkway

N

BLUE RIDGE PARKWAY

Great Craggy Mountains ×

Black Mountain ●

694

SWANNANOA RIVER

● Swannanoa

9

Asheville ●

40

5 MILES

240

74A

25

1 Milepost #361.2 – Glassmine Falls

2 Milepost #363.4 – Graybeard Mountain Overlook

3 Milepost #367.6 – Bee Tree Gap

Craggy Gardens Visitor Center

26

The Blue Ridge Parkway in the Newfound Mountains

[Fig. 19] Stretching from Blackstock Knob, milepost 358, to the French Broad River overlook, milepost 393.8, this section of the Blue Ridge Parkway is only 36 miles in length but lives up to the tradition of breathtaking views and overlooks. Blackstock Knob is part of the "fishhook" bend in the Black Mountains and at 6,325 feet is the highest point along the bend.

Two miles down the road, the Balsam Gap Parking Area is surrounded by a forest of red spruce and Fraser fir. Though a Fraser fir only averages 40 feet in height (and is therefore not as commercially useful as the twice-as-tall red spruce), it plays an important role in soil retention. This is particularly important to area residents, because the surrounding 20,000-acre area constitutes the Asheville Watershed, where mountain streams flow down steep terrain before being captured in reservoirs for use by the largest city in Western North Carolina.

There are more views at milepost 361.2, this time of Glassmine Falls [Fig. 19(1)]. Known as a "wet weather" falls, the 200-foot falls are primarily visible after a rain storm. "Glassmine" refers to the old Abernathy mine where early in the century mica, or isinglass, was mined.

Graybeard Mountain overlook, milepost 363.4 [Fig. 19(2)], affords a view of its namesake mountain with an elevation of 5,365 feet. Those living in its shadow tell stories of how they often can predict rain when the mountain's summit is covered in clouds resembling a gray beard. From here through the 245 feet of Craggy Pinnacle Tunnel and the 355 feet of Craggy Flats Tunnel, the Parkway passes by Craggy Dome and the Craggy Gardens Recreation Area. Five miles south of Bee Tree Gap, milepost 367.6 [Fig. 19(3)], and the entrance to Craggy Gardens Picnic Grounds, the Great Craggy range and the crest of the Swannanoa Mountains loom above the Swannanoa Valley below.

As the Parkway nears the Asheville environs, it takes on the role of a crosstown, east-west thoroughfare for residents of the area. The Parkway also serves as a destination for cyclists. Any bikers traveling the 470 miles of the Parkway from Virginia to Cherokee, North Carolina, climb a total of 48,000 feet, if every hill climbed en route is added together. The challenge increases with weather conditions that can change quickly any time of year. A flyer featuring the major elevations climbed and other safety tips and regulations is available from the Blue Ridge Parkway (*see* Appendix D, page 301).

WOLF LAUREL SKI AREA

[Fig. 21(7)] Mountains only a short drive north of Asheville cannot compete in height with those farther out west, but Wolf Laurel Ski Area still offers adventure to the beginner and expert skier. With 54 acres of skiable terrain, Wolf Laurel harbors 13 ski slopes requiring varying levels of expertise as well as a snowboard half-pipe and sled run. The top elevation reaches 4,650 feet with a vertical drop of 700-plus feet. The slopes stay busy throughout the winter season thanks to the resort's 100 percent snowmaking capabilities and lighted slopes for night skiing. The on-site ski school offers clinics and lessons at every level. Various instruction programs include racing clinics, snowboarding, and a children's ski school.

During the warmer months, Wolf Laurel offers hiking, mountain biking, fly-fishing, whitewater rafting, and other active programs on site and throughout the region. The Appalachian Trail traverses the resort.

Directions: From Asheville at the intersection of I-240 and US 19/23 north, travel 22 miles to where US 19 and US 23 split. Continue on US 23 for 8 miles; turn right at the Wolf Laurel sign and follow the signs for 4 more miles.

Activities: Skiing, snowboarding, sledding, hiking, mountain biking, horseback riding.

Facilities: Chair lifts, equipment rentals, lodge, restaurant, sport shop, day-care center.

Dates: Open year-round; Nov.–Mar. for skiing.

Fees: Packages vary.

Closest town: Mars Hill, 10 miles.

For more information: Wolf Laurel Ski Area, Rt. 3 Box 129, Mars Hill, NC 28754. Phone (704) 689-4111 and (800) 817-4111.

NORTHERN RED OAK

(Quercus rubra) Red oaks can be identified by tiny bristles on the tip of each leaf.

The Vance Birthplace offers a glimpse into the early homestead life in Western North Carolina.

VANCE BIRTHPLACE

[Fig. 21(12)] A visit to the birthplace of Zebulon B. Vance presents a window into eighteenth-century homestead life in the mountains of Western North Carolina. Zebulon Vance achieved a prominent military and political career (three terms as governor of North Carolina and three terms as the state's U.S. senator), but his birthplace offers a look into the more pastoral side of life in the Reems Creek Valley.

The homestead—a large two-story structure of hewn yellow-pine logs—has been reconstructed around the original chimney with its two enormous fireplaces. The furnishings and household items on display are representative of the period from 1790 to 1840 and feature a few pieces original to the home. Six log outbuildings are clustered about the grounds and include the corncrib, springhouse, smokehouse, loom house, slave house, and toolhouse. The grounds come to life throughout the year with special events highlighting seasonal activities of the Vance family's life. Costumed interpreters demonstrate the skills and occupations settlers practiced in the region. A visitor center hosts exhibits portraying the life of Vance.

Directions: From the town of Weaverville, travel south on Business 25 for approximately .5 mile, turn left onto Reems Creek Road, and continue for 5 miles. Vance Birthplace is on the right.

Facilities: Visitor center, gift shop, restrooms, covered picnic shelter.

Dates: Open year-round.

Fees: None.

Closest town: Weaverville, 5.5 miles.

For more information: Vance Birthplace, 911 Reems Creek Road, Weaverville, NC 28787. Phone (704) 645-6706.

Hot Springs Area

*The water at Hot Springs is abnormally warm mainly because
hot water, originating deep inside the earth, rises quickly through fissures in the crust.*

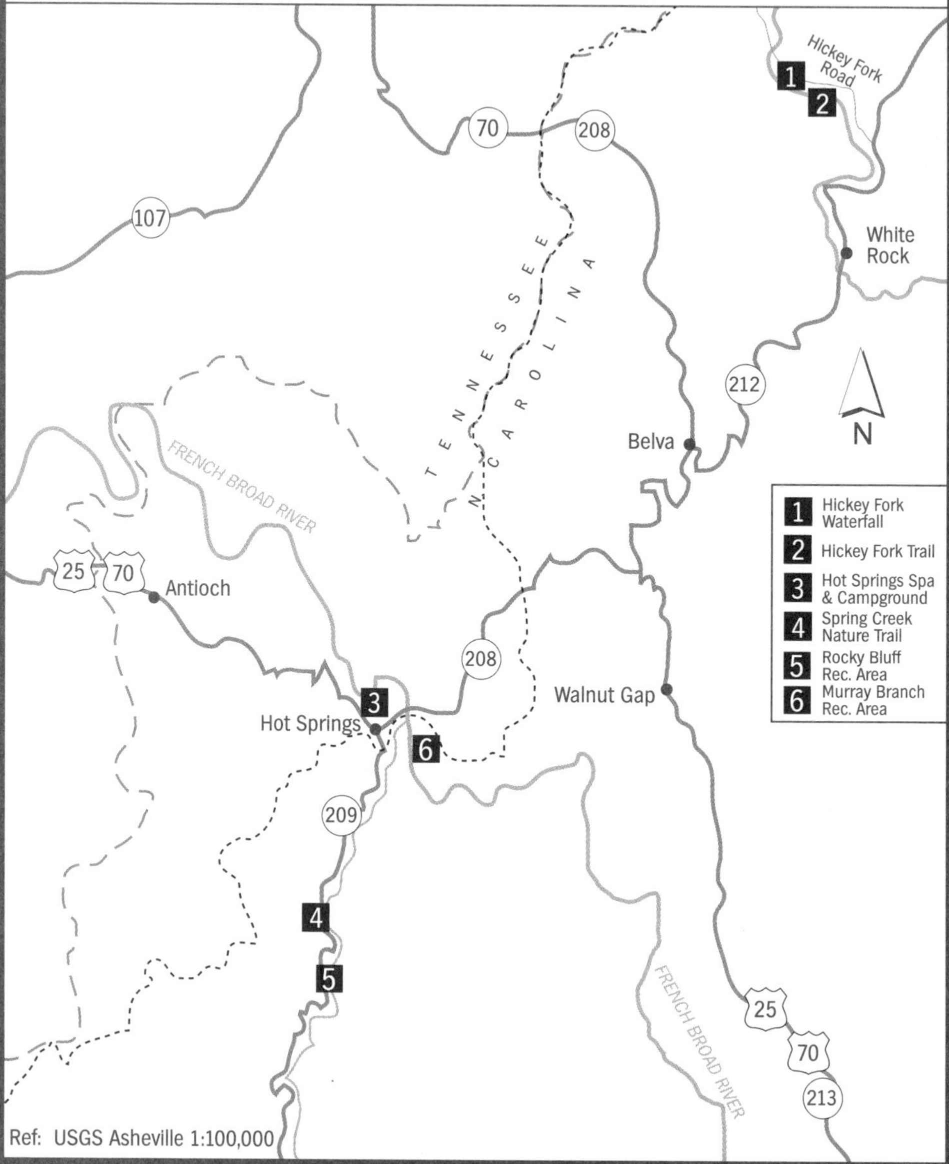

Hickey Fork Road

1
2

70
208

107

White
Rock

TENNESSEE
N CAROLINA

212

Belva

N

FRENCH BROAD RIVER

1	Hickey Fork Waterfall
2	Hickey Fork Trail
3	Hot Springs Spa & Campground
4	Spring Creek Nature Trail
5	Rocky Bluff Rec. Area
6	Murray Branch Rec. Area

25 70
Antioch

208

Walnut Gap

3
Hot Springs
6

209

4

5

FRENCH BROAD RIVER

25

70

213

Ref: USGS Asheville 1:100,000

Hot Springs

[Fig. 21(3), Fig. 20] Located on the French Broad River, the friendly town of Hot Springs has a history revolving around water, especially the geothermal waters that give the town its name. Geothermal hot springs have been used by humans for centuries. The Romans, for example, used hot springs and mineral baths for medicinal, bathing, and recreational purposes. The waters at Hot Springs are abnormally warm primarily because the hot water deep within the earth finds an easy conduit here, probably in the form of fractures within the earth, that allows it to rise to the surface more quickly. When the hot water escapes at ground surface, it forms a hot spring.

During the late 1800s, Hot Springs became famous as a health resort town. Doctors, patients, and vacationers from all over the world flocked to the town, believing the curative powers of the hot mineral waters would heal all of their ills. Over the years, many testimonials have been filed by visitors who claim that the mineral waters of Hot Springs brought them relief from stomach, liver, and gallbladder ailments, rheumatism, and arthritis.

People still enjoy these geothermal springs today at Hot Springs Spa and Campground [Fig. 20(3)]. The water, which maintains a natural temperature of 100 degrees Fahrenheit year-round, bubbles up into modern Jacuzzi tubs in secluded outdoor settings along the French Broad River and Spring Creek. In addition to leisurely soaks in the tubs, the spa also offers massage therapy and riverside camping.

Nestled among the loftiest peaks of the southern Appalachians, Hot Springs is a favorite with hikers on the Appalachian Trail (AT), which runs through town, providing hikers easy access to stores and supplies. Lovers Leap Rock, one of the most popular AT side hikes in the area, offers a grand view of the French Broad River 500 feet below. Lovers Leap Rock gets its name from a Cherokee Indian legend that tells of a maiden who threw herself from the steep cliff after learning her lover had been killed by a jealous beau. While this hike is only 2.6 miles round-trip, it is a strenuous hike, gaining 1,000 feet in elevation. From town, take Main Street north following the white blazes painted on the sidewalk. After the trail crosses the French Broad River Bridge, it curves under the bridge on Lovers Leap Road for .3 mile to Silver Mine Creek parking area. Continue through the U.S. Forest Service gate and follow the orange blazes which mark the trail to Lovers Leap Rock.

Rocky Bluff Recreation Area [Fig. 20(5)] offers camping, picnicking, hiking, nature study, and fishing in Spring Creek, as well as flush toilets, lavatories, and water fountains. The site was formerly residential farmland and, at one time, a school. The recreation area is open from mid-April to mid-November, and can be reached by driving south from Hot Springs on NC 209 for 3.3 miles.

The 1.6-mile Spring Creek Nature Trail [Fig. 20(4)] is located at Rocky Bluff Recreation Area and is an easy-to-moderate, yellow-blazed trail. At .5 mile, there is a nice vista of Spring Creek. Then the trail continues around the mountain, following along the side of the cascading stream. Keep a lookout for Eastern hemlock (*Tsuga canadensis*), basswood (*Tilia americana*), oaks, and an abundance of wildflowers including varieties of trillium.

Only 1.1 miles in length, the trail to Hickey Fork Waterfall [Fig. 20(1)] is strenuous. The falls are rich with growing mosses. The small grottos that can be spotted behind its mist provide a habitat for the spray-cliff natural community. From Hot Springs, head north on NC 208 until it intersects with NC 212, and take a right. Continue for 6.8 miles to NC 1310, which is known as Hickey Fork Road. Turn left and drive until you see the parking area on the right. The trailhead begins about 200 feet up the road, on the left. Hike in about 1 mile. At this point, a smaller yet beautiful cascade occurs on the right. To reach the main waterfall, continue another .1 mile. Some bushwhacking is necessary to reach the base of the waterfall. Hemlock, white pine (*Pinus strobus*), yellow-poplar (*Liriodendron tulipifera*), rhododendron (*Rhododendron catawbiense* and *maximum*), mountain laurel (*Kalmia latifolia*), dog-hobble (*Viburnum alnifolium*), and ferns are all common.

The Murray Branch Recreation Area [Fig. 20(6)] is located 6 miles down the French Broad River from Hot Springs. The area offers recreational opportunities for picnicking, fishing, and canoe access to the river. Facilities at Murray Branch, under the shade of pines, include picnic tables, grills, restrooms, water, and two picnic shelters for large groups. An easy, 1-mile loop trail is adjacent to the area, providing a bird's-eye view of the French Broad River and the surrounding valley.

The location of the town along the French Broad River also provides easy access for whitewater rafting, canoeing, and kayaking. A variety of outfitters have been established in the area to provide guided trips and rentals (*see* Appendix C, page 300).

Directions: From Asheville, head north on US 19/23 to the Marshall Exit (US 25/70). Travel north 17 miles to the town of Hot Springs.

Activities: Hiking, biking, whitewater rafting, canoeing, and kayaking.

Facilities: Spas, restaurants, accommodations, supplies, picnic areas. Two national forest campgrounds—Silvermine Campground and Rocky Bluff Campground—are located near Hot Springs, providing tent platforms, water, grills, tables, and toilets.

SILVERMINE GROUP CAMPGROUND. Silvermine Group Campground provides spaces for groups of 2 or more and is located near the French Broad River and 2 rafting outfitters. Only 1 group is permitted to use this campground at a time, and reservations are required. There is a charge for camping. Open Aug.–Oct.

For more information: Phone (704) 622-3202.

ROCKY BLUFF CAMPGROUND. Rocky Bluff Campground, part of the Rocky Bluff Recreation Area, is located on State Highway 209. This campground offers 30 campsites on a first come, first served basis. Two of the campsites can accommodate trailers up to 18 feet long. There is a charge for camping. Open May–Oct.

For more information: Phone (704) 622-3254.

HOT SPRINGS SPA AND CAMPGROUND. RV and tent camping are also available at the privately owned Hot Springs Spa and Campground. There is a charge for camping. A comfort station with hot showers is available.

For more information: Hot Springs Spa and Campground, One Bridge Street, Hot Springs, NC 28743-0428. Phone (704) 622-7676.

HARMON DEN AREA

[Fig. 21(25)] According to local legend, Harmon Den was named for a man, Harmon, who lived by himself under a large rock outcropping on what is now Harmon Den Mountain. Like other areas of the region, Harmon Den was heavily logged earlier this century. Timber companies cut all the forest in the Cold Springs Creek drainage and built logging roads, narrow-gauge railroads, and amenities for the logging crews and their families. Relief from this destruction came in 1936 when the USDA Forest Service purchased Harmon Den and operated a Civilian Conservation Corps camp in the area during the 1940s; corpsmen planted many of the white pines still evident today.

Although I-40 runs through much of Harmon Den Area, the lack of paved roads and developed communities keeps this remote area pristine and uncrowded. Twenty-one miles of the Appalachian Trail and 17 miles of trails such as the Buckeye Ridge Trail afford spectacular views of the surrounding Great Smoky, Snowbird, and Black mountains. The trail network features five horse trails and two additional hiking trails that serve mountain bikers as well. Following the old roadbeds through hardwood-hemlock forests and along streambeds, these trails open opportunities to experience the abundance of wildlife flourishing in this quiet area. The renowned Max Patch Trail (*see* Max Patch, page 106) is also part of the Harmon Den Area.

Directions: Take the Harmon Den Exit off I-40 near the North Carolina/Tennessee state line. Drive northeast on FR 148 (Cold Springs Road) approximately 3 miles to Harmon Den parking area on the left. Parking for trailers is also available at lower junction of FR 148 and FR 3526, Robert Gap Trailhead at junction of FR 148 and NC 1182, and Cherry Ridge Trailhead on NC 1182.

Activities: Hiking, biking, horseback riding, fishing.

Facilities: Primitive campsites only.

Fees: None.

Closest town: Hot Springs, approximately 40 miles; Waynesville, approximately 20 miles.

For more information: A detailed map of the Harmon Den Area is available from the U.S. Forest Service, French Broad District.

MAX PATCH

[Fig. 21(4)] Whether black clouds ominously color the surrounding mountains or a clear blue sky affords breathtakingly panoramic views of the Black, Bald, Balsam, and Great Smoky mountains, Max Patch is a favorite trail with hikers of all degrees of endurance. It is a gentle climb across the southernmost bald on the Appalachian Trail to its grassy summit at 4,629 feet. During the warmer seasons, the trail abounds with wildflowers. This relatively short hike can be extended by continuing either north or south on the Appalachian Trail.

The northern segment travels 20 miles to the town of Hot Springs. The first 7 miles along this segment are easy, gaining less than 1,000 feet in elevation, but the path soon climbs steadily toward the wooded summit of Walnut Mountain (elevation 4,280 feet). After a short stretch on an old roadbed, the trail reaches Catpen Gap and ascends Bluff Mountain (elevation 4,686 feet). From here the trail drops steadily, losing more than 3,000 feet along its 10-mile descent into Hot Springs. After a two-day hike, the Hot Springs Spa offers a luxurious change of pace (*see* Hot Springs, page 103).

Privately owned until 1982, the land covered by the trail had been used for grazing sheep and cattle. An offer to sell to a ski development was fortunately countered by the U.S. Forest Service, which bought the 392 acres for the Appalachian Trail.

Directions: From Hot Springs, travel south on NC 209 for 7 miles. Turn right onto NC 1175 and continue for 5 miles. Turn onto NC 1182 (Max Patch Road) and travel 3 miles to the parking area at the foot of the bald.

Activities: Hiking.

Facilities: None at Max Patch. Several shelters along the Appalachian Trail.

Fees: None.

Closest town: Hot Springs, 15 miles.

Trail distance and configuration: Connector trail from parking lot to the AT approximately .5 mile. The Max Patch–Hot Springs segment of the AT approximately 20 miles.

Elevation: 4,692 feet.

Degree of difficulty: Max Patch: Easy. AT to Hot Springs: Moderate.

Surface and blaze: Forest floor, pastureland; white blaze on the AT.

FLAME AZALEA
(*Rhododendron calendulaceum*)

RATTLESNAKE LODGE TRAIL

[Fig. 21(13)] The trail to Rattlesnake Lodge begins its gentle ascent up the Bull Gap range a short distance off the Blue Ridge Parkway on Ox Creek Road. Numerous switchbacks along a former carriage trail are as handy for today's walker as they were at the turn of the century for the family of Dr. Chase P. Ambler. A prominent pulmonary physician and noted conservationist, Ambler created a rough-hewn mountain estate for his family from the virgin land thick with oak, hickory, birch, black walnut (*Juglans nigra*), and American chestnut (*Castanea dentata*). The estate eventually included a two-story lodge, workshop, springhouse, log barn, corncrib, tenant's house, swimming pool, and tennis court, but it burned to the ground in 1925. All that stands today are the still-impressive stone foundations of the house, the walls of the springhouse, and a few apple trees from the orchards. The trail, which is part of the Mountains-to-Sea Trail system, features almost continuous mountain vistas and acres of pencil-straight hardwoods sheltering the trail. An impressive array of wildflowers, especially jewelweed (*Impatiens pallida* and *I. capensis*) and houstonia (*Houstonia purpurea*), hug the pathway, and each spring daffodils overtake the hollow where the estate stood. The National Park Service purchased 233 acres from Dr. Ambler's estate in the mid-1970s.

Dr. Ambler is recognized for his contributions to forestry conservation and wilderness preservation in the region. A 6,100-foot peak in the Great Smoky Mountains National Park is named in honor of his tireless efforts to establish the park, and the sign at the entrance to Curtis Creek Area (*see* Curtis Creek, page 93) recognizes his dedication to the preservation of national forest lands.

The Bull Gap area offers excellent opportunities for watching the spring songbird migration and is considered one of the best places in North Carolina's mountains for spotting cerulean warblers (*Dendroica cerulea*). The area harbors other late-spring and summer birds such as the pileated woodpecker (*Dryocopus pileatus*), downy woodpecker (*Dendrocopos pubsecens*), Carolina wren (*Thryothorus ludovicianus*), wood thrush (*Hylocichla mustelina*), indigo bunting (*Passerina cyanea*), and a variety of warblers.

Directions: At Blue Ridge Parkway milepost 376, turn left onto Ox Creek Road. Continue .9 mile to a small dirt parking area. A Mountains-to-Sea Trail sign marks the trailhead.

Activities: Hiking.

Facilities: None.

Dates: Open year-round.

Closest town: Asheville, approximately 12 miles.

Trail distance and configuration: A segment of the Mountains-to-Sea Trail; from parking lot to lodge, approximately 3 miles round-trip.

Elevation: 3,700 feet.

Degree of difficulty: Easy to moderate.

Surface and blaze: Forest floor; white blaze.

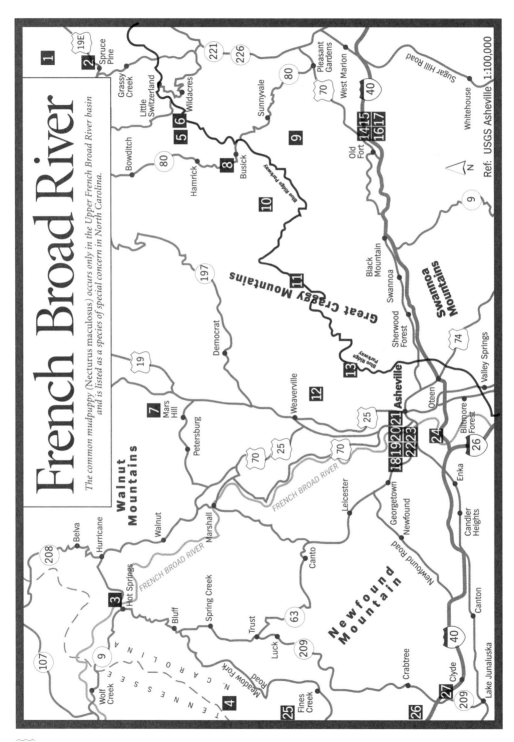

French Broad River

The common mudpuppy (Necturus maculosus) occurs only in the Upper French Broad River basin and is listed as a species of special concern in North Carolina.

Ref: USGS Asheville 1:100,000

1 Overmountain Victory National Historical Trail

2 Penland School of Crafts

3 Hot Springs

4 Max Patch

5 Crabtree Meadows

6 Crabtree Falls Trail

7 Wolf Laurel Ski Area

8 Carolina Hemlock Recreation Area

9 Curtis Creek

10 Mount Mitchell State Park

11 Craggy Gardens Recreation Area

12 Vance Birthplace

13 Rattlesnake Lodge/Bull Gap

14 Old Fort

15 The Mountain Gateway Museum

16 Grant's Indian Museum

17 Railroad Museum & Visitor Center

18 University Botanical Gardens at Asheville

19 Western North Carolina Nature Center

20 Folk Art Center

21 Colburn Gem Mine/Mineral Museum

22 Thomas Wolfe Memorial & Visitor Center

23 Cherokee Archaeological Site at Warren Wilson College

24 Biltmore Estate

25 Harmon Den

26 Cataloochee Ski Area

27 Rhododendron Garden & Arboretum at Haywood Community College

Blue Ridge Parkway

Craggy Gardens Recreation Area

[Fig. 21(11)] When summertime hits Asheville, northbound traffic on the Blue Ridge Parkway picks up as residents head for the Craggy Gardens Recreation Area only 15 miles away. The climb is steep from the lowlands around Asheville, and soon the summer swelter turns to cool, shady, and sometimes chilly conditions.

But Craggy Gardens isn't just for summertime—it is a popular destination any time of year, with high peaks and scenic views, rugged terrain, and heath balds covered with Catawba rhododendron. By mid- to late June, the mountainside is awash in pink and purple blossoms, perhaps the most spectacular display for miles around. In the fall, in addition to the carnival of color from deciduous trees turning gold, red, and orange, bouquets of bright red berries hang from the mountain-ash (*Sorbus americana*). Even in winter, the ice-encased branches of the gnarled hardwood forest of American beech (*Fagus grandifolia*), yellow birch (*Betula alleghaniensis*), buckeye (*Aesculus octandra*), and mountain-ash sparkle in bright sunlight.

The Craggies are widely regarded as one of the Parkway's most important botanical areas because they host a number of endangered and threatened plants. In addition to the rhododendron, the heath balds host mountain laurel, flame azalea (*Rhododendron calendulaceum*), and plentiful blueberry bushes (*Vaccinium*). Balds here are comprised primarily of grasses and wildflowers, which in some areas interweave through the heaths to form "pathways" through the rhododendron. Together the grasses and wildflowers form pieces in the puzzle of the southern Appalachian balds. Though many theories circulate about the origins of balds, the one that proposes some balds were man-made may apply here. In the Craggies, the balds were used cleared and used by early settlers for pasturing livestock during the summer months. Yet, most grazing ceased by 1920 and definitely stopped in 1950 when the National Park Service acquired the land, and the balds still exist. No one knows why.

The 700-acre site, recognized by the state as a Natural Heritage Area, includes a visitor center, picnic grounds, and several short but rewarding hiking trails. The Craggy Gardens Trail starts at the south end of the visitor center parking area or from the north end of the picnic area. From the south end of the visitor center parking area, the trail begins as a self-guiding nature trail with a moderate uphill climb to a large trail shelter, built by the CCC in 1935. The nature trail ends at the shelter, and a short spur trail crosses the rhododendron bald to spectacular views of the Black Mountain range. The main trail continues on a gradual descent into a mixed-hardwood forest to the picnic area. In this general area, violets, blackberry (*Rubus argutus*), mayapple (*Podophyllum peltatum*), and wild crabapple (*Malus angustifolia*) are just some of the colorful wildflowers that compete with the rhododendron for attention.

Craggy Pinnacle Trail delivers the most view for the least amount of walking. Only a moderate 20-minute walk is required from the upper level of the Craggy Dome Parking Overlook. From beginning to end, the trail is resplendent with tunnels of rhododendron, wildflowers, and more blueberries. The Lower Overlook, which is signposted after the last ascent, offers a different—and to some, more interesting—view of the geology and vegetation of the pinnacle. A reminder: as with all trails, though they appear lush and thriving, these are fragile environments. Stay on the designated trails and off the rocky outcrops. Even hard-to-see lichens and mosses play critical roles in our environment.

Longer trails include a segment of the Mountains-to-Sea Trail (MST) (*see* page 287); the Snowball Mountain Trail (8 miles round-trip), accessed a short distance off the MST crossing at the picnic area; and the Carter Creek Falls Trail (8 miles round-trip—also known as Douglas Falls Trail). Access for this trail is from the picnic area. Follow the MST north for 1.5 miles to its intersection with Carter Creek Falls Trail. The trail is strenuous but leads through a series of cascades and two virgin hemlock groves on its way to the 70-foot falls. Improved access to the Mountains-to-Sea Trail has recently been completed at the south end of the visitor center parking area where the trail branches off to the right after 100 yards.

PILEATED WOODPECKER
(*Dryocopus pileatus*)

The Parkway provides easy access to many excellent bird-watching sites, and Craggy Gardens holds an esteemed reputation for birds. This is due in part to the work of John S. Cairns who late in the nineteenth century conducted field studies nearby. The parking area of the visitor center is a great place for easy birding, even for those confined to wheelchairs. The common raven (*Corvus corax*), veery (*Hylocichla fuscenscens*), winter wren (*Troglodytes troglodytes*), cedar waxwing (*Bombycilla cedrorum*), Canada warbler (*Wilsonia canadensis*), rose-breasted grosbeak (*Pheucticus ludovicianus*), and catbird (*Dumetella carolinensis*) are just some of the birds typically found here in late spring and summer.

Directions: Off the Blue Ridge Parkway. Visitor center, milepost 364.6; picnic grounds, milepost 367.5; Craggy Pinnacle parking, milepost 364.1.

Activities: Hiking.

Facilities: Visitor center: restrooms, water, information, books and maps. Picnic grounds: several dozen tables and grills, restrooms, water.

Dates: Visitor center: May–Oct. All other facilities: year-round.

Fees: None.

Closest town: Asheville, 15 miles.

For more information: Blue Ridge Parkway, phone (704) 298-0398.

▦ BILTMORE ESTATE AND GARDENS

[Fig. 21(24)] A winding 3-mile route through woodland groves provides an idyllic approach to the Biltmore Estate. Double rows of tulip trees flank the wide front lawn of this French Renaissance chateau that George Vanderbilt first opened to his guests in 1895.

The 250-room mansion, designed by Richard Morris Hunt, is the largest private residence in the United States. Many of the original furnishings, art, and antiques are on display in this National Historic Landmark. Eight thousand acres of the original 125,000-acre estate remain, including 75 acres of landscaped gardens, forested walking trails, rolling wooded parks, formal pleasure gardens, and riverside fields designed by landscape architect Frederick Law Olmsted as his last and largest project.

The 4-acre English Walled Garden is brilliant with more than 50,000 tulips, 40 varieties of annuals, perennial borders, and 2,000 roses in more than 100 varieties. The 15-acre Azalea Garden contains one of the most complete collections of native and hybrid azaleas in existence. More than 1,000 azaleas represent 14 native species in this spectacular display. The vibrant colors are dazzling beneath a canopy of century-old pines.

The Biltmore Estate and Gardens is home to many native plant species in more than 75 acres of landscaped gardens and forested walking trails.

The sixteenth-century Italian Garden adds elegance with its reflecting pools and statuary, and the Conservatory offers a fragrant display of color with blooming tropicals and hothouse plants.

The Shrub Garden contains hundreds of native and exotic woody plants. A forest trail shows the care taken by the young forester, Gifford Pinchot, employed by the estate in one of the first organized attempts at forestry in the United States (*see* Cradle of Forestry, page 150).

The Bass Pond and Lagoon created from an old creek-fed millpond add another dimension of tranquil beauty to this magnificent estate. The Meadow Trail provides a high vista overlooking the pond where Canada geese (*Branta canadenis*), mallards (*Anas platyrhnchos*), and other waterfowl play. A waterfall drops in silvered beads to the creek below, and migrant songbirds, insects, and wildlife abound. Great blue herons (*Ardea herodias*), raccoons (*Pipilo erythrophthalmus*), gray and red foxes (*Urocyon cinereoargenteus* and *Vulpes fulva*), and beavers (*Castor canadensis*) have been spotted. The Estate Winery produces 75,000 cases of wine each year, using more than 200 tons of estate-grown grapes as part of the Biltmore philosophy of maintaining a self-sufficient, working estate.

Directions: From I-40: Take Exit 50 or 50B and travel 3 blocks north on Highway 25. From I-26: Take I-40 East, then Exit 50. Follow the signs.

Facilities: House, gardens, restaurants, gift shops, and winery. Handicapped accessible throughout.

Dates: Open year-round except Thanksgiving and Christmas.

Fees: There is an entrance fee.

For more information: The Biltmore Company, One North Pack Square, Asheville, NC 28801. Phone (704) 274-6333 and (800) 570-4780. Web site: www.biltmore.com.

THE UNIVERSITY BOTANICAL GARDENS AT ASHEVILLE

[Fig. 21(18)] This is a garden with heart. Since its inception in 1960, nature-loving volunteers have planted, transplanted, and cultivated an extraordinary sanctuary for native flora and a vital wildlife refuge near the center of busy downtown Asheville.

Across the 10 acres of varied terrain—from creekside bog, to forested hillside, to wildflower-filled glade—the gardens are a living tribute to the rich biodiversity of the Southern Highlands. From the rare and endangered shortia or oconee bells (*Shortia galactifolia*) to the common and nutritious stinging nettle (*Urtica dioica*), more than 700 plant species thrive in the botanical gardens.

On a typical spring afternoon an artist sets up an easel, a photographer poses a young couple before a field of creeping buttercup (*Ranunculus repens*), and a lone visitor engages in contemplation sitting beneath a giant sycamore (*Platanus occidentalis*). Flushed joggers speed past young families strolling along paths graced with little sweet betsy (*Trillium cuneatum*) and wake robin (*Trillium erectum*). The fragrance of lily of the valley (*Convallaria majalis*) sweetens the air and joyful birdsong harmonizes with the soothing sound of Reed Creek flowing over the rocks, its rippled water gilded by the afternoon sun.

An original log cabin, rebuilt on site, provides a glimpse of earlier mountain habitation, and memorial plaques beneath flowering trees honor some of those who loved these gardens and helped preserve them.

Golden club (*Orontium aquaticum*) thrives in the bog-side lily pond. Carolina hemlocks (*Tsuga carolinanian*) reach skyward and flame azaleas brighten the wooded slopes. Two-winged silverbells (*Halesia diptera*), delicately blooming in spring, buzz with honey bees. Eastern chipmunks (*Tamias striatus*) and gray squirrels (*Scirus carolinensis*) scamper beneath flowering dogwoods (*Cornus florida*) in a meadow bordered with violets (*Viola papilionacea*). Pinxter flower azaleas (*Rhododendron nudiflorum*) and red buckeyes (*Aesculus pavia*) add to the beauty. Even the common burdock (*Arctium minus*), pokeweed (*Phytolacca americana*), and poor man's pepper (*Lepidum virginicum*) have a place here.

Directions: Take I-240 to Merrimon Avenue Exit, go north to Weaver Boulevard, and go west past the university entrance. Located at 151 W. T. Weaver Boulevard, between Merrimon Avenue and Broadway, adjacent to the University of North Carolina at Asheville campus.

Facilities: 10-acre site with handicapped accessible, easy paths. Gift shop, library, auditorium, solarium, restrooms, designated picnic tables.

Dates: Open seasonally.

Fees: None.

Closest town: Asheville.

For more information: Botanical Gardens Visitor center, phone (704) 252-5190.

WESTERN NORTH CAROLINA NATURE CENTER

[Fig. 21(19)] Many natural events, both obvious and subtle, occur daily in the southern Appalachian Mountains. Their stories need telling and retelling for it is only through public education and subsequent public support that the environmental integrity of North Carolina's wild areas can be assured. Realizing this need, Buncombe County Recreation Services has provided the public with a first-class nature interpretation facility, the Western North Carolina Nature Center. The 42-acre facility evolved in the mid-1970s from the former Asheville City Zoo, which was in major need of renovation. Concerned citizens had been lobbying for remodeling of the zoo facility in keeping with "environmentally friendly" zoo modernization efforts under way around the nation. The Junior League of Asheville made the renovation project its priority in preparation for the July 4, 1976, bicentennial celebration. Today, as many as 90,000 visitors are received at the center each year.

A reception building that houses an information/ticket desk, gift shop, and restrooms opens the way to an array of choices. Inside the Main Exhibit Building, for example, live exhibits of reptiles, amphibians, and fish are complemented by hands-on areas where visitors can observe natural objects through microscopes, explore guessing boxes, or view the inner mechanisms of tree growth.

Back outside, paths lead to a turtle pond, various gardens, and the .6-mile Trillium Glen Nature Trail loop, which contains native southern Appalachian plants in a natural forest setting.

The biggest attraction of the nature center is its assemblage of native mammals and birds of prey. River otters (*Lutra canadensis*) bask on rocks or playfully swim in the water, and a special window enhances the viewing of the underwater antics of these graceful creatures. Visitors are also treated to habitats of the red fox, raccoon, white-tailed deer (*Odocoileus virginia*), black bear (*Ursus americanus*), cougar, bobcat (*Lynx rufus*), gray wolf (*Canis lupus*), and the endangered red wolf (*Canis rufus*). Feathered members of the menagerie include the peacock, wild turkey (*Meleagris gallopavo*), red-tailed hawk, great horned owl (*Bubo virginianus*), and golden eagle.

In other areas, the World Underground exhibit allows visitors to walk through dark subterranean wildlife habitats and experience what it is like to live within the hidden layers of soil and tree roots below the forest floor. The Educational Farm includes a barn that houses sheep, goats, and rabbits. A nearby corral area is open to kids and adults who want to approach and pet these creatures.

The nature center offers a series of creative programs throughout the year called Wild Weekends. Visitors who bring in an insect on Bug Day or a snake during the Snake Beauty Pageant earn free admission. (Insects are identified by a volunteer specialist, and snakes get a shot at winning the beauty pageant.) Other Wild Weekends include Farm Fun Day, Hey Day, and An Evening with the Reindeer. At the start of February, visitors are treated to a presentation on groundhog natural history and a chance to pet the center's resident groundhog (*Marmota monax*). Other programs offered by the nature center include indoor nature presentations and off-property day hikes.

Directions: Take I-240 to Exit 8 and travel north on US 74 to Swannanoa River Road (NC 81) for .75 mile. Turn right on Azalea Road, then turn right on Gashes Creek Road and follow to the WNC Nature Center entrance on right.

Facilities: Visitor center, nature exhibit rooms, wildlife habitat enclosures, gift shop, restrooms.

Dates: Open year-round. Closed some holidays.

Fees: A fee is charged for admission.

Closest town: Asheville.

For more information: Phone (704) 298-5600.

RIVER OTTER (Lutra canadensis)

Sociable animals, river otters wrestle, play tag, and roll around riverbanks and in water. Their streamlined bodies, webbed toes, and eyes and ears that can be closed underwater make them well suited for life in and around water.

Folk Art Center

[Fig. 21(20)] Set in the heart of a region where for generations the most beautiful things have been handmade, the Folk Art Center represents the finest in American crafts. Opened in 1980, the 30,500-square-foot center is filled with fine traditional and contemporary crafts—weaving, quilting, pottery, baskets, paper, glass, jewelry, woodworking, blacksmithing, and metalsmithing, among others—from the members of the Southern Highland Craft Guild.

The guild enjoys a long, creative history of setting milestones in the American craft movement. It was founded in 1930 by a group of who's whos in American craft who dedicated their lives to promoting indigenous crafts from the nine southern Appalachian states. Frances Goodrich was among them, a Presbyterian missionary and social worker from Ohio who came in 1895 with heart and mind open to ways of helping the economically impoverished area. She soon discovered that though the people were in need of many temporal things, they had much to share, most notably a woven double bowknot coverlet given to her in friendship. Struck by its quality and integrity, Goodrich began her life's work of fostering regional handicrafts and, in turn, saving many old crafts from extinction.

Goodrich organized a group of women to card, spin, dye, and weave wool and cotton coverlets for sale by mail order; she paid them on a piecework basis. By 1908 her Allanstand Cottage Industries had a permanent showroom in Asheville, and in 1931, upon her retirement, she donated it to the guild. Today, Allanstand Craft Shop occupies 3,000 square feet on the first level of the Folk Art Center, enjoying the distinction of being America's oldest continuously operated craft shop.

The Guild also spearheaded the revival of craft fairs in America, hosting its first

The 30,500-square-foot Folk Art Center is filled with some of the finest traditional and contemporary handicrafts one can find in the United States.

fair in 1948 across the Great Smoky Mountains in Gatlinburg, Tennessee. Every third weekend in July and October in downtown Asheville's Civic Center, the Craft Fair of the Southern Highlands spotlights the work of 150 traditional and contemporary craft artists and features demonstrations, regional music, and entertainment.

The center's second level hosts two exhibition spaces, the Main Gallery and the Focus Gallery. At least once a year, selections from the guild's 2,000-piece permanent collection of historic and modern crafts are featured. Future goals include an interpretive display in which pieces from the collection help tell the rich history of the guild. Classes, members' exhibitions, national juried shows, demonstrations, and lectures also help carry out the guild's commitment to education.

Visitors can get good travel advice from the staff at the Blue Ridge Parkway Visitor Center in the Folk Art Center's lobby, and a well-stocked bookstore features maps and books detailing the natural life along the Parkway.

Mountain folk arts have a strong tradition in Western North Carolina and there are many places to witness the fine handicrafts and traditions of the area. Above, a craftsman at the John C. Campbell Folk School in Brasstown, North Carolina.

A segment of the Mountains-to-Sea Trail (*see* MTS, page 287) runs adjacent to the center.

Directions: From I-40 East, Exit 55, turn left on Tunnel Road. Follow signs after 1 mile and head north on Blue Ridge Parkway. Located at Blue Ridge Parkway, milepost 382.

Facilities: Restrooms, Blue Ridge Parkway information center and bookstore, exhibitions, craft shop, programs.

Dates: Open year-round.

Fees: None.

Closest town: Asheville, 5 miles.

For more information: Southern Highland Craft Guild, PO Box 9545, Asheville, NC 28815. Phone (704) 298-7928.

French Broad River Area

[Fig. 21] The French Broad River is the largest watercourse in Western North Carolina. First settled by members of the Cherokee Nation and visited in 1540 by the treasure-seeking Spanish explorer Hernando De Soto, the river basin was ultimately occupied by English-speaking settlers. They gave the river its often-misunderstood name because it flowed west toward the Mississippi Valley lands claimed by French explorers and fur traders. With a rich and varied history, the river has had a major influence on human activities in the area and continues to do so today.

From the river's headwaters west of Rosman in Transylvania County to the border of Tennessee, the French Broad is about 70 miles in length. Its drainage basin includes 5,124 square miles, with 1,664 square miles occurring in North Carolina. At its highest elevation, the French Broad River reaches 6,400 feet, where one of its major tributaries, the Swannanoa River, begins below Potato Knob in the Black Mountains. The river's lowest North Carolina elevation, 1,240 feet, occurs at the Tennessee state line west of Hot Springs.

The French Broad River has several characteristics that are unusual for rivers of the southern Appalachians. Due to the nature of southeastern Blue Ridge topography, the river flows in a northward semicircle, cradled between the Tennessee Valley Divide and the Pisgah Ridge. Beginning at the junction of its first three major tributaries, the North, West, and East forks, the river flows first to the northeast, then turns north to Asheville, and finally sweeps to the northwest toward Tennessee.

Another of the French Broad's interesting characteristics is that it flows along a nearly level grade for much of its length. The river's southern portion has an average fall of only 3 feet per mile and, at some locations, as little as 1 foot per mile. This rate eventually increases between Asheville and the Tennessee line, where steeper gorges and narrower channels result in a fall of 16 to 30 feet per mile.

In addition, the river is wider by comparison than others in the region. The slow currents, together with the gently sloping topography, contribute to an expansive floodplain along the river's portion south of Asheville. This floodplain is especially wide in the area between the French Broad's junction with the Mills River and the Asheville vicinity.

Finally, the French Broad River occurs at a fairly low elevation, where winter temperatures are relatively moderate and summer temperatures approach those expected in the Piedmont and Coastal Plain provinces. This combination of geology and climate influences forest and animal species found along the river. While trees typically associated with the mountains such as basswood, tulip poplar, and various oaks are found here, so are a number of floodplain species—river birch (*Betula nigra*), sycamore (*Platanus occidentalis*), American hornbeam (*Carpinus caroliniana*), hazel alder (*Alnus serrulata*), and several species of willow.

A large variety of wildlife, especially birds, can be seen along the French Broad

River, the most notable being the wading birds. Great blue herons are numerous, and green (*Butorides virescens*) and little blue herons (*Florida caerulea*) appear as well. Egrets, which make their way inland after nesting in Coastal Plain habitats hundreds of miles to the southeast, are a special treat in the mountains. These magnificent white birds can be seen searching for fish and crustaceans along the banks of the French Broad's quiet waters.

Other water birds include the black duck (*Anas rubripes*), pied-bill and horned grebes (*Podilymbus podiceps* and *Podiceps auritus*), belted kingfisher (*Megaceryle alcyon*), osprey (*Pandion haliaetus*), wood duck (*Aix sponsa*), and, occasionally, the spotted sandpiper (*Actitus macularia*). The southern bald eagle historically nested along the river and still can be spotted today. Migratory woodland and riparian birds commonly seen and heard in summer include the white-eyed and red-eyed vireo (*Vireo griseus* and *V. olivaceus*), hooded warbler (*Wilsonia citrina*), worm-eating warbler, yellow-throated warbler, northern parula warbler (*Parula americana*), Acadian and great crested flycatcher (*Empidonax virescens* and *Myiarchus crinitus*), Louisiana waterthrush (*Seiurus motacilla*), and various swallow species.

One of the best ways to see the wading birds and ducks is from the river itself. There is good access to quiet water stretches at Sandy Bottom near the Bent Creek area. For those lacking the proper equipment, outfitters offer canoes and rafts plus put-in and take-out shuttles (*see* Appendix C, page 300). Two-hour trips, for example, take visitors along an easy route with just enough Class I rapids to make this a relaxed but fun family outing. Paddlers are treated to views of floodplain forest and river-edge vegetation and wildlife, as well as the historic Biltmore Estate property and mansion. Sharp eyes will spot river otters, white-tailed deer, and perhaps turtles basking on sunlit logs. Colorful red skimmer dragonflies often hover above the French Broad's waters which sparkle with tiny flakes of mica.

West of Asheville, paddlers are treated to a totally different experience. Intense whitewater excitement replaces the relaxed drifting and nature study possible below the city. For whitewater enthusiasts, numerous parks (both city and county) provide access points from Asheville to Hot Springs. There are also a number of whitewater river outfitters in Western North Carolina that offer guided trips through the various stretches of rapids (*see* Appendix C, page 300).

Once polluted and nearly lifeless, the beautiful French Broad River has been rehabilitated and now supports a wide variety of fish, including largemouth bass (*Micropterus salmoides*), brown and rainbow trout (*Salmo trutta* and *Oncorhynchus mykiss*), muskellunge (*Esox masquinongy*), and catfish. Riverlink, Inc., a nonprofit community organization, has been spearheading efforts to promote the health and use of the river, including converting former industrial areas along the Asheville riverfront into parks, riverside shops, and other businesses.

COLBURN GEM AND MINERAL MUSEUM

[Fig. 21(21)] The Colburn Gem and Mineral Museum, located on historic Pack Square in downtown Asheville, is one of the four museums of the Pack Place Education, Arts and Science Center. The museum showcases a diverse collection of gems and minerals from around the state and from numerous parts of the world.

Exhibits begin in the first room with a brief history on the development of the Dana Classification System of minerals. Along the left wall, various colorful minerals are grouped in classes labeled Halides/Borates, Carbonates, and Oxides/Sulfates, and there is an exhibit of crystallography, including an intriguing phenomenon known as "phantom" crystals. Between these exhibits are insets of specimens of the major mineral groups.

Separate floor exhibits feature beautiful, large crystals of emerald in its natural matrix, a quartz-aragonite that somewhat resembles an undersea finger coral, calcite crystals with sand inclusions, and a magnificent aquamarine weighing 376 pounds, one of the museum's premier possessions.

Another display features minerals that emit scintillating fluorescent tints when exposed to ultraviolet light controlled by the viewer. Nearby is another viewer-operated switch that demonstrates a sandstone that literally flexes without breaking.

Toward the rear of the museum, a popular permanent exhibit spotlights the minerals for which North Carolina is most famous. Entitled "North Carolina—The Gem State," this exhibit includes native emeralds, rubies, sapphires, and gold. The economically valuable spodumene, mica, feldspar, granite, olivine, and phosphate are also on display. A brief history of the nation's first gold rush, which occurred following the mineral's discovery in North Carolina, rounds out the exhibit. This area of the museum also has featured special or traveling displays, such as the Foster Sondley Gem Collection and the rarely shown Harvard Gold Collection.

The final exhibit room includes displays of cut and polished precious and semi-precious gemstones plus intricately fashioned articles of jade and lapis lazuli and examples of decorative and ornamental stones and pigments, such as those used in monuments, buildings, and paints. The left wall includes ores and minerals accompanied by derivative products in a display entitled "Resources of Modern Civilization."

The Colburn Museum holds two other outstanding exhibits. The world's largest star sapphire, the "Star of the Carolinas," is on view here. Listed in the *Guinness Book of World Records*, this black polished stone has a finish weight of 1,445 carats. Also displayed is a collection of the extremely rare mineral hiddenite.

The museum sponsors various programs and events, including lectures, teacher training, school outreach programs, field trips, mineral identification, and an annual mineral sale. The Starlab Planetarium also is operated under the auspices of the museum.

Directions: From I-240, take Exit 5A/Merrimon Avenue. Follow signs for US Highway 25 South, and follow Pack Place for 3 blocks to Pack Square.

Mining and Gems in Western North Carolina

North Carolina's mountains have a mining history that dates back 5,000 years to a time when Native Americans discovered steatite, or soapstone, outcrops. Rich in the soft mineral talc, soapstone was easily carved into bowls and other useful containers. When clay pottery became popular 3,000 years later, soapstone mining ceased.

Native Americans also mined significant amounts of mica for use as ornaments and for the graves of individuals of high status. Mica found in burial mounds from the Midwest to Florida came from these prehistoric mines in the Black Mountains.

In 1544, the Spanish explorer Hernando De Soto searched the North Carolina mountains unsuccessfully for gold rumored to occur there. Not until 1799 was the mineral discovered for the first time in the United States, in North Carolina's Piedmont. America's first gold rush began here in 1803, and eventually more than 600 mines and prospects were scattered over the Piedmont and mountains. North Carolina remained the only gold-producing state until 1828, when gold was discovered in Georgia and America's first major gold rush began there. North Carolina remained one of the most productive gold-producing states in the United States until 1849, when the state's experienced miners headed west to exploit California's newly found reserves.

A number of other minerals have been mined here since the region was settled. Some copper mining occurred following the discovery of the mineral in Ashe County around 1850. And soon after the 1789 discovery of magnetite near the town of Cranberry, small water-powered forges began producing iron from local magnetite mines. By 1930, when competition from the Great Lakes region forced the local iron industry to shut down, Cranberry mines had produced 1.5 million tons of iron ore.

But the most important commercial mining materials were micas, feldspars, olivine, and crushed stone. Micas, due to their electrical insulating qualities and transparency, were once mined in great quantities for use in electrical components and as windows in stoves and lanterns. Currently, tiny mica flakes are used in paints and in cement that binds gypsum within sheetrock panels. One of the most commercially valuable materials to come from mines today is crushed stone, which is surface mined in open pits and used as gravel for rural roads, as a base for modern highways, and as the main component of concrete and asphalt.

A thriving tourism industry has evolved among many inactive mines in the region. From spring through fall, families and individuals enjoy visiting these mines with their mineral museums and retail gem shops. Most of the mines house water-fed flumes where visitors sieve buckets of mined soil in search of gemstones. Mines that sell materials salted with gems from other regions advertise their materials as "enriched." The other mines, that is, the ones that do not say "enriched," have native materials. At some flumes, experts are present to identify and mount such treasures for personal jewelry.

(*See* Appendix F, page 302, for a listing of area mines and museums.)

Facilities: Mineral exhibits, restrooms, water, gift shop. Also at Pack Place: Asheville Art Museum, The Health Adventure, YMI Cultural Center, Diana Wortham Theatre.

Dates: Open year-round.

Fees: A fee is charged for admission.

Closest town: Asheville.

For more information: Phone (704) 254-7162.

THOMAS WOLFE MEMORIAL AND VISITOR CENTER

[Fig. 21(22)] In his epic autobiographical classic, *Look Homeward, Angel*, American novelist Thomas Wolfe chronicled his boyhood in Asheville and immortalized his mother's "Dixieland" boarding house where he spent many of his childhood years. The sprawling Victorian structure, located downtown, has been preserved almost intact, providing visitors with a glimpse of the experiences that shaped the legendary author—and of the memories that he kept alive in his work.

Next to the memorial, a newly opened visitor center features an audiovisual program about Wolfe's life. In addition, an exhibit hall showcases the contents of the writer's New York apartment and items from his father's stone monument carving shop which also figured prominently in his writing. All in-print books by Thomas Wolfe are available at the visitor center.

Directions: Traveling west on I-240, take the Merrimon Exit, which runs directly to Market Street. Traveling east on I-240, take the Merrimon Exit and turn left at the stoplight. At next stoplight, take a left on Woodfin. Take a right at the next stoplight, which is Market Street.

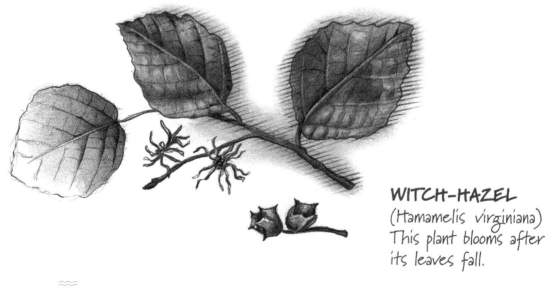

WITCH-HAZEL
(Hamamelis virginiana)
This plant blooms after its leaves fall.

Facilities: Historic home, visitor center, restrooms.

Dates: Open year-round.

Fees: A fee is charged for admission.

For more information: Thomas Wolfe Memorial, 52 N. Market St., PO Box 7143, Asheville, NC 28802. Phone (704) 253-8304.

CHEROKEE ARCHEOLOGICAL SITE AT WARREN WILSON COLLEGE

[Fig. 21(25)] Beneath the high peaks of the Great Craggy Mountains is a valley that has inspired community, creativity, learning, and a sense of harmony with the environment. Evidence exists of settlement in the Swannanoa Valley as early as the Middle Archaic period (5000–1500 B.C.) Today, Warren Wilson College students and others from across the country study the culture of those settlers by participating in the excavation of one of the most significant archeological sites in southern Appalachia.

Best known as the location of a prehistoric Cherokee village around A.D. 1350, the site has been operated as an archeological dig since 1965. In 1996, the Eastern Band of the Cherokee Indians accepted an invitation from Warren Wilson College to become partners in the project, making it the first excavation in North Carolina working in conjunction with the Cherokee people to define and teach cultural sensitivity to future archeologists.

Directions: Traveling east on I-40, take Exit 55. Drive underneath the interstate, and yield to the right at the US 70 intersection. Follow US 70 east for 2 miles. Turn left at the first traffic light onto Warren Wilson Road. After 2 miles, the campus is visible. Take a right at the south entrance and follow the road to a building labeled Laursen. Those interested in visiting the dig should check in at the college's Public Information Office, located in this building.

Dates: A field school is operated at the site for 4 weeks each summer (mid-June–mid-July).

Fees: There is a charge for attending the field school. There is no charge for visiting the dig.

For more information: Cherokee Archeology, Warren Wilson College, PO Box 9000, Asheville, NC 28815-9000. Phone (704) 298-3325, extension 421.

SHOWY ORCHIS
(Orchis spectabilis)
Bees and dragonflies thrust tongues
into the spur of this blossom for pollen.

Chimney Rock Park

[Fig. 25(4)] Chimney Rock—a private recreational facility owned and managed by the fourth generation of the family that originally developed the park—proudly bills itself as "the best of the mountains, in one place." In a region rich in natural treasures, that might seem to be pushing things a bit, yet Chimney Rock—with its unique geology, stunning long-range views, and abundant flora and fauna (including many rare species)—can legitimately make the claim.

The involvement of the Morse family fortunes with Chimney Rock can be traced back to 1900, when Lucius B. Morse, a physician from Chicago, paid $.25 to ride a mule to the top of the rock monolith looming over Hickory Nut Gorge. When he took in the 75-mile view from up above, it spawned a lifelong obsession.

Over the next several decades, Morse and his brothers (with the backing of investors) acquired thousands of acres of land, built neighboring Lake Lure, and gradually developed the park site, adding a road, a bridge, a three-story restaurant, and even the Cliff Dwellers Inn. The Great Depression seriously dented Morse's ambitious plans for a world-class resort in the gorge, but he hung onto his beloved rock, gradually adding facilities. One of the remarkable additions was the 258-foot elevator shaft bored and blasted through the rock from 1946 to 1948, which created almost instant access to the view from the top.

Predictably, the park's image has also changed with the times. Originally a 1920s-style rustic resort, it provided the backdrop for many early movies, including the *Blue Ridge Bandit* series. Ironically, wild animals were shipped to Chimney Rock for the filming. Through the lean Depression and postwar years, however, the park became a seasonal attraction operating on a shoe-string budget. The Chimney Rock Hill-Climb, a nationally known sports-car event, ran annually for 40 years until it was discontinued in 1995.

Today, the emphasis is firmly on ecotourism. A new Nature Center in the Meadows helps give visitors a better understanding of the park's uniqueness. Regular workshops, slide presentations,

CHESTNUT OAK (Quercus prinus)
This is also called rock oak because of its preference for a rocky habitat.

and guided walks highlight the park's many natural wonders. And a series of free brochures, available at the park entrance and the gift shop, helps visitors identify key features.

Naturally, the main attraction is the chimney itself, a 535-million-year-old pillar of igneous rock. At some point in the distant geologic past, a portion of the earth's molten interior congealed into a substantial mass of granite buried far below the surface. Over the ensuing quarter of a billion years, the intensive workings of temperature and pressure turned the granite into Henderson gneiss. As the earth's surface gradually eroded, the chimney and surrounding cliffs were exposed. Subsequent erosion has more clearly separated the chimney from the cliffs. Other notable view spots within the park include the crest of Hickory Nut Falls (2,450 feet) and Exclamation Point, the park's highest peak (2,480 feet), which offers a stunning window into the gorge below.

Chimney Rock has much to offer, including diverse flora and fauna, beautiful views, and dramatic geology such as the mass of granite pictured above.

The spectacular Hickory Nut Falls is a dancing ribbon of spume and spray plunging 404 feet against the sheer cliff face. Visitors may recognize the falls and some of the surrounding scenery from the 1991 film *The Last of the Mohicans.*

The park's 1,000 acres embrace a wide range of habitats, in large part because of the roughly 1,700-foot elevation range. The varied influences of water also play a part; the moist microclimate created on the high cliffs near the falls is one example.

That diversity enables a staggering variety of plant species to find homes at Chimney Rock. Round-leaf serviceberry (*Amelanchier sanguinea*), deerhair bulrush (*Scirpus cespitosus*, var. *callosus*), and choke cherry (*Prunus virginiana*) all inhabit the cool, wet cliffs. Biltmore sedge (*Carex biltmoreana*), until recently believed to be extinct in North Carolina, can be seen along the upper trails, as can Carey's saxifrage (*Saxifraga careyana*). A host of other rare plant species are found within the park boundaries (but not always near the trails), including bleeding heart (*Dicentra eximia*), spreading rockcress, white-leaf sunflower, sweet pinesap (*Monotropsis odorata*), fringetree (*Chionanthus virginicus*), two species of mock orange (*Philadelphus hirsutus* and *P. inodorus*), shooting star (*Dodecatheon meadia*), lesser rattlesnake orchid (*Goodyera repens*, var. *ophioides*), white irisette (*Sisyrinchium dichotomum*), pale honeysuckle (*Lonicera flava*), and divided-leaf ragwort (*Senecio millefolium*). A detailed free brochure lists hundreds of plants found in the park and tells when they bloom and where to look for them.

Chimney Rock is also home to a number of giant trees, including a tulip tree, a red oak (*Quercus rubra*), and a cucumbertree (*Magnolia acuminata*) believed to be more than three centuries old. Before Morse purchased the park lands, there were no roads on the mountain, and the trees' inaccessibility probably saved these arboreal behemoths from the loggers. Other tree species in the park include the chestnut oak (*Quercus prinus*), royal paulownia (*Paulownia tomentosa*), black locust (*Robinia pseudo-acacia*), sassafras (*Sassafras albidum*), basswood (*Tilia heterophylla*), black gum (*Nyssa sylvatica*), tupelo (*Nyssa aquatica*), and sweet buckeye (*Aesculus octandra*).

With its varied elevations and habitats, Chimney Rock offers outstanding bird-watching opportunities spring through fall, with more limited opportunities in the winter months. More than 100 species have been recorded in the park, and about a third of the species are known to breed there. Along the Rocky Broad River, yellow warblers (*Dendroica petechia*), yellow-throated warblers, and belted kingfishers may be seen. Higher up, the deciduous forests shelter scarlet tanagers and more than a dozen species of warblers and vireos, including the elusive cerulean warbler and Swainson's warbler (*Lymnothlypis swainsonii*), in the summer. Cerulean warblers are known to breed in the park, thanks to the discovery of a nest several years ago (only the second ever found in North Carolina).

Because of their unusually cool microclimate, Chimney Rock's sheer cliffs attract several bird species that usually breed only at much higher elevations. Birds here include the dark-eyed junco (*Junco hyemalis*) and common raven. A breeding pair of peregrine falcons (*Falco peregrinus*) first nested in the park in 1990, successfully raising three chicks in the cliffs beyond Devil's Head that summer. More common birds of prey include black vultures (*Coragyps atratus*) and turkey vultures (*Cathartes aura*), both residents in the park.

Spring and fall, when many species migrate through Hickory Nut Gorge, are the prime times for birding at Chimney Rock. Flocks of tanagers, vireos, and warblers move through on their way north in spring and return on their way south in the fall. Fall is especially notable for the spectacular hawk migrations, when hundreds of broad-winged hawks (*Buteo platypterus*) and smaller numbers of sharp-shinned hawks, Cooper's hawks (*Accipiter cooperii*), and red-shouldered hawks (*Buteo lineatus*) can be seen. On a single, memorable day in 1992, more than 3,000 broad-winged hawks were observed flying south. Another fall delight is the annual migration of monarch butterflies (*Danaus plexippus*).

Look for squirrels and chipmunks scampering among the trees along park trails. Due to the large number of park visitors, other local wildlife, such as groundhogs, white-tailed deer, and the nocturnal raccoons and gray foxes, are not so easy to spot.

Peregrine Falcons in Western North Carolina

Western North Carolina contains many diverse habitats that attract a wide range of bird species. The unique topography includes one feature particularly suitable for the magnificent peregrine falcon: isolated towering rocky ledges with widespread views ideal for the nesting sites required for these raptors. These ledges recently played a major role in one of the greatest success stories of the federal Endangered Species Act.

Falcons have shared a unique relationship with humans for nearly 4,000 years. The ancient Chinese and Persian civilizations perfected the art of hunting game birds with trained falcons. Later, falconry became popular with noblemen of medieval Europe.

The peregrine's sparse distribution and predator status contributed to its sudden decrease in population during the late 1950s and 1960s. The World War II development of organochlorides for use in DDT and other military pesticides was so successful in eliminating malarial mosquitos and other insect pests that the chemicals were later made available worldwide for agriculture and home use. The advantage of these compounds was that they remained potent for many years, reducing the need for reapplication.

This same characteristic led to environmental disaster for many animals, especially predatory bird species. Through a phenomenon called biomagnification, the insecticide accumulated in the tissues of animals as they progressed up through the food pyramid. The accumulation of poisons either killed outright peregrine falcons or, even worse, caused a calcium deficiency which resulted in clutches with thin eggshells. For the widely scattered peregrines, the impact was particularly great, and their population numbers dropped quickly.

It took a decade to solve the mystery of their demise and nearly another to ban DDT and its cousins and formulate a plan to bring the peregrine falcon back from its close brush with extinction. Using a two-part system of captive breeding and release through a method called hacking, a successful program began in the mid-1970s.

In North Carolina, hack boxes were placed in historic or likely nesting sites among the highest cliffs and ledges of the Blue Ridge Mountains. Young falcons were kept and fed in these boxes until they were able to fly. The boxes were then opened, but food was still provided until the birds were able to sufficiently hunt on their own, after which the boxes were permanently closed. The species made its recovery. By the early 1990s, more than 4,000 peregrine falcons had been released in the United States. As with wild populations, a much smaller percentage survived to reproduce on their own, but where only 60 nesting pairs were known to exist in the mid-1970s, 800 pairs were recorded in the nation by 1993. In North Carolina, captive-release programs were conducted at Grandfather Mountain, Hawksbill Mountain, Looking Glass Rock, Whiteside Mountain, and Chimney Rock. Today, these powerful birds are periodically sighted in these spots, as well as in the Shining Rock and Linville Gorge wilderness areas, the Graveyard Fields, Alum Bluff caves, and other suitable locations.

Several miles of nature trails enable visitors to immerse themselves in different park habitats. The Forest Stroll, an easy .75-mile walk along an old jeep trail, cuts through dense forest, highlighting interesting rock formations and notable plants en route to its terminus at the base of Hickory Nut Falls. The moderate-to-strenuous Skyline Trail hugs the cliffs up above, offering periodic breathtaking views on the way to the top of the falls. And, for other dedicated scramblers, the Cliff Trail provides an in-between route to the same destination, winding among the sheer, piled-up rocks. Between its flora and fauna, its unique geology, and its stunning views, Chimney Rock Park can keep the nature-loving visitor happily occupied for several hours or more.

Directions: From Asheville, take I-240 east to its terminus at US 74-A east. Continue on the beautiful (but twisty!) US 74 about 20 miles to the small town of Chimney Rock. The conspicuous park entrance is on the right.

Activities: Hiking.

Facilities: Hiking trails, nature center, picnic areas, gift shop, dining area.

Dates: Open daily year-round, except for Thanksgiving, Christmas, and New Year's Day.

Fees: A fee is charged for admission.

Closest town: Chimney Rock.

Elevation: 2,280 feet (chimney); 1,080 feet (ticket office).

For more information: Phone (800) 277-9611.

BOTTOMLESS POOLS

Set in the midst of a virgin forest within the beautiful Hickory Nut Gorge [Fig. 25(5)], the Bottomless Pools and waterfalls of Pool Creek have been a popular spot since they opened in 1916. The main attractions are the three separate pools each with its own waterfall and personality. Along the pathways to the pools, rhododendron, mountain laurel, and a variety of other evergreens form a thick understory over lush beds of wildflowers.

Unlike the watershed of the nearby Broad River, the 6-square-mile watershed of Pool Creek flowed slowly, which in turn carved the pools, or unusually large pot-holes, in the solid rock. As Pool Creek flows from its source higher in the mountains down to Lake Lure, it runs over many fractures, or joints, as geologists refer to them, in the underlying Henderson granite gneiss. Two sets of fractures are prominent in many places along the course of the stream. The flowing water can more easily erode along these fractures than on massive unjointed rock.

Not only is the weakness of the rock emphasized at the intersection of two fractures, but the course of the water is altered into a swirling motion. Pebbles and stones carried into the whirlpool intensify the erosion process, carving steep, circular walls as they cut deeper into the rock below.

Scientists do not agree on how long this process has been going on at the pools. Some say only 25,000 years while other contend 100,000 years. What they do agree on, after studying the surrounding rock and other factors, is that the pools are younger than a few hundred thousand years old.

Lake Lure, the 1,500-acre lake described by *National Geographic* as one of the most beautiful man-made lakes in the world, formed when a dam 115 feet high and more than 600 feet long was built across the Rocky Broad River. As deep as 100 feet in places, Lake Lure features a 27-mile shoreline with many small bays and inlets. Bass and trout fishing and all kinds of water sports are enjoyed in the lake and along its shores under the supervision of resident mallard ducks and great blue herons.

Nearby, the towns of Lake Lure and Chimney Rock offer a selection of bed and breakfast inns and restaurants that serve local trout, barbecue, and other dishes indigenous to the area. The town of Chimney Rock has been undergoing major changes, adapting to the changing interests of visitors, especially those attracted to the natural beauty of nearby Chimney Rock Park (*see* Chimney Rock Park, page 124). Lake Lure Inn, taking its name from the lake it overlooks, offers fine dining and accommodations.

Caution: Rocks in the creek bed are slippery, and visitors are encouraged to stay on the trails and to watch children closely.

Directions: From Lake Lure, travel 300 yards south on US 74 to the entrance on the right.

Activities: Hiking.

Facilities: Gazebo, covered bridge, restrooms, picnic area.

Dates: Mid-March–mid-Nov.

Fees: There is a charge for admission.

Closest town: Lake Lure.

For more information: Bottomless Pools, PO Box 5, Lake Lure, NC 28746. Phone (704) 625-8324.

BOBCAT (Lynx rufus) The bobcat is the most common wild feline in North America. A solitary animal, the bobcat's preys are usually rabbits and mice.

Balsam Mountains

The Great Balsams, located at the east edge of the Great Smoky Mountains, are one of several "backbone" ranges which form right angles to the northeast-southeast trend of the Appalachians.

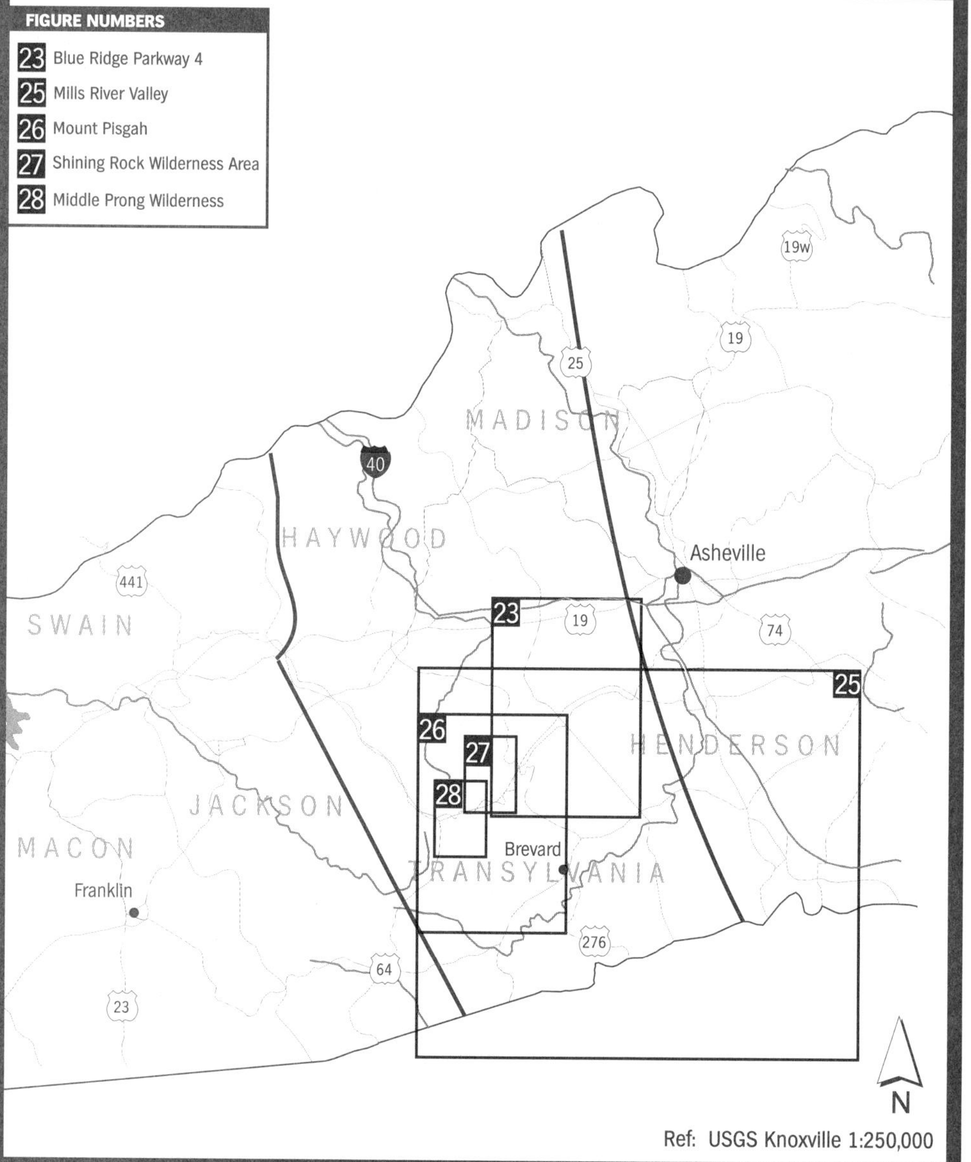

FIGURE NUMBERS
23 Blue Ridge Parkway 4
25 Mills River Valley
26 Mount Pisgah
27 Shining Rock Wilderness Area
28 Middle Prong Wilderness
19w
19
25
MADISON
40
HAYWOOD
Asheville
441
SWAIN
23
19
74
25
26
27
HENDERSON
28
JACKSON
MACON
Brevard
TRANSYLVANIA
Franklin
276
64
23
N
Ref: USGS Knoxville 1:250,000

The Balsam Mountains

Though the Balsam Mountains section [Fig. 22] is geographically smaller than others in this book, it is chock full of natural bounty. It is bordered by the Great Smoky Mountains National Park to the northwest and South Carolina just east of Tryon to the south. Two almost-parallel lines run southeasterly from the park to the border, one running south of Asheville and the other between the towns of Cherokee and Maggie Valley.

Confusion over names of mountains and mountain ranges is encountered in the Balsam Mountains section. Mount Pisgah, for example, is the highest peak on the Asheville horizon and is popularly identified as part of the Pisgah Mountains. Yet, others claim that there are no Pisgah Mountains and that the peak is part of the Pisgah Ridge or the Pisgah Ledge. Still others assert that Mount Pisgah is part of the Great Balsam Mountains.

[*Above:* Graveyard Fields near Brevard, North Carolina]

The chief cross ranges are the Pisgah Ledge (to choose one name) followed by the Great Balsam Range on the boundary of Haywood and Jackson counties. The Great Balsams, located at the east edge of the Great Smoky Mountains, are one of several "backbone" ranges that form right angles to the northeast/southwest trend of the Appalachians. Intersecting the Great Balsams are the Plott Balsams, named after a German family of settlers who came to the area in 1750. The Blue Ridge Parkway wends its way along the Great Balsams and bisects the Plott Balsams at milepost 458. Waterock Knob, at milepost 451.2 on the Blue Ridge Parkway south of the town of Maggie Valley, marks the joining point of the Plot Balsams and the Great Balsams.

The Balsam Mountains have at least seven forest types, in most part due to the variety of elevations found here, ranging from bogs found at lower elevations to spruce-fir on Balsam Knob topping out at 6,410 feet. A number of factors affect the development of these forests. The geology, for example, determines mineral content and thickness of the soil which in turn determines the species that can grow there. Topography affects what grows where: south-facing slopes, for instance, tend to be drier because the day-long presence of the sun evaporates soil moisture. On the other hand, north-facing slopes are more shaded and therefore more moist, but they take the brunt of sharp, cutting winds that impact the size and type of vegetation. Elevation and annual precipitation are also factors.

Oak-chestnut forests are perhaps the most common in Western North Carolina, hosting a number of oaks such as white (*Quercus alba*), scarlet (*Q. coccinea*), northern red (*Q. rubra*), black (*Q. velutina*), and chestnut (*Q. lyrata*). Other trees found in an oak-chestnut forest include hickories, red maple (*Acer rubrum*), white pine (*Pinus strobus*), black locust (*Robinia psyeudoacacia*), black walnut (*Juglans nigra*), Eastern hemlock (*Tsuga canadensis*), and American beech (*Fagus grandifolia*).

The cove hardwood forest develops in protected coves with damp soils, generally at low and middle elevations. The conditions here are ideal for an amazing diversity of trees—as many as 40 species in one forest. A sampling of the trees in the cove hardwood forest include yellow birch (*Betula lutea*), yellow buckeye (*Aesculus octandra*), sugar maple (*Acer saccharum*), yellow-poplar (*Liriodendron tulipifera*), and black cherry (*Prunus serotina*).

The floodplain forest, unique in Western North Carolina to the Asheville and French Broad River area, is related to the cove hardwood forest. It includes river birch (*Betula nigra*), box elder (*Acer negundo*), and American sycamore (*Platanus occidentalis*), among others, along the river banks.

One of the driest forests, the oak-pine forest, grows in thin and sandy soil that does not produce the lush vegetation usually so prevalent in the mountains. Blueberry bushes (*Vaccinium*), mountain laurel (*Kalmia latifolia*), and a limited number of hardy wildflowers are sufficiently drought resistant to grow here. Pines also grow well in dry conditions in part because their waxy needles conserve water. But they cannot tolerate shade. Once the canopy becomes dense, pines are replaced by the dominating oaks.

With its diverse trees and understory, the northern hardwoods forest resembles those forests found in New York and New England and features species common to the northern regions. Trees include yellow birch, yellow buckeye, and beech, among others. At Steestachee Bald, milepost 437.6, evidence of the yellow birch's ability to root in mossy boulders is evident. A variation on the northern hardwood forest, orchards, occurs when northern red oaks dominate areas where harsh weather stunts trees in ways that make them look like fruit orchards. An example of this is at Frying Pan Gap, milepost 409.6, just south of Pisgah Inn.

As discussed in the Black Mountains section, spruce-fir forests are only found at higher elevations and higher latitudes in places such as New England and Canada. As the name implies, the two main species are red spruce (*Picea rubens*) and Fraser fir (*Abies fraseri*) which dominate the summits.

Spruce appears at 4,500 feet elevation while the fir requires another 1,000 feet elevation before it can grow. In the Balsam Mountains, the highest overlook along the Parkway—Richland Balsam, milepost 431.4—and Devil's Courthouse Overlook, milepost 422.4, offer access to this forest type.

Finally, the tundralike bald is one of the most unusual environments in the mountains of North Carolina. Balds are defined as high-altitude, open areas devoid of trees occurring as either shrub-dominated areas or tundralike grasslands at or near the summits of the highest mountains at the edges of Canadian zone spruce-fir forests. Balds are enigmatic because no one seems to know how they were formed or why they persist. Although ecologists have offered many theories for the persistence of balds, no one theory has been universally accepted.

TULIPTREE OR YELLOW-POPLAR

(*Liriodendron tulipifera*)

Of eastern broadleaved trees, the tuliptree is one of the straightest and tallest and has one of the largest diameter tree trunks. Wind-borne seeds of the tulip poplar make their way into the openings in mountain forests to take over in areas denuded by heavy logging or disease.

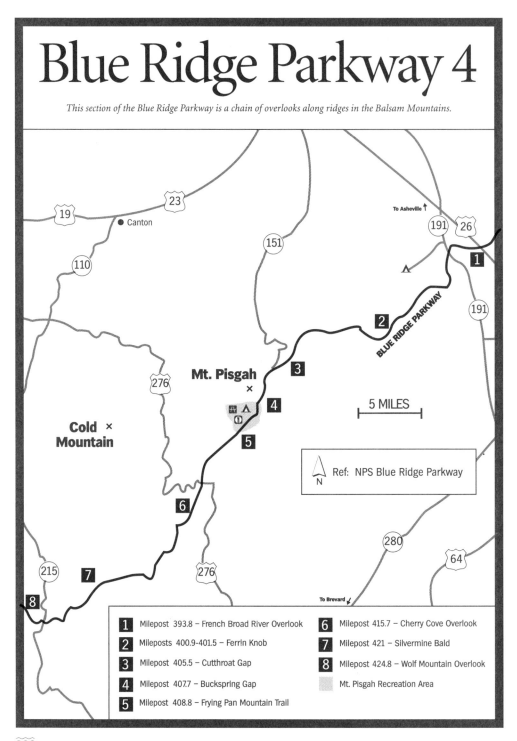

Blue Ridge Parkway 4

This section of the Blue Ridge Parkway is a chain of overlooks along ridges in the Balsam Mountains.

19
23
Canton
151
191
To Asheville
26
110
1
276
191
Mt. Pisgah
2
3
4
5
Cold Mountain
5 MILES
N Ref: NPS Blue Ridge Parkway
6
280
64
215
7
276
8
To Brevard

1	Milepost 393.8 – French Broad River Overlook		**6**	Milepost 415.7 – Cherry Cove Overlook
2	Mileposts 400.9-401.5 – Ferrin Knob		**7**	Milepost 421 – Silvermine Bald
3	Milepost 405.5 – Cutthroat Gap		**8**	Milepost 424.8 – Wolf Mountain Overlook
4	Milepost 407.7 – Buckspring Gap			Mt. Pisgah Recreation Area
5	Milepost 408.8 – Frying Pan Mountain Trail			

The Blue Ridge Parkway in the Balsam Mountains

Traveling from the French Broad River south to approximately milepost 440, this stretch of the Blue Ridge Parkway passes through 11 of the 25 tunnels in North Carolina and reaches its highest point at Richland Balsam Overlook, milepost 431.4, elevation 6,053 feet. Perhaps the most pronounced feature along this section of the Parkway is a long chain of overlooks stretching along the ridges like a beaded necklace and offering breathtaking vistas of many of the nearby parks and attractions such as the Mills River Valley, Mount Pisgah, Looking Glass Rock, and Devil's Courthouse.

The French Broad River Overlook at milepost 393.8 [Fig. 23(1)] features a beautiful vista of the wide, north-flowing river on the outskirts of Asheville. This is a popular spot for residents and visitors when fireworks light up the sky on the Fourth of July and other holidays. The historic Shut-In Trail begins near here, as well. Late in the nineteenth century this trail led from George Vanderbilt's Biltmore Estate to his Buck Springs hunting lodge near Mount Pisgah. Years after the trail fell into disrepair, volunteers reclaimed it along a 16-mile stretch of the Parkway from the French Broad River to milepost 407.6 at the Mount Pisgah trailhead.

The 25 tunnels in North Carolina (plus one in Virginia) represent a total of 2.25 miles of mountain carving carefully blasted with air drills and explosives and painstakingly dug out and carried away. At Ferrin Knob, mileposts 400.9 to 401.5 [Fig. 23(2)], it took three tunnels to do the job right.

Cutthroat Gap at milepost 405.5 [Fig. 23(3)] is named for the sharp, wintry winds that local folks swear blow in direct from the North Pole. This gap also is called Elk Pasture Gap referring to a small herd that once grazed nearby after George Vanderbilt imported them from Yellowstone National Park.

Vanderbilt chose a site atop the mountain at Buck Spring Gap, milepost 407.7 [Fig. 23(4)], for the lodge where he entertained dignitaries and artists, authors and scholars, and presumably escaped from the rigors of running his 250-room chateau below. Although he and his cohorts hunted and fished here, they actually left the land in better shape than they found it. Overhunting had taken its toll by the late nineteenth century, but Vanderbilt restocked the land with white-tailed deer (*Odocoileus virginia*), wild turkey (*Meleagris gallopavo*), and trout. Their descendants thrive here today.

Just past the Mount Pisgah Recreation Area, Frying Pan Mountain Trail, milepost 408.8 [Fig. 23(5)], ascends to a fire tower that offers dramatic vistas highlighted early and late in the day by the glow of a sunrise or sunset. The trail is a moderately strenuous hike at 3.8 miles round-trip. Like most mountain tales, stories about how the mountain and corresponding gap got their names vary. One cites the oddly shaped spring nearby, and another claims a frying pan was always left hanging at the camping area favored by local herders.

Humans aren't the only ones to flock here in late summer and early fall. Thousands of migrating monarch butterflies (*Danaus plexippus*) pass through on their 2,000-mile migration to central Mexico to overwinter. The Cherry Cove Overlook, milepost 415.7 [Fig. 23(6)], offers an excellent vantage point for viewing their flight during the month of September. Birds flock here, too. It seems conditions in the moist cove 1,000 feet below are ideal for growing black cherry trees as tall as 100 feet—as much as twice their average height. The trees' small white blossoms turn to dark reddish-black fruit in July and August, providing a feasting paradise for many species of birds.

Silvermine Bald, near milepost 421 [Fig. 23(7)], was once the site of a 60-foot-deep silver mine shaft worked at the turn of the century. This mine was typical of other mineral mines in the region—more lure than lode—and was eventually abandoned.

Fauna figures prominently in life along the Parkway, and several overlooks pay them tribute. According to U.S. Geological Survey maps, the 3 miles across the Balsams between mileposts 427.6 to 430.4 host at least 10 mountains, coves, and streams named after the bear. Bear Pen Gap, Bear Trap Gap, and Bear Trail Ridge are three popular examples. Wolf Mountain Overlook, milepost 424.8 [Fig. 23(8)], recalls days when wolves still roamed the mountains. During the Civil War when men were busy fighting among themselves, wolves thrived. Unfortunately, after the war, soldiers became hunters and farmers again and extirpated the wolves. (*See* Red Wolf Restoration, page 255.)

RUFOUS-SIDED TOWHEE
(Pipilo erythrophthalmus)
A loud "drink-your-tea" song coming from underbrush or thicket identifies the towhee.

The Pisgah National Forest

[Fig. 24] Anyone who has visited the lush forests of Western North Carolina would agree—it was a logical place to start securing public lands after the passage of the Weeks Act of 1911. The act was a Congressional response to the public outcry to restore forests endangered by wasteful logging and the ravages of fire and erosion. In 1912, when Congress authorized the first purchase east of the Mississippi, 8,100 acres on Curtis Creek (*see* Curtis Creek, page 93), Pisgah National Forest was born. Pisgah National Forest and Nantahala National Forest, the other national preserve in North Carolina's mountains, are two of the four national forests statewide.

Over the years, new lands were acquired but none more significant than the nearly 87,000 acres Edith Vanderbilt sold to the National Forest Service following the early death of her husband, George (*see* Biltmore Estate, page 112). Gifford Pinchot, Vanderbilt's former forest manager, then headed the agency (*see* Cradle of Forestry, page 150). Today, Pisgah National Forest, which takes its name from the mountain from which Moses saw the Promised Land, includes 495,979 acres divided in two by the city of Asheville and its more urban environs.

Four ranger districts serve the forest: Grandfather Ranger District with 186,735 acres in parts of McDowell, Burke, Caldwell, and Avery counties; Toecane Ranger District with 74,458 acres in four segments along the Tennessee/North Carolina border and the Blue Ridge Parkway; French Broad Ranger District with 78,683 acres in Madison and Haywood counties; and Pisgah Ranger District with 156,103 acres in Buncombe, Haywood, Henderson, and Transylvania counties. The Pisgah National Forest surrounds 100 miles of the Blue Ridge Parkway.

The quality of the natural beauty in the mountains of North Carolina is directly attributable to the substantial holdings of public lands—including those of the national forests, the Blue Ridge Parkway, and the state parks system. Mount Mitchell State Park, for example, with its namesake peak rising to the highest point east of the Mississippi (6,684 feet), is well known as a biological island, an isolated environment that the retreating glaciers of the Pleistocene epoch left behind. Certain subspecies of flora and fauna are found nowhere else, and 90 species of birds live in Pisgah National Forest. In addition, 39 of the 55 species of wild orchids found in North Carolina grow there.

Many of the sights and destinations within Pisgah National Forest are explored in detail in the Black Mountains, Newfound Mountains, and Balsam Mountains sections—not everything is included considering the forest encompasses more than 850 miles of trails, including 138 miles of the Appalachian Trail and numerous trails along the Mountains-to-Sea Trail as they course through the rich ecosystem of the forest. The forest also harbors three wilderness areas—Middle Prong (7,900 acres), Shining Rock (18,500 acres), and Linville Gorge (10,975 acres). Two new wilderness areas in the Grandfather Ranger District—Harper Creek and Lost Cove—are in the

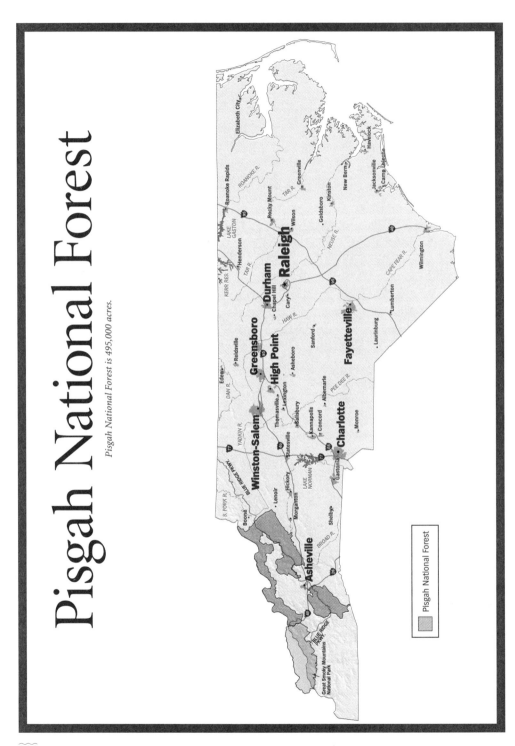

Pisgah National Forest

Pisgah National Forest is 495,000 acres.

Pisgah National Forest

proposal phase awaiting approval. All trails within the forest are open to hikers, and some paths are designated for horseback riding such as the steep, 17.5-mile Buncombe Horse Range Ridge Trail [Fig. 17(2)] on the slopes of the Black Mountains. In addition, nearly 100 miles of mountain biking trails wind through the forest. Whitewater is a popular activity, with the French Broad and Nolichucky rivers offering excellent opportunities through a number of experienced outfitters; for a calmer water experience, Wilson Creek and the South Toe River are favorites for swimming, tubing, and fishing. More unusual activities such as llama trekking and rock climbing are growing in popularity.

The Forest Heritage National Scenic Byway is a 79-mile loop that travels by forested slopes rich in forest history and outstanding scenery. Traversing Pisgah National Forest in Transylvania and Haywood counties via highways US 276, US 64, and NC 215, this byway offers many just-off-the-road scenic and educational attractions covered within this section such as the Cradle of Forestry [Fig. 26(2)], Looking Glass Rock [Fig. 26(11)], Sliding Rock [Fig. 26(6)], and Pisgah Center for Wildlife Education [Fig. 26(12)]. Much of the byway follows old settlement roads and logging railroads, and many camping and picnic areas off the road were once logging towns, sawmills, or mountain communities.

See Appendix D (page 301) for complete listing of National Forest Ranger Districts in Western North Carolina. A free brochure on the Forest Heritage National Scenic Byway is available through the Pisgah Ranger District.

The North Carolina Arboretum

[Fig. 25(3)] Just as the trails and bridges within its boundaries link surrounding mountains, forests, and waterways, the North Carolina Arboretum nurtures the interconnections between the designed and the natural world. The North Carolina General Assembly established the arboretum in 1986 as an interinstitutional facility of the University of North Carolina. Since then, it has developed as a regional center devoted to integrating education, landscape, and research.

Since the turn of the century, this area has played an important role in forest history and research. The 426-acre site of the North Carolina Arboretum was once part of the 125,000-acre Biltmore Estate [Fig. 21(24)]. More than 100 years ago, Frederick Law Olmsted, landscape architect for George Vanderbilt's Biltmore House, proposed an arboretum on the botanically rich property. Today, the arboretum sits within the Bent Creek Research and Demonstration Forest, a 6,300-acre tract established in 1925 as the first research area focused on the regeneration of southern Appalachian hardwoods. Ten state champion trees, which are the largest of their species in the state, grow there today. Trails within the Bent Creek Research Forest connect and lead up to the arboretum.

This rich heritage is shared through extensive programming and outreach activities that are projected to attract 1 million people annually over the next decade. A Visitor Education Center and Horticultural Support Facility provide space for traditional workshops and presentations for adults, children, students, and professionals. A network of hiking and biking trails accommodate people of all abilities while a core of formal gardens and wild natural areas allow for a broad range of interdisciplinary exercises that explore scientific, historical, and cultural issues. Diverse interpretive techniques such as the instructive plant identification markers in English and Braille, which also feature illustrations; audio tours of gardens; and hands-on, interactive family activities have been developed.

In the formal gardens, for example, school groups can learn about Western North Carolina's strong craft heritage through a specially tailored tour of the Quilt Garden planted with more than 2,000 annuals, perennials, bulbs, and grasses to create a different traditional Appalachian quilt pattern each year. The Spring Garden replicates the foundation walls of an abandoned mountain homestead built near a water source and surrounded by heirloom trees and flowers including periwinkle (*Vinca minor*), crabtree (*Malus angustifolia*), Kentucky coffee trees (*Gymnocladus dioica*), and several varieties of daylilies and roses that would have been planted by early settlers. A woodland mountain stream environment has been created in the third formal garden. Other gardens and trails serve as teaching tools for home gardeners and landscapers interested in cultivating native plants and trees. A low-maintenance garden that borders the road to the Horticultural Support Facility features more than 75,000 plugs of native grasses and wildflowers started in the arboretum's greenhouse. Over the years, the site will transform as the trees in the garden form a canopy cover and a forest ecosystem emerges.

Preservation and research and development activities are central to the arboretum's educational and operational efforts. As a member of the national Center for Plant Conservation, a network of 25 public gardens in the United States, the arboretum participates in conserving rare or endangered plant species. The National Native Azalea Repository, a gene pool collection of the 15 species native to North America, has been established at the arboretum. Also, a recently constructed cool chamber maintains a collection of endangered plants from the region's highest elevations.

Expansion of the arboretum's regional native plant collection is ongoing. Seeds and cuttings have been collected from North Carolina, Alabama, Florida, Georgia, and South Carolina. In addition to an on-site nursery, a field nursery developed in conjunction with Asheville's Warren Wilson College uses the bottomland near the Swannanoa River to cultivate nearly 300 specimen trees and shrubs grown without the use of chemicals or irrigation.

Directions: From I-26, take Exit 2 (marked Blue Ridge Parkway–Brevard Road–Highway 191). Go south onto 191. Go approximately 2 miles, past the Biltmore Square Mall, until the highway narrows from 4 lanes to 2. At the light across from a

Baptist church, take a right onto Bent Creek Ranch Road toward Lake Powhatan. Follow Department of Transportation signs to the arboretum (approximately 1.5 miles). Bear left at the fork where the road becomes Wesley Branch Road. At the arboretum, turn left for the Visitor Education Center and Core Gardens, right for the Horticultural Support Facility.

Activities: Hiking, mountain biking.

Facilities: Visitor Education Center, Horticultural Support Facility, hiking and biking trails.

Dates: Open year-round.

Fees: No fee for individual visitors; various group fees for special tours.

Closest town: Asheville, approximately 10 miles.

For more information: The North Carolina Arboretum, PO Box 6617, Asheville, NC 28816. Phone (704) 665-2492.

YELLOW BUCKEYE

(Aesculus octandra) Growing as tall as 90 feet, the yellow buckeye has 4- to 6-inch leaves and yellow flowers and produces seeds protected inside smooth capsules. Buckeye seeds resemble chestnuts, but they are round while chestnuts have a pointed tip.

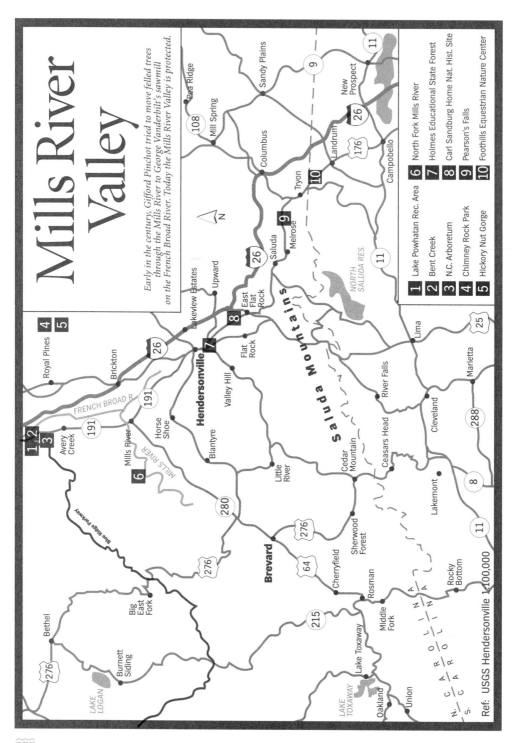

Mills River Valley

Early in the century, Gifford Pinchot tried to move felled trees through the Mills River to George Vanderbilt's sawmill on the French Broad River. Today the Mills River Valley is protected.

1	Lake Powhatan Rec. Area	6	North Fork Mills River
2	Bent Creek	7	Holmes Educational State Forest
3	N.C. Arboretum	8	Carl Sandburg Home Nat. Hist. Site
4	Chimney Rock Park	9	Pearson's Falls
5	Hickory Nut Gorge	10	Foothills Equestrian Nature Center

N

Ref: USGS Hendersonville 1:100,000

North Fork Mills River

[Fig. 25(6)] Early this century, Gifford Pinchot designed two splash dams along Big Creek, one of the major tributaries of the North Fork Mills River, as a means of moving felled timber down to the deeper Mills River. From the Mills River, the logs were floated via the French Broad River to an Asheville sawmill owned by George Vanderbilt. The splash dams held back moderate amounts of water which were then released to create a temporary surge to float the logs down the shallow Big Creek streambed.

The plan ultimately backfired, though, as the logs and flood waters eroded creekside vegetation and caused major silting downstream. When the logs reached the Mills River, heavy rains flooded the river sending the valuable timber out into adjacent farmlands. Irate farmers refused to allow the retrieval of the logs, and many sued Vanderbilt for property damage.

Fortunately, today this area within the valley shaped by Laurel Mountain on the south and Seinard Mountain to the east is protected and peaceful. The mountains drained by North Fork Mills River and its extensive tributary creeks offer numerous backcountry opportunities. Ranging from well-maintained hiking trails to gated forest roads, these trails provide access to hiking, mountain biking, trout fishing, and horseback riding. With the help of Pisgah National Forest maps, loops of varying length (at least 25 miles of hiking trails and 50 miles of mountain biking trails) can be created.

North Fork Mills River is a popular, medium-to-large fishing stream with easy access from the North Mills River campground. Two other creeks in the area, Big Creek and Fletcher Creek, are classified Wild Trout Waters. They are more remote, however, and require a 2-mile trek either on foot or on bike.

Directions: From Pisgah Forest north of Brevard, travel approximately 11 miles north on NC 280 to North Mills River Road. Turn left and continue for almost 5 miles to the campground.

Activities: Hiking, mountain biking, horseback riding, camping.

Facilities: 31 campsites with picnic table and grill. Flush and pit toilets and water spigots.

Dates: Open Apr.–Nov.

Fees: A fee is charged for campsites.

Closest town: Brevard, 20 miles.

For more information: Phone (704) 877-3265.

PERSISTENT TRILLIUM
(Trillium persistens)
A rare flower, it grows under or near rhododendrons.

Lake Powhatan Recreation Area/Bent Creek

[Fig. 25(1,2)] Thirteen man-made lakes and ponds provide added opportunities for water sports and recreation along the Blue Ridge Parkway, and Lake Powhatan, with its multifaceted recreation area, is one of the most popular.

Rather than a primitive wilderness experience, the Lake Powhatan Recreation Area offers easy access to a variety of outdoor activities such as fishing, hiking, swimming, and mountain biking. In addition, connector trails lead to the 6,300-acre Bent Creek Research and Demonstration Forest, The North Carolina Arboretum, and less heavily visited areas in the Pisgah National Forest.

Fishing is one of Lake Powhatan's primary draws. Anglers more interested in dropping a hook in the water than trekking through thickets to find remote mountain streams enjoy several casting spots on its shores as well as a handicapped-accessible fishing pier near the dam. Also, Bent Creek, a small-to-medium 5-mile stream, flows just north of the lake and into the French Broad River. Both the lake and creek are well stocked with rainbow (*Oncorhynchus mykiss*) and brown trout (*Salmo trutta*).

Lake Powhatan Recreation Area is a favorite destination for mountain bikers who make regular use of the single-track and forest-road trails. In addition, they find Lake Powhatan a good base camp for trips out into the more rugged trails and logging roads beyond nearby gated forest roads accessible to hikers and mountain bikers.

A system of loop trails in the recreation area provides hikers of all levels with an extensive range of options, with most trails rated easy to moderate. New routes emerge regularly as the Cradle of Forestry in America Interpretive Association continues to build additional trails. Maps are available at the Lake Powhatan gatehouse. Hikers can obtain more information at the Bent Creek Research and Development Center on NC 191 just outside the recreation area between Lake Powhatan and the Blue Ridge Parkway.

Along the southern edge of the recreation area, the Shut-In Trail is a longer hike that is also part of the Mountains-to-Sea Trail system. Open only to hikers, the trail was originally part of George Vanderbilt's estate, providing access from the Biltmore House through isolated and sometimes rough terrain to his hunting lodge near Mount Pisgah. Though the full hike, which passes through a black bear sanctuary, is 16.3 miles one-way, connecting spurs and access at Blue Ridge Parkway overlooks make it possible to hike smaller sections. For 20 years, black bear research in this section has been tracing the blood lines, heritage, population numbers, and health of the species.

Even visitors who never venture far beyond the rolling wooded hills of the campground and banks of Bent Creek can enjoy active spring and summer bird life. The creek is home to the great blue heron (*Ardea herodias*), green heron (*Butorides virescens*), wood duck (*Aix sponsa*), and spotted sandpiper (*Actitis macalaria*). In the surrounding woodland, the yellow-throated warbler (*Dendroica dominica*), white-eyed vireo (*Vireo griseus*), and Acadian flycatcher (*Empidonax virescens*), among many others, are often seen.

Directions: At Blue Ridge Parkway milepost 393.7, take the exit ramp to NC 191 and travel west. Go .3 mile to Bent Creek Ranch Road (NC 3480); a Forest Service sign will mark the turn. Turn left and continue .3 mile until the road forks. Go left onto Wesley Branch Road (SR 3484). The recreation area entrance is 2.3 miles ahead.

Activities: Hiking, mountain biking, fishing, swimming, picnicking.

Facilities: Picnic area, beach, 97 campsites that accommodate tents and motor homes, restroom/shower facilities with hot water and flush toilets.

Dates: Open Mar. 21–Oct. 31.

Fees: There is a charge for camping and recreation day-use parking.

Closest town: Asheville, approximately 10 miles.

For more information: Lake Powhatan Recreation Area, 375 Wesley Branch Road, Asheville, NC 28806. Phone (704) 667-0391.

ROSEBAY RHODODENDRON (Rhododendron maximum)

With evergreen leaves and clusters of white to pink flowers, this rhododendron grows on slopes.

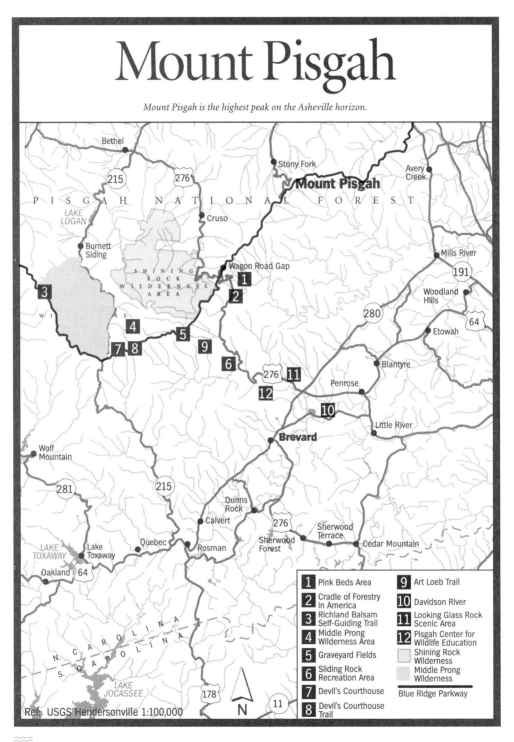

Mount Pisgah

Mount Pisgah is the highest peak on the Asheville horizon.

Mount Pisgah

[Fig. 26] In 1776, General Griffith Rutherford led an expedition into Western North Carolina against the Cherokee Indians. A Scots-Irish Presbyterian minister named Reverend James Hall accompanied the band, and, according to local folk history, Hall was awestruck by the view of the French Broad River Valley as seen from the area's highest peak. Reminded of the biblical Mount Pisgah from which Moses viewed the Promised Land after his 40-year odyssey through the desert wilderness, Hall gave the North Carolina mountain peak its present name. Pisgah was subsequently applied to the surrounding forest lands.

Perched below Mount Pisgah's 5,721-foot outline and overlooking the Pink Beds area, George Vanderbilt constructed a large hunting lodge, the Buck Spring Lodge, for his family and guests. To reach the lodge, he commissioned a trail to connect with the Biltmore Estate at the present-day site of Bent Creek Recreation Area [Fig. 25(2)]. The trail became known as the Shut-In Trail due to the dense rhododendron (*Rhododendron catawbiense* and *R. maximum*) foliage through which it passed. It remains today as a popular recreation trail that parallels the Blue Ridge Parkway for more than 16 miles (*see* Shut-In Trail, page 135).

From the Mount Pisgah parking area, the 1.6-mile Mount Pisgah Trail rises 712 feet through a northern red oak forest before giving way to a heath bald at the peak. It earns a moderate to strenuous rating because the last half of the climb grows particularly steep and rocky, but spectacular views of the Shining Rock Wilderness [Fig. 26] to the west-southwest and the French Broad River Valley to the north and east make the climb well worth the effort.

Also accessible from the southern end of the parking area, the Buck Spring Trail leads through a mixed forest of hemlock and oak past the site of the Buck Spring Lodge. Hikers can create a number of shorter hikes with the help of the map boards in both the Pisgah Inn and campground parking lots.

This area is rich with varying elevations and habitats enhanced by easy access to good viewing sites. The parking lot at the nearby Pisgah Inn, for example, serves as a good spot for watching the American woodcock (*Philohela minor*) perform its courtship displays at dusk even for those who cannot travel long treks. Other late-spring and summer birds include the downy woodpecker (*Dendrocopos pubsecens*), white-breasted nuthatch (*Sitta carolinensis*), ruby-throated hummingbird (*Archilochus colubris*), cedar waxwing (*Bombycilla cedrorum*), and several species of warblers. The campground across from the Pisgah Inn is also an ideal spot for observing birds accustomed to high elevations such as the brown creeper (*Certhia familiaris*), veery (*Hylocichla fuscenscens*), rose-breasted grosbeak (*Pheucticus ludovicianus*), and Canada warbler (*Wilsonia canadensis*). Visitors to the parking lot of the Pisgah picnic grounds report seeing scarlet tanager (*Piranga olivacea*), red crossbills (*Loxia curvirostra*), and common ravens (*Corvus corax*).

Directions: Blue Ridge Parkway mileposts 407.4–408.6.

Activities: Camping, picnicking, hiking.

Facilities: At milepost 408.6: The Pisgah Inn, restaurant, coffee shop, gas station, supply store, 70 tent and 70 RV camping sites, restrooms.

Dates: Trails: Open year-round, weather permitting. Facilities: May–Oct.

Fees: A fee is charged for camping and at the lodge.

Closest town: Asheville, 25 miles.

MOUNT PISGAH TRAIL

Trail distance and configuration: Blue Ridge Parkway milepost 407.4, 2.5 miles round-trip.

Elevation: 5,721 feet. Change of 712 feet from Mount Pisgah parking area to peak.

Degree of difficulty: Strenuous.

Surface: Natural forest floor to bare rock. Caution: Rocks are very slippery when wet!

BUCK SPRING TRAIL

Trail distance and configuration: Blue Ridge Parkway portion (milepost 407.4), 2.2 miles round-trip. Forest Service portion from Pisgah Inn parking lot to US 276, 6.2 miles one-way.

Elevation: 5,000 feet at parking lot.

Degree of difficulty: Blue Ridge Parkway and Forest Service portions: moderate.

Surface: Natural forest floor to bare rock.

For more information: Pisgah Ranger District Phone (704) 877-3265 and (704) 235-8228 (Mount Pisgah Inn).

Graveyard Fields

[Fig. 26(5)] Water is nature's driving force, a fact readily apparent in the mountains of Western North Carolina. The region's ample rainfall produces high humidity and fuels countless springs, streams, and rivers that in turn support the lush evergreen and deciduous forests. While water has promoted the evolution of forests, logging and fire have permanently altered them. Nowhere is this more evident than in a beautiful narrow valley known as the Graveyard Fields.

Prior to 1925, extensive logging of the American chestnut (*Tsuga canadensis*) and other prime hardwood timber occurred in the area leaving behind huge, moss-covered stumps. In 1925, a great fire swept through the area and eventually burned more than 25,000 acres of forest. The fire occurred at the start of the trout fishing season, and many of the 200-plus fishermen taking part in the season's opening day were caught in the valley. They survived by immersing themselves in the pools of the Yellowstone Prong, repeatedly surfacing into the searing heat for a brief gasp of air before plunging under again. Once the fires were out, the desolate valley and its dark stumps from a distance resembled a huge tombstone-studded graveyard, which gave the area its name.

The Graveyard Fields is easily one of the most popular hiking areas in Western North Carolina. A scenic stream, the Yellowstone Prong, enters the Graveyard Fields with one waterfall, the Upper Falls, then passes over another set, Second Falls, and exits through a third, Yellowstone Falls. These falls are quite spectacular and photogenic, especially considering the small size of their parent stream.

The Yellowstone Prong got its name from the color of lichens and minerals found on the rocks within and adjacent to the stream. Various colors and unusual erosion patterns can be seen, and these offer photogenic scenes, as well.

The high precipitation, shallow peaty soils, and historic disturbance in the area have produced an unusual mix of forest, shrub, and wetland vegetation. Trees include yellow birch (*Betula lutea*), serviceberry (*Amelanchier arborea*), mountain-ash (*Sorbus americana*), flowering dogwood (*Cornus florida*), various oaks, white pine, Fraser fir, and red spruce.

Pink and purple blooming mountain laurel and rhododendron thrive throughout the valley as do many wildflowers, such as bluets (*Houstonia caerulea*), galax (*Galax aphylla*), and a number of asters and honeysuckles. Other groundcover plants include the hay-scented fern (*Dennstaedtia punctilobula*), ground pine (*Lycopodium obscurum*), and running clubmoss (*Lycopodium clavatum*).

One delight in the Yellowstone Prong floodplain is the wild berry shrubs that have colonized the area. Hikers along the river enjoy summer and fall harvests of blackberries (*Rubus argutus*), gooseberries, and blueberries. These fruit-bearing shrubs also attract a variety of wildlife, including white-tailed deer, which munch on them from dusk till dawn.

Bird watchers report some unusual bird sightings here, including the belted kingfisher (*Megaceryle alcyon*), bald eagle (*Haliaeetus leucocephala*), peregrine falcon (*Falco peregrinus*), northern goshawk (*Accipiter gentilis*), and spotted sandpiper. Along the meadowlike areas in late spring and summer, northern bobwhite (*Colinus virginianus*), eastern bluebird (*Sialia sialis*), common yellowthroat (*Geothlypis trichas*), and indigo bunting are regulars.

The three waterfalls in the Graveyard Fields are easily accessible from the Blue Ridge Parkway. The main trail descends from a parking area by means of steps that give way to an asphalt path, necessary due to the popularity of the area. Many parts of the trail beyond the asphalt portion have been worn into deep ruts which are often muddy due to the frequency of precipitation. For those who wish to hike beyond the Yellowstone Prong Valley, the spur off the Graveyard Field Trail, the Graveyard Ridge Trail, leads to, among several places, Black Balsam Knob and Tennent Mountain where spectacular views, buckets full of blueberries, and grassy balds await.

Directions: Blue Ridge Parkway milepost 418.8.

Activities: Hiking, picnicking.
Facilities: Parking, trailhead signage.
Dates: Open year-round.
Fees: None.
Closest town: Brevard, 24 miles.

▨ GRAVEYARD FIELDS TRAIL

Trail configuration and mileage: 3.2-mile loop from parking area trailhead.
Elevation: 5,200 feet (at trailhead and Upper Falls) to 4,800 feet (at Yellowstone Falls).
Degree of difficulty: Moderate.
Surface and blaze: Asphalt, steps, changing to moist or muddy soil with occasional bridges or boardwalks; blue blaze.
For more information: Pisgah Ranger District Phone (704) 877-3265

The Cradle of Forestry in America

"Here was my chance. Biltmore could be made to prove what America did not yet understand, that trees could be cut and the forest preserved at one and the same time." —Gifford Pinchot

[Fig. 26(2)] Western North Carolina history and culture cannot be separated from its forests. These woodlands have shaped, and have been shaped by, the inhabitants of the area since prehistoric times, and their history is interwoven with fascinating stories.

Native Americans first made an impact upon the forests with their mica and soapstone mining activities and their use of forest fires set intentionally to flush game out to waiting hunters. Later, European settlers brought changes through mining, clearing, and agricultural practices. But these activities had little effect on the overall ecology of the region. The rugged mountainous terrain that discouraged settlement also protected the region, for a time, from large-scale commercial exploitation. The transportation of products derived from the area's natural resources to Piedmont and Coastal markets was just too difficult and uneconomical.

It wasn't until the late nineteenth century that man's activities, precipitated by two factors, profoundly changed these mountains and their inhabitants. First, a growing population and a corresponding increase in consumer demand for forest products was depleting the great forests of the northern Appalachians and the Midwest. Second, the railroad finally forged its way into the mountains of North Carolina.

Faced with a supply shortage, northern timber and paper pulp interests turned to the southern Appalachians, buying up thousands of acres of old-growth forests. For the first time, these mountains and their forests were viewed by outside interests as a commodity. The untapped forests were a valuable resource, and the timber companies had the technology to harvest this resource and transport it to the market.

A new, powerful "geared locomotive," designed for narrow-gauge railroad tracks, could easily pull seven cars loaded with logs up and down slopes and around tight, switchback curves. As many as 600 company logging towns were established throughout Western North Carolina and other mountain states, luring much of the local population away from their subsistence lifestyles. In a few short years, these people were transformed from self-sufficient farmers into employees who were wholly dependent upon large private corporations. The reward was better pay and steady work, while the distant urban public enjoyed a variety of quality forest products.

But these rewards came at a high price. By the late 1880s, uncontrolled logging began taking its toll on the area. Forests were cut but not replanted, resulting in topsoil erosion, washed-out gullies, and silting of streams. By 1920, the forest slopes of North Carolina were depleted of most of their quality lumber, and many of the large companies went out of business or moved to the virgin forests of the Pacific Northwest. The local mountain ecology and economy were devastated, and much of the population found itself suddenly unemployed and impoverished.

Even as the logging boom began gaining momentum, though, the solution to its disastrous effects was being developed in the mountains southeast of Asheville. In 1889, George Vanderbilt, the wealthy grandson of railway promoter and financier Cornelius Vanderbilt, began purchasing large tracts of land on which to build his 250-room French chateau, the Biltmore House. During his European travels, Vanderbilt had been impressed with the forests overseas. As in America, those forests once had been depleted by the logging practices of earlier generations, but since then they had been reclaimed through careful management.

Vanderbilt hired a young American named Gifford Pinchot, who had studied forestry in Europe, to develop a sound management plan for the Biltmore property which at the time totaled about 8,000 acres. On Pinchot's advice, Vanderbilt continued buying surrounding mountainous terrain until his estate eventually included 125,000 acres of woodlands known as the Pisgah Forest. The area drew its name from Mount Pisgah (also purchased by Vanderbilt), the highest peak for many miles around. Soon after beginning his work at the estate, however, Pinchot became more interested in formulating a national forestry policy and left Biltmore to enter the political arena.

On the recommendation of influential contacts, Vanderbilt hired a German forester, Dr. Carl Schenck, to replace Pinchot. Schenck began the seemingly insurmountable task of rejuvenating the devastated forests and soils and, in the process, laid the foundation for modern forestry in the United States. Simultaneously, Schenck created the first school of forestry in the nation. The Biltmore Forest School, as it was called, exposed its students not only to classroom lectures but also practical work experience in the wonderful outdoor laboratory of the Pisgah Forest. These students became indispensable in the great forestry experiments Schenck was conducting, and many went on to become prominent foresters in their own right.

Schenck's pioneer forestry methods were centered below Mount Pisgah in a lush area of cove forests and streams that form the headwaters of the Mills River. Known as the Pink Beds [Fig. 26(1)] (*see* Pink Beds, page 153), the area was once a sparsely populated mountain farm community.

An old community schoolhouse which Schenck converted into his forestry classroom still stands today along with the community church where he delivered Sunday sermons to the local inhabitants who worked on the Biltmore property. In addition to these structures, there is an old store, several cabins that housed the students, and a beautiful cabin constructed by Schenck. He named it the Black Forest Lodge after Germany's famous Black Forest where Schenck had once studied forestry. Several of these lodges were eventually constructed throughout Pisgah Forest to house wardens who guarded the Biltmore property against poachers, arsonists, and other intruders.

The Biltmore Forest School operated in Pisgah Forest for 11 years. In 1909, Schenck was dismissed by Vanderbilt, and the school might have ended. Schenck, however, expanded the school's role by holding classes in such locations as Germany, Switzerland, France, and in the forests of New York, Michigan, North Carolina, and the Pacific Northwest. Finally, in late 1913, Schenck closed the Biltmore School. There was not enough demand for practical forestry education to fund its continued operation.

But the story does not end there. Gifford Pinchot, Schenck's predecessor at the Biltmore Estate, went on to serve as chief of the U.S. Forest Service under President Theodore Roosevelt. Thanks to his efforts and those of other citizens and conservation organizations, in 1916 Congress established the first forest reserve in the eastern United States. Named Pisgah National Forest, the reserve received a big boost when, following George Vanderbilt's untimely death, his widow, Edith, made available for purchase 87,000 acres of the Vanderbilt property. Eventually, Congress purchased more than 250,000 acres of the Appalachian Mountains in Western North Carolina.

In 1968, Congress set aside 6,500 acres of Pisgah National Forest land, including the Pink Beds campus area, to commemorate Schenck's Biltmore Forest School. The Cradle of Forestry in America, as the area is now called, is a National Historic Site open to the public from spring through fall.

The history of forestry is interpreted at the Cradle of Forestry through films, interactive exhibits, and two short trails. The Biltmore Campus Trail winds its way among the historic buildings and grounds of the forestry school where periodically craft makers demonstrate weaving, natural dying, quilting, and toy making. On the Forest Festival Trail, visitors climb aboard the 1915 "Climas" narrow-gauge locomotive as they hear Preacher Rose, an eightysomething logging train historian and former lumberman, tell childhood stories of the logging days. At the Cantrell Creek Lodge near the parking area, woodcarvers and basket makers demonstrate their skills throughout the season.

Inside the visitor center, a new $900,000 exhibition gallery treats kids and adults to state-of-the-art displays and interactive stations on habitats, natural cycles, wilderness camping, and environmental issues. A carpeted tunnel burrows under a remarkably lifelike great white oak to reveal habitats of the red fox (*Vulpes fulva*), star-nosed mole (*Condylura cristata*), groundhog (*Marmota monax*), and eastern cottontail rabbit (*Sylvilagus floridanus*). A retired Huey helicopter simulates flying over an actual forest fire, and Discovery Theater features a wide selection of nature films.

The legacy of the efforts of Pinchot and Schenck, of course, far exceeds the boundaries of the Cradle of Forestry and even Western North Carolina. Their once-revolutionary methods of forest management and replanting have been adopted by the timber and pulpwood industries nationwide. As a result, depleted forests across the country have grown lush. Moreover, a young nation woke up to the fact that its rich resources required thoughtful stewardship to keep them bountiful.

Directions: At Blue Ridge Parkway milepost 412, turn south on US 276. Travel 4 miles to the Cradle of Forestry entrance on left.

Facilities: Interpretive exhibits, history film, guided tours, gift and book shop, cafe, restrooms.

Dates: Open daily, mid-April–mid-Nov.

Fees: A fee is charged for admission; group rates are available.

Closest town: Brevard, 14 miles.

For more information: Cradle of Forestry, 1002 Pisgah Highway, Pisgah Forest, NC 28768. Phone (704) 877-3130.

PINK BEDS AREA

[Fig. 26(2)] Adjacent to the Cradle of Forestry, the Pink Beds are a network of upland bogs supporting habitats more like those found on the Coastal Plain than the mountains. In the shadow of looming formations such as Looking Glass Rock and Mount Pisgah, the Pink Beds are remarkably level, making them a popular destination for hiking and mountain biking. A network of trails lacing through the area include the Pink Beds Loop Trail, South Mills River Trail, and a segment of the Mountains-to-Sea Trail (*see* MST, page 287).

Trails pass through lush stands of rhododendron and mountain laurel. One legend has it that their pink and white blooms give the area its name. Another legend, however, claims this was meadowland filled with all kinds of flowers and that Scots-Irish settlers typically used the word "pink" to describe flowers in general. Above this understory flourishes a mixed canopy of red maple, yellow-poplar, northern red oak, southern red oak (*Quercus falcata*), Eastern hemlock (*Tsuga canadensis*), and white pine. At South Fork Mills River's junction with its tributary, Bearwallow Brook, a grove of huge white pines dominates in a beautiful and peaceful setting.

Thick, shiny-leafed stands of dog-hobble (*Leucothoe axillaris*) droop over the streams as if protecting them from intruders. Nearby numerous mats of ground pine (*Lycopodium obtusum*) cover areas free of understory, and occasional rosettes of rattlesnake plantain (*Goodyera pubescens*) can be found as well. There are also a number of shortleaf pines (*Pinus echinata*) scattered throughout the area closest to the US 276 parking-area trailhead. These trees grow extremely straight and, because they drop their lower limbs under the shaded canopy, are easily harvested for telephone poles.

The Pink Beds Loop Trail was once a 5-mile walk. However, a newly constructed beaver (*Castor canadensis*) dam has flooded the northeastern end and reduced the hike to 3.2 miles. The Mountains-to-Sea Trail now forms the farthest end of the loop.

Directions: At Blue Ridge Parkway milepost 412, turn south on US 276. Travel approximately 3.5 miles to the Pink Beds parking area on the left.

Activities: Hiking, mountain biking, fishing, camping, picnicking.

Facilities: Wildlife viewing areas, picnic areas, primitive camp sites along FR 476, and backcountry camping permitted.

Dates: Open year-round, though mountain biking on some trails is restricted mid-Oct.–mid-Apr.

Closest town: Brevard, 13 miles.

PINK BEDS LOOP TRAIL

Trail distance and configuration: 3.2 miles along South Fork of Mills River.

Elevation: 3,280 feet at US 276 trailhead to 3,200, at Mountains-to-Sea Trail intersection.

Degree of difficulty: Easy.

Surface and blaze: Level stream floodplain, occasional muddy sections; orange blaze. When connecting with the Mountains-to-Sea Trail, white blaze.

BUTTERFLY WEED
(Asclepias tuberosa)
This plant is often found in home gardens because its bright orange, star-shaped flowers attract butterflies. The plant's roots have been used in India as a cure for pleurisy and for other pulmonary ailments.

Mountain Bogs

The mountain bog ecosystem ranks as one of Western North Carolina's most rare and endangered habitats. These precious wetlands contain soils and plants that are very different from the communities surrounding them. Because the soil is highly acidic, low in nutrients, and saturated with water, only plants adapted to these conditions can survive here. In spite of such restrictions, however, as many as 90 species of rare, threatened, or endangered plants find a home in these mountain bogs.

North Carolina's mountain bogs are broken down into two groups: those in the northern mountains and those in the southern range. The plants in the northern type contain species typically associated with the northern United States, such as the cranberry (*Vaccinium macrocarpon*). The southern bogs support plants commonly found among the southern coastal counties, such as sundew (*Drosera intermedia*). In keeping with nature's never-ending diversity, some bogs produce a mixture of each.

Water is the lifeblood of a bog ecosystem. Bogs, therefore, are found in depressions or among level areas within river and stream floodplains. Though the water level in a bog often varies with rainfall, it is groundwater, rather than precipitation, that influences these wetlands. Groundwater enters slowly from springs and underground seeps. Estimated to have once totaled 5,000 acres, North Carolina's mountain bogs have been drained or partially altered over the centuries. There are now only 500 acres of bogs remaining in the region.

Plants common to most bogs include cinnamon fern, horsetails (*Equisetum* spp.), ground pine (*Lycopodium obscurum*), and various species of sedges and small orchids. Showy or rare species include dragon's mouth (*Arethusa bulbosa*), grass pink (*Calopogon pulchellus*), and Gray's lily (*Lilium grayi*). Due to the lack of nutrients within the peaty soils, it is not unusual to find insectivorous plants in a bog setting. These plants augment their food supply with highly nutritious insects trapped on, or within, their structures. Sundew is a diminutive plant with tiny droplets of sticky nectar on its leaf surfaces. When attracted to the nectar, hapless insects become stuck and are then absorbed by the plant. The mountain sweet pitcher plant (*Sarracenia purpurea*) is another carnivorous variety that traps insects within its long, slender, tube-shaped leaves. This plant is so rare that it occurs in only a few sites in the world, many of which are within the mountains of North Carolina, South Carolina, and Georgia. Bogs also support an interesting mix of animals, including the rare bog turtle.

Fortunately, efforts are now under way to protect many of these valuable mountain wetlands and to restore some that have been partially altered. McClure's Bog, located in Henderson County and owned by The Nature Conservancy, is currently undergoing restoration. It is hoped that as more people become aware of mountain bogs and of their ecological importance, these protective efforts can increase.

Shining Rock Wilderness

Shining Rock Wilderness has five mountain peaks rising higher than 6,000 feet, with Grassy Cove Top being the highest at 6,040 feet.

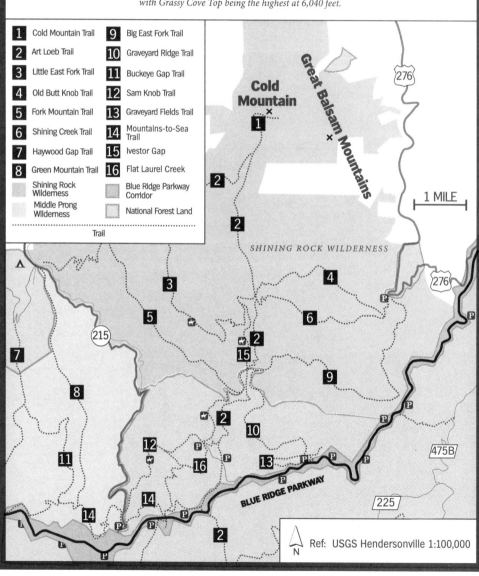

1 Cold Mountain Trail	**9** Big East Fork Trail
2 Art Loeb Trail	**10** Graveyard Ridge Trail
3 Little East Fork Trail	**11** Buckeye Gap Trail
4 Old Butt Knob Trail	**12** Sam Knob Trail
5 Fork Mountain Trail	**13** Graveyard Fields Trail
6 Shining Creek Trail	**14** Mountains-to-Sea Trail
7 Haywood Gap Trail	**15** Ivestor Gap
8 Green Mountain Trail	**16** Flat Laurel Creek

Shining Rock Wilderness

Middle Prong Wilderness

Blue Ridge Parkway Corridor

National Forest Land

Trail

Cold Mountain

Great Balsam Mountains

1 MILE

SHINING ROCK WILDERNESS

BLUE RIDGE PARKWAY

Ref: USGS Hendersonville 1:100,000

Shining Rock Wilderness Area

[Fig. 22(27), Fig. 27] Few words fire man's imagination more than the term "wilderness." Once defined as wild areas unexplored by humans, wilderness today generally refers to areas that have been left relatively undisturbed or those which have recovered from man's activities.

For the average person, though, wilderness has several meanings: It is a place to escape the pressures of civilization, to study a wondrous variety of plants and animals, to experience nature by "taking only photographs and leaving only footprints," or to physically challenge oneself with survival on nature's own occasionally harsh terms.

Acknowledging these contemporary views of wilderness, Congress in 1964 passed the Wilderness Act which elevated the concept of wilderness to a level of special significance. The act provided for the protection of areas according to Congress's own legal definition of wilderness. According the Wilderness Act of 1964, a wilderness area is defined as undeveloped federal land, at least 5,000 acres in size, which retains its primeval character and influence without permanent improvements or human habitation. With this act, the groundwork was laid for the establishment of one of the nation's first wilderness areas, Shining Rock Wilderness. This area was later joined by the adjacent Middle Prong Wilderness Area. The 18,500-acre Shining Rock and the 7,900-acre Middle Prong wilderness areas make up the northwestern corner of Pisgah National Forest.

The rugged terrain of the Shining Rock Wilderness includes five mountain peaks rising higher than 6,000 feet, with Cold Mountain at 6,030 feet as the highest. The 10-mile range known as Shining Rock Ledge offers spectacular vistas and diverse habitats, including what was once one of the most impressive stands of spruce-fir forest in the South. Around 1900, spruce trees towered above the forest floor, some as high as 100 feet with 4-foot diameters. But that all changed a little later in the century due to unrestricted logging.

In 1906, the Champion Fibre Company began buying huge tracts of land for a paper pulp and tannin processing operation at Canton. They established a company town named Sunburst as a base of operations at the junction of the Right Hand Prong and Middle Prong of the Pigeon River's West Fork.

The quality and quantity of pulpwood proved inadequate, and in 1911 the land was sold to Champion Lumber Company. The Sunburst community moved downstream to what is now Lake Logan, where a band sawmill was set up to process timber for the construction market. The original mill location is currently the site of the Sunburst Campground and Picnic Area.

The logging era of the area not only depleted the spruce but also many of the hardwoods, hemlocks, and Fraser firs. The forest ecology was further disrupted when, in 1925, a major forest fire covered the region. Eventually the area became associated with other southern Appalachian tracts collectively referred to as "the land that nobody wanted." Finally, in 1935, at the height of the Great Depression, the area was purchased by the federal government for inclusion in the Pisgah National Forest. But a final insult to the land came in 1942 when the worst series of fires in recent history swept Western North Carolina, permanently altering the Shining Rock and Middle Prong vegetation.

The forest fires at Shining Rock destroyed the former lush forest, creating open patches of shrub communities that have persisted for many decades. Many of its slopes support masses of blueberry bushes which attract black bears and hungry hikers alike. For many years, the low vegetation allowed white quartz outcrops to reflect colorful light from sunsets, but maturing trees have now hidden most of this "shining rock." Of the eight hiking trails traveling more than 35 miles through the wilderness, several trails lead to these outcrops on Shining Rock Ledge, the center-piece of the area, and vistas that make long hikes worthwhile. Part of the Art Loeb Trail [Fig. 27(2)] (*See* Art Loeb, page 168) also traverses Shining Rock Wilderness, and all trails within the wilderness either connect with or have access to the Art Loeb Trail. For those seeking solitude, the Little East Fork [Fig. 27(3)], Fork Mountain [Fig. 27(5)], Old Butt Knob [Fig. 27(4)], and Cold Mountain [Fig. 27(1)] trails are reported to be the least used within the wilderness.

The easier the access, the more popular the trails. Such is the case with the four trails leading off the Black Balsam parking area: Art Loeb [Fig. 27(2)], Ivestor Gap, Flat Laurel Creek, and Sam's Knob [Fig. 27(12)] trails. The Black Balsam parking area is located where FR 816 ends, approximately 1.2 miles from the Blue Ridge Parkway milepost 420.2.

Highlights of the trails within the wilderness include cascades and pools of the Pigeon River along the Little East Fork Trail [Fig. 27(3)]; a profusion of rhododendron and laurel along Fork Moun-tain Trail; and wildflowers and mighty basswood and locust trees on Fire Scald Ridge Trail. Big East Fork Trail offers numerous camping areas near the rapids and clear pools of

HIGHBUSH
BLUEBERRY
(Vaccinium
corymbosum)

the East Fork of the Pigeon River, where excellent fishing is reported. Shining Creek Trail [Fig. 27(6)] courses along the banks of Shining Creek where wildflowers thrive under the canopy of hickory, birch, rhododendron, and spruce. Equestrian use is limited to two trails: Ivestor Gap (to the wilderness boundary) and Little East Fort trails.

The establishment of a wilderness in the region is an excellent example of man's ability to correct past mistakes. Half a century of natural growth and forest management have helped to heal the southern Appalachian forests. In addition, the 1984 North Carolina Wilderness Act increased Shining Rock acreage from 13,600 to 18,500 acres and created the Middle Prong Wilderness, reflecting the increasing importance that the American public places on its special wilderness areas.

Directions: At Blue Ridge Parkway milepost 412, turn northwest on US 276. Travel approximately 1.25 miles to Big East Fork Parking Area. For a less strenuous access, exit the Blue Ridge Parkway at milepost 420.2 onto FR 816. Travel 1 mile to parking area. The Ivestor Gap Trail leads into the wilderness.

Activities: Hiking, camping, fishing, horseback riding.

Facilities: Parking, camping, picnic tables.

Dates: Open year-round.

Fees: None.

Closest town: Brevard, 20 miles.

For more information: District Ranger, USDA Forest Service, 1001 Pisgah Highway, Pisgah Forest, NC 28768. Phone (704) 877-3265.

YELLOW BIRCH
(Betula alleghaniensis) The unique bark of the birch is thin and shreddy. This bark is flammable even when wet, so it is useful for campsites.

Middle Prong Wilderness

The Middle Prong Wilderness, a 7,900-acre section of the Pisgah National Forest, became a federally designated wilderness area in 1984.

Ref: USGS Hendersonville 1:100,000

N

NATIONAL FOREST

97

WEST FORK PIGEON RIVER

215

SHINING ROCK WILDERNESS

× Big Beartrail Ridge

1 Sunburst Recreation Area

2 Fork Mountain Trail

3 Beartrail Ridge Gap

4 Haywood Gap Trail

5 Green Mountain Trail

6 Buckeye Gap Trail

7 Little Bearpen Gap

8 Rough Butt Bald

9 Haywood Gap

10 Sam Knob Trail

11 Mountains-to-Sea Trail

12 Buckeye Gap

Middle Prong Wilderness

Shining Rock Wilderness

Blue Ridge Parkway Corridor

National Forest Land

Trail

215

MIDDLE PRONG WILDERNESS

BLUE RIDGE PARKWAY

1 MILE

Middle Prong Wilderness Area

[Fig. 28] Experienced backcountry travelers who know Middle Prong Wilderness value the secluded tract for what it lacks: designated campsites, blazed and well-maintained trails, and established picnic spots. The one sought-after amenity it does offer—almost without fail—is solitude.

In 1984, this 7,900-acre section of the Pisgah National Forest became a federally designated wilderness area, falling under the 1964 Wilderness Act. The designation preserves Middle Prong Wilderness in its natural, primitive state as more of a safe-haven for native plants and animals than a recreation spot for throngs of day-hiking visitors.

Throngs, in fact, are not allowed. The isolated nature of this wild environment is maintained in part by limiting groups to 10 people. Those who do use the area should be experienced hikers with the strong orienteering skills necessary to navigate unmarked routes safely.

In this central portion of the Richland Balsam Mountains, two rugged north-south trails intersect with a section of the Mountains-to-Sea Trail [Fig. 28(11)] at the southern edge of the area. Connections with trails leading into Shining Rock Wilderness to the northeast, just across the West Fork of the Pigeon River, are also possible, providing opportunities for lengthy backpacking and camping expeditions.

The Sunburst Campground and Picnic Area [Fig. 28(1)], situated on NC 215 approximately 9 miles west of the Blue Ridge Parkway, provides camping (with water and toilets) and picnic areas and serves as a base camp for treks into the wilderness. To hike Haywood Gap Trail [Fig. 28(4)], for example, start at the south end of the campground and continue 1.6 miles on FR 97; the route climbs two switchbacks and, after the third one, turns left off FR 97 onto a primitive path that crosses Little Beartrap Branch and soon enters the wilderness boundary. From here Haywood Gap Trail continues another 3.4 miles to the intersection with Buckeye Gap Trail [Fig. 28(12)]. Both trails connect with the Mountains-to-Sea Trail and travel through rhododendron groves and forests of birch, cherry, maple, beech, and the occasional spruce and fir. Adjacent to Shining Rock Wilderness Area, Middle Prong contains the highest peak within these two wilderness areas and the highest in the Pisgah Ranger District: Balsam Knob, which rises to 6,410 feet.

Within this federal preserve, the state of North Carolina has designated 800 acres as the Mount Hardy–Fork Ridge Natural Area, recognizing its biological diversity. Remnant spruce-fir forests can be found at Mount Hardy's 6,110-foot peak (technically just outside the southern border of the wilderness). Other ridgetops feature grass and heath balds. Mixed southern Appalachian hardwood forests, various shrub populations, and high-elevation seeps and bogs support rare plant life including pink azalea (*Rhododendron nudiflorum*). Blueberries grow in the meadows of Fork Ridge's eastern escarpment, and wretched sedge takes root in rock crevices.

Since much of the area was logged in the early 1900s, the forests that exist in Middle Prong Wilderness today are primarily second growth. Sunburst, to the north, was a lumber town for Champion Fibre Company whose 10 camps harvested hemlock, poplar, and American chestnut. Parts of the old railroad and skid grades and logging equipment remain strewn throughout the area. The leftover symbols of human encroachment into this now wild landscape are protected by the Antiquities Act, which bans their removal.

Middle Prong Wilderness serves as a sanctuary for black bears. Bobcats also exist in the area along with more common white-tailed deer, opossums (*Didelphis marsuialis*), and raccoons (*Procyon lotor*). Though this wilderness has not been studied extensively by ornithologists, it is considered prime bird-watching territory. Yellow-bellied sapsucker (*Sphyrapicus varius*), black-capped chickadee (*Parus atricapillus*), brown creeper, and wild turkey are seen regularly.

Nine miles of trout streams flow through the wilderness. The West Fork of the Pigeon River is a medium-to-large, hatchery-supported stream with steeply sloping banks of craggy rock. Middle Prong, a smaller, clear Wild Trout Water stream, runs swiftly through the center of the area, keeping the waters cool enough to support the native brook trout.

Though Middle Prong Wilderness is much less heavily used than adjacent Shining Rock Wilderness, protecting the solitude and natural state that the Wilderness Act intended requires that visitors, no matter how few in number, make efforts to minimize their impact. No open fires are allowed, though camp stoves may be packed in. Recreational vehicles are also prohibited. Visitors typically do not bring electronic devices into the wilderness and strictly follow Leave No Trace camping techniques.

Directions: The Blue Ridge Parkway provides trail access, with trailheads at Buckeye Gap (milepost 425.5) and Haywood Gap (milepost 426.7). The nearby Sunburst Campground also provides trailheads. To reach the campground, exit Blue Ridge Parkway milepost 423.3 onto NC 215. The campground is 8.6 miles to the north, with the entrance on the left.

Activities: Hiking and fishing.

Facilities: 14 miles of hiking trails.

Closest town: Waynesville, 30 miles.

Elevation: Ranges from 3,200 feet to 6,410 feet.

For more information: District Ranger, USDA Forest Service, 1001 Pisgah Highway, Pisgah Forest, NC 28768. Phone (704) 877-3265.

DWARF GINSENG
(Panax trifolius)
Believed by some to be an aphrodisiac, ginseng has been overcollected.

SLIDING ROCK

[Fig. 26(6)] Whether they were weaving river cane baskets or hand-crafting wooden dulcimers, Western North Carolina's early settlers drew on the resources of the mountains for every aspect of their lives. Each summer, adventurous kids and kids at heart still rely on natural resources for old-fashioned fun at Sliding Rock.

A cascade of 11,000 gallons of water a minute fuels this 60-foot rock water slide, emptying sliders into a 6-foot-deep pool in Looking Glass Creek. The 50-degree to 60-degree water temperature makes this cool mountain attraction one of the Pisgah National Forest's most popular spots at the height of summer.

Sturdy sliding gear (cutoff jeans are recommended) wears better than bathing suit material during the shoot down the slick yet somewhat rough surface. Those who want to completely avoid minor bumps and bruises can share in the exhilaration—and perhaps capture it on film—from the viewing platform at the base of the slide.

Many generations have enjoyed the innocent fun of shooting down Sliding Rock near Brevard.

Directions: At Blue Ridge Parkway milepost 412, turn south on US 276. Travel for approximately 6 miles to the Sliding Rock Recreation Area.

Activities: Swimming.

Facilities: Observation area and bathhouse.

Dates: Accessible year-round. Lifeguard on duty and facilities open Memorial Day–Labor Day, daily.

Fees: There is a charge per vehicle or per person for large vans or buses; season passes available from the Pisgah Ranger Station.

Closest town: Brevard, approximately 10 miles.

For more information: Pisgah Ranger Station, 1001 Pisgah Highway, Pisgah Forest, NC 28768. Phone (704) 877-3265.

LOOKING GLASS ROCK SCENIC AREA

[Fig. 26(11)] Its glistening surface, whether reflecting the winter sun off a coating of ice or bouncing rays of light from its spring rain-drenched sides, makes Looking Glass Rock one of Pisgah National Forest's most striking landmarks. The towering structure is sought out by rock climbers, hikers, photographers, and sightseers alike.

This 3,969-foot granite dome is part of a larger mass called Whiteside Granite, a body of igneous rock formed 390 million years ago from crystallized magma nearly

14 miles below the earth's surface. Looking Glass, visible only in the last few million years, was carved into place as weather and water eroded the softer gneiss around it. An exfoliation process, which broke and stripped the surface of the dome according to concentric faults, caused the rounded shape.

A strenuous, 6.2-mile (round-trip) trail climbs through mixed hardwood forests and mountain laurel to the outcrop's crest, providing hikers with lofty views of the surrounding forest and the Davidson River Valley. In recent years, peregrine falcons have nested on Looking Glass following a reintroduction program. They may be spotted between mid-March and mid-September, with their greatest activity in March and April. Peregrine falcons nest underneath overhangs just above the tree line.

Several of Transylvania County's scores of waterfalls, caused by the area's erosion-resistant rock and its wide variations in elevation, tumble and crash nearby. Looking Glass Falls is, perhaps, the most visited with its easy access from US 276; Moore's Cove Falls and Sliding Rock are also along Looking Glass Creek. All are highly rated and thoroughly explored in Kevin Adams's book, *North Carolina Waterfalls*.

Directions: Looking Glass Rock can be viewed from Blue Ridge Parkway milepost 417.1. To reach the trailhead, exit Blue Ridge Parkway at milepost 412. Travel south on US 276 until its intersection with FR 475. Take 475 .4 mile to the parking area on the right.

Activities: Hiking, rock climbing.

Closest town: Brevard, approximately 10 miles.

DEVIL'S COURTHOUSE/DEVIL'S COURTHOUSE TRAIL

[Fig. 26(7,8)] Over the centuries in the southern Appalachians, rugged rock faces, forbidding overhangs, and serpentine pathways nearly enclosed by boulders have given rise to dark legends of evil spirits. Cherokee folklore names a rough outcropping in the Balsam Range as the inner sanctum of the Devil himself.

The bare summit that rises from the source of the French Broad River, according to the Cherokee, contains a cave in its bowels where the evil Judaculla held court, passing judgment on those lacking courage or virtue. (*See* Judaculla Rock, page 202.)

As if to substantiate the myth, a steep and taxing hike to the massive rock's storied peak passes through the skeletons of a Fraser fir forest where the trees have been all but destroyed by the balsam woolly aphid. The aphid was accidentally introduced to this area in the 1950s and has wreaked havoc on fir trees ever since. Once infested, most firs die, leaving behind only bare, gray snags as a grim reminder of the aphid's presence. Some scientists are encouraged, however, that the firs will be able to stage a comeback, as each new generation grows increasingly resistant to the menace.

The 360-degree view from the top presents very little sign of civilization, and the scene is majestic. Besides North Carolina, three states are visible—South Carolina to the south, Georgia to the southwest, and Tennessee to the west. Hawks, ravens, vultures, and occasionally eagles and peregrine falcons ride the hot air currents that rise from the valley. Rock climbing is also popular here.

Research into the size, weight, and numbers of the northern flying squirrel is regularly conducted in the higher elevations surrounding Devil's Courthouse. The endangered species, which averages 10 inches in length and 5 ounces in weight, lives on seeds, lichens, and mushrooms. Active mostly at night, the northern flying squirrel is rarely seen gliding through the air, using folds of skin running from its front to back legs much like a parachute with its tail as rudder.

Directions: Blue Ridge Parkway milepost 422.4; park in the lot to the west of the Devil's Courthouse peak, which can be seen clearly. The trail begins by running north along the Blue Ridge Parkway and then ascends into the woods.

Closest town: Pisgah Forest/Brevard, approximately 15 miles.

Trail configuration and distance: Approximately 1.7 miles round-trip.

Elevation: 5,720 feet.

Degree of difficulty: Strenuous.

Surface and blaze: First portion of the trail paved, wooded portion rock and forest floor; no blaze.

Davidson River Area

[Fig. 26(10)] There is at least one spot in Western North Carolina where visitors are as likely to float along the edge of a Forest Heritage National Scenic Byway on an inner tube as they are to drive the route in a car. Cutting through a picturesque section of the Pisgah National Forest just north of Brevard, the Davidson River is the focal point for an active recreation area and one of the district's most popular campgrounds.

East of the Pisgah Center for Wildlife Education, a host of tributaries—Laurel, Shuck, Daniel Ridge, Cove, and Caney Bottom—flow together to create the Davidson River. For the next 10 miles west, anglers show up in all seasons, fishing this mountain stream for hatchery-reared and native brook trout (*Salvelinus fontinalis*). No size limits or bait restrictions exist for hatchery-stocked areas, but fishing in the natural trout water nearer the Davidson River Campground is all catch and release. A detailed river map outlining changing restrictions is available at the Pisgah Ranger Station across from the campground.

Though the river's consistent, shallow depth doesn't attract paddlers, it is considered a prime tube-floating river throughout the summer. In addition to the allure of the easy-flowing current, regulars are drawn by the cool water and wooded banks that provide an ideal spot for rest or play even on summer's hottest days.

A Davidson River Trail Guide, also available at the Ranger Station, lists nine area hikes that range from short interpretive loops to full-day hikes and overnight backpacking trips, all with starting points near the campground. The North Slope Trail, one of the most accessible, is an easy day hike that runs from the bottomland environment of sycamore and poplar up to the drier forests of primarily chestnut oak (*Quercus lyrata*) on top of North Slope Ridge.

Campers don't have to venture far beyond the river's plateau to observe a variety of birds in spring and summer. Mourning doves (*Zenaidura macroura*), blue-gray gnatcatchers (*Polioptila caerulea*), American redstarts (*Setophaga ruticilla*), and ruby-throated hummingbirds, among many others, are common near the campground. Other birds less commonly spotted include hooded warblers (*Wilsonia citrina*) and yellow-breasted chats (*Icteria virens*). Peregrine falcons, which were successfully reintroduced to the area several years ago, nest at nearby Looking Glass Rock and can sometimes be seen flying overhead. An Eastern screech-owl (*Otus asio*) or great horned owl (*Bubo virginianus*) may be heard after nightfall.

From Memorial Day through Labor Day and on weekends into the fall, the nonprofit Cradle of Forestry in America Interpretive Association offers a diverse array of programming at the Davidson River Campground. Focusing on local culture and the area's natural history, activities include guided hikes, stream investigation, and Friday and Saturday evening events such as square dancing and live bluegrass music. Guest speakers on animal rehabilitation and special children's programs are also presented.

Directions: Exit the Blue Ridge Parkway at milepost 412. Travel south on US 276 approximately 14 miles. The campground will be on the right, across from the Pisgah Ranger Station. Or from Brevard, travel east on US 64/US 276 approximately 3 miles to the stoplight in Pisgah Forest; turn left and travel north 1.2 miles on US 276. The campground will be on the left.

Activities: Fishing, tubing, hiking.

Facilities: 161 campsites which can accommodate tents and RVs, bathhouses with warm-water showers and flush toilets, dump station, no electrical hookups.

Dates: Open year-round.

Fees: A fee is charged for camping.

Closest town: Brevard, 4 miles.

For more information: Pisgah Ranger Station, 1001 Pisgah Highway, Pisgah Forest, NC 28768. Phone (704) 877-3265. Davidson River Campground, phone (704) 862-5960; Camping/Recreation Center Reservations, phone (800) 280-2267.

PISGAH CENTER FOR WILDLIFE EDUCATION

[Fig. 26(12)] Pisgah Center for Wildlife Education is a new and modern facility operated by the North Carolina Wildlife Resources Commission with a mission to teach how human activities affect and are affected by wildlife and the natural environment. The center is due to be finished in the summer of 1998, offering to the public the 17-acre educational and interpretive center featuring exhibits, programs, and hiking trails. It also serves as a gateway to the Wildlife Commission's adjacent Pisgah Trout Hatchery, explaining the hatchery's operation and function as well as the North Carolina Wildlife Commission's larger role in managing the state's wildlife and inland fish populations.

The center is located at the base of an impressive geologic feature known as John Rock. This dome-shaped outcrop is part of the larger rock mass, Whiteside Granite— a 390-million-year-old igneous rock mass that cooled and crystallized from molten rock deep within the earth's crust. Several mountain-building episodes, followed by weathering and erosion, exposed John Rock and nearby Looking Glass Rock (*see* Looking Glass Rock, page 163). John Rock is the centerpiece of the John Rock Scenic Area, a 435-acre area surrounding the center. To reach John Rock, hike the Cat Gap Loop Trail, accessed from the east end of the center's parking lot, for 1 mile until the junction with John Rock Trail. The yellow-blazed John Rock Trail climbs steeply through hardwoods, laurel, and shrubs en route to its namesake. Views of the fish hatchery, the Davidson River valley, and the other monolith in the area, Looking Glass Rock, are spectacular. A word of caution: water seeps from the mosses, making the rock's surface slippery. Staff members at the center suggest backtracking the trail to the parking lot, at least for first-time hikers, for a hike of approximately 5 miles round-trip.

The theme of this state-of-the-art facility centers around "Mountain Streams, Where Water and Life Begin," emphasizing the importance of clean water to the environment, wildlife, and people. The flow of water is tracked from its beginnings as rainfall and snow on mountains, down through the streams and rivers of the Piedmont and Coastal Plain to the Atlantic Ocean, and eventually to its reconversion into rain. Stations feature interactive displays, demonstrations, and hands-on activities on the state's ecosystems designed in a manner that allows visitors from across the country to relate the concepts to their own ecosystems.

The Pisgah Center for Wildlife Education also serves as an outdoor classroom and meeting place for environmental education workshops for the Wildlife Commission. Outdoor exhibits focus on wildlife management and protection, fish culture, and conservation education. Permanent and changing displays present general scientific concepts illustrated through specific examples relating to the Blue Ridge Mountains as implemented by the Wildlife Commission.

At the heart of the wildlife center, the outdoor interpretive exhibit on a .5-mile loop walkway incorporates a mountain stream, native plant and animal life, and the trout-rearing raceways. The raceway exhibit is one of three cold-water facilities in the state devoted to raising trout. (Other state hatcheries produce warm-water species including largemouth bass, striped bass, sunfish, and catfish.) Hatchery stockings enhance the angling experience by providing more trout than would be produced by natural reproduction.

During the spawning season at the hatchery, ripe eggs are hand-stripped from female trout and milt (sperm-containing fluid) is stripped from the males. Once the eggs are gently mixed with the milt and fertilized, they are placed in stacks of shallow incubation trays where they receive a constant flow of cool, clean water. The eggs begin to hatch about 30 days after fertilization. A newly hatched fish is called a sac fry because, even though the fish has emerged from the egg, it still feeds from the attached yolk sac. The young fish are kept inside the hatchery for four to five months until they become fingerlings, 2 to 3 inches in length. Fingerlings are then moved to outside raceways, elongated concrete fish-rearing ponds with a constant flow of fresh water, where they are kept for up to one and a half years. When the fish are old and large enough, they are removed for stocking in public trout waters.

More than 400,000 trout weighing more than 180,000 pounds are stocked from the Pisgah Forest Fish Hatchery each year. Hatchery-supported waters are stocked with a ratio of 40 percent rainbow, 40 percent brook, and 20 percent brown trout.

Directions: Exit the Blue Ridge Parkway at milepost 412. Travel south on US 276 approximately 10 miles. Turn right onto FR 475; the center is 1 mile on the left. Or from Brevard, travel east on US 64/US 276 approximately 3 miles to the stoplight in Pisgah Forest. Turn left, and travel 5 miles on US 276 to the junction with FR 475. Turn left; the center is 1 mile on the left.

Facilities: Exhibits, trails, raceways, auditorium, gift shop, restrooms.

Dates: Mar.–Nov.

Fees: None.

Closest town: Brevard, 9 miles.

For more information: PO Box 1600, Pisgah Forest, NC 28768. Phone (704) 877-4423.

ART LOEB TRAIL

[Fig. 26(9), Fig. 27(2)] Blustery bald mountaintops, gaps filled with sun-scorched grasses, river lowlands of bee-balm (*Monarda didyma*) and cone flower (*Rudbeckia hirta*), and open groves of sourwood (*Oxydendrum arboreum*), hickory, and maple. Those passionate about the Art Loeb Trail value it for its diversity—a captivating mix of breathtaking vistas and peaceful valleys, of challenge and tranquillity.

Designated a National Recreation Trail in 1979, this 30-mile trek through the Pisgah National Forest was named for Arthur J. Loeb, an active hiker and former leader of the 65-year-old Carolina Mountain Club. The Art Loeb Trail's four contrasting sections, determined by the Forest Service, begin at the Davidson River Campground and run northward. The trail connects with 13 other trails, climbing to an elevation of 6,030 feet along the trail to the summit of Cold Mountain on the north end. For a slightly less strenuous hiking or backpacking experience with a lesser elevation gain, the trail can be hiked north to south, starting at the Daniel Boone Boy Scouts Camp.

The Blue Ridge Parkway and several other roads and highways intersect with the trail, providing access points for shorter, customized hikes. The trail's first section begins in the cool, forested valley of the Davidson River, crosses several streams, and passes through woods of locust and oak and undergrowth of blackberry before winding to the summit of Rich Mountain. On the north side of Pilot Mountain, at the beginning of the second section, pink azaleas bloom in mid-May. Lower elevations feature the brilliant blossoms of dogwoods and Fraser magnolias (*Magnolia fraseri*).

Black Balsam Knob and Tennent Mountain, in the trail's third section, both provide spectacular panoramas at more than 6,000 feet before the trail enters Shining Rock Wilderness. Though this federally preserved wild area is heavily used, short paths that diverge from the Art Loeb Trail provide more of an isolated backwoods experience. Northern harriers and rare golden eagles (*Aquila chrysaetos*) can sometimes be seen on Black Balsam Knob. In the fourth section, the trail descends to the source of Sorrell Creek, passing small waterfalls, blankets of ferns, and wildflowers including painted trillium (*Trillium undulatum*), umbrella leaf (*Diphylleia cymosa*), and golden Alexanders (*Zizia aurea*).

Campers may pitch tents most places along the trail. A Pisgah District Trail Map plots Art Loeb's main route and a variety of connector trails through some of North Carolina's most picturesque terrain.

Directions: Exit the Blue Ridge Parkway at milepost 412. Travel south on US 276 approximately 14 miles. The campground is on the right, across from the Pisgah Ranger Station. Or from Brevard, travel east on US 276 approximately 3 miles to the stoplight in Pisgah Forest; turn left and travel north 1.2 miles. The campground is on the left. Once in the campground, take a left before the bridge to go to the Art Loeb Trail parking lot. For a less strenuous access, exit Blue Ridge Parkway at milepost 420.2 onto FR 816. Travel 1 mile to parking area.

Trail: Approximately 30 miles one-way.

Elevation: 5,500 feet (excluding the connector trail to Cold Mountain).

Degree of difficulty: Strenuous.

Surface and blaze: Varied surface; white blazes except within Shining Rock Wilderness (last 8 miles), where blazes are not allowed.

Closest town: Brevard, approximately 4 miles.

For more information: Pisgah Ranger Station, 1001 Pisgah Highway, Pisgah Forest, NC 28768. Phone (704) 877-3265.

AMERICAN TOAD
(Bufo americanus)
Despite popular myth, toads do not cause warts.

▨ RICHLAND BALSAM SELF-GUIDING TRAIL

[Fig. 26(3)] Perched near the top of the Great Balsam range, Richland Balsam Overlook at 6,053 feet is the highest point on the Blue Ridge Parkway. The self-guiding trail from this overlook winds through spruce-fir forests, past flora and fauna more akin to Canada than the South, to the 6,292-foot summit of Richland Balsam. The experience is tarnished somewhat by the dead and downed trees surrounding the summit, where the struggle between the Fraser fir and the balsam woolly aphid is painfully evident.

The brighter side of this story is, of course, that life's natural cycle continues. Dead trees open space to new life that would otherwise not get enough sun, allowing blackberry and elderberry (*Sambucus pubens*) to thrive, ferns and trees to sprout, and the forest to continue its renewal. Rotting logs contribute to the cycle, too, providing homes for beneficial insects, rodents, salamanders, and other wildlife. Wildflowers and shrubs along the trail vary with the season—speckled wood lily (*Clintonia umbellulata*) in May, climbing false buckwheat (*Polugonum scandens*) in July, and hobblebush (*Viburnum llantanoides*) and red-berried elder (*Sambucus racemosa pubens*), both sporting white spring flowers that develop each fall into deep red berries, a favorite with the birds.

Saw-whet Owl

The Great Balsam range in general is an excellent area for spotting the saw-whet owl. A 14-mile stretch of the Parkway from mileposts 419 through 433 is a sure bet from late March through June for hearing these northern owls in the evening and into the night.

Other birds known to inhabit the region include the winter wren (*Troglodytes troglodytes*), red-shouldered hawk (*buteo lineatus*), yellow-bellied sapsucker, black-billed cuckoo (*Coccyzus erythropthalmus*), and pine siskin (*Spinus pinus*). The red squirrel (*Tamiasciurus hundsonicus*) lives here and the tracks of white-tailed deer have been spotted in the soft, rich soil from which "Richland" takes its name.

Directions: Blue Ridge Parkway milepost 431.4.

Activities: Hiking.

Facilities: Parking area, self-guiding trail.

Dates: Open year-round; Parkway closes often in the winter.

Fees: Trail guide for sale at the trailhead.

Closest town: Waynesville, approximately 18 miles.

Trail distance and configuration: 1.5-mile loop trail.

Elevation: 6,292 feet at the summit.

Degree of difficulty: Moderate to strenuous.

Surface and blaze: Forest floor, no blaze.

THE RHODODENDRON GARDEN AND ARBORETUM AT HAYWOOD COMMUNITY COLLEGE

[Fig. 21(27)] Dazzling white to lilac. Creamy yellow then magenta. Flaming red and back to white. The honey bees' dizzying excitement is contagious at Haywood Community College's Rhododendron Garden. The bees are the lucky ones. They get to come every day and watch 75 varieties of rhododendron unfold from early April through May. The garden was designed to extend the blooming season as long as possible, but once the rhododendron have given their all, colorful wildflowers and cultivars take over.

The Rhododendron Garden follows a delicate rhythm in harmony with nature. Careful landscaping gives the effect of a long, leisurely walk deeper and deeper into the forest even though the walk only measures .33 mile. The woodland canopy of tall oak, poplar, and hickory filters sunlight onto the rhododendrons which filter it yet again onto the herbaceous layer below, dense with ferns and wildflowers such as bleeding heart (*Dicentra eximia*), foamflower (*Tiarella cordifolia*), and bloodroot (*Sanguinaria canadensis*).

At the heart of the garden lies Ogden Circle, a council ring 24 feet in diameter surrounded by four walls tapering up from the earth. The walls define four paths that cross here, radiating from a centered millstone. Tall, columnar boxwoods punctuate the circle. Students contribute hanging baskets, wooden flower boxes of impatiens and lobelia, and a living sculpture of annual plants atop the millstone.

Structures within the garden, such as the wooden arbor supporting Dutchman's pipe vines or the split-rail fences dividing cinnamon ferns (*Osmunda cinnamonea*) and periwinkle, work with the native plants. The Rockery hosts lichen- and moss-covered rocks, thick ferns, and wildflowers. A virtual wall of Eastern hemlock glows bright green with tips of new spring growth. Queen Anne's lace (*Daucus carota*) grows near the trail's end.

The Rhododendron Garden is part of the 80-acre Haywood Community College Campus Arboretum which serves as a living laboratory for the students, faculty, and community. In addition to the Rhododendron Garden, the Campus Arboretum includes the Freedlander Dahlia Garden (peaks in September), Class of '74 Rose Garden (July), new Water Garden, dwarf conifer collection, vegetable gardens, perennial garden, herb garden, fruit tree orchard, greenhouse conservatory, and picturesque Mill Pond surrounded by weeping willow (*Salix babylonica*) and river birch (*Betula nigra*).

Landscape architect Doan Ogden designed the campus for industrialist A. L. Freedlander, who donated funds for the college with the stipulation that the property's sizeable oak forest be preserved. An early inventory recorded 880 trees including 22 native species (most averaging 100 years old) to which the Campus Arboretum staff has added 100 new species of trees, shrubs, and ground covers.

Directions: From US 19-23 in Clyde (5 miles east of Waynesville and 25 miles west of Asheville), take the Jones Cove Road Exit and follow signs to Freedlander Drive and the campus entrance. Pass the Mill Pond on the right, turning into the third driveway on the left (opposite Sawmill Road on the right). Follow signs to Rhododendron Garden.

Dates: Open year-round.

Fees: None.

For more information: Haywood Community College, Freedlander Drive, Clyde, NC 28721. Phone (704) 627-2821.

CATALOOCHEE SKI AREA

[Fig. 21(26)] High atop Moody Top, Cataloochee Ski Area holds the distinction of being the first ski slope in the South. Tom and Judy Alexander opened the slope in 1954 adjacent to their famed Cataloochee Ranch, a 1,000-acre resort that got its start in the late 1920s as North Carolina's first tourist camp in the newly legislated Great Smoky Mountains National Park. Five years later, when the federal government consolidated its holdings in the park, the Alexanders had to move and took the valley's name with them. They settled across the divide on Fie Top, where the elevation surpasses 5,000 feet and an ocean of breathtaking mountain ranges surrounds. Cataloochee, after all, is a Cherokee word meaning "wave upon wave."

The ski area is no longer part of the ranch, but it continues to offer excellent skiing on nine slopes. At 5,400 feet with a vertical drop of 740 feet, Moody Top is the highest. Other less-daunting slopes suit beginners and intermediates better; skiing instruction is also available.

Directions: From I-40 7 miles west of Clyde, take Exit 20 from the west or Exit 27 from the east. Cataloochee is 4 miles off US 19 overlooking Maggie Valley.

Activities: Skiing, hiking trails to the adjacent Great Smoky Mountains National Park.

Dates: Winter season, hours vary.

Facilities: Lodge, ski rentals, skiing school, snow-making equipment.

Closest town: Maggie Valley, 4 miles.

Elevation: 5,400 feet at the summit.

For more information: Route 1, Box 502, Maggie Valley, NC 28751. Phone (800) 768-0285 or (704) 926-0285.

HOLMES EDUCATIONAL STATE FOREST

[Fig. 25(7)] Created during the Depression-stricken 1930s, Holmes Educational State Forest got its start as a seedling nursery run by the Civilian Conservation Corps (CCC). In 1972 the land received both a new name and a new purpose as one of six educational forests in North Carolina. Named in honor of John S. Holmes, one of the state's first foresters, the 235-acre forest treats visitors to a series of well-marked trails that, as they loop through the forest's abundance of hardwoods and wildflowers, are as informative as they are scenic.

The rugged geology of the area consists primarily of gneiss metamorphosed from granite approximately 430 million years ago by the forces of continental collision. Flecked with flaky, black mica, this gneiss is sometimes banded by layers of rock with eye-shaped depressions of minerals. Accessible by a steep .25-mile trail, Wildcat Rock is a good example of these outcroppings that typify the region.

An altitude change of 450 feet within its boundaries allows Holmes to support a wide variety of plant life. Hardwoods such as oak, hickory, and red maple flourish in the uplands while lower in the forest, coves of yellow-poplar, basswood (Tilia *americana*), and silverbell (*Halesia carolina*) thrive. Flowering dogwood grows throughout. Lovers of wildflowers will also find troves of colorful specimens. More than 50 species of blossoms have already been identified trailside, among them rhododendron, flame azalea (*Rhododendron calendulaceum*), trout lily (*Erythronium americanum*), yellow lady slipper (*Cypripedium calceolus*), jack-in-the-pulpit (*Arisaema triphyllum*), trillium, bloodroot, and violet.

In addition to the trail leading to Wildcat Rock, Holmes offers four other trails. On the Talking Tree Trail, a push of a button prompts trees to "tell" stories about themselves and the forest in which they live. Forestry practices are explained on the 3.5-mile Forest Demonstration Trail, while the handicapped-accessible Crab Creek Trail features equipment such as a helicopter and a fire tower used in battling forest fires. A 200-foot boardwalk crosses trillium-laden wetlands on the Soil and Water Trail. Ranger-conducted programs are also available to groups visiting the forest.

Directions: From the junction of US 64 and US 25 in downtown Hendersonville, travel south on US 25 for .5 mile. Turn right at junction with Kanuga Road, which later becomes Crab Creek Road (NC 1127). Continue 9 miles to the forest entrance.

Activities: Hiking, volleyball net, horseshoe pits, picnicking.

Facilities: Educational trails and exhibits, 2 amphitheaters (each 30-person capacity), picnic shelter (for 80–100 people) with massive stone fireplace, 20 picnic tables and grills, restrooms, walk-in tent campsites on mountaintop (call to reserve a site).

Dates: Mid-Mar.–Fri. before Thanksgiving.

Fees: None.

Closest town: Hendersonville, 9 miles.

For more information: Holmes ESF, Route 4, Box 308, Hendersonville, NC 28739. Phone (704) 692-0100.

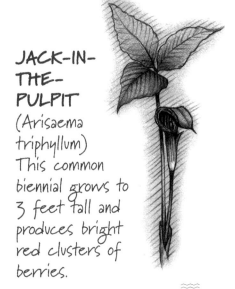

JACK-IN-THE-PULPIT (*Arisaema triphyllum*) This common biennial grows to 3 feet tall and produces bright red clusters of berries.

Carl Sandburg Home National Historic Site

[Fig. 25(8)] Carl Sandburg, one of America's most beloved poets, drew great inspiration from the quiet beauty of Connemara, his 264-acre home in Flat Rock. Since 1968, the year Congress established the Carl Sandburg Home National Historic Site (one year after Sandburg's death), visitors have been able to share his experience. The site is administered by the National Park Service.

The name Flat Rock refers to the smooth outcroppings of Henderson gneiss which served as Cherokee Indian ceremonial grounds and later a trading area with European settlers. The town of Flat Rock, the State Theatre of North Carolina, Flat Rock Playhouse, and Connemara all rest atop these impressive outcroppings of granite.

Several easy and well-maintained trails course through the wooded property, encircling the Front Lake and heading to the summits of Glassy Mountain and Little Glassy Mountain. Along the way, shiny patches of galax, violet, rattlesnake plantain, periwinkle, and robins-plantain (*Erigeron pulchellus*) grow beneath the rhododendron, mountain laurel, huckleberry, and dogwood understory. A second-growth, oak-hickory climax forest associated with many large rock outcroppings forms the canopy.

The varied habitat here offers a haven for permanent resident and migratory birds. Available at the bookstore is a free folder containing a listing of 100 species of birds that have been spotted in the park, noting their seasons and abundance. From uncommon double-crested cormorant (*Phalacrocorax auritus*), great blue heron, and broad-winged hawk (*Buteo platypterus*) to regulars such as golden-crowned kinglet (*Regulus satrapa*), great crested flycatcher (*Regulus satrapa*), and downy woodpecker, the grounds are an excellent place for bird-watching.

From the parking area, the trail meanders uphill to the Main House and barn area where the bleating kids and goats beckon even the most avid hikers for a short detour. Today's goats are descendants of the prize-winning herd Sandburg's wife, Paula, raised. The well-marked trail to Glassy Mountain begins at the Main House and climbs steadily but comfortably with benches along the way. While the view en route is best before foliage, the vista from the summit offers a spectacular year-round panorama of Mount Pisgah and its neighboring peaks. Connecting trails for a longer hike lead to Little Glassy Mountain and around the Front Lake where beavers, Canada geese (*Branta canadensis*), and mallard ducks (*Anas platyrhynchos*) make their home.

For a special lunch or dinner after touring Connemara, Highland Lake Inn is less than a mile away. Many ingredients for the fresh cuisine are picked daily from the colorful and fragrant organic gardens on the grounds. Traveling north on US 25 from Flat Rock, turn right onto Highland Lake Drive. Turn right at the dam and waterfalls.

Directions: Travel 3 miles south of Hendersonville on US 25 and turn right onto Little River Road at the Flat Rock Playhouse. Parking and the visitor information center is on the left. The visitor contact station is up the hill at the house.

Activities: Hiking.

Facilities: Visitor information center, visitor contact station, house tours, bookstore, restrooms, drinking water.

Dates: Open year-round.

Fees: A fee is charged for the house tour; no fee to tour grounds and hike trails.

Closest town: Flat Rock.

GLASSY MOUNTAIN TRAIL

Trail distance and configuration: 2 miles round-trip from visitor contact station.

Elevation: 2,783 feet at the summit.

Degree of difficulty: Moderate.

Surface and blaze: Forest floor, rocky in places; no blaze.

LITTLE GLASSY MOUNTAIN LOOP TRAIL

Trail distance and configuration: .75 mile.

Elevation: 2,220 feet at summit.

Degree of difficulty: Easy.

Surface and blaze: Forest floor, rocky in places; no blaze.

FRONT LAKE LOOP TRAIL

Trail distance and configuration: approximately .5 mile.

Elevation: 2,145 feet.

Degree of difficulty: Easy.

Surface and blaze: Forest floor; no blaze.

For more information: Carl Sandburg Home National Historic Site, Flat Rock, NC 28731. Phone (704) 693-4178.

PEARSON'S FALLS

[Fig. 25(9)] In 1931, this family-owned glen and surrounding forest were in danger of being sold to a timber company. The Tryon Garden Club intervened, protecting the secluded valley and 250 acres of woodland for generations of picnickers, hikers, bird watchers, and students. It remains under the club's ownership and management today.

Designated a North Carolina Heritage Area, the park's centerpiece is a thundering falls of nearly 90 feet. The lush, water-sprayed environment surrounding it is filled with more than 200 varieties of ferns, wildflowers, algae, and mosses, many outlined in a booklet sold at the gatehouse.

Approximately 14,000 visitors come to Pearson's Falls each year to see the lush, water-sprayed environment surrounding the 90-foot falls, which is filled with more than 200 varieties of ferns, wildflowers, algae, and mosses.

The park's 14,000 visitors each year include bus loads of young science students on field trips. In addition, the area, which is also a wildlife preserve, serves as an outdoor laboratory for nearby college and university botany programs.

Directions: On US 176, travel 4 miles north of Tryon or 3 miles south of Saluda. A small sign on the Pacolet River side of the road marks Pearson Falls Road (NC 1102). Follow this road for not quite 1 mile to the park entrance.

Activities: Light hiking, picnicking.

Facilities: Picnicking, .25-mile hiking trail.

Dates: Open year-round, except Jan.

Fees: A fee is charged for admission.

Closest town: Saluda, 5 miles.

For more information: Polk Country Visitor Information Center, 425 N. Trade Street, Tryon, NC 28782. Phone (800) 440-7848, or Pearson's Falls Gatehouse, phone (704) 748-3031.

Foothills Equestrian Nature Center

[Fig. 25(10)] Tucked between the rolling countryside of the Piedmont region and the edge of the Blue Ridge province, the Foothills Equestrian Nature Center (FENCE) is a year-round private refuge devoted to the preservation, study, and enjoyment of the foothills. Thousands of people each year are attracted to programs and activities at this 220-acre learning and recreation center.

FENCE sits in the heart of North Carolina horse country, where stables, riding schools, and horse farms are a long-standing tradition. FENCE's award-winning equestrian facilities are showcased in nearly 20 horse shows each year. Some of the hunter/jumper and dressage shows and driving rallies are produced by FENCE, others by outside riding clubs. The Tryon Riding and Hunt Club's Steeplechase has been a spring tradition in the area for more than 50 years.

Each year, more than 2,000 schoolchildren from surrounding counties participate in the outdoor programming. A 5-mile system of nature trails, hummingbird and culinary herb gardens, and a wildlife pond provide a variety of hands-on learning settings. The pond and surrounding natural marsh are home to nesting birds as well as herons, kingfishers, and occasionally ducks. And members of an active beaver population often work on trees nearby.

Individual visitors are welcome, too. An indoor exhibit space hosts permanent displays of rocks, gems, and birds of prey, along with changing exhibits including live animals that are briefly held and then released into their natural habitats. An indoor classroom and workshop space in a restored 1860s log cabin house seasonal programming and demonstrations on everything from herbs to mushrooms.

The staff conducts regular flower and bird walks.

In addition to its on-site programming, FENCE sponsors bird walks in nearby communities and natural history trips around the world. Recent excursions have taken participants to Scotland, England, and Peru.

Directions: Traveling south on Interstate 26, take SC Exit 1, toward Landrum, S.C. Travel 1.5 miles, and take the first right onto High Farms Road. Follow the road .6 mile to the end. Turn right onto Prince Road. After .5 mile, take the second left onto Hunting Country Road. Proceed 1 mile to the FENCE entrance on the right.

Activities: Hiking, horseback riding.

Facilities: Equestrian facilities, indoor exhibit area and nature classroom, gift shop, outdoor stage.

Dates: Open year-round.

Fees: No fees for viewing exhibits and using grounds, but annual membership encouraged; various fees accompany special events and workshops.

Closest town: Tryon, NC, and Landrum, SC, each approximately 3 miles.

For more information: FENCE, 500 Hunting Country Road, Tryon, NC 28782. Phone (704) 859-9021.

Nantahala Mountains

The Nantahala Mountains are south of the Great Smoky Mountains National Park.

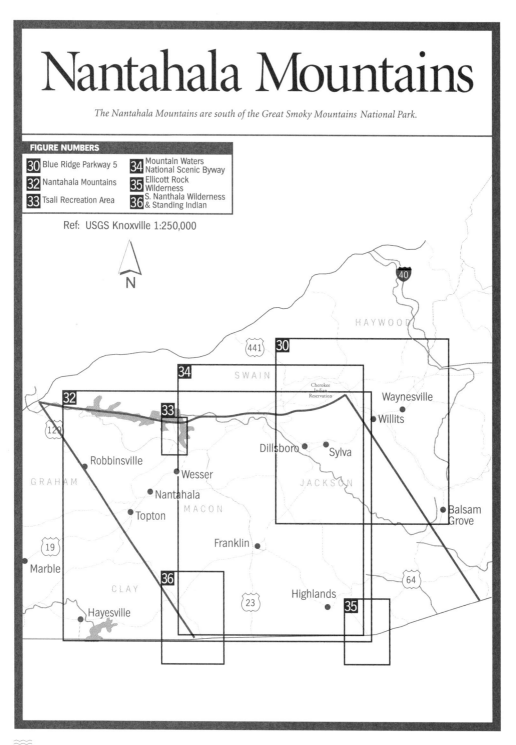

FIGURE NUMBERS

30	Blue Ridge Parkway 5	**34**	Mountain Waters National Scenic Byway
32	Nantahala Mountains	**35**	Ellicott Rock Wilderness
33	Tsali Recreation Area	**36**	S. Nanthala Wilderness & Standing Indian

Ref: USGS Knoxville 1:250,000

N

40

HAYWOOD

441
30

34

SWAIN

32

Cherokee
Indian
Reservation

Waynesville

33

Willits

129

Robbinsville

Dillsboro
Sylva

Wesser

GRAHAM

Nantahala

JACKSON

Topton

MACON

Balsam
Grove

19

Franklin

Marble

64

36

CLAY

Highlands

35

23

Hayesville

The Nantahala Mountains

The Nantahala Mountains section [Fig. 29] is bordered by the Great Smoky Mountains National Park to the northwest and the Georgia and South Carolina borders to the south. The boundary for this section runs southeasterly from the park to the state lines, one running between the towns of Cherokee and Maggie Valley and the other through the Nantahala River Valley just east of Robbinsville. The Blue Ridge Parkway winds down to its terminus here (or gets its start, depending on your perspective). Framed on the northwest and southeast by the Smoky Mountains and Blue Ridge Mountains, respectively, the major cross ranges of this section include the Nantahala, Cowee, and Cheoah mountains.

The diversity of plants and animals found here and throughout the mountains of Western North Carolina is due in part to the tremendous volume of precipitation that occurs here each year. This is especially true in the gorges of Nantahala National

[*Above*: Whitewater Falls near Cashiers, North Carolina]

Forest. In fact, the southwestern mountain slopes that give rise to the headwaters of the Savannah River likely receive the heaviest rainfall in the entire Blue Ridge province from Virginia to Georgia. Some areas of the region receive as much as 100 inches of precipitation per year, approaching that of the Pacific Northwest rainforests and ranking Western North Carolina among the wettest of the contiguous 48 states. Where does this water come from and why does it fall here?

The story begins in the Gulf of Mexico and the southern Atlantic coastal plain states, where offshore moisture rises into the atmosphere and moves northward, forming thick cloud layers. As this warm, saturated air meets the cooler temperatures of the southern Appalachians, it condenses in the form of fog, rain, and snow because cold air cannot hold as much moisture as warm air. Thanks to this frequent and abundant odyssey of water, the mountains of Western North Carolina are lush with a diversity of plant species greater than that found in all of Europe.

It was not always known that precipitation is the source of mountain springs and rivers. Homer speculated on the origins of this water as early as 1000 B.C. and began what was known as the "subterranean school" of groundwater geologists. Aristotle proposed that the interior of mountains somehow condensed rainwater to produce the moisture seen in springs. Kepler theorized that a large, ocean-dwelling animal drank sea water and passed it up to higher elevations where it was excreted as freshwater springs. Nearly as improbable was Kirchner's theory that whirlpools near Norway fed Europe's springs via underground caverns. By the 1700s, the subterranean school of thought became obsolete.

MOUNTAIN LAUREL
(Kalmia latifolia)

Geologists finally proved that precipitation is the true source of mountain springs and rivers. By the early twentieth century, numerous experiments showed a direct correlation between the amount of rainfall in a drainage basin and all of the resulting stream flows in the same basin. The only precipitation the streams did not account for was shown to be lost through evaporation from the forest leaves, transpiration (the pumping of water out of the soil by plants), and the absorbent capabilities of the soil.

Through hindsight, this process is easily seen today. The mountain forest canopy trees are the first to receive precipitation, catching much of it on a vast network of leaves and branches. Once saturated, the canopy allows the excess to fall on the understory dogwoods, silverbells, birches, basswoods, mountain laurels, and rhododendrons. Yet, even these cannot catch all of the moisture, so the groundcover ferns, mosses, partridgeberries, and wildflowers then get their share.

The rain continues to fall, soaking into forest floor leaves and humus and the thin soil layers that overlie massive schist, gneiss, and granite rock foundations. When even these spongy soil layers become saturated, the excess water leaching through may be halted by impermeable underlying rock and begin flowing along this underground boundary. Where opportunity presents itself, this underground water surfaces in the form of springs.

Meanwhile, on the soil surface, there are no more plant barriers to halt the downpour, and the excess water flows in sheets down the broad mountain slopes. Detouring at every swale, ditch, and gorge, the various sheet flows and springs gather and grow, forming vast mountain capillaries of creeks and streams. These join together and, upon reaching lower elevations, eventually carry enough water to earn the label "river."

Some of this water eventually makes its way over cliffs and sheer rock walls, forming the abundance of waterfalls for which Western North Carolina is renowned. In some regions, such as the Nantahala Mountains, the underlying rocks are composed of hard metamorphic rock, and the number of waterfalls far surpasses those in areas with softer, sedimentary rock, such as that found in the Snowbird Mountains. The abundance of precipitation and the topography of the region also contribute to the number of waterfalls.

Throughout the book, terms such as cataract, cascade, and rapid are used to describe water flow. While local preferences often win out over more scientific explanations, the following definitions are a general rule of thumb. Cataract refers to the largest volume of water, as in Rainbow Falls near Sapphire. A cascade is a smaller waterfall that tends to flow over boulders rather than sheer cliffs and generally does not have a pool or basin. Rapids, such as those found within the Nantahala River, are intermittent areas of whitewater. Slides occur when the water flows in sheets along the surface of the rockface; Sliding Rock in the Balsam Mountains section is an excellent example. The word "shoal" shows up often in the names of areas or roads. A shoal is generally a shallow, rocky area on a river. Whatever the size or shape, waterfalls play an important role in oxygenating the water, which provides habitats for some of the wide-ranging flora and fauna that thrive in Western North Carolina.

Blue Ridge Parkway 5

On the weathered rock outcrops along the Blue Ridge Parkway, mica glitters from dikes and sheets of coarsely crystalline pegmatite and granite.

276
209
40
LAKE JUNALUSKA
19 Maggie Valley
Waynesville
110
276
1
WRIGHTS CREEK
2
3
4
215
441
5 **6** **7**
10 MILES
BLUE RIDGE PARKWAY
74 23
Sylva
441
TUSKASEGEE RIVER

1 Milepost #458.2 – Wolf Laurel Gap

2 Milepost #452.1 – Cranberry Ridge

3 Milepost #451.2 – Waterrock Knob Overlook

4 Milepost #439.7 – Pinnacle Ridge Tunnel

5 Milepost #435.7 – Licklog Gap

6 Milepost #435.3 – Flat Gap

7 Milepost #432.7 – Lone Bald

Great Smoky Mountains National Park

NANTAHALA NATIONAL FOREST

281

WOLF CREEK LAKE

BEAR CREEK LAKE

107

THORPE LAKE

N Ref: NPS Blue Ridge Parkway

The Blue Ridge Parkway in the Nantahala Mountains

[Fig. 30] The Blue Ridge Parkway reached its highest point at Richland Balsam Overlook, but now it begins gradually winding down toward its terminus. Anyone who has spent time on the Parkway can attest to feeling a growing sadness as the scenic highway comes to an end. Rest assured, though, that the trip remains exciting to the last mile.

Lone Bald, milepost 432.7 [Fig. 30(7)], once had a lone red spruce (*Picea rubens*) growing atop. When the tree fell, the name changed to Lone Bald. Over the years, though the area has sprouted low shrubs and a variety of trees, the name still stands.

Flat Gap, milepost 435.3 [Fig. 30(6)], offers views of Doubletop Mountain and the historic site of the Cherokee village Tuckasegee (Tsi-ksi-tsi) along the river below. The name is said to mean "terrapin place," referring to the slow pace of the river here. There was nothing slow, however, about the attack of 150 American soldiers who in 1781 destroyed the village during the Revolutionary War. The Cherokee were allies of the British.

Licklog Gap, milepost 435.7 [Fig. 30(5)], is said to have once hosted its namesake, the licklog—a log with holes cut in it by herders and filled with salt for cattle. Twenty-three miles down the Parkway, Lickstone Ridge, milepost 458.9, earned its name from something similar—the lickstone. A stone instead of a log was used as a place for the cattle's supply of salt.

At milepost 439.7, Pinnacle Ridge Tunnel [Fig. 30(4)], the first of six tunnels in this section, runs 895 feet long. Sherrill Cove Tunnel, milepost 466.3, the last tunnel (or first if starting near Cherokee) on the Parkway, cuts through 590 feet of mountain. At the Waterrock Knob Overlook, milepost 451.2 [Fig. 30(3)], the namesake mountain sits astride both the Plott Balsams and the Great Balsam ranges. Waterrock Knob offers a 360-degree panorama of the most spectacular proportions: the Great Balsams, Great Smokies, Cowees, and Nantahalas. The Newfound, Blacks, and Craggies are all visible on a clear day. A plaque at the overlook recognizes H. Getty Browning, who led a well-researched campaign to route the Parkway through North Carolina rather than share it with neighboring Tennessee. Nearby Browning Knob was named in his honor.

Cranberry Ridge, milepost 452.1 [Fig. 30(2)], is named for the small cranberry (*Vaccinium oxycoccos*) that grows along the higher-elevation slopes. Small pinkish flowers of this creeping, woody perennial bear edible red berries in late summer and early fall, especially popular with wildlife.

At Wolf Laurel Gap, milepost 458.2 [Fig. 30(1)], a spur road carries travelers to the Mile-High Overlook and a spectacular view of the Smokies and the Balsams, teasing travelers with the majestic peaks that lie ahead in the Smokies: Clingmans

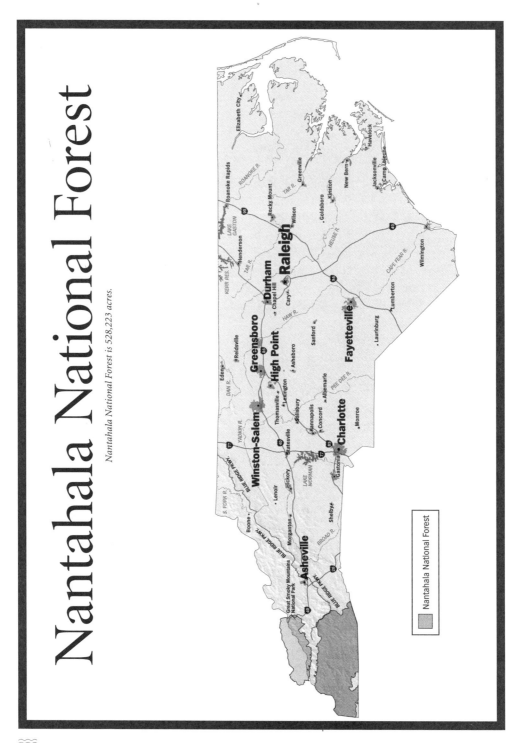

Nantahala National Forest

Nantahala National Forest is 528,223 acres.

Nantahala National Forest

Dome, Mount LeConte, Mount Kephart, and Mount Guyot. The spur road continues past a view of Maggie Valley below and of Lake Junaluska, a lake named in honor of the Cherokee warrior who first fought against the European settlers and later became their ally in the War of 1812. Andrew Jackson swore his gratitude to Junaluska, yet later as president he signed away the rights to the Cherokee's homeland, and the tragic Trail of Tears ensued (*see* Qualla Boundary, page 187).

The remaining miles of the Parkway are steeped in Cherokee legend as they wend their way toward the terminus at milepost 469, elevation 2,000 feet. True to its grand nature, the Blue Ridge Parkway doesn't just peter out but delivers its visitors to the natural beauty and native bounty of The Great Smoky Mountains National Park and Qualla Boundary of the Cherokee Indians, a noteworthy finale for this magnificent highway.

The Nantahala National Forest

[Fig. 31] An outline of the Nantahala National Forest more closely resembles coffee spatters than official survey lines. More than 516,000 acres span from Waynesville to Murphy, Fontana Village to Cashiers, across the crest of mountain ranges and over hundreds of waterfalls to the river valleys and lakes below. The state's largest national forest, Nantahala National Forest includes topography ranging from a high of 5,800 feet at Lone Bald to a low of 1,200 feet on the Tusquitee River.

The Nantahala National Forest was established in 1920 and took its name from the Cherokee word *nondayeli,* meaning "noonday sun." The Cherokee word is appropriate because of the number of steep gorges in the forest that only receive sunlight when the sun stands directly overhead. The Nantahala, Cullasaja, Chattooga, and Tuskasegee gorges confirm the relevance of the forest's name.

Three wilderness areas lie within the Nantahala National Forest: 3,930-acre Ellicott Rock [Fig. 35] near Highlands, 12,076-acre Southern Nantahala [Fig. 36] southwest of Franklin, and 13,132-acre Joyce Kilmer/Slickrock Wilderness Area [Fig. 38] near Robbinsville. Four ranger districts cover the forest: Wayah Ranger District, with 133,894 acres in Macon, Swain, and Jackson counties; Tusquitee Ranger District, the largest district with 158,348 acres primarily in Cherokee County but including Clay and Graham counties as well; Highlands Ranger District, with 105,084 acres in Macon, Jackson, and Transylvania counties; and Cheoah Ranger District, with 120,110 acres in Graham and Swain counties. In 1981 the Highlands Ranger District acquired 40,000 additional acres and created what is now referred to as the Roy Taylor Forest, in honor of the U.S. congressman's love and respect for the mountains.

The diversity of the Nantahala National Forest is explored in the Nantahala Mountains, Snowbird Mountains, and Long Trails sections of this book. The Standing Indian Basin [Fig. 36], for example, is honeycombed with hiking and riding trails, and the Fires Creek Rim Trail [Fig. 32(16)] follows a 25-mile ridge around its namesake to scenic views, heath and grassy balds, and a hardwood forest filled with wildflowers. Water sources here include the rugged Nantahala, Chattooga, and Horsepasture rivers, a chain of lakes lapping gently in the shadow of the mountains, and waterfalls roaring and tumbling down to basins below. The Mountain Waters Scenic Byway [Fig. 34] winds for 61.3 miles through southern Appalachian hardwood forest, rural countryside, two spectacular river gorges—Cullasaja and Nantahala—and numerous scenic waterfalls. The route leads from the town of Highlands along US 64 west to NC 1310 and US 19, where it ends at Fontana Lake.

It is difficult to isolate only a few of the awe-inspiring features found throughout the Nantahala National Forest, though two natural wonders beg a mention: Joyce Kilmer Memorial Forest and Whiteside Mountain. Joyce Kilmer, near Robbinsville, is one of America's most magnificent old-growth forests, featuring 100 species of trees, some soaring more than 100 feet high with a circumference exceeding 20 feet (*see* Joyce Kilmer, page 229). Rising nearly 5,000 feet above the earth, Whiteside Mountain, between Cashiers and Highlands, offers spectacular vistas along rocky crags that share the sky with soaring hawks and falcons (*see* Whiteside, page 205).

(See Appendix D, page 301, for a complete listing of National Forest Service Ranger Districts in Western North Carolina.)

AMERICAN MOUNTAIN-ASH
(Sorbus americana)
Found along swamp borders as well as on mountainsides, the mountain-ash produces clusters of orange-red fruit for birds and rodents.

Qualla Boundary of the Eastern Band of the Cherokee

The Cherokee and their predecessors were the region's first naturalists. For thousands of years before European settlers arrived, these native inhabitants hunted, fished, and farmed a vast territory. In the process, they amassed an encyclopedic knowledge of the indigenous plants and animals, and an equally comprehensive grasp of the rugged landscape they inhabited, with its specific weathers and seasons.

Today, about 11,000 of their descendants carry on some of these Native American traditions within the 56,000 acres of the Cherokee reservation known as the Qualla Boundary (*Qualla* is the Cherokee approximation of Polly, the name of a settler who once lived in the area) and in neighboring communities in Cherokee, Graham, and Swain counties. With its wide variety of cultural, recreational, and tourist attractions (clustered in Cherokee, North Carolina, just a few miles from the Oconaluftee Visitor Center in Great Smoky Mountains National Park), Qualla Boundary makes a convenient base of operations for visitors to the area.

To archeologists, the earliest inhabitants of these mountains are variously known as the Pisgah Culture, the Hiawassee People, the Upper and Middle Valley People, and so on. Opinions vary as to when the Cherokee emigrated to the area, but they had a thriving and sophisticated culture in place when Hernando De Soto came through in 1540.

At its height, the Great Cherokee Nation, the largest of all the southern tribes, had an estimated population of 25,000 and included some 135,000 square miles, extending from the Ohio River as far south as Alabama.

Like most native peoples, the Cherokee (who identify themselves as *Ani Yunwiwa*, "The Principal People") lived in harmony with nature. These wise stewards allocated much of the land they controlled for hunting and religious uses, concentrating their activities in towns. They built rectangular log houses, and each town also boasted a much larger council house. On their extensive, communally held farms, they raised corn, beans, squash, and potatoes and even cultivated peaches.

The Cherokee, however, also manipulated their environment, such as using controlled burning to clear farmland and give hunters easier access to game. Some have even theorized that the burning helped create the distinctive, treeless southern Appalachian balds, whose origins are still in dispute. In any case, the burning did enrich the soil and encourage certain species, such as pines and nut- and acorn-producing trees.

The Eastern Band of the Cherokee developed in reaction to the infamous Trail of Tears, when 18,000 Cherokee were forcibly removed to Oklahoma by the U.S. Army in 1838 (more than 7,000 died en route). But some determined holdouts stayed behind, hiding out in remote coves and valleys. Eventually, they were granted formal

The influence of the Cherokee Indians is found throughout Western North Carolina, with many rivers, mountains, and other natural features bearing Cherokee names.

recognition by the same government that had brutalized them, and their descendants keep this ancient culture alive in their beloved "Land of the Blue Mist."

The Oconaluftee River (a corruption of the Cherokee word *Ekwanulti*, meaning "Place by the River") follows the Oconaluftee Fault through the Smokies, from the Newfound Gap area to Smokemont. The shattered rocks created by the fault eroded more easily and gave way to form the beautiful Oconaluftee River Valley. Descending from the Smokies, the river cuts across Cherokee lands before joining the Tuckasegee River near the Ela community (Cherokee for "earth"). Just below the confluence is the approximate site of the ancient Cherokee town of Katuwha, perhaps 1,000 years old. (The remains of a ceremonial mound are visible behind an old airplane hangar along US 19, just outside the Qualla Boundary.)

In spring, this area, known as Governor's Island or Ferguson Fields, is rich in migrating bird species, including the American bittern (*Botaurus lentiginosus*), great blue heron (*Ardea herodias*), green heron (*Butorides virescens*), and many more. Rare species sighted in the area include the lesser golden plover (*Pluvialis dominica*) and henslow's sparrow (*Passerherbulus henslowii*).

The Oconaluftee River Valley, in general, shelters many bird species, especially in spring. Look for warblers, fly catchers, tanagers, vireos, and belted kingfishers (*Megaceryle alcyon*), which inhabit the area year-round. Other animals commonly seen in the area include the groundhog (*Marmota monax*), black bear (*Ursus americanus*), white-tailed deer (*Odocoileus virginianus*), and red fox (*Vulpes fulva*).

Water figured prominently in Cherokee religious ceremonies, and it is an abiding presence on Qualla Boundary lands, where several picturesque waterfalls can be seen. The best-known waterfall is 150-foot Mingo Falls. One of the more spectacular cataracts in the Smokies, it can be reached via an easy 10-minute stroll from the Mingo Falls Campground on Big Cove Road, 5 miles outside the town of Cherokee. The smaller, less-accessible Soco Falls, partially visible in winter from US 19, hosts many wildflowers growing at its base. Inquire at the Visitor Center in Cherokee (US

19 at Business 441) for more information about these and other nearby falls.

An easy way to explore local flora is to visit the Cherokee Botanical Garden [Fig. 44(4)], which features an herb garden among its more than 16,000 plants. Some 150 species are identified along the gentle, .5-mile loop trail, which winds through a mixed-pine and hardwood forest along the slopes of Mount Noble and past an old Cherokee cabin and offers periodic scenic views.

Adjacent to the Botanical Garden on US 441 is Oconaluftee Indian Village. Much of the inner life of contemporary Cherokee communities is invisible to the casual tourist, but a visit here provides a vivid introduction to traditional ways. Indians in native costumes serve as guides through a recreated eighteenth-century village, complete with rustic log cabins, a sweat lodge, and a seven-sided Council House. Cherokee crafters chip flint into arrowheads, carve spoons and bowls, and practice traditional basket making, fingerweaving, and bead work. Visitors can even see a dugout canoe being hollowed out the traditional way, using fire and heavy axes.

Down the hill from these attractions (US 441 at Drama Road) stands the Museum of the Cherokee Indian [Fig. 44(5)]. More than 20 audiotape and videotape presentations, including six mini-theaters, lead viewers through some 10,000 years of indigenous history. Among the museum's treasures are a rare eagle-feather coat and a 250-year-old dugout canoe.

Here visitors can learn about Cherokee mythology and history, including such little-known highlights as the Thomas Legion, a band of Cherokee soldiers who fought under Confederate Colonel William Holland Thomas during the Civil War. Thomas, a European trader who spoke and wrote Cherokee, was adopted by Chief Yonaguska and eventually elected chief of the Eastern Band.

The museum also highlights the contributions of noted Cherokee leaders, such as Junaluska—who saved future-President Andrew Jackson's life at the Battle of Horseshoe Bend during the War of 1812 (ironically, it was Jackson who signed the Removal Treaty banishing the Cherokee to Oklahoma, a quarter century later) and Sequoya, who created the Cherokee written language.

Cherokee Medicine

The Cherokee pharmacopoeia included more than 600 species of native plants. From the mayapple (*Podophyllum peltatum*), for example, they made a treatment for warts; today, we use chemicals obtained from the plant to treat cancer. Hundreds of other plants were used for dying cloth, making body paints, concocting poisons for spears and arrowheads, weaving baskets and other crafts, and of course, eating. One savory specialty, which they passed on to early European settlers, was chestnut dumplings, featuring the produce of the now virtually extinct American chestnut (*Castanea dentata*), the victim of a fungus accidentally imported earlier this century.

The museum's gift shop contains an impressive collection of books and reference materials about the Cherokee and other southern tribes, as well as handsome works by contemporary artists and master crafters.

Across Drama Road from the museum stands Qualla Arts & Crafts Mutual Inc., an Indian-owned and -operated cooperative offering a wide variety of locally made craft items—including baskets, dolls, jewelry, and woodcarvings, as well as fine Native American crafts from other regions. Other popular attractions include the Cherokee Heritage Museum and Gallery (Big Cove Road, off US 441 N) and *Unto These Hills*, an outdoor drama staged mid-June through late August in the Mountainside Theatre, next to Oconaluftee Village.

The reservation also offers outstanding recreational opportunities. Cherokee and environs are a paradise for hiking, horseback riding, tubing, and whitewater rafting. The Qualla Boundary boasts 28 campgrounds and both developed and backcountry camping possibilities abound in the adjacent Great Smoky Mountains National Park.

It's the trout fishing, though, that most stands out among Cherokee's recreational offerings. In fact, both the North Carolina record brook and brown trout were plucked from Cherokee waters. The brook or speckled trout (*Salvelinus fontinalis*) is native to these mountains, though wild ones are now relatively rare. Rainbows (*Onocorhynchus mykiss*) have been stocked in North Carolina streams since the 1880s (the wild ones have an end-to-end, reddish-orange stripe, black spots, and red around the gills). Brown trout (*Salmo trutta*) have been stocked in mountain streams since the turn of the century. Each year, hundreds of thousands of brook, brown, and rainbow trout raised in the reservation's hatchery on Straight Fork are released along 33 miles of streams and in several ponds. Thanks to this ambitious stocking program, the Tribal Enterprise Waters are so well supplied with fish that it is hard not to catch something. A $5 tribal permit is good for up to 10 trout per day, using any type of bait or lure. Permits and detailed information are available on the reservation.

Hikers wishing to connect with the timeless spirits who inhabit the Qualla Boundary can explore the Mount Noble Trail, which starts in the parking lot of Oconaluftee Village. The 4.5-mile round trip can be hiked in conjunction with the Cherokee Arboretum Trail. The Mount Noble Trail ascends through hardwood forests to the 4,066-foot summit, where a fire tower affords hikers sweeping views.

Directions: To Cherokee, NC from Asheville: Take I-40 to Exit 27 and go south on US 23/74, continue to US 19, exit and go west to Cherokee.

Dates: The following attractions are open year-round: Museum of the Cherokee, and Qualla Arts & Crafts. Oconaluftee Village and Botanical Garden: May 15–Oct. 25.

Fees: Admission to the Botanical Garden is free; a fee is charged for the museum and Oconaluftee Village.

For more information: Cherokee Visitor Center, PO Box 460, Cherokee, NC 28719. Phone (800) 438-1601. Museum of the Cherokee Indian, phone (704) 497-3481. Oconaluftee Village, phone (704) 497-2315. Qualla Arts & Crafts, phone (704) 497-3103.

Fontana Lake

[Fig. 32] Nestled in the shadow of the Great Smoky Mountains, the limpid waters of Fontana Lake (the largest lake in Western North Carolina) reflect the splendor of those ancient knobs and peaks. Don't be surprised if the spectacular views hereabouts seem strangely familiar: portions of several recent films, including *Nell* and *The Fugitive*, were shot here. Today, Fontana and environs constitute a world-class playground, drawing boaters, fishing enthusiasts, hikers, and mountain bikers from far and near.

Ironically, the peaceful vistas created by the lake are actually the fruits of war. Fontana was built in the wake of the Japanese attack on Pearl Harbor, to provide power for the war effort (specifically, Oak Ridge, Tennessee, where top-secret work on the atomic bomb was being conducted under heavy security). When the Tennessee Valley Authority completed the 480-foot-tall Fontana Dam late in 1944, it was the fourth largest hydroelectric facility in the world.

Today, those wartime concerns seem remote. Fontana Village—built to house the thousands of workers who labored round the clock, seven days a week to complete the dam in record time—is now the most comprehensive, year-round family resort in the Smokies, boasting a range of lodgings (from campsites to cottages to a full-service inn), extensive sport facilities, and more traditional activities (including classes in Appalachian crafts, music, and clogging). Fontana Village Resort offers 30 miles of mountain biking trails, as well as horseback riding and even escorted hikes.

But the lake itself remains the main attraction. Held back by the massive dam (the highest east of the Mississippi), the waters of the Little Tennessee River spread out along the coves and inlets to create the 29-mile-long artificial lake with its 240-mile rugged shoreline. Two other rivers, the Nantahala and the Tuckasegee, also feed the lake, as do numerous creeks descending from the Smokies to the north and from the geologic jumble of the Yellow Creek, Cheoah, and Nantahala mountains to the south.

Geologically, the area around Fontana Dam is similar to what one finds in most of the neighboring Smokies, including dark black slates and schists. Copper was mined along Eagle Creek (on the Smokies side) from 1927 until the dam was built. The sulfidic rock formations common in the area are what road builders call "hot rock": when exposed by construction, they can produce acid runoff, which eats through drain pipes and culverts and can be lethal to aquatic life and roadside vegetation.

Among the area's more intriguing geologic features are the Indian Caves in the lower Nantahala Gorge, just above the eastern end of the lake. The caves, a series of connected chambers scoured out of the Nantahala slate cliffs, were sacred to the Cherokee and later housed workers building the rail line through the gorge. The caves are located near the foot bridge on US 19, about 50 yards north of the tracks.

Warbler watchers will be in seventh heaven here—in the summer, the area hosts more

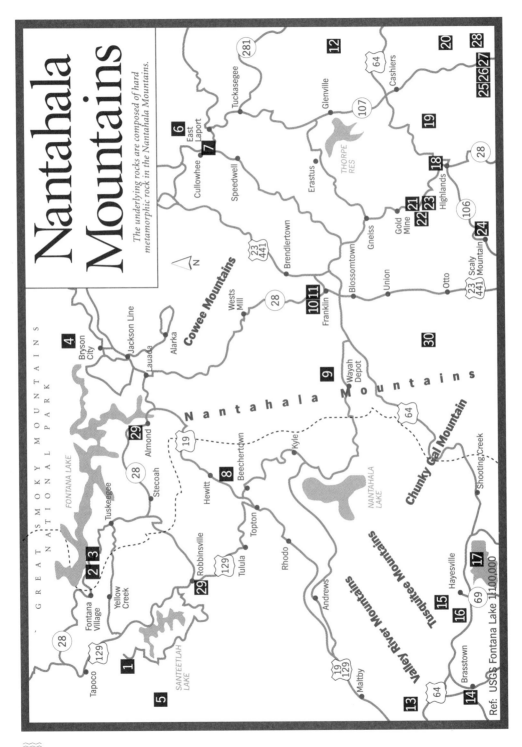

Nantahala Mountains

The underlying rocks are composed of hard metamorphic rock in the Nantahala Mountains.

1 Joyce Kilmer–Slickrock Wilderness Area

2 Cable Cove Recreation Area

3 Tsali Recreation Area

4 Deep Creek Area

5 Snowbird Area/Big Snowbird Trail

6 Judaculla Rock

7 Mountain Heritage Center

8 Nantahala Gorge

9 Wayah Bald Area

10 Ruby City Gems

11 Franklin Gem & Mineral Museum

12 Panthertown Valley Falls

13 Peachtree Mound & Village Site

14 Campbell Folk School

15 Leatherwood Falls

16 Fires Creek

17 Jackrabbit Mountain Recreation Area

18 Highlands Nature Center

19 Whiteside Mountain & Devil's Courthouse

20 Horsepasture River Bridge

21 Cullasaja Falls

22 Bridal Veil Falls

23 Dry Falls

24 Glen Falls Scenic Area

25 Ellicott Rock Wilderness

26 Ellicott Rock Trail

27 Bad Creek Trail

28 Whitewater Falls

29 Indian Lakes Scenic Byway

30 Coweeta Hydrologic Laboratory

- - - - - - - Appalachian Trail

than 20 species, including Cerulean (*Dendroica cerulea*), black-throated green (*D. virens*), yellow-throated (*D. dominica*), golden-winged (*Vermivora chrysoptera*), blue-winged (*V. pinus*), worm-eating (*Helmitheros vermivorus*), and Swainson's (*Limnothlypis swainsonii*). Spring and summer are the best times, though there are birding opportunities year-round along NC 28 and other local roads. Look for the bulb-shaped nests of the cliff swallow (*Petrochelidon pyrrhonota*) in the shelter of Fontana Dam.

The Nantahala Mountains—which run north from the Georgia border for about 25 miles, terminating near Fontana's eastern end—also offer diverse birding opportunities, with less competition from fellow bird lovers. Away from the lake, try the central Nantahalas, especially the area around Wayah Gap (*see* Wayah Bald, page 219).

The last known mountain lion (*Felis concolor*) in the Smokies was killed near Fontana Village, though unconfirmed sightings are periodically reported within the park boundaries.

Not surprisingly, Fontana Lake is best known for its recreational opportunities. Walleye, three kinds of bass—smallmouth (*Micropterus dolomieui*), largemouth (*M. salmoides*), and white (*Morone chrysops*)—as well as channel catfish (*Ictalurus punctatus*), flathead catfish (*Pylodictis olivaris*), and bluegill (*Lepomis macrochirus*) are abundant. Trout thrive in the many streams that feed the lake on the Smokies side. A state-record, 41-pound muskellunge (*Esox masquinongy*) was nabbed here in 1994. Two sites along NC 28, Tsali and Cable Cove recreation areas [Fig. 32(2,3)] (see below), provide access to the lake, as well as hiking, camping, and biking opportunities. *(Directions to these and other local attractions may change as the four-laning of NC 28 is carried out over the next several years.)*

The Appalachian Trail runs across Fontana Dam. Hikers might also explore a

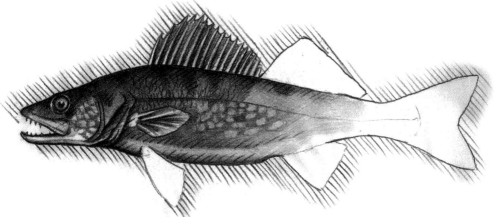

WALLEYE (*Stizostedion vitreum*)
With a common name stemming from its large eye, the walleye is sometimes erroneously called a "walleyed pike." Walleye can grow to 2 feet long and up to 20 pounds.

number of connected trails out of Fontana Village, including the Look (or Lookout) Rock Trail (off NC 1246, at the far end of Fontana Village) and the Lewellyn Cove Nature Trail, which features 50 trees and shrubs labeled for easy identification. Ask at the front desk for a free trail map and written material about these and other Fontana trails.

Directions: From Asheville, take I-40 to Exit 27 (Highway 74) go west past Bryson City, then turn right on NC 28. Go about 23 miles to Fontana Village billboard, turn left at stop sign. After about 3 miles, turn left at Texaco station, go up hill to parking lot.

Activities: Mountain biking, hiking, horseback riding, fishing, boating, swimming, water skiing, camping, tennis, volleyball.

Facilities: Marina, fitness center, picnic, indoor/outdoor pools, tennis, miniature golf, crafts, campground, cabins, cottages, inn, restaurants, museum, post office, store, laundry.

Dates: Open year-round.

Closest town: Robbinsville, 22 miles.

Elevation: 1,800 feet (water level fluctuates by about 130 feet).

For more information: Fontana Village Phone (800) 849-2258; Cheoah Ranger District, phone (704) 479-6431; Great Smoky Mountains National Park, phone (704) 497-1900.

Tsali and Cable Cove Recreation Areas

[Fig. 32(3), Fig. 33] Tsali, an internationally renowned mountain biking facility, derives its name from a Cherokee hero martyred in connection with the infamous Trail of Tears, when thousands of Cherokee were rounded up for forced removal to Oklahoma. The historical record is impossibly murky, but Tsali and some members of his family were apparently executed by their own people, perhaps to placate military authorities, in the aftermath of a scuffle in which one or more U.S. soldiers were killed. Some accounts say Tsali willingly sacrificed his life so that some of his countrymen could remain amid their beloved mountains. In any case, he has become a symbol of Cherokee resistance to oppression.

Today, intrepid off-road cyclists plunge down sharp ravines and catch glimpses of Fontana's sparkling waters through the trees where Cherokee and infantry once dueled. These bikers share Tsali's four trail loops—Tsali Left (11.9 miles), Tsali Right (11 miles), Mouse Branch (6.5 miles), and Thompson (7.7 miles)—with equestrian users, alternating on specified days. (Call the ranger station, or check the information at the trailhead.) Shorter 4- and 8-mile loops off Tsali Right are also possible. Hikers may enjoy the trails at all times, though it is wise to keep an eye and ear out for onrushing cyclists and skittish horses.

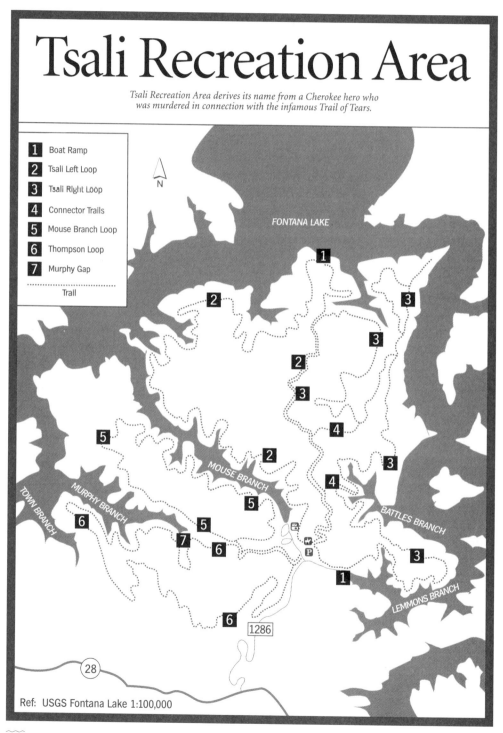

Tsali Recreation Area

Tsali Recreation Area derives its name from a Cherokee hero who was murdered in connection with the infamous Trail of Tears.

1 Boat Ramp
2 Tsali Left Loop
3 Tsali Right Loop
4 Connector Trails
5 Mouse Branch Loop
6 Thompson Loop
7 Murphy Gap
········· Trail

N

FONTANA LAKE

MOUSE BRANCH

TOWN BRANCH

MURPHY BRANCH

BATTLES BRANCH

LEMMONS BRANCH

1286

28

Ref: USGS Fontana Lake 1:100,000

Tsali's 3,000 acres straddle the Swain County/Graham County line, amid some of the more rugged terrain in the eastern United States. The topography within the recreation area, however, is gentler than the topography of much of the land around it, and, consequently, this acreage was once intensively farmed. That explains the abundance of southern yellow pine or shortleaf pine (*Pinus echinata*), one of the first species to reclaim abandoned farmlands. Recently, however, the southern pine beetle has been inflicting significant damage. In general, Tsali's vegetation is typical of lower-elevation, southern Appalachian hardwood forests, with their white oak (*Quercus alba*), hemlock (*Tsuga caroliniana*), poplar (*Populus gileadensis*), sourwood (*Oxydendrum arboreum*), and white pine (*Pinus strobus*). Other vegetation includes mountain laurel (*Kalmia latifolia*), sumacs, and scattered berry patches.

Wildflowers are abundant, among them sunflower (*Helianthus tomentosus*), coneflower (*Rudbeckia hirta*), wild phlox (*Polemoniaceae*), horsemint (*Collinsonia canadensis*), downy false foxglove (*Aureolaria virginica*), soapwort (*Saponaria officinalis*), henbit (*Lamium amplexicaule*), gentian (*Gentiana decora*), orchids, and violets. Ruffed grouse (*Bonasa umbellus*), wild turkey (*Meleagris gallopavo*), and assorted songbirds can be seen, especially feasting on insects in grassy areas. Larger animals include white-tailed deer, an occasional wild boar (*Sus scrofa*), and black bear that sometimes swim across the lake.

About 20 miles west of Tsali stands the much smaller (40 acres) Cable Cove Recreation Area [Fig. 32(2)] which, like Tsali, provides a boat ramp and a somewhat more primitive campground. Vegetation includes white pine and yellow-poplar and abundant wildflowers. In May, the mountain laurel and rhododendron (*Rhododendron catawbiense* and *maximum*) bedeck the slopes in blooms. Cable Cove is also a good area for spotting warblers and other neotropical migrant bird species.

Directions: From Bryson City, take US 19 south 9 miles, turn right on NC 28 for 5.5 miles. Turn right at sign for Tsali Recreation Area on FR 521 (gravel) for 1.5 miles. For Cable Cove, continue another 20 miles on NC 28. Directions to these sites may change as the four-laning of NC 28 is carried out over the next several years.

Activities: Mountain biking, horseback riding, hiking, camping, boating, fishing.

Facilities: Tsali: bike-washing station, campground (hot showers/flush toilets), boat ramp, picnic tables, stables. Cable Cove: boat ramp, campground (flush toilets, no showers), picnic tables.

Dates: Open Apr.–Oct.

Fees: Tsali: A fee is charged for camping (tent and RV) and for horse or bike use of trail (no charge for hikers). Cable Cove: A fee is charged for camping.

Closest town: Tsali is about 20 miles from Bryson City; Cable Cove is about 15 miles from Robbinsville.

For more information: Cheoah Ranger District, phone (704) 479-6431.

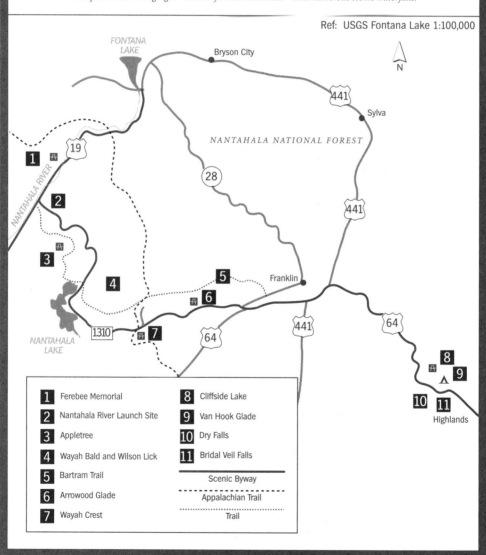

Mountain Waters Natl. Scenic Byway

The Mountain Waters National Scenic Byway winds for 61.3 miles through two spectacular river gorges—Cullasaja and Nantahala—and numerous scenic waterfalls.

Ref: USGS Fontana Lake 1:100,000

FONTANA LAKE

Bryson City

441

Sylva

NANTAHALA NATIONAL FOREST

19

1

NANTAHALA RIVER

28

2

441

3

4

5

Franklin

6

441

64

1310

7

64

441

64

NANTAHALA LAKE

8

9

10 11

Highlands

1 Ferebee Memorial		**8** Cliffside Lake
2 Nantahala River Launch Site		**9** Van Hook Glade
3 Appletree		**10** Dry Falls
4 Wayah Bald and Wilson Lick		**11** Bridal Veil Falls
5 Bartram Trail		———— Scenic Byway
6 Arrowood Glade		- - - - Appalachian Trail
7 Wayah Crest		········ Trail

Nantahala Gorge

[Fig. 32(8), Fig. 34] A drive through the Nantahala Gorge offers some of the most breathtaking scenery in Western North Carolina. Winding roads present leisurely views of sheer rock faces towering over crystal clear waters. Fresh fruit and vegetable stands, fly-fishermen, and rustic cabins dot the riverside, while whitewater enthusiasts of all kinds delight in the waterfalls and swirling rapids of the Nantahala River.

The Nantahala River Gorge is a 9-mile stretch of the Nantahala River running from Beechertown to Fontana Lake. Often referred to by locals as the "Nanty," the Nantahala River originates in Nantahala National Forest, the largest of four national forests in North Carolina. The water then flows into Aquone Lake, the highest lake in North Carolina, where it is dammed and then piped down the mountain to the Nantahala Power and Light Company. Running at a refreshing 45-degree angle, this mountain-canyon river next flows through the heavily forested Nantahala River Gorge for 9 miles where it ends at Fontana Lake. The cold water often creates a mysterious fog on warm days, rising as far as 3 feet above the water.

The Nantahala River Gorge is nationally known for its world-class whitewater. Since the Nantahala is a controlled-release river, there is always predictable whitewater from spring until fall, making it one of the most heavily used whitewater rivers in the region. The 8-mile river trip through the Class I, II, and III rapids takes about three hours. More than 10 commercial outfitters are established along the river, offering a variety of services including outfitting and guiding, boat rentals, instruction, restaurants, and overnight accommodations.

The U.S. Forest Service provides three river-access sites: the Nantahala River Launch Site, located off US 19 and NC 1310 at Beechertown, at the beginning of the run; Ferebee Memorial Recreation Area, 4 miles north of Topton, midway through the Nantahala Gorge; and the take-out landing located on US 19 at Wesser.

One of the focal points of the Nantahala Gorge is the Nantahala Outdoor Center (NOC). While there are numerous outstanding outfitters in the region, it is difficult not to single out NOC based on the scope and reputation of its offerings. NOC is the nation's largest paddling school, where everyone from beginners to experienced paddlers comes to learn and sharpen whitewater skills. Courses range from one-day canoe and kayak samplers to week-long clinics. Over the years, operations have expanded to include whitewater rafting trips on four other outstanding rivers in the southern Appalachians.

In addition to instruction, NOC also offers guide-assisted raft trips; raft rentals and funyack rentals; rock-climbing and backpacking courses; fly-fishing workshops; bicycle tours; a corporate team-building program with ropes course, retreat, and meeting facilities; and three restaurants.

The Nantahala National Forest lands that surround the Nantahala Gorge offer miles of adventurous single-track trails and gated forest roads ideal for mountain biking. Also, the renowned Tsali Recreation Area (*see* Tsali, page 195), located 8 miles from Nantahala Outdoor Center, offers more than 40 miles of rolling single-track along Lake Fontana Lake's shores.

The Nantahala River is renowned for trout fishing. The Nantahala Gorge is stocked with more than 6,000 fish from March to August, and fish grow quickly due to the quality of the food supply. The gorge is also the only part of the Nantahala River and the only trout water in North Carolina that permits night fishing.

Directions:. To reach the Nantahala Gorge portion of the Nantahala River, follow US 19/129 north from Andrews. Continue on US 19 when US 129 splits northeast. US 19 connects with the Nantahala River just north of Beechertown.

Facilities: NOC provides many services such as 3 restaurants, meeting facilities, supply store, launch sites. The U.S. Forest Service provides 3 river access sites.

Fees: A fee is charged for public access to the Nantahala River Launch Area.

For more information: See Appendix C, page 300, for a list of commercial rafting outfitters on the Nantahala River.

PANTHERTOWN VALLEY AND FALLS

[Fig. 32(12)] The fragile and biologically significant Panthertown Valley is recognized by leading botanists and national environmental organizations and publications as one of the more magnificent areas in the southern Appalachians. Since becoming caretakers of this valuable resource in 1988, the U.S. Forest Service has worked to maintain the delicate balance of allowing public access and protecting the area from the potentially devastating effects of too much traffic.

The Nature Conservancy began negotiating to purchase the 6,380-acre Panthertown Valley tract from Liberty Life Insurance in 1986, when Duke Power suddenly bought the valley for $10 million. Eventually, the Conservancy succeeded in purchasing the property and, in turn, sold the land to the U.S. Forest Service. A 230-kilovolt transmission line across one end, however, remains as a reminder of the power company's ownership.

At 4,000 feet, this flat valley supports unique and endangered communities. A rare, high-elevation bog, covered with a mat of sphagnum moss, is surrounded by a granitic dome of steep rock outcrops, where pinkshell azalea (*Rhododendron vaseyi*) and federally endangered rock gnome lichens cling.

Only 33 patches of rock gnome lichens exist in the United States, 26 in the mountains of Western North Carolina and the remainder in eastern Tennessee. The patches typically occupy less than 3 square feet, and that size is shrinking each year. Scientists believe increasing air pollution is the cause of the decline of the rock gnome lichens—filters of pollutants and indicators of air quality. In addition, heavy foot traffic can destroy an entire community.

Several mountain streams bordered by white sand beaches curl throughout the valley—some streams forming waterfalls. Schoolhouse Falls is the most easily accessible and spectacular. Fragile spray-cliff communities, surviving on the mosses and liverworts that are the earliest settlers of rock faces, are also in danger of being trampled by visitors who explore behind the falls.

Many of the valley's old railroad grades and logging roads are covered with forest growth or partially filled with young trees, blueberry bushes (*Vaccinium*), and greenbriers. More recently used roads that are now closed to vehicle traffic form trails throughout the valley.

Directions: 2 miles east of Cashiers on US 64, turn left (north) on Cedar Creek Road (NC 1120). Continue 2.2 miles and bear right (northeast) on NC 1121 (Breed-love Road). Continue 3.4 miles on NC 1121 to parking area at a gap where national forest boundary begins.

Activities: Hiking, catch-and-release fishing. Though mountain biking is permitted, no designated trails exist. Plans are under way for making trail designations that will prohibit biking on all but designated areas.

Closest town: Cashiers, approximately 10 miles.

For more information: Highlands Ranger District, 2010 Flat Mountain Road, Highlands, NC 28741. Phone (704) 526-3765.

MOUNTAIN HERITAGE CENTER

[Fig. 32(7)] In the eighteenth century, Scots-Irish immigrants found home in the glens and hollows of the Appalachian Mountains. The traditions and folkways they brought with them are a rich part of the cultural legacy of Western North Carolina. At the Mountain Heritage Center at Western Carolina University, a permanent exhibit focuses on the Scottish and English migrants who settled in Northern Ireland in the seventeenth century and whose descendants immigrated to Western North Carolina generations later.

In addition, temporary exhibits illustrate both the natural world and mountain societies of the past and present, centering around themes such as the environmental and cultural history of an Appalachian watershed and the southern Appalachian handicraft movement. The more than 10,000 artifacts in the center's collection include heirlooms of hundreds of Western North Carolina families, providing abundant material for changing displays.

To expand its reach, the Mountain Heritage Center publishes books and tapes and develops multi-image shows and media presentations for schools, civic organizations, and conferences. Educational programs such as a monthly children's cultural-arts program plus concerts, lectures, and other special events are offered on site, as well. And each fall, Mountain Heritage Day, a festival of mountain music, food, crafts, and storytelling, attracts 35,000 celebrators.

Directions: Traveling west on I-40 from Asheville, take Exit 27 to US 74. Continue on US 74 until the Cullowhee/Western Carolina University Exit. From the exit, take NC 107 south and follow the signs to the university. The Mountain Heritage

Center is on the ground floor of the Robinson Administration Building, the first building off the four-lane highway.

Dates: Open year-round.

Fees: None.

For more information: Mountain Heritage Center, Western Carolina University, Cullowhee, NC 28732. Phone (704) 227-7129.

JUDACULLA ROCK

[Fig. 32(6)] Nobody knows what it says, but over the years it has been the subject of a lot of talk. Judaculla Rock is a large soapstone slab carved with pictographs that have yet to be translated. Though the carvings predate Cherokee recorded history, the Cherokee contend that the fearful giant Judaculla (corrupted from the Cherokee *tsulkalu* which means "slant eyes") jumped from his mountaintop home on Tanasee Bald at the convergence of Haywood, Jackson, and Transylvania counties. He is said to have landed at what is today Caney Fork Creek and left the markings on the soapstone. The many other theories circulating about what the rock is—a boundary marker, peace treaty memorial, battle commemoration—take a back seat to the more popular story of jumping Judaculla.

Directions: From US 107 in Cullowhee, travel south approximately 4 miles and turn left at NC 1737, Caney Fork Road. Follow the signs along the 3-mile drive through a farm to an open shed covering the rock.

Dates: Open year-round.

Fees: None.

Closest town: Cullowhee, approximately 7 miles.

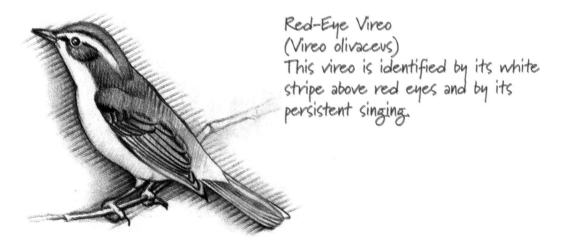

Red-Eye Vireo
(Vireo olivaceus)
This vireo is identified by its white stripe above red eyes and by its persistent singing.

Horsepasture River Trail and Waterfalls

[Fig. 32(20)] The Horsepasture River is, perhaps, the crowning jewel of North Carolina's mountain rivers, not for its size but for its waterfalls. This river, designated a Wild and Scenic River, lies within one of several extremely rugged river gorges that drain into the equally wild Lake Jocassee in South Carolina. Five spectacular waterfalls, some consisting of a series of cascades, occur alongside a 2.8-mile stretch of the Horsepasture's churning currents and are connected by a main trail with short spur trails to each falls.

The name "Horsepasture" is derived from the name of the alluvial plain created by the river's confluence with Toxaway River and Laurel Fork Creek. Now flooded by Lake Jocassee, this level area was once referred to as the Horse Pasture, its steep mountain walls serving as a natural corral for livestock.

The Horsepasture gorge supports a variety of wildflowers which take advantage of the sunny openings created by the river. Delightful colonies of bluet (*Houstonia caerulea*) occur on the moist banks and amid grassy islands in the river. Sweet white violet (*Viola blanda*) often occurs in these areas, and nodding trillium (*Trillium cernuum*) can usually be seen on wooded slopes near some of the waterfalls during spring.

Birds commonly seen or heard high in the tree canopy during late spring and summer include the red-eyed vireo (*Vireo flavoviridis*), downy woodpecker (*Dendrocopos pubsecens*), hooded warbler (*Wilsonia citrina*), ovenbird (*Seiurus aurocapillus*), wood thrush (*Hylocichla mustelina*), and northern parula warbler (*Parual americana*). Year-round resident species encountered range from the tufted titmouse (*Parus bicolor*), white-breasted nuthatch (*Sitta carolinensis*), and Carolina wren (*Thryothorus ludovicianus*) to the blue jay (*Cyanocitta cristata*), northern cardinal (*Richmondena cardinalis*), and rufous-sided towhee (*Pipilo erythrophthalmus*). Bird-watching is best away from the falls, since these produce a roar that drowns out any bird calls.

In spite of its rugged beauty, the river was almost lost to an electrical power project. Congress, in an attempt to curb its infamous pork barrel water projects tradition that had resulted in ecologically destructive and expensive dams and reservoirs, encouraged the renovation of old, small-scale mill and power dams for new sources of energy. Unfortunately, a loophole in the law also allowed for construction of dams in areas previously undisturbed.

In 1984, the California-based Carrasan Power Company obtained permits to build a water-operated turbine facility on this stretch of the river. Rather than using a reservoir, the plant would divert all of the river's water for its generators. Area power companies insisted that the resulting electricity would not be needed. A local resident, Bill Thomas, quickly organized a group called Friends of the Horsepasture that gained the attention of other citizens, organizations, business interests, and congressional representatives and ultimately stopped the project. Because of their efforts, 4.5 miles of the Horsepasture were included in both state and federal Wild and Scenic River Systems, giving the area permanent protection.

The five waterfalls of the Horsepasture are Drift Falls, Second Falls (or Turtleback Falls for its turtleshell-like rock formation), Rainbow Falls, Stairstep Falls, and Windy Falls. Drift and Turtleback falls occur near the trail access point on Bohaynee Road (NC 281). They are popular scenic falls and are used as swimming and sliding rocks from spring through fall.

Rainbow Falls, located in the southwestern corner of Transylvania County, is among the most spectacular in North Carolina. Its waters drop nearly 200 feet into a deep pool, pounding out a thunderous roar and producing a rising mist that forms beautiful and varied rainbows under the midday sun. The falls can be viewed at the bottom near a grassy bank that also supports a wildflower community. A strong railing has been installed here for safe viewing and to provide a site for excellent photography. The mist created by the falls is blown by a strong wind through a gap in the gorge, soaking those who observe from the railing.

Viewing the next two sets of falls is not easy. The side trail to Stairstep Falls is somewhat confusing, while the final 1.3 miles to Windy Falls is dangerous and recommended only for the most experienced and hardy hikers. Stairstep Falls is appropriately named since it consists of a series of seven cascades that resemble steps 10 feet wide. Once again, photographers will find good sites from which to shoot pictures of these falls. Windy Falls is another matter entirely. Even if one manages to overcome the extremely strenuous trail, it is not possible to photograph the entire falls. The series of cascades at Windy Falls tumbles a combined total of 700 feet down a narrow gorge, creating strong wind-tunnel like air currents.

Warning! It should be noted that the main trail along the Horsepasture River and the short spur trails to the waterfalls can be dangerous. Rain and ice make the trail surface treacherous, especially where bare rock or precipitous ledges occur. Drift Falls and Turtleback Falls may offer good swimming opportunities, but deaths have occurred when swimmers were knocked unconscious against the rocks and then drowned in the deep pools. Some swimmers, unable to stop after sliding down Turtleback, have been swept over Rainbow Falls just downstream, and hikers stepping too close to the top of Rainbow Falls have plummeted to their deaths, as well.

Directions: From Sapphire, travel east on US 64 and turn right (south) on NC 281 to Horsepasture River Bridge. Parking and trailhead just north of bridge.

Activities: Swimming, hiking.

Dates: Open year-round.

Fees: None.

Closest town: Sapphire, 1.8 miles.

Trail distance and configuration: Main trail is 5.6 miles round-trip.

Elevation: Change of 1,280 feet.

Degree of difficulty: Moderate to strenuous.

For more information: Highlands District Ranger, phone (704) 526-3765.

Whiteside Mountain

[Fig. 32(19)] The cliffs of Whiteside Mountain are some of eastern North America's highest, rising more than 2,100 feet to the summit at 4,930 feet, with massive crags extending 400 to 750 feet along the southeastern summit. Whiteside has attracted humans for centuries—Indians used its peak as a campsite; legend has it that Hernando De Soto and his explorers stopped at the mountain; and since the first recorded climb in 1971, expert rock climbers have been scaling the cliff's sheer faces.

Commonly called "whiteside granite," the igneous rock that formed the cliffs is actually a quartz diorite gneiss. It is composed primarily of feldspar, quartz, and mica, which appear as white streaks on the mountain's south face. Weathering, drying wind, and sun have left little vegetation on the south side, making the natural blue-gray color of the rock visible. The darker appearance of the north side is due to the mosses and lichens that grow in its more moist environment.

Whiteside Mountain supports two distinct botanical communities. Northern red oaks (*Quercus rubra*) are particularly dominant in the forest. Yellow birch (*Betula alleghaniensis*), American beech (*Fagus grandifolia*), and witch-hazel (*Hamamelis virginiana*) are also common. And prior to the blight of the American chestnut, the area had an abundance of chestnut trees. In late spring and summer, these woodlands

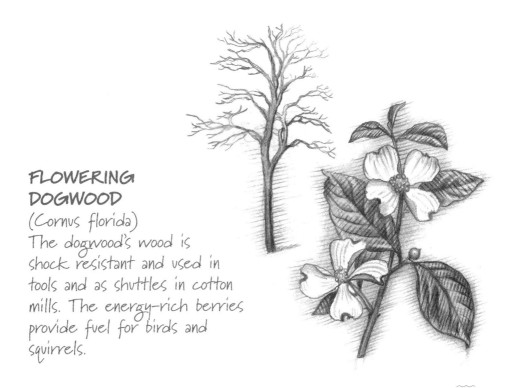

FLOWERING DOGWOOD

(Cornus florida)
The dogwood's wood is shock resistant and used in tools and as shuttles in cotton mills. The energy-rich berries provide fuel for birds and squirrels.

are a good place for watching the eastern phoebe (*Sayornis phoebe*), Canada warbler (*Sayornis phoebe*), American goldfinch (*Spinus tristis*), and rose-breasted grosbeak (*Pheucticus ludovicianus*) among many other forest-dwelling birds.

A second community exists among the rock outcrops along the cliffs—a separate habitat of shrubs such as rosebay rhododendron, mountain laurel, and flame azalea (*Rhododendron calendulaceum*). Plants such as lily of the valley (*Convallaria montana*), bluet (*Houstonia caerulea*), and wild strawberry (*Fragaria virginiana*) are plentiful. More rare and fragile forms of vegetation such as Allegheny sand myrtle (*Leiophyllum buxifolium*) also cling to the soil in these areas. Salamanders, including the mountain dusky (*Desmognathus ochrophaeus*) and Jordan's (*Plethodon jordani*), inhabit wet rock surfaces, and raptors such as red-tailed and broad-winged hawks (*Buteo jamaicensis* and *B. platypterus*), occasional golden eagles (*Aquila chrysaetos*), and peregrine falcons (*Falco peregrinus*), which were reintroduced to the area in the 1980s, make their homes among the cliffs.

Like many of its rugged counterparts throughout the area, Whiteside Mountain, a mountain landmark on the Eastern Continental Divide, is the center of legend and myth. The Cherokees believed it was part of a vast rock bridge that the wicked monster Utlunta was building across the mountains. Tales also place the devil's throne in a cave in Whiteside Mountain. Similar legends tell of a Devil's Courthouse in the Balsam Mountains, though the chamber at Whiteside is considered to be supreme.

A 2-mile moderate loop trail to the summit features magnificent views from ridgetops. Below, the Chattooga, a nationally designated Wild and Scenic River, begins its course down the Blue Ridge escarpment.

Directions: Take US 64 east out of downtown Highlands. Go 5.5 miles to the Whiteside Mountain Road sign and turn right on NC 1600. After .6 mile, bear left at the Wildcat Ridge Road sign and travel .35 mile farther. The gravel trailhead parking lot is on the left.

Activities: Hiking.

Facilities: Parking area, toilet.

Dates: Open year-round.

Fees: A fee is charged for parking and for season passes.

Closest town: Highlands, approximately 7 miles.

Trail distance and configuration: 2-mile loop trail.

Elevation: 4,930 feet.

Degree of difficulty: Moderate.

Surface and blaze: Forest floor, old road grade, some steps; formerly gray-blazed.

For more information: Highlands Ranger District, 2010 Flat Mountain Road, Highlands, NC, 28741. Phone (704) 526-3765.

▨ WHITEWATER FALLS

[Fig. 32(28)] For those interested in visiting the numerous waterfalls of North Carolina, Whitewater Falls has to top the list. Praise for Whitewater knows no bounds: it is reputed to be the highest falls in the Blue Ridge Mountains, measuring 411 feet from top to bottom, and has been described as the most spectacular falls east of the Rockies because of its unmatched water volume, height, and viewing pleasure.

It is one of the most accessible waterfalls as well. A short (.2 mile) trail leads from the parking area to the impressive overlook. The wide trail is paved and handicapped accessible. The overlook offers a distant, wide-angle view of the entire waterfall, an opportunity not available at most other cataracts.

A path to the left of the overlook offers a hike on a continuation of the 80-mile Foothills Trail. This path extends to a ford across the river a short distance upstream from the falls, but there is no safe way to view the cataract from the top. Another trail at the upper overlook leads very steeply down to a lower overlook that offers an even better view. Both sites are excellent for shooting photographs. This trail continues down to the river, but, as with the upper trail, there is no safe way to approach the base of the falls. Attempts to do so may also cause injury to a fragile ecosystem known as a spray-cliff community.

Spray-cliff communities support plants that require or tolerate the specific moisture conditions found near waterfalls. It may take decades for ferns, mosses, and wildflowers to take hold of, and build soil on, the moist rocks found here. Yet, it takes only a second for a hiker's shoe to tear such delicate colonies loose. Visitors are urged to stay on the trails.

Directions: From US 64 at Sapphire, turn south on NC 281. Follow 8.6 miles to Whitewater Falls Scenic Area entrance on left.

Activities: Hiking, trout fishing.

Facilities: Restrooms, picnic tables, overlook.

Fees: A fee is charged for parking and for season passes.

Closest town: Sapphire, approximately 9 miles.

Trail: .4 mile round-trip. Handicapped accessible. Foothills Trail connects with overlook (trailheads on right and left).

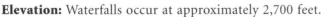

PITCH PINE
(Pinus rigida)

Elevation: Waterfalls occur at approximately 2,700 feet.

Degree of difficulty: Easy to overlook.

Surface: Paved to overlook. Steep soil and rock, forest floor on Foothills Trail.

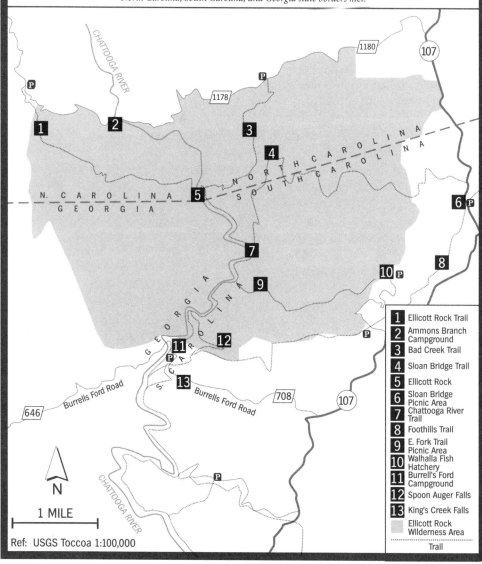

Ellicott Rock Wilderness

*The Ellicott Rock once was considered the point where
North Carolina, South Carolina, and Georgia state borders met.*

1 Ellicott Rock Trail
2 Ammons Branch Campground
3 Bad Creek Trail
4 Sloan Bridge Trail
5 Ellicott Rock
6 Sloan Bridge Picnic Area
7 Chattooga River Trail
8 Foothills Trail
9 E. Fork Trail Picnic Area
10 Walhalla Fish Hatchery
11 Burrell's Ford Campground
12 Spoon Auger Falls
13 King's Creek Falls

Ellicott Rock Wilderness Area

Trail

1 MILE

N

Ref: USGS Toccoa 1:100,000

Ellicott Rock Wilderness

[Fig. 32(25), Fig. 35] The Ellicott Rock Wilderness encompasses one of the Southeast's premiere river gorges and includes national forests from three different states—North Carolina, South Carolina, and Georgia. It also harbors one of the oldest trails in the East and a wonderful variety of plants and animals.

The Ellicott Rock Wilderness straddles the 15,000-acre Chattooga Wild and Scenic River corridor known for its high rocky cliffs, powerful cascades, and luxuriant mixed evergreen-deciduous forests. The area contains old-growth white pine, hemlock, tulip poplar, and other hardwood specimens. Thick, impassable tangles of great rhododendron understory form over creeks and on slopes, giving the colloquial term "rhododendron hell" true meaning. At times, these shrubs form a tunnel over the well-maintained trails.

For those interested in day hiking or primitive camping, the area offers excellent trails free of motorized vehicles, horses, and bicycles, making it as much of a true wilderness experience as possible. Campsites must be located at least 50 feet from water courses or designated trails.

The Ellicott Rock Wilderness was expanded from a much smaller scenic area first created in 1966. This 1975 expansion brought the area under the protection of the 1960 Wilderness Protection Act and increased the area to 9,012 acres. Nearly half (3,900 acres) of the tract lies in North Carolina. The Chattooga River was given Wild and Scenic River status in May 1974. Since then, the U.S. Forest Service has proposed acquiring an additional 2,000 acres to the south and east of the present boundaries.

The area is reached from North Carolina via the Ellicott Rock Trail or the Bad Creek/Fowler Creek Trail [Fig. 35(3)], the latter joining with the former just before crossing into South Carolina. The trail and wilderness area get their name from a rock on the east bank of the Chattooga River that was inscribed with the letters "NC" by a surveyor named Ellicott. Ellicott Rock was marked erroneously as the point at which the three states of North Carolina, South Carolina, and Georgia meet. The correct intersection is at Commissioner's Rock, which lies 10 feet downstream and is inscribed with the markings "Lat 35 AD 1813 NCSC."

The Ellicott Rock Trail [Fig. 32(26), Fig. 35(1)] begins just outside the wilderness boundary on Forest Service Road FR 1178 and extends for 3.5 miles to the three-state intersection. After following an old road for more than 2 miles, the trail follows a left fork away from the road and slopes down into the Chattooga River Gorge. After crossing over to the east bank of the river, the trail joins with the Bad Creek/Fowler Creek Trail to form the Chattooga River Trail [Fig. 35(4)]. Ellicott Rock is encountered on the riverbank soon after this junction. This stretch of trail, extending 3.5 miles south from the Bad Creek Trail and ending at the East Fork Trail in South Carolina, is part of a former Cherokee Indian trail, which makes this one of the oldest trails in the region.

Indian Pipe

Indian pipe (*Monotropa uniflora*) is a delightful, translucent white plant that appears trailside throughout summer. Unusual for a flowering plant, Indian pipe lacks chlorophyll and therefore cannot manufacture its own food. Instead, its roots obtain nutrition from decayed organic material, a feeding trait more commonly associated with saprophytic mushrooms.

Other trails within the North Carolina segment of Ellicott Rock Wilderness Area include the Slick Rock Trail, an easy, .2-mile trail off of Bull Pen Road, approximately 6 miles from Highlands. This short walk on an unmarked trail leads to massive rock formations affording scenic views of the Chattooga River. Two other trails offer a moderate hike to picturesque views of the Chattooga River with its cascades and pools, sandbars and boulders.

The trailhead for the Chattooga River Trail and Chattooga River Loop Trail can be found off Bull Pen Road at the Chattooga River bridge, marked by an information board. After .7 mile, the Chattooga River Trail connects with the Chattooga River Loop Trail, which completes the loop with an additional 1 mile of trail.

Numerous wildflowers appear along the wilderness area trails. Rattlesnake plantain (*Goodyera pubescens*), a tiny orchid that grows on a 1-foot spike, is spectacular for its evergreen basal (ground level) leaves which show a pattern perhaps reminiscent of a snake skin. Mountain camellia (*Stewartia ovata*) is a rare shrub with a beautiful, large white flower similar to the southern magnolia (*Magnolia grandiflora*). It occurs sparsely on river bluffs or wooded stream margins.

The area also supports a diverse wildlife population. The ample water supply guarantees a number of mammals, including raccoons (*Procyon lotor*), white-tailed deer, and black bears. Numerous species of birds reside in or pass through the Ellicott Rock Wilderness, and one, the Swainson's warbler (*Limnothlypis swainsonii*), is of special interest. This bird was first described near Savannah, Georgia, around 1801 in the drawings of naturalist John Abbot, who named it the "swamp worm-eater." His illustrations were not discovered, however, for nearly a century. In 1833, naturalist Reverend John Bachman reported the Swainson's warbler on the Edisto River in South Carolina, but it was not sighted again until ornithologists William Brewster and Arthur Wayne reported the species nearly 50 years later.

Brewster theorized that this and other lost birds might be found in the southern Appalachian Mountains, and began searching near the present Ellicott Wilderness. But it was another 50 years before the warbler's presence was established in some mountain rhododendron communities, and not until 1960 were they found in large numbers in the escarpment gorges of the Chattooga and other nearby rivers.

Directions: Ellicott Rock Trail: From Highlands, travel southeast on East Main Street which becomes Horse Cove Road as it leaves town. Follow to intersection with two gravel roads; Whiteside Cove Road joins from left, and Bull Pen Road joins from right. Follow Bull Pen Road about .5 mile to bulletin board at trailhead on right. Bad Creek Trail: From Cashiers, drive south on NC 107 from its intersection with US 64. After 6.7 miles turn right on NC 1100. Follow 2.3 miles to trailhead on left.

Activities: Hiking, primitive camping, trout fishing.
Closest town: Highlands, approximately 4.5 miles.
Fees: None.
Closest towns: Highlands, 4.5 miles, and Cashiers, 9 miles.

ELLICOTT ROCK TRAIL
Trail distance and configuration: Approximately 3.5 miles round-trip.
Elevation: 2,270 feet at Ellicott Rock.
Degree of difficulty: Moderate.
Surface and blaze: Old roadbeds, narrowing to natural forest floor; no blaze.

BAD CREEK TRAIL
Trail distance and configuration: 3.7 miles round-trip.
Elevation: 2,760 feet at Bad Creek trailhead.
Degree of difficulty: Moderate.
Surface and blaze: Old roadbeds, narrowing to natural forest floor; no blaze.

HIGHLANDS NATURE CENTER
[Fig. 32(18)] The center offers daily programs for children and adults, including lectures, nature classes, tours of the botanical gardens, and outings. The center offers exhibits on local archeology, geology, and biology, including live salamanders, snakes, and fish. Fresh wildflower arrangements are available to help visitors identify local plants. Next door is the Appalachian Environmental Art Center, where one may enroll in classes in nature and landscape photography.

Directions: On Horse Cove Road, an extension of East Main Street in Highlands.
Dates: Open June–Labor Day, Mon.–Sat.

GLEN FALLS
[Fig. 32(24)] Rare plants thrive in the high-altitude rainforest of the Highland Plateau in Macon County. Peregrine falcons nest in the ledges and crevices of ancient mountains that tower to 5,000 feet, and waterfalls abound, particularly around the pleasant resort town of Highlands, which holds a well-deserved reputation for its rambling old inns, modern bed and breakfast accommodations, and gourmet dining.

The Glen Falls Scenic Area in the Nantahala National Forest provides wonderful views of the Blue Valley. Among the abundant mountain laurel grow majestic trees including the Carolina hemlock (*Tsuga caroliniana*), basswood (*Tilia heterophylla*), the rare pignut hickory (*Carya glabra*), and northern red oak.

The well-maintained trail to the cascading falls is steep. Hikers have the option to take the first trail to the top of the upper falls or to descend to its base, then to the base of the middle falls, and on down to the lower falls. The cold water plunges 640 feet from the East Fork of Overflow Creek in just .5 mile, and the three waterfalls with connecting cataracts drop 70, 60, and 15 feet for an awesome and refreshing experience.

Directions: From the corner of NC 106 and Main Street in Highlands, take NC 106 west 1.6 miles and look for U.S. Forest Service "Glen Falls Scenic Area" sign on left. Turn left and immediately turn right onto a gravel road, SR 1618. Drive 1.1 miles to where the road ends at the parking area.

Dates: Open year-round.

Fees: None.

Closest town: Highlands, 2.7 miles.

Trail distance and configuration: 2.8 miles round-trip.

Elevation: Highlands, 4,118 feet.

Degree of difficulty: Moderate to strenuous.

Surface and blaze: Forest floor; unblazed.

Wedgwood Pottery

The Cowee Valley of Macon County is well known for its gemstones, but few people are aware of the high-quality clay that is also found there. This clay literally found its way to the dinner tables of European royalty.

In the 1760s, a Georgia potter named Andrew Duche learned of the Cowee Valley kaolin soils and scouted the Cherokee Indian territory in search of the clay. He had heard that it was comparable to the clay used in Chinese porcelain and obtained the rights from the Indians to mine the clay. Word of this agreement reached Josiah Wedgwood, an English potter, who sent a South Carolina agent to Western North Carolina to negotiate a similar deal.

Quick to realize that they held a valuable resource, the Cherokee chiefs offered the rights to the clay at a premium price. Wedgwood was forced to pay similarly high prices to transport the clay overland to a port for shipping.

Despite the costs, Wedgwood ultimately purchased a significant tonnage of Cowee Valley kaolin. He used it to manufacture very high quality china, which debuted under the name Queensware. Wedgwood's china catapulted him to great fame and provided the basis for the high-quality standard carried out by his successors. His North Carolina clay was also used to produce a dinnerware service for Russia's Catherine the Great. Although Wedgwood eventually located a European source for kaolin of similar quality, his original Cowee Valley pottery products have become priceless museum art pieces.

Bridal Veil Falls, Dry Falls, Cullasaja Gorge and Falls

Waterfalls are abundant along the brink of the Blue Ridge escarpment of the southern Appalachian Mountains. Several impressive cascades in the Nantahala National Forest are accessible within a few miles of the resort town of Highlands. This Macon County community, situated at about 4,118 feet, receives twice the rainfall of mountain-sheltered valleys. The combination of high altitude and rain-forest climate provides habitat for numerous rare plant species, including the dwarf polypody fern (*Grammitis nimbata*), found nowhere else in North America.

This region is the native land of the Cherokee, and many legends and names reflect that heritage. Cullasaja, for example, is the corrupted version of the Cherokee word *Kaulsetsiyi*, meaning "honey locust place." The Cullasaja River flows westward from Highlands, paralleled by the Mountain Waters Scenic Byway. The first 7.5 miles of this route wind along US 64/28 through the beautiful Cullasaja Gorge with spectacular scenic views of the river and its waterfalls. The Spanish explorer Hernando De Soto passed this way in 1540, as did the intrepid pioneers during the gold rush after the discovery of gold in North Carolina in 1799.

Bridal Veil Falls [Fig. 32(22), Fig 34 (11)], just 2.5 miles west of Highlands, is a gentle beauty. In Cherokee lore, a maiden who walks under the falls in the spring will be married before the turning of the year. An old

Cullasaja Falls in Macon County

section of highway routed beneath the falls provides a unique opportunity to drive under the flowing water. The 120-foot falls sometimes displays a rainbow in the afternoon, and it has been known to freeze during the winter.

Another mile or so along this curvy, two-lane section of US 64 is the plunging tumult of water known as Dry Falls [Fig. 32(23), Fig. 34(10)]. Accessible by a paved and fenced path, the rushing water falls 75 feet to the boulder-strewn river. The cascade is surrounded by schist and gneiss, rock that is estimated to be 800 million years old. The five-minute walk continues along the recessed ledge behind the not-so-dry falls. The freshness of the air and the cool spray of the roaring water is invigorating at this close range.

Beyond Dry Falls toward the town of Franklin, the highway hangs on a rock ledge over the Cullasaja Gorge in one of the most hazardous sections of road in these mountains. Below, the river cascades over the boulders in a foaming, tumbling flow, and it is worth the extra trouble to find a safe parking space (using extreme caution) for a more leisurely view of Cullasaja Falls [Fig. 32(21)].

Directions: Take US 64/28 west from Highlands. Bridal Veil Falls is along the edge of the highway with a roadside pull-off and handicapped-accessible view. Dry Falls is less than 1 mile farther (3.25 miles from Highlands), with an abrupt turn off the highway into a parking area. Cullasaja Falls is another 5.5 miles (8.75 miles from Highlands). Drive beyond the falls and stop along the right, then carefully walk back for a roadside view.

For more information: Highlands Chamber of Commerce, phone (704) 526-2112; or the Highlands Ranger District, phone (704) 526-3765.

Fees: A parking fee is charged at Dry Falls.

Gem Mines of Macon County Area

The Franklin area has long been known for its rich deposits of minerals. The region is popular with gem hunters, and an important tourism industry has developed around the mineral resources of Macon County.

The first commercial mining in the area was conducted in the late 1800s. Prior to that time, residents of the Caler Fork section of Cowee Valley had known about the red stones that commonly occurred in the creek's gravel beds. In 1893, however, a Tiffany's of New York representative named George Frederick Kunz produced a report on the value of the valley's rubies, which created great interest in the area. Many local people began sending their stones to Tiffany's for cutting and polishing.

In 1895, New Jersey mining expert W. E. Hidden began supervising work on Cowee Valley lands and old claims that were newly purchased by the American Prospecting and Mining Company. The company intended to find the source of the rubies and sapphires by digging experimental shafts and test holes uphill and away from Caler Fork. Similar testing was performed by the United States Mining Company and other mining interests. Despite these attempts, the source for the gemstones was never located.

In 1912, the state of North Carolina conducted a geological survey of the area and confirmed the presence of corundum, the mineral of which rubies and sapphires are the red and blue gem varieties, respectively. Because corundum approaches the hardness of diamonds, it was used for abrasives, bearings, and watch movements, as well as for gemstones. Neither the survey results nor the expensive mining company explorations revealed significant commercial quantities of corundum, though the mineral was mined for a time. The development of less expensive synthetic abrasives ultimately reduced the demand for corundum. The mining companies, therefore, halted their Cowee Valley operations early in the twentieth century.

Rock hounds and the tourism industry are the main beneficiaries of these early prospecting activities. Today, numerous old mines have been reopened and adapted to the desires of visitors wishing to mine their own gems. Some of these mines offer digs for native minerals only, while others offer "enriched" stream sediment, which contains minerals from other parts of the state or world. At some of these mines, visitors search for minerals from the creekbeds, while others sell buckets of stream sediment for washing and sieving at a flume.

Directions: Mines are located in the Franklin area. See Appendix F (page 302) for listings.

Activities: Gem/mineral hunting.

Facilities: Flumes, gem cutting, gift shops, concessions, picnic tables/shelters, restrooms. Some mines have handicapped access.

Dates: Open year-round or seasonal.

Fees: A fee is charged for admission to the mines.

Closest town: Franklin.

For more information: Franklin Area Chamber of Commerce, Inc., 180 Porter Street, Franklin, NC 28734. Phone (704) 524-3161.

Gems Unique to the Macon County Area

The creeks and valleys around the town of Franklin are reputed to contain the largest variety of minerals in the world. Though there are not enough large or contiguous deposits to make industrial mining profitable, minerals and gemstones occur in sufficient quantities to support a large tourism trade for amateur gem hunters.

Among the minerals and gemstones found in the Macon County area are kyanite, sillimanite, granular mica, quartz varieties, rutile, corundum, and magnesium-aluminum garnet. The gems most often associated with the Franklin area, however, are rubies and sapphires, which are the red and blue gem varieties (respectively) of corundum, an extremely hard aluminum-oxide mineral. The various colors found in ruby and sapphire gemstones are caused by the presence of trace amounts of elements such as chromium, iron, and titanium, among others.

Cowee Valley's unique geology has endowed the area with equally unique rubies and garnet gems. While rubies of various reddish tints have been found at mines in other parts of the world, none has produced the deep red ruby variety found in the Caler Fork area of Cowee Valley. These rubies are of extremely high quality.

The same holds true for the garnets that occur here. Rhodolite garnets are found in Macon County, but are very unusual and highly sought after. The name rhodolite is derived from the Greek *rhodon*, for rose (which also gave rise to the name for the rhododendron flower), and rhodolite garnets exhibit a very light to very dark rose color. As with Franklin-area rubies, rhodolite gemstones occur elsewhere, but the best specimens known to date are found only in the Cowee Valley area.

🏵 RUBY CITY GEMS

[Fig. 32(10)] Ruby City Gems, a retail gem and jewelry business in Franklin, features an astounding museum display of gems, minerals, and stone carvings. The extensive exhibit includes minerals from the Franklin area and from around the world, as well as North American Indian, Columbian, and pre-Columbian artifacts. The museum is open to the public at no charge, and the exhibit is displayed in a single large room located downstairs at the rear of the store.

Two features about this exhibit stand out. A number of the stones on display are giant-sized. One amethyst geode stands several feet tall and weighs more than 800 pounds. The lavender-tinted crystals inside the geode are several inches in diameter. Other large minerals and stunning agates are also on display here.

The second unique feature of the museum is its collection of mineral spheres. These large, highly polished spheres are derived from many different rocks and minerals. The elaborate patterns seen within the minerals were created not by artists, but by nature's own remarkable processes. The spheres themselves were masterfully created by the late Earnest F. Klatt, the founder of Ruby City Gems. His son, also named Earnest, continues to operate the store and museum. Visitors will also enjoy a store-level display of ivory carvings, jade sculptures, and huge polished slabs of red rhodochrosite. In addition, an adjacent room contains a wide variety of lapidary tools and equipment for sale to those interested in cutting and polishing their own minerals and gems.

Directions: Located at 44 East Main Street, Franklin.

Facilities: Museum, stone examination, custom jewelry designing/repairs. Free maps, mining information.

Dates: Open Apr. 1–Dec. 31.

Fees: There is no charge for admission.

For more information: Phone (704) 524-3967.

Mining has a long history in Western Carolina, where rich deposits of a wide variety of minerals and gems have attracted prospecting and mining activities for more than 170 years.

The Fascinating Diverse World of Salamanders

Western North Carolina's abundant rainfall and high humidity produce cold, fast-flowing streams, damp rock crevices, and moist woodlands filled with decaying logs and leaf litter. These are all perfect habitats for members of the highly diverse order of amphibians known as salamanders.

Salamanders are extremely shy creatures, preferring to hide under submerged rocks, in damp caves, and beneath fallen leaves, limbs, and tree trunks. Like all amphibians, they were among the first creatures to inhabit the continental land masses. Their evolution from the fishes coincided with the appearance of the first forests during the Devonian Period more than 345 million years ago. Salamanders provide an important link in the food web. They prey on numerous aquatic and terrestrial insects, crayfish and other crustaceans, worms, mollusks, and the eggs of frogs and other salamanders. Salamanders are also sought after as prey by birds, mammals, and fish.

More than 35 salamander species are known to inhabit the mountains of North Carolina. Aquatic salamanders spend their entire lives in water, while terrestrial species inhabit damp upland forests. In between are those that live in moist caves, crevices, or woods but visit streams, ponds, and bogs in order to breed. Curiously, the eastern newt (*Notophthalmus viridescens*) lives and breeds as an adult in lakes, ponds, and streams, but its subadult form, or "eft," is terrestrial, preferring moist woods.

Depending upon the species (and the opinion of the observer), a salamander's appearance may vary from the ugly (hellbender) and the bizarre (mudpuppy) to the beautiful (spotted, red, and two-lined salamanders, and eastern newts). The high mountain ridges play a part in restricting the distribution of some salamander species and in causing variations among others. The shovelnose (*Leurognathus marmoratus*), a North Carolina endangered species, is limited to the four westernmost counties of the state, while the rare zigzag salamander (*Plethodon dorsalis*) is found only in Henderson, Buncombe, and Madison counties. Usually associated with limestone areas in Tennessee, this may be a relict species.

Two salamander species, while reported in limited areas of Virginia, occur in a specific region of the North Carolina mountains. The green salamander (*Aneides aeneus*) is known only in Macon, Jackson, Transylvania, Henderson, and western Rutherford counties. Its occurrence is not widespread in these counties, but it appears in isolated populations. The common mudpuppy (*Necturus maculosus*) occurs only in the Upper French Broad River basin and is listed as a species of special concern in North Carolina.

Salamanders are delicate creatures and are easily injured. Observe them carefully, and avoid removing them from their habitat. Their importance to the stream and woodland ecosystems warrant the same respect given to larger and more familiar creatures of nature. These fascinating creatures hold clues for scientists studying man's early evolution from sea creatures.

FRANKLIN GEM AND MINERAL MUSEUM

[Fig. 32(11)] Gemologists and rock hounds will enjoy a visit to the Franklin Gem and Mineral Museum in Franklin, with its collection of countless precious and semiprecious stones found in this mineral-rich region of North Carolina as well as other areas in and out of the state. The museum, housed in the old Franklin jail building, opened its doors to the public in 1976. As visitors enter the small lobby from the street, they are greeted by a volunteer host from the Gem and Mineral Society of Franklin. Gems and minerals are organized by rooms such as "The North Carolina Room," "The States Room," "The Indian Room," and "The Fluorescent Room."

Step into the fluorescent room, press the button, and listen to a tape describing the minerals that respond to long- and shortwave ultraviolet rays given off by the black light. Behind the glass, visitors are treated to a truly dazzling display of beautiful colors and phosphorescent effects produced by the various minerals.

Upstairs, an authentic jail cell holds a display entitled "Rocks Used to Make Glass," while other rooms contain worldwide minerals, as well as fossils from plants, insects, ocean-dwelling organisms, and even mammoths. There is also a display case interpreting famous stones of ancient Greece and the Mideast. Souvenir minerals can be purchased, and information can be provided by the volunteer hosts.

Directions: Located at 25 Phillips Street, Franklin.

Facilities: A limited number of gems and minerals for sale, restrooms.

Dates: May 1–Oct 31.

Fees: None.

For more information: Phone (704) 369-7831.

COWEETA HYDROLOGIC LABORATORY

[Fig. 32(30)] Established in 1934, Coweeta Hydrologic Laboratory is a unit of the Forest Service's Southeastern Research Station. In cooperation with more than 130 scientists throughout the nation, it helps determine the effects of human use on forest growth and ecology. Visitors can drive through the experimental forest for most of the year to see forest-management practices in hydrology, engineering, and silviculture. Silviculture is the tending of forests from an ecological standpoint and involves efforts such as regeneration and management practices for sustainability. A self-guiding brochure is available at the station office.

Directions: The office is located on Coweeta Lab Road, which is accessed by turning right off US 441 South, 10 miles south of Franklin. The lab is 3 miles down the Coweeta Lab Road.

Dates: Office open Mon.–Fri.

For more information: Phone (704) 524-2128.

Wayah Bald Area

[Fig. 32(9), Fig. 34(4)] The Wayah Bald Area became part of the Nantahala National Forest domain soon after the passage of the Weeks Act in 1912. A stone observation tower at the summit of the area's highest point, Wayah Bald (5,385 feet), frames the awesome vistas of the Great Smoky and Unicoi mountains towering above the Nantahala and Little Tennessee river valleys. Built in 1937 by the Civilian Conservation Corps, the tower was originally used for fire detection and rose 60 feet above the summit. Over the years, water damaged the structure, and in 1947 the top two floors were removed; in 1983, a hemlock-beam and cedar-shake roof was added. The bald continues to be a popular destination for hikers and those seeking the natural beauty so evident in May and June when the rhododendron, azaleas, and other wildflowers bloom. (For more on balds, see the Natural History of the North Carolina Mountains, page 1.)

Evidence of Indian use of the bald as hunting grounds dates back to 300 B.C. *Wayah* is a Cherokee word for "wolf," an appropriate name prior to the arrival of European settlers. Red wolves roamed in abundance here until the middle of the nineteenth century when a bounty on them led to their eradication.

Though Wayah is called a bald, strictly speaking the bald area is rather small. It is surrounded by oaks, though they are stunted and pruned by the strong winds and icy winter weather. Birds along the bald include late-spring and summer varieties such as the ruffed grouse, rufous-sided towhee, white-breasted nuthatch, ovenbird, veery (*Hylocichla fuscenscens*), solitary vireo (*Vireo solitarius*), scarlet tanager (*Piranga olivacea*), golden-crowned kinglet (*Regulus satrapa*), a variety of warblers, and sometimes the yellow-bellied sapsucker (*Sphyrapicus varius*).

The Appalachian Trail and Bartram Trail cross here, and a number of shorter trails radiate from the area (*see* Long Trails, page 283).

Directions: From Franklin, travel west on US 64 for 3 miles to Old Murphy Road where there is a Wayah Bald sign. Turn right and drive .2 mile to Wayah Road (SR 1310). Turn left and continue for 9 miles to Wayah Gap and FR 69. (Wayah Crest Picnic Area is on the left.) Turn right onto FR 69 and drive 4.4 miles to the Wayah Bald parking area. The road can be rugged in places, though the area is well traveled.

Activities: Hiking, picnicking.

Facilities: Pit toilets on the paved road to the summit, small picnic area.

Dates: Open year-round.

Fees: None.

Closest town: Franklin, 15 miles.

HELLBENDER (Cryptobranchus alleganiensis)
The hellbender grows to 29 inches.

Southern Nantahala & Standing Indian

The Standing Indian basin is a horseshoe-shaped drainage formed by the Nantahala and Blue Ridge mountains with several peaks higher than 5,000 feet.

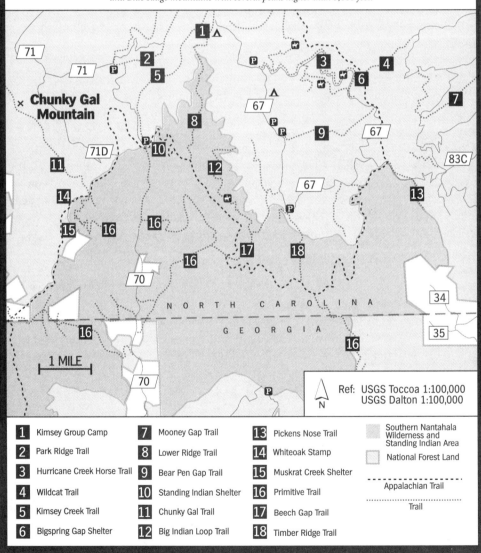

× Chunky Gal Mountain

NORTH CAROLINA

GEORGIA

1 MILE

Ref: USGS Toccoa 1:100,000
USGS Dalton 1:100,000

N

1 Kimsey Group Camp	**7** Mooney Gap Trail	**13** Pickens Nose Trail
2 Park Ridge Trail	**8** Lower Ridge Trail	**14** Whiteoak Stamp
3 Hurricane Creek Horse Trail	**9** Bear Pen Gap Trail	**15** Muskrat Creek Shelter
4 Wildcat Trail	**10** Standing Indian Shelter	**16** Primitive Trail
5 Kimsey Creek Trail	**11** Chunky Gal Trail	**17** Beech Gap Trail
6 Bigspring Gap Shelter	**12** Big Indian Loop Trail	**18** Timber Ridge Trail

Southern Nantahala
Wilderness and
Standing Indian Area

National Forest Land

- - - - - - - - - -
Appalachian Trail

....
Trail

Southern Nantahala Wilderness Area/ Standing Indian Area

[Fig. 36] The Southern Nantahala Wilderness was created by the 1984 Wilderness Acts in both North Carolina and Georgia and is managed as part of the Nantahala National Forest in North Carolina and the Chattahoochee National Forest in Georgia. It includes 23,714 acres at the southern end of the Blue Ridge Mountains. Elevations range from 2,400 feet to 5,499 feet on Standing Indian Mountain. The area includes numerous peaks taller than 4,000 feet and is characterized by steep, rugged terrain dissected by several streams and drainages that feed the Nantahala, Tallulah, and Hiwassee rivers. Typically, the forest cover is dense and varies from spruce-fir and grass-heath balds at the higher elevations to mixed hardwoods at middle elevations.

Standing Indian Mountain, the highest point in the Southern Nantahala Wilderness, stands as a sentinel, watching over the diverse range of habitats and wildlife on its descending slopes and in the wetlands and river basin below. According to Cherokee myth, the 5,499-foot peak is the stone remains of an actual watchman, an Indian warrior sent to the mountaintop to keep a lookout for the winged monster that had stolen a village child. When the Great Spirit answered the village's prayers and destroyed the monster with a furious lightning storm, the mountain was shattered and the lone scout was turned to stone. The legend also "explains" the treeless heath or shrub bald summit, covered primarily with purple rhododendron.

Farther below, the ridge supports pine and hemlock groves, mountain laurel, and red and white oak forests with fern, azalea, and blueberry understory. Some drier, almost bare soil areas down the 1.5-mile ridgeline are covered with a rare tundra species, the three-leaved cinquefoil (*Potentilla tridentata*). This threatened plant exists here at the southern periphery of its range.

The Standing Indian basin is a horseshoe-shaped drainage formed by the Nantahala and Blue Ridge mountains, which include several peaks higher than 5,000 feet. Numerous trails wind through the basin along old roadbeds, including 17.7 miles of orange-blazed trails designated as horse trails: Big Indian Loop Trail [Fig. 36(12)] (8 miles, moderate to difficult), Blackwell Gap Trail (4.2 miles, moderate) and Hurricane Creek Loop Trail (5.5. miles, moderate). The abundance of trails, higher elevations and the resulting cooler temperatures, and beautiful scenery through the forest and along streambeds makes this a popular destination for horseback riders from across the Southeast. Primitive camping featuring 20 sites and 40 hitching posts for horses is available at Hurricane Creek beyond the developed Standing Indian Campground.

A network of loop trails throughout the area connects with the strenuous, 5-mile (round-trip) hike to the top of Standing Indian. (Standing Indian Area trail maps are available through the Forest Service.) In addition, the Appalachian Trail, at its highest point south of the Smoky Mountains, skirts the southern and eastern ridge of the basin, serving as a master connector route. The purple rhododendron and flame azalea make this section of the Appalachian Trail especially stunning in late spring and early summer. Off the trail, deep in the ridge forest, pits remain as relics of a time when mica was mined in the area.

The Nantahala River, which flows through the Standing Indian Basin (and through the Standing Indian Campground), provides excellent trout-fishing opportunities. Along the river's upper route, varieties of salamanders, frogs, turtles, and rare plants thrive in the area's bogs, swamps, and marshes. The hardwood forests create habitats for a range of wildlife including bear, wild boar, white-tailed deer, ruffed grouse, owls, and hawks.

Forests in this area are virtually all second growth. In the 1920s, the Ritter Lumber Company began operating one of its main logging camps out of the basin and removed most of the virgin timber by the early 1930s. Today, 11,944 acres are protected in North Carolina as the Southern Nantahala Wilderness Area (additional acreage lies in Georgia). The beautifully landscaped Standing Indian Campground is on the site of the former logging camp.

Nearby, the second-largest poplar in the United States survives. The John Waslik Memorial Poplar, named after a former Wayah District ranger, was too large for the company's oxen to haul out, so it was left standing. The giant tree is 25 feet in circumference and, until a storm blew its top off, was 125 feet tall.

Directions: To reach the Standing Indian Campground, take US 64 west out of Franklin for approximately 9 miles. Take a left on Wallace Gap Road (sign will say "Old US 64") and follow it 1.5 miles to FR 67. Turn right and go 1.5 miles to the entrance.

Activities: Hiking, fishing.

Facilities: Standing Indian Campground: 84 campsites, picnic area, hiking trails. Hurricane Creek primitive camping for horses.

Dates: Wilderness area open year-round. Campground open Apr. 1–Nov.

Fees: A fee is charged for campsites.

Closest town: Franklin, approximately 10 miles.

For more information: U.S. Forest Service, 90 Sloan Road, Franklin, NC 28734. Phone (704) 524-4410.

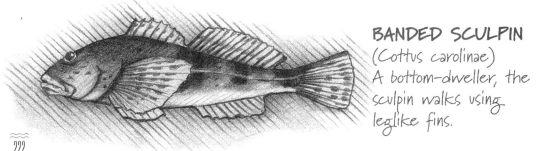

BANDED SCULPIN
(Cottus carolinae)
A bottom-dweller, the sculpin walks using leglike fins.

Little-Known Fishes of Western North Carolina

As with so many other plants and animals found in Western North Carolina, the freshwater fish that occur here are more diverse than those found in other parts of the United States. The unique geology of the Blue Ridge Mountains and the rivers within them contributed to this wide range of fish species, as well as their distribution.

Disjointed ridges and valleys created by mountain-building activities that occurred millions of years ago separated various river drainage systems. Fish populations in these systems were either cut off from one another or entered new river basins and slowly evolved into different species.

While the term "freshwater fish" usually brings to mind such game fish as largemouth bass or sunfish, there are, in the southern Appalachians, a far greater number of small fish. These fish are well adapted to shallow, fast-running mountain creeks and tributaries. Often called minnows, and believed by many to be one type of fish species, there are, in fact, dozens of different species and subspecies, many exhibiting vividly colorful patterns.

There are several groups of small fish that many call minnows. The Cyprinid family contains, among others, minnows, shiners, dace, and chub. The Percid family includes perch but is almost entirely composed of darters. The snail darter found in the Little Tennessee River became the most famous of this group during the controversial construction of the Tellico Dam in the 1970s. It was believed that the dam would wipe out the endangered snail darter, but construction was completed nonetheless. Other snail darter populations were subsequently found in nearby drainages.

Streams are made up of different habitats, including deep, swift-flowing runs, deep quiet pools, and riffles—shallow fast-flowing currents that flow over boulders and rocks. Darters are found in riffles, bass and sunfish prefer pools, and minnows generally inhabit runs. Some minnows reach several feet in length, although the various minnows found in Western North Carolina mountain streams average only about 4 inches. About 25 species of minnows can be found in the state's mountain tributaries and rivers, including both carnivorous and herbivorous varieties.

Darters, so named for their quick movement, live and feed on the bottom of streams and are not easy to spot from above the surface. There are more than 20 species that occur in Western North Carolina, some restricted to small areas.

Ichthyologists, those who study the fishes, believe that populations of various darters and minnows were separated or combined by stream capture. The rivers flowing to the Atlantic have eroded faster than those flowing into the Mississippi basin, and at various times in the past, the eastern-flowing rivers have intercepted the headwaters of westward flowing rivers, thus capturing those streams. This interception may have influenced differences in such species as the turquoise, sea green, and Swannanoa darters. That all three species are similar implies that this separation occurred relatively recently.

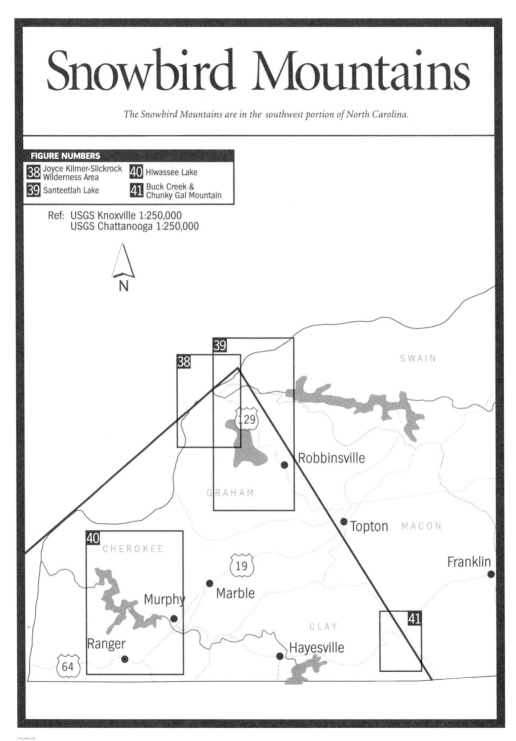

Snowbird Mountains

The Snowbird Mountains are in the southwest portion of North Carolina.

FIGURE NUMBERS

38	Joyce Kilmer-Slickrock Wilderness Area	**40**	Hiwassee Lake
39	Santeetlah Lake	**41**	Buck Creek & Chunky Gal Mountain

Ref: USGS Knoxville 1:250,000
USGS Chattanooga 1:250,000

The Snowbird Mountains

The Snowbird Mountains section [Fig. 37] lies in the extreme southwestern portion of the state, shaped primarily by the Great Smoky Mountains and the Unicoi Mountains (the southernmost mountains in the Unaka range). The Snowbird Mountains are a less significant cross range, but they were chosen to identify this section because the name Snowbird is associated with this area of the state. Other ranges that define this rugged and isolated region include the Cheoah and Yellow Creek mountains. The states of Georgia and Tennessee and the Great Smoky Mountains National Park form most of this section's geographic boundaries.

Some of the state's most spectacular forests thrive here, in part because this area is decidedly less developed than other parts of Western North Carolina. Certainly the forests and wildlife benefit from less human intervention, but the other side of the coin is less money to maintain the resources and foster their appreciation.

[*Above*: Huge poplars grow in the Joyce Kilmer–Slickrock Wilderness Area]

This section, for example, does not include the Blue Ridge Parkway; however, the Snowbird Mountains section recently saw the opening of a new road that is already bringing new opportunities. Opened in October 1996, the 17.5-mile Cherohala Skyway runs from Santeetlah Gap in North Carolina to Beech Gap at the Tennessee state line. The skyway ranges in elevation from 3,000 feet at Santeetlah Gap, to its highest point at Haw Knob at 5,472 feet, and down again to 4,490 feet at Beech Gap. The name Cherohala is a combination of the names of the national forests through which it runs—Cherokee in Tennessee and Nantahala in North Carolina.

The U.S. Forest Service has given the same attention to blending the road in with its environment as workers did earlier this century on the Blue Ridge Parkway. Guardrails are a natural rusted brown to blend with the earth and trees. Scenic overlooks are defined by attractive rock walls. Some overlooks, such as the one at Spirit Ridge, are handicapped accessible and offer expansive views of the magnificent landscape of Joyce Kilmer–Slickrock Wilderness and Snowbird Creek basin. Other overlooks connect with hiking trails such as the one to Hooper Bald, elevation 5,429 feet, near where the wild Russian boar was first introduced to North Carolina (*see* Snowbird Area, page 225). Interpretive stations, restrooms, and picnic areas are also planned.

The Joyce Kilmer–Slickrock Wilderness [Fig. 37(38), Fig. 38] is perhaps the best-known destination in the Snowbird Mountains section. The magnificent virgin and old-growth forests, mercifully preserved in spite of the overlogging experienced throughout Western North Carolina, harbor ancient trees that grow to a height of more than 150 feet and a girth of 20 feet. A number of man-made lakes—Fontana, Cheoah, Calderwood, and Santeetlah—are also popular sites for camping, fishing, and hiking.

COPPERHEAD
(*Agkistrodon contortrix*)
The copperhead is a pit viper with a sensory pit between its eyes that detects prey.

CATAWBA RHODODENDRON
(Rhododendron catawbiense)
This shrub forms dense thickets on mountain slopes.

Rangers within the national forests are continually working to maintain and improve these natural treasures. At the Beech Creek Seed Orchard, located west of Murphy off FR 307, improved tree seeds for reforestation are developed and later supplied to the southern Appalachian forests. These genetically improved seeds of white, shortleaf, and Virginia pines provide foresters with an opportunity to grow more and better wood throughout the national forests. The orchard has extensive hardwood clone banks of black cherry, oak, and yellow-poplar.

In 1994, the North Carolina Department of Transportation designated a scenic byway through the area known as Indian Lakes Scenic Byway, taking its name from the lakes along its route. The picturesque, though sometimes sharply curving, route courses through the Stecoah Valley along NC 28 west from Almond to Fontana Lake and past the Cheoah Lake and Dam. The destination-rich route then continues on US 129 south to the Santeetlah Dam and Lake, through the town of Robbinsville, and past Tallulah (Cherokee for "cry of the frog") Creek, which joins Sweetwater Creek to form the Cheoah River. At US 19/74 the route ends just south of the Nantahala Gorge.

For more information on hiking, picnicking, boating, fitness/jogging trails, and historical and forest-management interpretive trails within this section as well as the wilderness, backcountry, and lakes, contact the Cheoah Ranger Station, phone (704) 479-6431. The office is located adjacent to Lake Santeetlah on SR 1116, 2 miles north of Robbinsville off US 129. Office hours are 8:00 to 4:30, Monday through Friday, year-round. Extended summer-season days and hours are possible. A Civilian Conservation Corps campsite, Camp Santeetlah, which previously occupied the site, is interpreted by a 2.5-mile trail to a scenic overlook of the mountains.

Joyce Kilmer– Slickrock Wilderness

The U.S. Forest Service purchased 13,055 acres in the Little Santeetlah Basin from Gennett Lumber Company in 1935 for $28 an acre, thereby preserving what is now the Joyce Kilmer–Slickrock Wilderness.

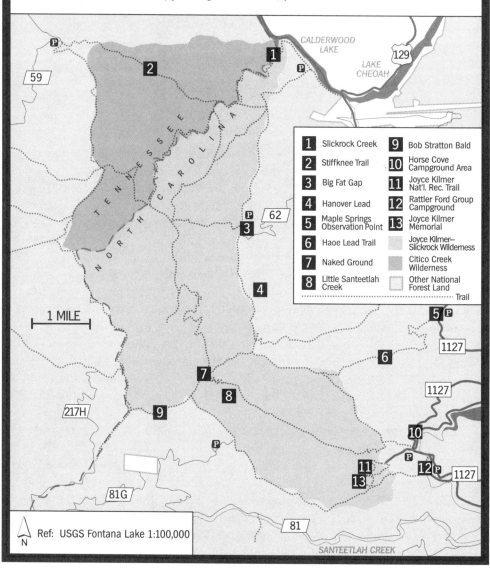

1	Slickrock Creek	**9**	Bob Stratton Bald
2	Stiffknee Trail	**10**	Horse Cove Campground Area
3	Big Fat Gap	**11**	Joyce Kilmer Nat'l. Rec. Trail
4	Hanover Lead	**12**	Rattler Ford Group Campground
5	Maple Springs Observation Point	**13**	Joyce Kilmer Memorial
6	Haoe Lead Trail		Joyce Kilmer–Slickrock Wilderness
7	Naked Ground		Citico Creek Wilderness
8	Little Santeetlah Creek		Other National Forest Land

1 MILE

Ref: USGS Fontana Lake 1:100,000

N

Joyce Kilmer–Slickrock Wilderness Area

[Fig. 37(38), Fig. 38] Joyce Kilmer–Slickrock was designated a wilderness area with the passage of the 1975 Wilderness Act. Nine years later, when the 1984 North Carolina Wilderness Act went into effect, the original 14,033 acres increased to the present 17,013 acres. Joyce Kilmer–Slickrock shares a common boundary along the Unicoi Mountains with the Citico Creek Wilderness in the Cherokee National Forest in Tennessee. Portions of the Joyce Kilmer–Slickrock Wilderness Area are actually in the Cherokee National Forest, although the majority of its lands are in the Nantahala National Forest in North Carolina.

The two dominant watersheds in the wilderness area are the Little Santeetlah Creek and Slickrock Creek, which are joined by a common ridgeline at their headwaters. Their basins are steep and rugged, with elevations ranging from only 1,086 feet at the mouth of Slickrock Creek to 5,341 feet on Stratton Bald. Rock outcrops are common, and a network of streams dissect the terrain. Only in the higher ridges do heath or grass balds break the dense hardwood forests that blanket the slopes.

The shining star of this wilderness area is the Joyce Kilmer Memorial Forest—the kind of place that brings out the poet in all of us. The 3,840-acre preserve was named after the poet who wrote the poem "Trees," although Kilmer never saw the virgin poplar and hemlocks here that have graced the earth for 400 years, some reaching 150 feet in height and 20 feet in circumference. Inside their sheltered canopy, the atmosphere is decidedly different from other forests. It is quieter, the birds so high in the treetops that their songs are hard to hear. The understory is markedly different, too, not nearly so lush or overwhelming as in second-growth forests still evolving. To say the forest is like a cathedral is no literary excess—its majesty and peacefulness create an other-worldly atmosphere. Tall trees form columns and arches that seem to draw thoughts and energy skyward. A soft carpet of bright green moss and multihued lichens soften our earthbound existence.

Much of the surrounding land in the region was logged by timber companies. Babcock Land and Timber Company, which logged the surrounding Slickrock Creek area, owned the Little Santeetlah Creek basin that forms the Joyce Kilmer Memorial Forest. Over the years, other timber companies have held the deed, yet, for a variety of reasons, they never logged it.

Officially, the memorial forest was saved from destruction in 1936 after a long series of seemingly unrelated events that ranged from bankruptcy and bravery to warfare and the welfare of a small mountain river basin. Alfred Joyce Kilmer wrote his now-famous poem "Trees" in honor of a magnificent white oak tree on the campus of Rutgers College in New Jersey, where he attended school from 1904 to 1906. He eventually became an editor at the *New York Times* and continued to write and publish his poetry. "Trees" was first published in his second book of poetry in 1914, the year that World War I began. In 1917, when the United States entered the war, Kilmer enlisted and went to France, where, on July 30, 1918, he was killed during a reconnaissance mission. The French government awarded him the *Croix de Guerre* for his bravery.

The brave yet gentle spirit of Kilmer was not easily forgotten. In 1934, a New York chapter of the Veterans of Foreign Wars petitioned the federal government to find an appropriate memorial for Kilmer. The government agreed and asked the U.S. Forest Service to locate a tract of virgin forest in the eastern United States—not an easy task given the unregulated logging the mountains had suffered. By chance the forest in the Little Santeetlah basin had been spared. A series of odd circumstances contributed to its survival, such as the construction of two lakes—Calderwood and Santeetlah— that flooded the rail system necessary for transporting the timber out of the region and the bankruptcy of a logging company just before it was ready to use its recently constructed splash dams to float out the trees. Finally, the U.S. Forest Service purchased 13,055 acres in the Little Santeetlah basin from Gennett Lumber Company in 1935 for $28 an acre—an exorbitant price at a time when most land was selling for only $4 an acre. But it was worth it, and the Joyce Kilmer Memorial Forest was dedicated on July 30, 1936, 18 years to the day after the poet's death. In 1975, Congress designated the Joyce Kilmer–Slickrock Wilderness, which included the memorial forest.

The Joyce Kilmer National Recreation Trail [Fig. 38(11)] is an easy 2-mile trek through the forest along two loops: the 1.25-mile lower loop and the .75-mile upper loop coursing through Poplar Cove, a rich, fertile grove hosting the largest trees in the forest. The two loops converge at the Joyce Kilmer Memorial [Fig. 38(13), Fig. 39(1)], a large boulder with a plaque to the fallen soldier-poet. In spring, before the canopy filters out the sunlight, wildflowers are abundant along the pathways. A variety of violets, trilliums (of proportions as impressive as the trees), solomon's seal

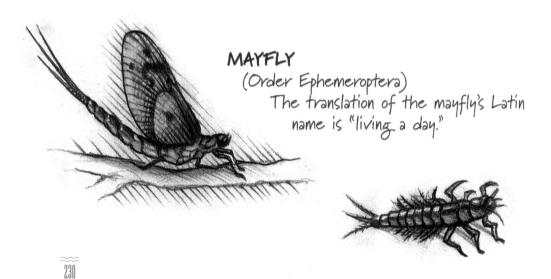

MAYFLY
(Order Ephemeroptera)
The translation of the mayfly's Latin name is "living a day."

Naturalists in Western North Carolina

The rich and diverse forest communities in Western North Carolina have long attracted important visitors to the region. Of the early naturalists, John Bartram and his son William are especially prominent. The Bartrams traveled through Western North Carolina and other southeastern colonies, describing the local ecology and collecting plant specimens. In 1791, after his final southern pilgrimage, William published an extensive account describing the Southeast based upon his and his father's explorations. *Bartram's Travels* established his credibility as a leading naturalist in both North America and Europe, and the work has become a literary classic of natural history.

In May of 1785, botanist André Michaux left pre-Revolutionary France to study the plants of the New World and quickly focused on the southern Appalachians' unique plants. When Michaux reached the summit of Grandfather Mountain in 1794 after a four-day climb, his emotions burst forth. "Reached the summit of the highest mountain of all North America," his diary notes, "and, with my companion and guide sang the 'Marseillaise' and shouted 'Long live America and the Republic of France, long live liberty, equality, and fraternity.'" Grandfather Mountain, of course, is not the nation's highest, but at 5,964 feet it certainly must have seemed so to Michaux. During his life in America, Michaux prepared and sent back to France 60,000 plant and seed specimens, many of which he discovered in the mountains of North Carolina. These included purple rhododendron (*Rhododendron catawbiense*), a buttercup (*Ranunculus hispidus*), crabapple (*Malus angustifolia*), and an elderberry species (*Sambucus pubens*).

Michaux collected and described a rare specimen that lay unknown in his collection in France for many years after his death. Eventually, an early- nineteenth-century scientist named Asa Gray discovered the plant in Michaux's herbarium and published a description, naming it after Kentucky botanist Charles Short. *Shortia galicifolia*, commonly known as oconee bells, suddenly became a treasure, and many botanists and gardeners searched the Blue Ridge region for years in hopes of finding the plant. It was finally rediscovered in several areas in North Carolina and South Carolina. Rare even in Michaux's time, oconee bells remains an endangered species today. While numerous other naturalists studied North Carolina's mountain ecology, two others are of special significance. Asa Gray was most notable for publishing *Gray's Manual of Botany* which remains a standard college reference.

Eighteenth-century Scottish botanist John Fraser made several trips through the region and has been honored by having a native fir tree named after him. Fraser fir (*Abies fraseri*) is the only fir native to the southern Appalachians and has become one of the most popular Christmas trees widely grown by Western North Carolina farmers and nurseries. The umbrella tree (*Magnolia fraseri*), a mountain magnolia with large graceful leaves, also bears his name.

(*Polygonatum biflorum*), galax (*Galax aphylla*), crested dwarf iris (*Iris cristata*), jack-in-the-pulpit (*Arisaema triphyllum*), and carpets of ferns fill the understory.

In addition to the mighty yellow-poplar (*Liriodendron tulipifera*) and Eastern hemlock (*Tsuga canadensis*), the forest harbors red oak (*Quercus rubra*), basswood (*Tilia americana*), red maple (*Acer rubrum*), American beech (*Fagus grandifolia*), yellow birch (*Betula lutea*), Carolina silverbell (*Halesia carolina*), dogwood (*Cornus florida*), and witch-hazel (*Hamamelis virginiana*), among others. Birds are hard to spot in these tall treetops, but the songs of the downy woodpecker (*Dendrocopos pubsecens*), wood thrush (*Hylocichla mustelina*), solitary and red-eyed vireo (*Vireo solitarius* and *Vireo flavoviridis*), ovenbird (*Seiurus aurocapillus*), golden-crowned kinglet (*Regulus satrapa*), scarlet tanager (*Piranga olivacea*), and brown creeper (*Certhia familiaris*) have been reported.

COMMON FOXGLOVE

(Digitalis purpurea) This is the source of digitalis, a drug used to treat heart disease.

Never is the sound of water far away, either—the rushing Little Santeetlah closer to the trailhead or the trickling tributaries on their way toward bigger waters. While the trail is only 2 miles in length, the walk takes much longer than average because there is so much to see along the way. (And the frequent craning to see mighty treetops has caused more than a few stiff necks!) Even the dead and down trees are like magnificent sculpture, coming to life again with a host of mosses, lichens, fungi, and wildflowers growing in their decaying mass.

Because the forest is in a designated wilderness, dead or dying trees are not removed. Sadly, some of the huge trees are dying, which increases the potential for falling limbs and trees. A large sign at the trailhead cautions against walking here on windy days or after a snowfall or ice storm when branches and trees are more likely to fall. Also watch out for hunters. Hunting and fishing are popular in the memorial forest and the Slickrock Wilderness, especially bear and boar hunting from mid-October until the end of the year (except for two weeks in late November and early December set aside for deer season).

The trail network within the entire Slickrock Wilderness Area offers more than 60 miles of trails carefully laid out to allow access to the many topographic regions within the wilderness, such as rock outcrops; rich, moist coves; virgin and old-growth forests; boulder-strewn creeks; and grass and heath balds. The trails also were designed to interconnect and, therefore, allow extended hikes through the wilderness. Because this is a wilderness area, with the exception of the paths at Joyce Kilmer Memorial Forest, the trails are primitive, rugged, and virtually unmarked. Some are easy to follow or are used enough to make the pathway obvious. Others, however, are more difficult, and like any wilderness experience, they require a topographic map and compass.

Wilderness areas are often associated with serenity and solitude. As interest in this area grows, however, some trails and sections are more popular than others. According to the Joyce Kilmer–Slickrock map from the U.S. Forest Service, the trails within the wilderness that offer the least opportunity for solitude include Joyce Kilmer National Recreation Trail, Naked Ground [Fig. 38(7)], Big Fat Gap [Fig. 38(3)], Hanover Lead [Fig. 38(4)], Slickrock Creek [Fig. 38(1)], Stiffknee Trail [Fig. 38(2)], and Falls Branch Falls Trail. Stratton Bald, on the other hand, offers a journey into virgin forest on a quiet and peaceful trail. The trailhead is found easily just across the Santeetlah Creek from the Rattler Ford Group Campground near Joyce Kilmer. Though it is rated "most difficult," other than a few rocky segments, it is a moderate, easy trail into a pristine virgin forest.

Bears and wild boars populate the wilderness and adjoining national forest. The wild boars (*Sus scrosa*), or "hogs," as they are referred to locally, were first introduced to the region in 1912, when 13 were imported to a private game preserve below Hooper Bald. Ox-drawn wagons carried the boars to their new home along with a number of buffalo, elk, mule deer, bears, wild turkeys, and thousands of ring-necked pheasant eggs. Eight years later, 100 boars escaped the confines of the preserve and over the years have multiplied into a growing problem. They are a hardy species, learning, adapting, and breeding quickly. A 125-pound boar can eat as much as 1,300 pounds of food in a six-month period, which, given the way they forage for food, tears up vast amounts of ground and disrupts plants and soil. This foraging in turn destroys groundcover and habitats and causes erosion and siltation. Boars thrive in all types of elevations and forests and as omnivores, on all kinds of food. Though they favor nuts, they will eat insects, salamanders, eggs, and small mammals, as well as wild yams and bulbs and roots of wildflowers.

As the hogs' numbers have grown, so have efforts to control them. In the nearby Great Smoky Mountains National Park, hunting, trapping, fencing, and luring have been tried with differing degrees of success and popularity. Some boars have been relocated from the park to the national forests, where they can be hunted. The efforts are ongoing as rangers at the national forest and Great Smoky Mountains National Park work toward a balanced solution.

Just outside the wilderness area in the Nantahala National Forest, Maple Springs Observation Area [Fig. 38(5)] offers a spectacular 180-degree view of the surrounding mountains. An easy 5-mile drive north of Joyce Kilmer on SR 1127, this is literally a road to nowhere. It began as part of the road first envisioned in the 1950s that today is known as Cherohala Highway. Construction began in 1965, but when the area was designated as wilderness, the road had to be rerouted along the Unicoi Crest. As a result, this earlier road now ends at the Maple Springs parking area; en route to its end, it also serves as access to the Haoe Lead Trail [Fig. 38(6)].

From the parking area, a wooden deck leads to a magnificent view of the surrounding mountains including the Snowbird, Great Smoky, Unicoi, and Cheoah ranges. On a sunny day, Santeetlah Lake glistens in the valley to the right, and the abundant mountain laurel (*Kalmia latifolia*) explodes with pink and white blossoms in early June.

This deck is handicapped accessible and offers easy access to a rewarding vista. At an elevation of 3,520 feet, the overlook affords opportunities to watch from above the aerial aerobics of a variety of summer birds such as the broad-winged and red-tailed hawk (*Buteo platypterus* and *B. jamaicensis*), cedar waxwing (*Bombycilla cedrorum*), great crested flycatcher (*Myiarchus crinitus*), American goldfinch (*Spinus tristis*), indigo bunting (*Passerina cyanea*), pileated woodpecker (*Dryocopus pileatus*), downy woodpecker, scarlet tanager, and numerous warblers.

Primitive camping sites are abundant throughout the wilderness area, and U.S. forest campgrounds are near the boundary. In addition, the U.S. Forest Service Horse Cove Campground Area [Fig. 38(10)] offers 17 units adjacent to the rushing mountain stream, Little Santeetlah Creek. The campground is located directly across from the entrance to Joyce Kilmer picnic area. Fishing is popular along and in the Little Santeetlah Creek and Slickrock Creek, as well as at nearby Santeetlah Lake (*see* Santeetlah Lake, page 237).

Directions: To Joyce Kilmer Memorial Forest: take US 129 north approximately 1 mile past Robbinsville. Turn left onto NC 143 west (marked with a sign for Joyce Kilmer). After approximately 3.5 miles, turn left onto SR 1127 and continue for approximately 9 miles. The entrance is well marked on the left. To access the wilderness's southern perimeter, start at the Cheoah Ranger Station and turn left onto SR 1116. Travel 2.4 miles and turn right onto SR 1127. Continue for 6.9 miles to an unmarked road; turn left and then turn immediately right onto FR 81 (gravel road). Travel 6.8 miles to FR 81F and turn right at the forest service sign. Wolf Laurel Hunter Camp is ahead 4.4 miles on the left, and the parking area, signboard, and trailhead for Wolf Laurel Trail another .5 mile. To enter the northern portion of the wilderness, travel on US 129 for 5.6 miles north of where it intersects Old US 129. At a bridge across the Cheoah River, turn left onto a narrow, gravel road, FR 62. Continue for 7.2 miles to a parking area and the trailhead for Big Fat Gap Trail.

Activities: Hiking, picnicking.

Facilities: Parking, picnic tables and grills, restrooms, water.

Fees: None.

Closest town: Robbinsville, 17 miles.

For more information: Cheoah Ranger Station, Route 1, Box 16A, Robbinsville, NC 28771. Phone (704) 479-6431. Tim Homan's *Hiking Trails of Joyce Kilmer–Slickrock and Citico Creek Wilderness Areas*.

Snowbird Area

[Fig. 32(5)] The Snowbird backcountry area lies in the Snowbird Creek basin near the convergence of the Snowbird and Unicoi mountain ranges. For centuries the area was hunted by the Cherokee, and due to its steep and rugged terrain, it was one of the last areas in Western North Carolina to be settled by European pioneers.

In the nearby town of Robbinsville lies the grave of Chief Junaluska, the Cherokee chief who saved Andrew Jackson's life in the 1814 Battle of Horseshoe against the Creek Indians. Years later, Jackson betrayed his rescuer when he signed the Indian Removal Act, and in turn the great Cherokee leader earned the name we know him by—Junaluska, meaning "he tried repeatedly but failed." A short walk from NC 143 just west of town leads up a flight of steps to the well-maintained grave and memorial plaque to the chief; his wife, Nicie, is buried next to him. During the Trail of Tears when the Cherokee were moved to Oklahoma, a number of Cherokee, led by Tsali (*see* Tsali, page 195), escaped exile by hiding in the remote wilderness of the Snowbirds. Today, approximately 300 direct descendants of these families live in the Little Snowbird community.

In 1943, the federal government acquired the Snowbird area as part of the Nantahala National Forest. Seven hiking trails covering 37 miles ascend the surrounding ranges and follow the Snowbird and Sassafras creeks. Like the nearby wilderness trails, these are purposely kept primitive and rugged; they are rated "easiest," "more difficult," and "most difficult" on the forest service map of the area. Big Snowbird Trail [Fig. 32(9)], for example, crosses the stream numerous times without the aid of bridges or footlogs. After heavy rains, trails may be impassable. Other trails in the area include Burntrock Ridge, King Meadows, Middle Falls, Mitchell Lick, Sassafras Creek, and Snowbird Mountain. Snowbird Creek offers excellent fishing opportunities for brook trout, rainbow trout (*Oncorhynchus mykiss*), and brown trout (*Salmo trutta*), although some fishing sites are accessible only by hiking along Big Snowbird Trail or wading upstream.

Sassafras Falls, Big Falls, Middle Falls, and Upper Falls are four waterfalls within the Snowbird Creek basin. These falls are all accessed off Big Snowbird Creek Trail, and some strenuous hiking is required to reach them. For a complete guide to their accessibility and beauty rating, refer to Kevin Adams's book, *North Carolina Waterfalls*.

For those wishing for a break from the wilderness experience, fine lodging and dining are available near Santeetlah Gap at the historic Snowbird Mountain Lodge. Listed on the National Register of Historic Places, the 22-room lodge features breathtaking views from a number of decks and overlooks, comfortable accommodations, and gourmet dinner and breakfast to rival any found in more likely locations such as Asheville or Highlands.

Directions: From the ranger station near Robbinsville, turn left (west) onto NC 143. After 2.3 miles turn right onto SR 1127. Travel slightly more than 2 miles and

Santeetlah Lake

The construction of Santeetlah Lake flooded the rail system necessary for transporting timber out of this region.

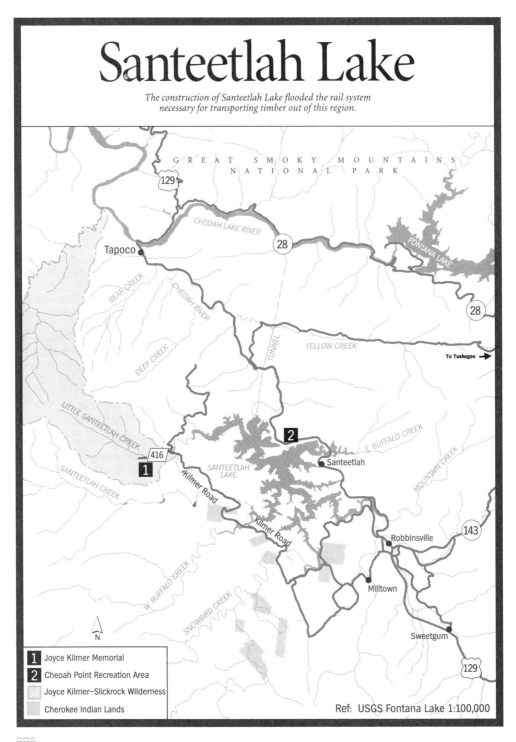

GREAT SMOKY MOUNTAINS
NATIONAL PARK

129

CHEOAH LAKE RIVER

28

Tapoco

FONTANA LAKE

28

BEAR CREEK

CHEOAH RIVER

TUNNEL

YELLOW CREEK

To Tuskegee →

DEEP CREEK

LITTLE SANTEETLAH CREEK

2

E. BUFFALO CREEK

416

1

SANTEETLAH LAKE

Santeetlah

MOUNTAIN CREEK

SANTEETLAH CREEK

Kilmer Road

Kilmer Road

Robbinsville

143

W. BUFFALO CREEK

Milltown

SNOWBIRD CREEK

Sweetgum

N

129

1 Joyce Kilmer Memorial
2 Cheoah Point Recreation Area
Joyce Kilmer–Slickrock Wilderness
Cherokee Indian Lands

Ref: USGS Fontana Lake 1:100,000

bear left at a fork onto SR 1115. After 2 miles the road turns sharply to the left. After another mile, cross a bridge and turn right (and cross another bridge) onto SR 1120. The road dead-ends after 6 miles (4 miles of which is gravel) at the trailheads.

Activities: Hiking, fishing, camping, picnicking.

Facilities: None.

Fees: None.

Closest town: Robbinsville, 13 miles.

Elevation: Snowbird Creek, 2,200 feet, to Hooper Bald, 5,429 feet.

Santeetlah Lake

[Fig. 39] In the midst of the lush, green mountain slopes, 3,000 acres of open water ideal for fishing, canoeing, and kayaking comprise Santeetlah Lake. (Its name is derived from an Indian word meaning "blue waters.") Santeetlah Lake is formed by the Santeetlah Dam across the Cheoah River on the northern end of the lake, and, like many of the man-made lakes in the mountains, Santeetlah makes its way into numerous picturesque coves and inlets. Most of the shoreline is undeveloped and part of the Nantahala National Forest, where ample camping opportunities abound. Cheoah Point [Fig. 39(2)], for example, can be reached 6 miles north of Robbinsville off US 129.

Both cold- and warm-water species of fish flourish here, including largemouth bass (*Micropterus salmoides*), smallmouth bass (*M. dolomieui*), walleye (*Stizostedion vitreum*), bluegill (*Lepomis macrochirus*), brown trout, and rainbow trout. Reports of osprey (*Pandion haliaetus*) and spotted sandpiper (*Actitis macalaria*) near the boating access area have been recorded in the spring and summer, and great horned owls (*Bubo virginianus*) have been spotted in the winter. During migration shorebirds and waterfowl including green herons (*Butorides virescens*), prothonotary warblers (*Protonotaria citrea*), and red crossbills (*Loxia curvirostra*) stop by the shallow coves of the many-fingered lake.

Directions: There are numerous access points. To reach Cheoah Point Recreation Area, travel on US 129 north from Robbinsville for 5 miles to the junction with SR 1145. Turn left and travel almost 1.5 miles to the campground on the left and the boat ramp ahead.

Activities: Hiking, camping, fishing, swimming, canoeing, kayaking.

Facilities: Boat ramp, swimming beach, campground. Cheoah Point Campground features 26 sites with picnic tables and grill, pit toilets, no shower.

Fees: There is a charge for camping.

Closest town: Robbinsville, 7 miles.

Elevation: 1,940 feet.

PEACHTREE MOUND AND VILLAGE SITE

[Fig. 32(13), Fig. 40(3)] According to experts, settlement at the convergence of the Peachtree Creek and the Hiwassee River in Cherokee County dates back to the Archaic period (8000 to 1000 B.C.), with ongoing occupation continuing until historic times.

Unfortunately, an unscientific exploration of the village site and mound in 1885 resulted in the removal of significant archeological material. In 1933, however, the Smithsonian Institution conducted a more careful excavation of the site, which investigators concluded was the ancient Cherokee village of Guasili. Numerous recorders of Hernando De Soto's gold expedition to the area in 1540 mention Guasili, where they report they were graciously received and entertained. The Smithsonian team found nearly 250,000 pieces of pottery at the Peachtree Village site and discovered 68 burial sites, some enclosed in stone-lined graves.

Indians built earthen mounds that were often used as burial sites. The Peachtree Mound, according to the Smithsonian report, was a multilevel ceremonial structure. At the base, a hard-packed floor was the foundation for a wood and stone building, covered by a earthen mound about 60 feet in diameter. A sand strata separated the first mound from a larger mound which was built later and appeared to have undergone at least two major periods of construction. Evidence of superimposed floors indicated that the second mound supported three separate ceremonial structures.

Directions: From Murphy, take Highway 64 east 2 miles. An historic marker on the right side of the road tells of Hernando De Soto's stop in the area. The mound is visible from the marker.

Closest town: Murphy, 2 miles.

For more information: Cherokee County Historical Museum, 205 Peachtree Street, Murphy, NC, 28906. Phone (704) 837-6792.

CAMPBELL FOLK SCHOOL

[Fig. 32(14)] Earlier this century, settlement schools were established in the mountains of North Carolina as a means of bringing improved education to the isolated coves and valleys. Farming practices and craft instruction, for instance, were taught in an effort to elevate the depressed economies of the region.

The Campbell Folk School in Brasstown grew out of the efforts of John C. Campbell, his wife Olive Dame, and their friend Marguerite Butler. At the turn of the century, Campbell and his new bride studied mountain life from Georgia to West Virginia. While John interviewed farmers about their agricultural practices, Olive collected mountain ballads and studied regional handicrafts.

The Campbells were intrigued by an approach to education in Denmark that had helped transform the countryside into a vibrant and creative force: the folk school, or "school for life." It was their hope that this alternative to traditional education, when applied to the southern Appalachians, would help change the pattern that had developed that led intelligent young people away from their family farms to work in the cities. John died in 1919, but Olive Dame and Marguerite Butler continued to study folk schools in Denmark, Sweden, and other countries.

When they returned to America full of enthusiasm, these two dynamic women had the wisdom to know that the effective implementation of such plans had to grow out of a genuine collaboration with the people. While exploring several potential locations, Miss Butler made a trip to Brasstown, where she explained the idea to local merchant, Fred O. Scroggs. Before leaving, she told him she would be back in a few weeks to see if any interest had been shown. The 200 people who later greeted her at the local church offered a resounding "Yes!" They pledged labor, building materials, and other support, including 75 acres of land donated by the Scroggs family. In 1925, the Folk School began its work.

That work continues today, although its focus has shifted with the times. Now designated an Historical District by the National Register of Historic Places, the Folk School's 27 buildings are the scene of many services to the community, a variety of special events, and an internationally recognized crafts instruction program. The 372-acre campus features fully equipped craft studios where people from all over the world come to learn pottery, weaving, spinning, dyeing, blacksmithing, stained glass, basketry, wood carving, woodworking, broom making, dollmaking, quilting, and many other crafts. In addition to crafts, the Folk School has been instrumental in preserving mountain music and dance traditions. A sawmill, meeting rooms, covered outdoor dance pavilion, nature trail, craft shop, vegetable garden, and rustic lodgings are scattered across the picturesque campus. While many buildings are in the style of typical Appalachian farm buildings, some were designed by a Belgian architect in a Romantic European style, adding to the unique ambiance and quickly impressing on any first-time visitor that something special is going on here.

Campbell Folk School and other settlement schools in the area—Penland School of Crafts (see page 80) and Arrowmont School of Art & Craft in nearby Gatlinburg, Tennessee—were originally founded by urban social workers to teach country people city ways. Ironically, today these schools are in great demand to teach weary city dwellers the ways of these magnificent mountains.

Directions: From Murphy, travel east on US 64 for 5 miles. Turn right at Tri-County Community College onto Old US 64. Travel 2 miles to Brasstown Road. Turn right; the entrance is on the left.

Sports: Hiking, dancing, nature walks.

Facilities: Lodging, studios, dance pavilion, craft shop, meeting rooms.

Fees: There is a charge for classes.

Closest town: Brasstown.

Elevation: 1,600 feet.

For more information: Campbell Folk School, One Folk School Road, Brasstown, NC 28902-9603. Phone (800) FOLK-SCH.

Hiwassee Lake

Hiwassee Lake is 6,090 acres and has almost 180 miles of shoreline;
it measures 22 miles long and more than 200 feet deep in places.

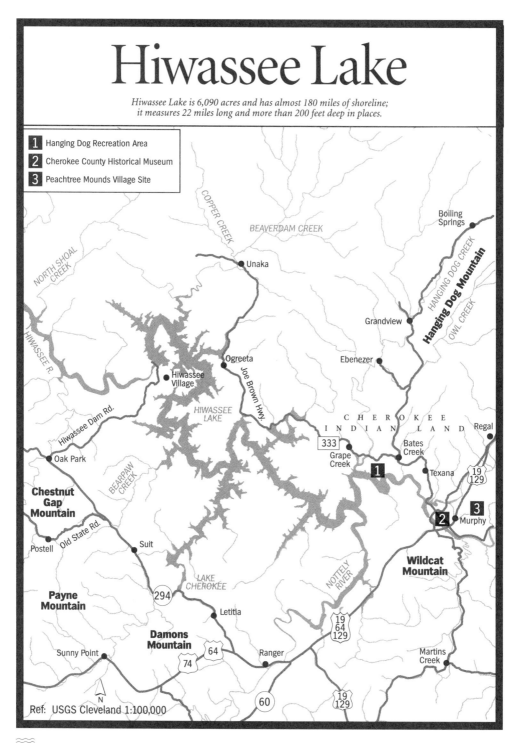

1 Hanging Dog Recreation Area
2 Cherokee County Historical Museum
3 Peachtree Mounds Village Site

COPPER CREEK

BEAVERDAM CREEK

Boiling
Springs

NORTH SHOAL CREEK

Unaka

HANGING DOG CREEK

OWL CREEK

Hanging Dog Mountain

Grandview

HIWASSEE R.

Ogreeta

Ebenezer

Hiwassee
Village

Joe Brown Hwy.

HIWASSEE
LAKE

C H E R O K E E
I N D I A N   L A N D   Regal

333

Bates
Creek

Hiwassee Dam Rd.

Grape
Creek

1

Oak Park

Texana

19
129

BEARPAW CREEK

**Chestnut
Gap
Mountain**

2 Murphy

3

Postell   Old State Rd.   Suit

LAKE
CHEROKEE

**Wildcat
Mountain**

NOTTELY RIVER

**Payne
Mountain**

294

Letitia

19
64
129

**Damons
Mountain**   64

Sunny Point

Ranger

Martins
Creek

74

60

19
129

N

Hiwassee Lake and River

[Fig. 40] Surrounded by the Nantahala National Forest, Lake Hiwassee offers spectacular scenery and tranquility. Fed primarily by the Hiwassee, Nottley, and Valley rivers, this beautiful, green mountain lake covers 6,090 acres with almost 180 miles of shoreline; it measures 22 miles long and more than 200 feet deep in places. The Tennessee Valley Authority dam, also named Hiwassee, was completed in 1940 for flood control and electric power. At 307 feet, it is the highest overspill dam in the world. As its waters head west, Lake Hiwassee feeds into Appalachia Lake. In conjunction with Lake Chatuge (*see* Lake Chatuge, page 248), these three lakes along the Tusquitee River are collectively referred to as the Chain of Lakes, offering boating, water-skiing, swimming, and fishing opportunities against a picturesque mountain backdrop.

The National Freshwater Fishing Hall of Fame lists a record catch of a 54-pound striped bass (*Morone saxatilis*) from Lake Hiwassee. Other fish within the reservoirs include bluegill, yellow perch (*Perca flavescens*), and muskie (*Esox masquinongy*). Boating and canoeing/kayaking enthusiasts will find easy access to the water at the Hanging Dog Recreation Area on Lake Hiwassee with a campground, picnic area, hiking trails, and a boat launching ramp. In Murphy access is available to the Hiwassee River. This Class I and II whitewater river is 18.3 miles long with a 3-mile stretch designated as a Trophy Trout Stream. Family rafting and tubing trips can be arranged by outfitters in the area. Because Appalachia Lake has no developed recreation areas, it is an excellent option for those seeking solitude during the busy summer season.

The Unicoi Turnpike once ran by the source of the Hiwassee River in Unicoi Gap on its way to Great Echota, the ancient capital and sacred Peace Town of the Cherokee Nation. The Cherokees called the river *Ayuhwa'si*, meaning a "savannah or meadow."

Directions: To reach the Hanging Dog Recreation Area [Fig. 40(1)], from Murphy travel 4.4 miles northwest on Peachtree Road (later becomes Joe Brown Highway). The entrance is on the left.

Activities: Camping, hiking, boating, water skiing, tubing, and fishing.

Facilities: Three public docks and boat launching ramps; boat rentals; bait and equipment shop. Camping at Hanging Dog Recreation Area includes 66 sites on 4 loops in a wooded area along the shore with restrooms but no showers.

Fees: There is a charge for camping.

Closest town and mileage: Murphy, 4.4 miles.

EARLY MOREL

(Verpa bohemica)
Growing up to 4 inches tall, this morel is identified by a yellow-brown, bell-shaped cap atop a hollow, light-colored stem. It grows in wet areas.

Fires Creek

[Fig. 32(16)] Serious outdoors lovers take note: The Fires Creek area—tucked away in the extreme southwest corner of North Carolina amid some of the most remote and pristine scenery in the eastern United States—offers varied opportunities for superb interaction with the natural world. Its more than 21,000 acres, which shelter abundant flora and fauna, are ideal for hiking, backpacking, camping, hunting, and fishing.

The most unusual geological feature in Fires Creek is the "bowls" or basins occurring atop Potrock Bald (reached via the Trail Ridge Trail from Bristol Horse Camp). Local legend says these unique depressions, of uncertain origin, were used by the Cherokee,

Fairy Crosses

In spite of the legends and superstitions that surround fairy crosses (also known as fairy stones and fairy tears), these unique, cross-shaped stones do have a scientific explanation. Found in rocks that have been subjected to great heat and pressure, fairy stones are composed of staurolite, a combination of silica, iron, and aluminum. Together, these minerals often crystallize in twin form and appear on the stones in a crosslike structure.

Staurolite stones (from the Greek word *Stauros*, meaning "cross") are most commonly shaped like St. Andrew's and Roman crosses. For many years, people have used fairy stones as good luck charms, believing that they protect the wearer against witchcraft, sickness, accidents, and disaster. It is claimed that three U.S. presidents carried fairy stones as talismans.

The Cherokee are particularly fond of these stones. One Cherokee legend explains that fairy crosses are the fallen tears of the Yunwi Tsunsdi, or Little People, tiny, fairylike spirits known for their shy, timid nature and their ability to find lost people. According to the legend, the Little People were gathered near the town of Brasstown for a day of singing and dancing when a foreign messenger arrived with news of the Crucifixion. The horrible story made the Little People weep, and their tears fell to the earth as small crosses. Their hearts were so filled with sorrow that they did not notice the tiny crosses on the ground when they left. An excellent collection of fairy crosses is on display at the Cherokee County Historical Museum in Murphy, phone (704) 837-6792.

In addition to the Brasstown area, staurolite stones have been discovered throughout the Blue Ridge Mountains of North Carolina, Georgia, and Virginia. Fairy Stone State Park (Route 2, Box 723, Stuart, VA 24171-9588, phone 540-930-2424) in Stuart, Virginia, claims to be the best place for fairy cross hunting, and rangers provide free informational handouts on the unique history of the stones. Despite how frequently they appear in this region, fairy stones remain largely uncommon throughout most of the world.

perhaps for cooking. A similar (and more easily reached) formation is the Indian Wash Pot on the bank of Fires Creek near Leatherwood Falls. Supposedly, the Indians used it to heat water for bathing, though it's now filled in with leaves and debris. The falls themselves, about 35 feet high, make a pleasant picnic spot. In addition to the usual southern Appalachian hardwoods, six kinds of pine, hemlock, mountain laurel and rhododendron, ferns, and a dazzling array of wildflower species thrive here.

Fires Creek is a designated bear sanctuary, and as development in surrounding areas limits their habitat, still more black bears (*Ursus americanus*) will be driven into this protected territory. The rare Appalachian water shrew (*Sorex palustris*) can be seen in the fast-moving, high-elevation streams, as can the southern pygmy shrew (*S. hoyi*). Other local fauna include all the small game typical of the area: squirrels, wild turkey (*Meleagris gallopavo*), white-tailed deer (*Odocoileus virginia*), and ruffed grouse (*Bonasa umbellus*), as well as both copperhead (*Agkistrodon contortrix*) and timber rattlers (*Crotalus horridus*). The pristine streams shelter native brook trout, rainbow trout, and brown trout. Among the many bird species here are numerous varieties of warblers, hawks, owls, and woodpeckers.

The Rim Trail, a roughly 26-mile loop, circumscribes the Fires Creek basin, intersecting with other shorter trails en route. Although many more equestrians than hikers use the trail, backpackers could spend several pleasurable days exploring the loop. Camping is prohibited in designated wildlife openings. And, as always along ridgeline trails, hikers are advised to carry plenty of water (though, at 8 pounds per gallon, it makes its presence felt in a backpack). There is a dependable spring near the intersection of the Shinbone Ridge and Rim trails, about 100 feet below the rim, and several other springs that may require a longer detour to reach.

Directions: From Murphy, take US 64 East toward Hayesville. After about 9 miles, turn left at the green forest service sign (and Citgo service station) onto NC 1302. After about 4 miles, make another left (also marked) onto NC 1344. It's about 1 mile to Hunters Camp, and another .7 mile to the Leatherwood Falls parking area. About 5 miles farther on is Bristol Horse Camp.

Activities: Backpacking, hiking, fishing, camping, hunting, picnicking.

Facilities: Leatherwood Falls: picnic tables, grills. Hunters Camp: pit toilets. Bristol Horse Camp: camping, facilities for horses.

Fees: There is a charge for some campsites.

Closest town: Hayesville, about 9 miles.

For more information: Tusquitee Ranger District, 201 Woodland Drive, Murphy, NC 28906. Phone (704) 837-5152.

BLACK BEAR (Ursus americanus)
This bear grows to 300 pounds.

LEATHERWOOD FALLS

[Fig. 32(15)] Heading west from Transylvania, Macon, and Jackson counties, the number of waterfalls drops off as precipitously as the hundreds of cascades left behind. The reason for this drastic change is found in the geology rather than in factors such as amount of rainfall. (Clay County, for example, does experience a somewhat reduced amount of rainfall, but not enough to be the cause of this difference.) Here, as in the Great Smoky Mountains, more sedimentary rock is present. Unlike the harder, more erosion-resistant metamorphic and igneous rock in the regions to the east and north, sandstone does not hold up as well to weathering and wear. The water wears the rock down instead of creating dramatic cascades. In addition, without the higher elevation plateaus found farther east, streams do not have time to become wide and strong enough to form waterfalls before they flow into the valleys.

Nonetheless, Leatherwood Falls in Clay County is a beautiful, if less dramatic, example of nature and gravity. Leatherwood Falls is located in the Fires Creek Recreation Area, part of the Nantahala National Forest. The 25-foot falls is visible from the picnic area or along a barrier-free, paved trail alongside the creek. The ice-cold water of Fires Creek provides an invigorating swim for hearty souls, particularly under the bridge where it is 6 or 7 feet deep. Leatherwood is a common family name in the area, and generations of local children have frolicked in the creek or fished for trout along its banks.

Colorful wildflowers are everywhere, and huge mossy logs, remnants of the once-abundant chestnut tree, add to the beauty. For a short walk, the .7-mile loop trail along the creek is easy and enjoyable.

Fires Creek is a sanctuary for the American black bear. Other wildlife, including white-tailed deer and the Russian boar, roam among the rhododendron thickets and in forests of yellow-poplar, birch, and oak trees. The pileated woodpecker, assorted warblers, vultures, and hawks can also be seen here.

CARDINAL FLOWER

(Lobelia cardinalis) A favorite stop for hummingbirds, this flower grows up to 5 feet tall.

Directions: From Murphy, take US 64 East toward Hayesville. After about 9 miles, turn left at the green forest service sign (and Citgo service station) onto NC 1302. After about 4 miles, make another left (also marked) onto NC 1344. It's about 1 mile to Hunters Camp, and another .7 mile to the Leatherwood Falls parking area.

Activities: Hiking, swimming, fishing (trout stamp required).

Facilities: Parking, picnic tables, vault toilets, water spigots.

Closest town: Hayesville, 9 miles.

For more information: Tusquitee Ranger District, 201 Woodland Drive, Murphy, NC 28906. Phone (704) 837-5152.

Songbird Migration

The mountains of North Carolina offer ample opportunities for watching the annual bird migrations. Overlooks and parking lots, riverbeds and gorges, meadows and backyard feeders welcome thousands of temporary residents each season on their way up from Central America and down from Canada. Concern is growing, however, as the birds' populations grow smaller each year. Surveys over many decades in the Maryland/Washington, D.C., area, for example, have documented the disappearance of several warbler varieties and drastically reduced numbers of wood thrushes, scarlet tanagers, and red-eyed vireos. The reasons for the decline are complex, but certainly two factors are the loss of habitat and use of pesticides, especially those banned in the United States but used in countries more lax in their regulations. A tragic report of as many as 20,000 Swainson's hawks (*Buteo swainsoni*) dying in Argentina in one season because of a toxic chemical used to kill the grasshoppers on which they feed is just one such story. While many birds and other wildlife are experiencing losing their habitats as the tropical rainforests are harvested or cleared for agriculture, habitat problems occur in the United States, as well. For instance, birds dependent upon the Texas coast as a place to rest and feed after their exhausting trip over the Gulf of Mexico now find farmlands that lack the food and shelter they require. In addition, many forests and wetlands throughout the United States are being drained and developed.

That's the bad news. The good news is that a wide range of community and environmental groups are getting involved to make much-needed changes. The National Audubon Society kicked off a campaign earlier in the decade called Birds in the Balance, which is being implemented by all 515 of its chapters in the United States and Latin America. The goal is to protect not only endangered birds but also species that are still abundant. Individuals get involved by building better backyard habitats featuring native plants, ponds, feeders, baths, and houses for the birds. Successful community-based projects include efforts ranging from conducting bird surveys and lobbying legislatures to building plaster of paris nests for cliff swallows (*Petrochelidon pyrrhonota*) when bridge repairs destroyed their colony site.

Education and negotiations in and with Latin American countries are also reaping rewards. One of the most promising programs in Central America is the campaign to show how well-managed coffee fields in shaded, forestlike environments—rather than sunny plantations—can also serve as havens for wildlife. The shade-loving coffee bush thrives as an understory plant, setting it apart from other tropical products such as bananas or sugar that require the clearing of rainforest land for fields, leaving birds and other wildlife neither food nor shelter. According to a story in the November-December 1994 issue of *Audubon*, a single shaded coffee field can support 66 species of trees and shrubs and 73 wildlife species.

Buck Creek & Chunky Gal Mountain

Chunky Gal Mountain gets its name from the Cherokee legend of a plump Indian maiden who fell in love with a brave and followed him over the mountain after the brave was banished from camp.

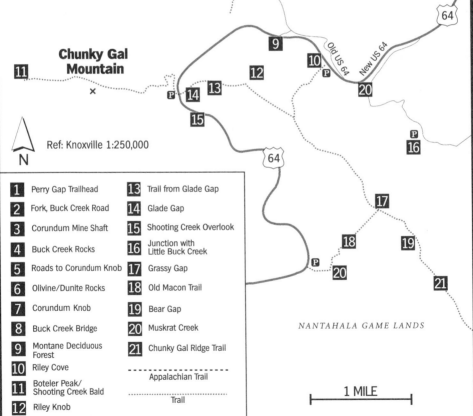

Chunky Gal Mountain

Ref: Knoxville 1:250,000

N

1 Perry Gap Trailhead
2 Fork, Buck Creek Road
3 Corundum Mine Shaft
4 Buck Creek Rocks
5 Roads to Corundum Knob
6 Olivine/Dunite Rocks
7 Corundum Knob
8 Buck Creek Bridge
9 Montane Deciduous Forest
10 Riley Cove
11 Boteler Peak/ Shooting Creek Bald
12 Riley Knob

13 Trail from Glade Gap
14 Glade Gap
15 Shooting Creek Overlook
16 Junction with Little Buck Creek
17 Grassy Gap
18 Old Macon Trail
19 Bear Gap
20 Muskrat Creek
21 Chunky Gal Ridge Trail

- - - - - - - Appalachian Trail
············· Trail

NANTAHALA GAME LANDS

1 MILE

Chunky Gal Mountain Area

[Fig. 41] Chunky Gal Mountain gained its evocative name from a Cherokee legend about a chubby maid who fell in love with a young man from another tribe. Her parents attempted to snuff the budding romance, but the determined young woman abandoned her family to follow her heart, finding her way across the mountain's slopes to be with her beloved.

Chunky Gal forms a roughly 8-mile ridge that runs between the Appalachian Trail and US 64 (at Glade Gap, in the Fires Creek area). The geology of this little-known area helps explain its considerable botanical significance. Outcrops of amphibolite account in part for the relatively high pH of the area's soils, which allows them to support rich cove forests. In those cove and upland forests, many rare plant species can be found, such as the dwarf ginseng (*Panax trifolius*), American columbo (*Frasera caroliniensis*), yellowwood (*Cladrastis lutea*), Goldie's fern (*Dryopteris goldiana*), and glade fern (*Athyrium pycnocarpon*).

Another geologic feature, the world-class deposit of olivine in the Buck Creek area, deserves special mention. Dunite, the rock that contains the olivine, accounts for the presence of rubies, as well as garnets, sapphires, and other gem stones at Buck Creek. Much of the area is under lease (hence, off limits), but at Corundum Knob, a public rock-hunting area, people dig along the creek, as well as higher up the mountain (commercial activity is prohibited, as is disturbing the creek banks).

The unusual geology supports an equally distinctive plant community called a serpentine barren, which is home to many rare species. Southern Appalachian bogs, with their own distinctive species, are also found on Chunky Gal.

Rare insects include the mountain catch fly (*Silene ovata*), found at the break between the rich cove and montane oak forests, and several species of butterflies: the large, distinctive diana fritillary (*Speyeria diana*), the silvery blue (*Glaucopsyche lygdamus*), and the early hairstreak (*Erora laeta*).

Beaver activity is evident along Buck Creek, and the new habitat created by these industrious builders attracts blue-winged teal (*Anas discors*) and wood ducks (*Aix sponsa*). The area also supports a strong wild turkey population, and cerulean warblers (*Dendroica cerulea*) have been spotted here.

The 22-mile Chunky Gal Trail [Fig. 41(21)] offers abundant opportunities for extended backpacking expeditions. The moderate-to-strenuous trail can be combined with others in the adjoining Fires Creek area, as well as portions of the Appalachian Trail. Many of these trails are not well maintained, however, and there are no developed facilities. The Chunky Gal trailhead is accessed off US 64. At a gravel road (unmarked FR 71) .3 mile west of the Macon/Clay county line, turn left and travel for 6.8 miles to the junction with the Appalachian Trail in Deep Gap. The trailhead begins at the parking and picnic area.

Directions: From Hayesville, drive east on US 64 for about 8 miles; at Chunky

Gal Mountain, the road starts to ascend. There is no formal parking area, but at Glade Gap there are plenty of places to pull off and park. Rock hounds should turn left on Barnett Creek Road, and continue 1–2 miles to a parking area.

Activities: Backpacking, hiking, fishing, camping, hunting, rock hunting.

Facilities: None.

Fees: None.

Closest town: Hayesville, approximately 9 miles.

For more information: Tusquitee Ranger District, 201 Woodland Drive, Murphy, NC 28906. Phone (704) 837-5152.

Lake Chatuge/Jackrabbit Mountain Recreation Area

[Fig. 32(17)] In Cherokee legend *Tusquitee* refers to the place "where the water dogs laughed." This area, now a part of the Nantahala National Forest in Clay County, has one of the most scenic lakes in the Tennessee Valley Authority (TVA) system. The 130 miles of shoreline around Lake Chatuge is magnificently framed by the nearby Tusquitee Mountains and "the Great Blue Hills of God," as the Cherokee called the Blue Ridge Mountains. The Chatuge Dam is 144 feet high, and the lake supports water sports and recreation. The fishing is good with more than 32 species in the lake. Jackrabbit Mountain Recreation Area is situated on a pine-wooded peninsula with hiking trails that offer pleasing views of Lake Chatuge. It isn't just the abundant salamanders who find reason for mirth in this popular family recreation area. Clay County Recreation Park is also popular with families.

Directions:. Jackrabbit Mountain: From Hayesville, travel east on US 64, turn south and travel 2.5 miles on NC 175, turn right on SR 1155. Clay County Recreation Park: 6.2 miles east from Hayesville on US 64 (turn right onto NC 175).

Activities: Fishing, swimming, skiing, camping, boating, hiking.

Facilities: Clay County Recreation Park: 25 campsites, picnic shelters, ball field, swimming area, and a boat-launching ramp. Jackrabbit Mountain: 103 camping sites, swimming beach with showers, hiking trails, picnic areas, and a boat launching ramp.

Fees: There is a charge for camping.

Closest town: Hayesville, approximately 6 miles.

JACKRABBIT MOUNTAIN SCENIC TRAIL

Trail distance and configuration: 2.4 miles.

Degree of difficulty: Easy.

Elevation: 1,200 feet.

Surface and blaze: Forest floor; blue blaze.

Monarch Migration

The monarch butterfly (*Danaus plexippus*), long appreciated for its beauty, has gained additional recognition in recent years for its startling migratory abilities. Previously, the southward movement each fall of these bright orange and black butterflies had been observed, but their winter destination remained a mystery. The mystery was finally solved with the discovery of overwintering grounds 9,000 feet up in the Sierra Madre mountains of Mexico. Like many insects, monarch butterflies undergo a four-stage metamorphosis, evolving from egg to larval, pupal, and finally adult stages. The larvae have voracious appetites and literally increase their weight 3,000-fold in only 14 days' time.

During this larval stage, the monarch caterpillar feeds exclusively on various species of the milkweed plant. This plant contains an organic compound that is poisonous to birds and causes a violent reaction if ingested. One such distasteful experience is enough to discourage a bird from ever again pursuing a monarch as a meal.

A monarch's wings are covered with tiny, colorful, overlapping scales that are the "dust" that comes off on the hands when holding a butterfly too firmly. The wing patterns formed by these scales define a monarch's appearance and give the insect its beauty. But of even greater significance, the scales help predatory birds quickly recognize the insect and serve as a warning that this is one butterfly to avoid.

Anywhere from three to five generations of monarchs may be produced during a single summer season. The last generation of a given season will not reach sexual maturity, and this generation will follow a powerful instinct to migrate southward, sometimes flying more than 2,500 miles to reach the Mexico wintering site. Apparently, a dormant period in the relatively mild winter of this mountainous region is required for the butterflies to become sexually mature. When spring arrives, the insects then begin the northward return journey, mating and producing offspring en route. It is one of these newer generations that actually reaches the southern Appalachians each summer. It remains both a mystery and a miracle as to how the season's final generation makes the southern migration without ever having been to Mexico.

Much of the recent information on monarch migration has been gained through the pioneering efforts of Fred and Nora Urquhart of the University of Toronto. They developed miniature lightweight tags, attached them to the butterflies' wings, and have been compiling migration data for many years. In Western North Carolina, zoologist Dr. Hal Mahan and his wife, Laura, a botanist, have cooperated in this research effort, tagging hundreds of monarchs over the years, many of which have been recovered in Mexico. The mountains of North Carolina lie directly along the migration route, making the area perfect for monarch tagging. Such efforts have helped unlock some of the secrets of the monarch and provided insight into other species as well. (For information on sites where you can watch the monarch migration, *see* Doughton Park, page 25; Chimney Rock Park, page 124; and Cherry Cove Overlook, page 136.)

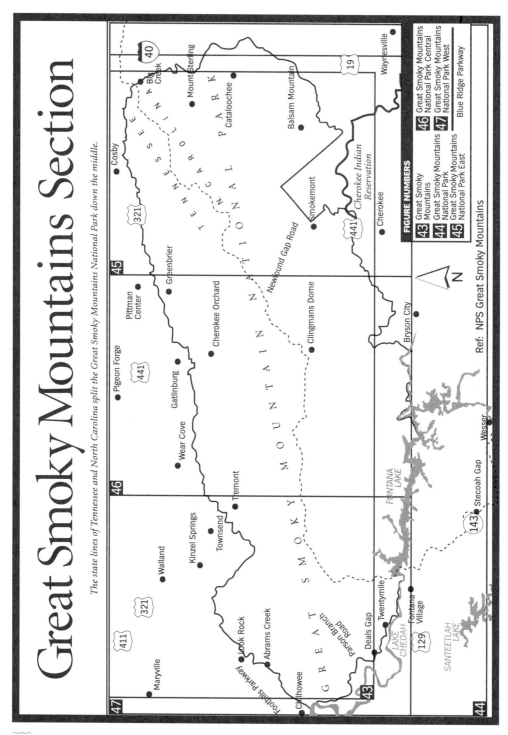

Great Smoky Mountains Section

The state lines of Tennessee and North Carolina split the Great Smoky Mountains National Park down the middle.

Ref: NPS Great Smoky Mountains

FIGURE NUMBERS

43	Great Smoky Mountains
44	Great Smoky Mountains National Park
45	Great Smoky Mountains National Park East
46	Great Smoky Mountains National Park Central
47	Great Smoky Mountains National Park West
	Blue Ridge Parkway

The Great Smoky Mountains

The Great Smoky Mountains National Park [Figs. 42–47], though geographically part of the Blue Ridge province, is a world unto itself. Maybe this land was always extra blessed with wildlife and breathtaking terrain (hosting 17 peaks with elevations of 6,000 feet or higher), but more likely its elevated status stems from the fact that more than 520,000 acres have been protected from man's continuing intervention. As a result, visitors can enjoy 110,000 acres of old-growth forest, 1,600 species of flowering plants, 2,000 different fungi, 300 kinds of mosses, 200 varieties of birds, 60 species of fur-bearing mammals, 48 types of fish, 38 species of reptiles, 27 kinds of salamanders, and 12 endangered species. Of particular note,

[*Above*: Rhododendron thickets in the Smoky Mountains]

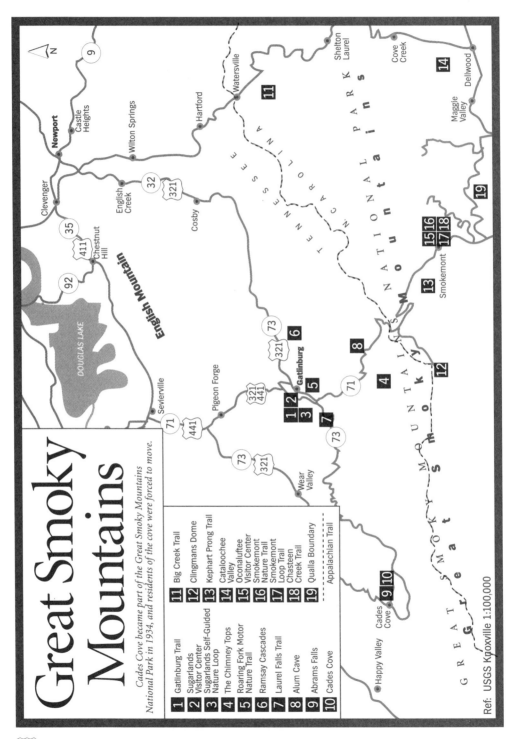

Great Smoky Mountains

Cades Cove became part of the Great Smoky Mountains National Park in 1934, and residents of the cove were forced to move.

1 Gatlinburg Trail
2 Sugarlands Visitor Center
3 Sugarlands Self-Guided Nature Loop
4 The Chimney Tops
5 Roaring Fork Motor Nature Trail
6 Ramsay Cascades
7 Laurel Falls Trail
8 Alum Cave
9 Abrams Falls
10 Cades Cove
11 Big Creek Trail
12 Clingmans Dome
13 Kephart Prong Trail
14 Cataloochee Valley
15 Oconaluftee Visitor Center
16 Smokemont Nature Trail
17 Smokemont Loop Trail
18 Chasteen Creek Trail
19 Qualla Boundary

- - - Appalachian Trail

Ref: USGS Knoxville 1:100,000

approximately 500 black bears live in the park, and their presence should be a consideration throughout any visit.

The geology of the region varies, too, from the lands east of the park, although the basic formation process was the same. First came the periods of continental collision and mountain building in which sedimentary rock layers hundreds of miles in length and 40,000 feet deep became folded, broken, and overturned; then, millions of years of erosion followed up through today. The total acreage of the park is divided between North Carolina (276,063 acres) and Tennessee (244,345 acres), and it is primarily in Tennessee that some variations in the geologic makeup begin to appear. Of the three basic bedrocks found in the park, the Precambrian basement rock, more than 1 billion years old, consists chiefly of schists, gneisses, and some granitic rocks. The late Precambrian rocks of the Ocoee Series, however, ranging in age from 500 million to 1 billion years, are dominant in the park and include more sedimentary, less metamorphosed rocks such as shales, slates, and sandstones in the northwestern areas of the park. Finally, the sedimentary rocks of the Valley and Ridge, deposited during the Paleozoic Era and only 300 to 500 million years old, are found primarily in the westernmost portions of the park.

Fossils are also somewhat more prevalent here, because fossils usually occur in sedimentary rock younger than 600 million years that has not experienced metamorphism. Most of Western North Carolina, and the Blue Ridge province, is composed of metamorphic and igneous rocks, which limits the numbers of fossils dramatically.

Weathering and erosion over millions of years have reduced the Blue Ridge Mountains to only a shadow of their original grandeur. One particularly interesting effect of this erosion lies in the Cades Cove area where, as in the Grandfather Mountains Window in the Black Mountains section, layers of younger Paleozoic limestone underlie the older metamorphosed rock. This resulted when ancient upheavals and collisions thrust the younger rock underneath the older, and over millions of years the older rock has worn away to open "windows" into the layers of younger rock.

The park's geologic history and climate (which results from the area's geographic location) strongly influence the diverse plants and animals that live here. The mountain-building periods produced a confusing jumble of splintered ridges and coves that created many protected pockets of diverse life zones. The broad range of plant communities found in the park include floodplain habitats, mixed pine-hardwood forests, hemlock-heath communities, bog wetlands, cove hardwood habitats, northern hardwood forests, boulderfields, spruce-fir communities, and mountaintop balds. While many animal species can overlap these communities, each ecosystem also supports wildlife specially adapted to a particular set of conditions.

Weather systems that collide with the southern Appalachian Mountains also work to create a number of unique wildlife ecosystems. The exposed peaks are subject to tremendous winds (up to 100 mph) and excessive precipitation each year. Moisture is greatest on the southwest slopes, where rainfall arriving from the Gulf of Mexico

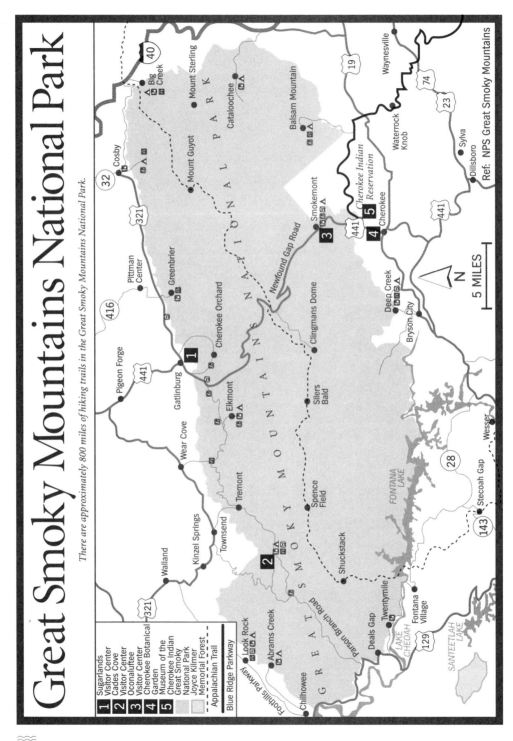

Great Smoky Mountains National Park

There are approximately 800 miles of hiking trails in the Great Smoky Mountains National Park.

1 Sugarlands Visitor Center
2 Cades Cove Visitor Center
3 Oconaluftee Visitor Center
4 Cherokee Botanical Garden
5 Museum of the Cherokee Indian

Great Smoky National Park
Joyce Kilmer Memorial Forest
Appalachian Trail
Blue Ridge Parkway

Ref: NPS Great Smoky Mountains

N

5 MILES

The Red Wolf Restoration

When European explorers first reached the New World's wilderness, they found it surprisingly rich in animal life. They must have been surprised to encounter diverse wildlife including alligators, black bears, raccoons, and bison.

One mammal, however, was not a surprise. In fact, this animal had become highly feared following centuries of folklore and myth that produced terrifying stories of human and wolf confrontations. The wolf, as it happens, is native to both Europe and North America, and the mentality that led to its demise in the Old World was easily transplanted by colonists to the New World.

Beginning with the very first settlements, the two eastern species of North American wolves, the gray wolf (*Canis lupus*) and red wolf (*Canis rufus*), suffered from methodical attempts to eradicate them. For the red wolf, these attempts were very nearly successful.

At one time, the red wolf was extremely common throughout the Southeast. Its northern range formed a line that extended from central New Jersey to Illinois and Texas. Over the years, bounty-hunting, habitat destruction, and genetic decline through interbreeding with coyotes led to steep decline of the species.

By 1970, it was estimated that fewer than 100 genetically pure wolves remained in a small coastal area on the Texas/Louisiana border.

Biologists predicted total extinction unless drastic measures were taken. A captive-breeding-and-release program resulted in the capture of about 400 wolves, which were then checked for health and genetic purity. Of these, 43 were chosen for the breeding program. Further health problems, hybrid litters, and a lack of proper breeding facilities reduced the number of breeding stock to 14.

Eventually, more than 30 breeding facilities were established, and in 1992 the Western North Carolina Nature Center of Asheville was added as one of these sites. Red wolves are continually relocated to the center for breeding. Adults and pups are then moved from the nature center to national wildlife refuges on the North Carolina, South Carolina, and Florida coasts, as well as in the Great Smoky Mountains National Park.

The restoration program has met with great success in the coastal areas but limited success in the Smokies. It appears that the animals making up the wolves' diet—rabbits, raccoons, and white-tailed deer—are more plentiful among coastal forests and wetlands than in the higher elevations of the North Carolina mountains.

Still, wolves are continually being released in some areas in the Great Smokies, and consideration is being given to release programs in Pisgah, Cherokee, and Nantahala national forests as well. While captive-breeding programs will need to be continued indefinitely, the red wolf restoration program has thus far preserved the species from oblivion.

first encounters the mountains. A similar situation occurs in the south-oriented Blue Ridge Escarpment, where Atlantic coast moisture is dumped among the mountains of Georgia, North Carolina, and South Carolina.

The other climatic influence on the region, that of temperature, relates to latitude and, once again, geology. In low-lying areas, the warm southern temperatures encourage plants normally found in Piedmont and Coastal Plain provinces. On the other hand, at higher altitudes in the park the temperature can be as much as 15 degrees Fahrenheit cooler, reflecting an average decrease of 3 degrees Fahrenheit for every rise of 1,000 feet in elevation. In the Smokies, land at high altitudes harbors species more typical of northern latitudes.

No one questions that the park is a national treasure. On the contrary, the real problem is too many visitors and not enough money in the budget. New ideas are being developed to help finance much-needed improvements and expanded programming required to serve the 9.3 million visitors who came in 1996 alone (more than double the number of visitors to the Grand Canyon). Careful planning and appropriate funding are vital to keeping the park truly the Great Smoky Mountains.

The park offers an outstanding network of facilities for camping, picnicking, information, and the general welfare of visitors. Not every facility can be covered within this section—only those that are located close to trails and attractions being described. No hunting is allowed in the park; fishing of nonnative fish (no brook trout fishing) is allowed and requires either a Tennessee or North Carolina permit. For more information, consult the park's newspaper, *Smokies Guide*, available for $.25 at all visitor centers or contact the National Park Service, 107 Park Headquarters Road, Gatlinburg, TN 37738. Phone (423) 436-1200. Website www.nps.gov/grsm/homepage.htm.

CATALOOCHEE VALLEY

[Fig. 43(14)] The Cataloochee Valley is one of the most remote, and therefore least visited, parts of the Great Smoky Mountains National Park. The area is of a rural rather than wilderness nature, having once supported a close-knit family community of 1,200 residents, some of whom lived in the valley as recently as the 1960s. The valley's pastoral roots are evident in several old buildings, including a school, a church, and a number of former homes and barns. The name Cataloochee is derived from the Cherokee phrase *god-a-lu-chee*, which generally translates into English as "wave upon wave of mountains" and refers to the distant views of the region as seen from the higher mountain peaks.

The Cataloochee drainage basin is defined by the Balsam Mountain Range which extends along the western border north to Tricorner Knob at the Smokies Crest. The Mount Sterling Ridge, north of the valley, and the Cataloochee Divide on the southeast, both extend from the Balsam Range to form additional boundaries.

The area provides access to a number of hiking and horse trails and the Cataloochee Primitive Campground, which includes 27 campsites. There is also a ranger station, located in what was formerly a home, built in 1916 from chestnut beams and paneling. An old church graveyard lies on a hill on the right just past the Palmer Chapel and puts on a showy display of pink lady slipper (*Cypripendium acaule*) in the spring.

Thirty-seven miles of trails course through Cataloochee Valley, including the popular Boogerman Loop, Rough Fork Trail, and Cataloochee Divide Trail. Cataloochee Creek, Caldwell Creek, and Palmer Creek offer excellent fishing opportunities, subject to park regulations.

Directions: Take I-40 west from Asheville to Exit 20 onto US 276. Follow US 276 north .1 mile to Cove Creek Road (NC 284) on the right. Travel 5.8 miles along this narrow, winding gravel road to Cove Creek Gap, which marks the boundary of the national park. Continue another 1.7 miles to a paved road. The campground entrance is 3.1 miles ahead and the ranger station another .5 mile.

Activities: Camping, hiking, fishing, horseback riding.

Facilities: Ranger station, campground.

Fees: There is a charge for camping.

Closest town: Dellwood, NC, 11 miles.

BIG CREEK TRAIL

[Fig. 43(11)] As Big Creek drops more than 1,200 feet on its way toward its confluence with the Pigeon River, it creates one of the most beautiful watersheds in the Great Smoky Mountains National Park. The creek is noted for its effervescent cascades, whitewater falls, and excellent fishing opportunities. Brown trout (*Salmo trutta*) and rainbow trout (*Oncorhynchus mykiss*) are visible in its clear, cold waters. The native brook trout (*Salvelinus fontinalis*) lives here as well, but it is illegal to fish the native species.

Like so many areas of these mountains, logging operations made camp in Big Creek early this century. From 1908 to 1918, the Crestmont Lumber Company established homes, a school, and a mill here before depleting the mighty timber. (Trees once grew to diameters as large as 10 to 12 feet.) In the 1930s, the CCC made camp here, improving roads and trails in the area. Big Creek Trail is the main trail in the area, connecting with several other side trails. The 5.8-mile trek (one-way) starts at Big Creek Campground on the former Crestmont site just past the ranger station (1,700 feet elevation) and climbs steadily yet gently to Walnut Bottom (3,080 feet). Along the way, the trail follows Big Creek on old logging railroad beds to beautiful stops such as Midnight Hole, an 80-foot-wide, deep and dark pool of water fed by two small falls cascading over huge boulders. A little farther, Mouse Creek Falls pours between the boulders in a picturesque hourglass shape. The trail continues through rhododendron (*Rhododendron catawbiense* and *R. maximum*) and dog-hobble (*Viburnum alnifolium*) thickets on its way to Brakeshoe Spring, so named for the fountainlike effect created by a brakeshoe placed in a depression in the rock. The story goes that sometime before 1918, an engineer of a logging train placed the brakeshoe to create a fountain when the water rushed through, making his twice-daily stops for drinking water a little easier. The brakeshoe disappeared in the mid-1970s, but the name remains intact. The clear water harbors trout, salamanders, crawfish, and other aquatic life that thrives in the park. Like much of the park, this is also bear and snake country, and appropriate arrangements should be made for food storage.

The trail continues through hardwood forests with wildflowers along the creek-bed before reaching Walnut Bottom, where backcountry campsites under stands of yellow buckeye (*Aesculus octandra*) and Eastern hemlock (*Tsuga canadensis*) are popular with hikers.

Directions: Take I-40 west from Asheville, approximately 50 miles, to the Waterville Exit. After crossing the Pigeon River bridge, turn left and continue on the road past an electric power plant to an intersection (approximately 2 miles from the interstate). Travel straight up a narrow road past the Ranger Station to the campground ahead.

Activities: Hiking, camping, horseback riding, fishing, picnicking.

Facilities: Camping, picnic area, restrooms, water.

Fees: There is a charge for camping.

Closest town: Waterville, 4 miles.

Trail distance and configuration: 11.6 miles round-trip.

Elevation: 1,700 feet at campground.

Degree of difficulty: Moderate.

Surface and blaze: Roadbed, forest floor.

DEEP CREEK AREA

[Fig. 32(4)] To some, the Deep Creek Area offers a peaceful walk and tubing down the creek. To the more hardy, it offers a 12-mile trek with an elevation gain of 2,820 feet—or an even longer hike, as numerous trails interconnect with Deep Creek Trail. One of the first trails constructed in the newly legislated park in 1932, Deep Creek Trail is also the historic site of Kituhwa, one of the Cherokee settlements William Bartram visited in the early nineteenth century (*see* Naturalists, page 230). Like many of the popularly named mountains, ridges, and streams, Deep Creek is not necessarily the deepest creek in the region—it just seemed that way to the local folks who named it. The easier hike, Deep Creek–Indian Creek Loop, is a 3.9-mile river walk following the creek before ascending Sunkota Ridge and looping back to the parking area along Indian Creek Trail.

From the trailhead at the parking lot, an old roadbed courses through the gentle river valley and soon passes Tom Branch Falls on the right. The lacy waters glisten as they cascade 80 feet down a series of six rocky tiers on the way to join Deep Creek.

The trail continues along the creek, at times adjacent to and at other times overlooking the rushing waters. Wildflowers are abundant along the pathway, including a variety of trilliums, blooming at different times, and the airy spikes of foamflower (*Tiarella cordifolia*) punctuating the ground cover of galax (*Galax aphylla*), crested dwarf iris (*Iris cristata*), beard tongue (*Penstemon canescens*), cinquefoil (*Potentilla canadensis*), bloodroot (*Sanguinaria canadensis*), bluet (*Houstonia caerulea*), and blue-eyed grass (*Sisyrinchium augustifolium*). Jack-in-the-pulpit (*Arisaema triphyllum*) is abundant yet hard to spot among the wild geranium (*Ceranium maculatum*), clinton's lily (*Clintonia borealis*), and large houstonia (*Houstonia purpurea*). Jacks or Indian turnips, as they are commonly called, vary considerably in appearance, ranging from slender, short varieties to thick-stemmed, 3-foot-high plants. These interesting-looking plants also have a unique sexual life—they can reproduce asexually and can change their sex from season to season. They can be male, female, neuter, or both male and female. Their ability to alter their sex allows them to adapt to a changing environment and offers the female, who gave her all bearing fruit last season, a chance to regain her strength.

Dog-hobble, solomon's seal (*Polygonatum biflorum*), and false solomon's seal (*Smilacina racemosa*) are prevalent near the creek bed, but as the trail rises in elevation along Sunkota Ridge and Indian Creek Trail, the canopy of hemlocks, oaks, and maples dominates an understory of rhododendron, mountain laurel (*Kalmia latifolia*), flame azalea (*Rhododendron calendulaceum*), and many of the same wildflowers as found along the riverbed.

As the loop approaches its end, Indian Creek Falls, near the confluence of Deep Creek and Indian Creek, flows frothy and white. Trout live in these waters, though they are primarily the imported brown trout, the native brook trout having retreated to more remote, colder streams because of siltation and warmer waters resulting from logging activities.

Directions: From downtown Bryson City on US 19, turn north at the Swain County Courthouse, turn right after crossing the bridge, and follow the Deep Creek signs for 3 miles.

Activities: Hiking, biking, tubing, fishing, picnicking, horseback riding, camping.

Facilities: Parking, camping, restrooms. Nearby Bryson City features several good restaurants, accommodations, and shopping. The Smoky Mountain Railway has a depot in town.

Fees: There is a charge for camping.

Closest town: Bryson City, 3 miles.

Trail distance and configuration: 3.9-mile loop.

Elevation: 1,990 feet at parking lot.

Degree of difficulty: Easy to moderate.

Surface and blaze: Roadbed, forest floor.

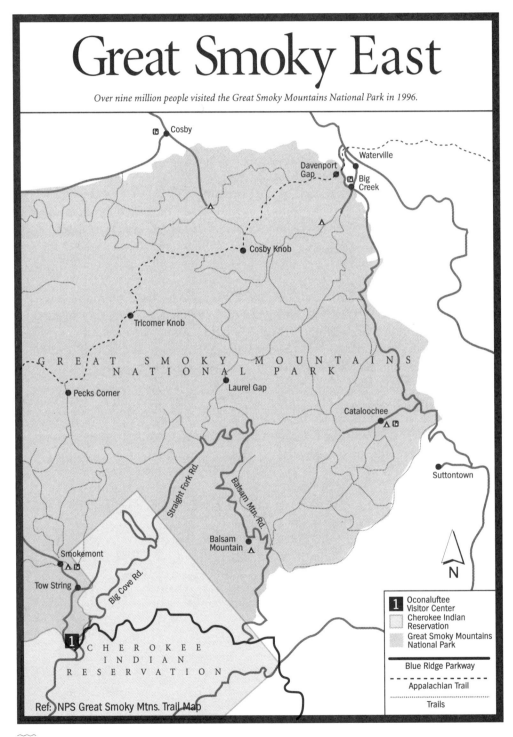

Great Smoky East

Over nine million people visited the Great Smoky Mountains National Park in 1996.

Cosby

Waterville

Davenport Gap

Big Creek

Cosby Knob

Tricomer Knob

G R E A T   S M O K Y   M O U N T A I N S
N A T I O N A L   P A R K

Pecks Corner

Laurel Gap

Cataloochee

Suttontown

Straight Fork Rd.

Balsam Mtn. Rd.

Balsam Mountain

Smokemont

Tow String

Big Cove Rd.

1

C H E R O K E E
I N D I A N
R E S E R V A T I O N

N

1 Oconaluftee Visitor Center
Cherokee Indian Reservation
Great Smoky Mountains National Park
Blue Ridge Parkway
Appalachian Trail
Trails

Ref: NPS Great Smoky Mtns. Trail Map

The Oconaluftee Visitor Center

[Fig. 43(15), Fig. 44(3), Fig. 45(1)] The Oconaluftee Visitor Center sits on a fertile tract of land whose flatness is accentuated by the mountains that rise on all sides, its pastoral greens a bright contrast to the darker hues of the forests beyond. When compared to some of the Great Smokies' more craggy locales—their unsuitability to farming vividly captured in such names as Rocky Spur, Stony Gap, and Long Hungry Ridge—it seems even more of an arable oasis. Land that any pioneer would have been pleased to stumble upon, it is the fitting home to a living mountain farm museum that pays tribute to the self-sufficient ways of the settlers who once scrabbled out a life here by growing corn and raising cattle.

Changing exhibits inside the visitor center depict wildlife in the park as well as chronicle the area's pioneers and loggers, who were often just as colorful, not to mention as ornery, as any black bear. A short way from the center lies the museum and a collection of turn-of-the-century buildings assembled by the National Park Service from former Great Smokies settlements and arranged for historical accuracy. The farmstead includes a cabin dwelling, a barn, corncribs, a spring house, and a meat house. A plotted garden grows a short way from a crop of corn and sorghum cane, used to make molasses. A strutting rooster or two, chickens, a pig, and a plodding team of horses populate the barnyard. During the summer and fall, old-time methods of farming and housekeeping are demonstrated regularly. At other times, visitors can stroll the grounds to peer inside the buildings and wonder at how life used to be.

Weary hikers might find in the flatness of the land a reprieve of another kind. The Oconaluftee River Trail, which begins just behind the farmstead, is only 1.5 miles long and is level enough to be handicapped accessible. While easy, the hike is also rewarding. Following close by the river, the trail travels among Eastern hemlock, yellow buckeye, Eastern sycamore (*Platanus occidentalis*), white basswood (*Tilia americana* var. *heterophylla*), flowering dogwood (*Cornus florida*), and tuliptree or yellow-poplar (*Liriodendron tulipifera*).

More than 40 species of wildflowers have been identified along the trail, making it an especially worthwhile walk in spring and fall. Blossoming in spring are varieties of trillium, jack-in-the-pulpit, squirrel corn (*Dicentra canadensis*), stonecrop or sedum (*Sedum ternatum*), mayapple (*Podophyllum peltatum*), as well as several species of other sedum and violets; in fall, asters are the main attraction. Spring also brings a variety of recently migrated warblers to the trail, whose songs, when joined by the odd "cock-a-doodle-doo" wafting down from the farm, create an odd aural juncture of nature and history.

The Oconaluftee River flows southeast and drains the valley between Thomas Divide and Hughes Ridge. Its name represents a juncture, too, this one between past and present. It evolved from the Cherokee word *Egwanulti*, which means "by the river" and was once used to refer collectively to the various Cherokee communities that thrived on the banks of the river in the years before the American Revolution. Corrupted by the pronunciation and spelling of the European settlers who arrived in the early 1800s, the word became Oconaluftee and soon, by association, grew to mean the river itself.

Approximately .5 mile up the road from the center is another testament to days gone by: the Mingus Mill. Built in 1886, the gristmill was used by the nearby mountain community for more than 50 years to grind corn and wheat into meal and flour, its turbine powered by the flow of Mingus Creek through its redwood millrace. Demonstrations are still held from late spring to fall at the mill, which was rehabilitated by the National Park Service in 1968. Hikers are discouraged from using the nearby Mingus Creek Trail. No longer included on park maps, the trail passes a law-enforcement target range as well as the water-supply treatment area for the town of Cherokee, making it neither safe nor pleasant to walk on.

Directions: From US 19 in Cherokee, turn right on US 441. Follow 2 miles to visitor center on right.

Activities: Hiking, fishing.

Facilities: Visitor center with exhibits and information, sales area, restrooms, mountain farm museum, working gristmill (approximately .5 mile away), backcountry permits.

Fees: None.

Closest town: Cherokee, 2 miles.

Trail distance and configuration: 3 miles round-trip.

Elevation: 2,000 feet.

Degree of difficulty: Easy, handicapped accessible.

SMOKEMONT NATURE TRAIL

[Fig. 43(16)] The Smokemont Self-guiding Nature Trail is short, interesting, and convenient for overnight campers and day visitors to the Smokemont Campground. This loop trail is only about 1 mile in length and involves little climbing, making it easy for young children and adults alike.

The trailhead is located halfway into the campground on the left side. The trailhead is marked by a kiosk where a box contains interpretive brochures with 12 numbered descriptions that correspond to numbered posts along the trail.

The brochure explains how the combination of moisture, sunlight, and soil at Smokemont have determined which plant species dominate. It also highlights the changes that have occurred in the area. Smokemont was the name of a logging community carved out of the forest by the Champion Fibre Company in the early 1900s. The Nature Trail and brochure interpret the devastating changes logging brought to this ecosystem, and the forest's subsequent response to these changes. Unique trees and shrubs are also noted along the trail.

Directions: Go to the southern terminus of the Blue Ridge Parkway at Great Smoky Mountains National Park. Turn right on Newfound Gap Road, follow to Smokemont Campground, 3.2 miles past Oconaluftee Visitor Center.

Activities: Camping, hiking, trout fishing.

Facilities: Ranger office, restrooms. Campground includes picnic tables, trailer/ tent sites. No showers, trailer hookups.

Fees: There is a charge for camping.

Closest town: Cherokee, 5 miles.

Trail distance and configuration: 1-mile loop.

Elevation: Approximately 2,600 feet.

Degree of difficulty: Easy.

Surface: Forest floor.

SMOKEMONT LOOP TRAIL

[Fig. 43(17)] The Smokemont Loop Trail takes hikers through magnificent creekside cove hardwood forests as well as drier oak- and hickory-dominated ridge-tops. The easy, level hike along the first portion is followed by a long and moderately steep climb up and down Richland Mountain.

The trail begins at a gated gravel road at the rear of Smokemont Campground on Newfound Gap Road. The first 1.7 miles is actually the Bradley Fork Trail and follows along the east bank of a wide creek bearing that name. A sign at the gate indicates the mileage to the junction with Smokemont Loop proper, as well as other trails in the area.

The dominant trees along Bradley Fork are northern red oak (*Quercus rubra*), scarlet oak (*Q. coccinea*), and tulip poplar. Several floodplain species are common here as well, including sycamore (*Platanus occidentalis*), river birch (*Betula nigra*), and American hornbeam (*Carpinus caroliniana*).

HIGHBUSH BLACKBERRY
(*Rubus allegheniensis*) This bramble produces a delectable fruit that is popular food for wildlife.

Where ample sunlight penetrates, the trail edges are lush with herbaceous growth. Wildflowers such as foamflower, wild geranium, buttercup (*Ranunculus hispidus*), and lyre-leaved sage (*Salvia lyrata*) are common here. The ever-present mountain laurel and rhododendron are joined by other shrubs such as witch-hazel (*Hamamelis virginiana*) and buffalo nut (*Pyrularia pubera*). Understory trees and saplings include flowering dogwood, basswood (*Tilia heterophylla*), sugar maple (*Acer saccharum*), and striped maple (*A. pensylvanicum*).

After 1 mile, a large, mossy rock can be seen a short distance to the right of the trail. The rock is shaped like a bench and may have been placed there for that reason in the days when Smokemont was home to Champion Fibre's huge timbering operation. This area once held a hotel, boarding house, company store, and other structures related to the industry. All that remains are a few small clearings, which are being reclaimed through natural plant succession.

At 1.2 miles another sign indicates mileages to trails, including the Smokemont Loop, which joins at .5 mile farther. At that point, the loop begins by heading downhill and across a bridge over Bradley Fork. New York ferns (*Thelypteris noveboracensis*) grow in huge colonies along the creek here, and occasional clumps of squawroot (*Conopholis americana*) can be seen as well.

The trail then climbs steadily away from the creek until it reaches an extension of the ridge that forms Richland Mountain. Along the way hikers pass through thick stands of black cherry (*Prunus serotina*), yellow birch (*Betula alleghaniensis*), and Eastern hemlock. Higher up, the dominant species are pignut hickory (*Carya glabra*), white oak (*Quercus alba*), scarlet oak, and tulip poplar. At the ridge itself, chestnut oak (*Quercus montana*) becomes codominant.

The trail makes a long descent down the southwest side of the ridge, eventually joining a gravel service road that leads across Bradley Fork Creek and into the Smokemont Campground. En route, hikers pass through an area with many fallen American chestnuts (*Castanea dentata*), remnants of old-growth giants that succumbed to blight earlier in the century. Also occurring on this stretch are the oldest tulip poplar trees on the trail and a spur trail leading to an old cemetery that dates back to the 1800s.

The Smokemont Loop hike is completed by turning left at the campground and walking .6 mile to the rear parking area where the Bradley Fork Trail began.

Directions: Go to the south terminus of the Blue Ridge Parkway in Great Smoky Mountains National Park. Turn right on Newfound Gap Road, follow to Smokemont Campground, 3.2 miles past Oconaluftee Visitor Center.

Activities: Camping, hiking, trout fishing.

Facilities: Ranger office, restrooms. Campground includes picnic tables, fireplaces, water, trailer/tent sites (no showers or trailer hookups).

Fees: There is a charge for camping.

Closest town: Cherokee, 5 miles.

Trail distance and configuration: 6-mile loop.

Elevation: 2,200 feet at Smokemont Campground, 3,460 feet at Richland Mountain.

Degree of difficulty: Bradley Fork Trail portion: easy. Smokemont Loop Trail proper: moderate to strenuous.

Surface: Forest floor.

CHASTEEN CREEK TRAIL

[Fig. 43(18)] The Chasteen Creek Trail can be accessed approximately 1.2 miles into the Smokemont Loop Trail/Bradley Fork Trail, which originates from the Smokemont Campground. After another 1.2 miles on the Chasteen Creek Trail, at a place with hitching posts for horses, a well-used side trail leads to an impressive view of the Chasteen Creek cascade. From here, the trail continues its steady rise toward Hughes Ridge, traveling along the creek's channel through rhododendron and mountain laurel and a second-growth hardwood forest of Eastern hemlock, tulip-trees, oak, mountain-ash (*Sorbus americana*), and, in the wetter areas, sycamore. The trail can get narrow, rocky, and sometimes strenuous as it travels upstream, but it is worth it. This appealing trail harbors hundreds of species of birds and wildflowers, as well as white-tailed deer, black bear, and other mammals of the park. Once atop the crest of Hughes Ridge, the creek narrows considerably from its earlier 10-foot width, and ferns, mosses, lichens, and fungi are abundant. Backtrack to the campground or make a longer, 14.8-mile loop by turning right onto the Hughes Ridge Trail. This trail intersects Chasteen Creek Trail on the ridge, and hikers can follow it back to the campground. A left turn at the intersection will continue 4.7 miles on Hughes Ridge Trail to Peck's Corner on the Appalachian Trail.

Directions: Go to the south terminus of the Blue Ridge Parkway in Great Smoky Mountains National Park. Turn right on Newfound Gap Road, follow to Smokemont Campground, 3.2 miles past Oconaluftee Visitor Center.

Activities: Hiking.

Closest town: Cherokee, 5 miles.

Trail distance and configuration: 10 miles round-trip on Chasteen Creek Trail; Chasteen Creek Trail/Hughes Ridge Trail, 14.8-mile loop.

Elevation: 2,360 feet at trailhead, 4,660 feet at Hughes Ridge.

Degree of difficulty: Moderate to strenuous.

Surface and blaze: Old roadbed, forest floor.

CHARLIES BUNION VIA KEPHART PRONG TRAIL

[Fig. 43(13)] Running along a branch of the Oconaluftee River, the Kephart Prong Trail is a short trail that gains an elevation of only 830 feet. Yet, in its 2 miles, it manages to introduce much of the recent history of the Great Smokies.

In the Depression era, a barracks-style camp of the Civilian Conservation Corps (CCC) was located in the woods just .2 mile past the trailhead. In a stand of Eastern hemlock, traces of the camp remain: a small stone entrance sign, a few low walls, a water fountain, and a chimney and hearth. The work performed by this organization has proved more durable than the camp—many of the footbridges crossed by the trail are buttressed by CCC stonework. Another goodworks project along Kephart Prong, a fish hatchery run by the Works Project Administration, was also active in the 1930s, hatching trout and bass to replenish mountain streams.

The trees in the forest are small and old railroad irons are strewn near the end of the trail, evidence of the extensive logging that occurred here before the advent of the CCC and the creation of the park. To remove cut timber to the sawmills, Champion Fibre Company built hundreds of miles of railroad track to crisscross the mountains. Near the trail's end grows another reminder of logging: a stand of Norway spruce. Planted by Champion to replace depleted acreage of red spruce, these Norway spruce are nonnative to the Smokies and are being removed by the National Park Service.

A mixed forest of oak and hemlock, with an understory including heaths of rhododendron, laurel, and dog-hobble, is now coming to maturity. While the trees are not yet prepossessing, the wildflowers that line this trail are. Spring sightings include foamflower, wild geranium, Rue anemone and wood anemone (*Anemonella thalictroides* and *Anemone quinquefolia*), large-flowered bellwort (*Uvularia grandiflora*), and three species of trillium. Flame azalea, Turk's cap lily (*Lilium superbum*), and speckled wood lily (*Clintonia umbellulata*) come into bloom with the rhododendron in June.

The creek and rich thickets of heath along the Kephart Prong Trail are attractive to wildlife. A number of warblers frequent the area, including the chestnut-sided warbler (*Dendroica pensylvanica*), the hooded warbler (*Wilsonia citrina*), and the black-throated green warbler (*Dendroica virens*). Louisiana waterthrush (*Seiurus motacilla*) can be spotted along Kephart Prong. Salamanders dwell here, too, one of them Jordan's salamander (*Plethodon jordani*), a red-cheeked variety found exclusively in the Smokies.

Kephart Prong flows down the side of Kephart Mountain. Both the mountain and the waterway are named for Horace Kephart, an early park enthusiast whose book *Our Southern Highlanders* is a classic study of mountain culture. By following Kephart Prong Trail to Grassy Branch and Dry Sluice Gap trails, hikers can reach Charlies Bunion, a famous rock outcropping on the Appalachian Trail that is most commonly accessed from Newfound Gap. Coincidentally, Kephart was present in the party of hikers who, when struck by the sight of this bare rocky spire, christened it for a long-suffering companion's protruding bunion.

The view from Charlies Bunion, sitting at an elevation of 5,400 feet, sweeps across state lines to both the North Carolina and Tennessee sides of the park. A spruce-fir forest grows here, including other species such as yellow birch. Raven (*Corvus corax*), turkey vultures (*Cathartes aura*), and hawks all favor this higher elevation.

This jagged and rakish outcrop is part of the Anakeesta Formation (*see* Chimney

TURKEY VULTURE
(Cathartes aura)
The vulture's wings form
a "V" when gliding.

Tops, page 272). Unlike Thunderhead Sandstone, which is metamorphosed from sand deposits and is extremely durable, Anakeesta was formed from oceanic mud and its slate layers are easily cloven.

A lumber company fire that swept up here from Kephart Prong heightened the starkness of Charlies Bunion. The hold of the trees in this rocky soil was already precarious when the fire ravaged the hillside. Stripped of vegetation, the soil washed away, and it is estimated that it may take centuries for equally deep soil pockets to develop. For now, pin cherries (*Prunus pensylvanica*) and mountain-ash have gained a foothold.

Directions: From Oconaluftee Visitor Center, travel north on US 441 (Newfound Gap Road) for 7.5 miles. Trailhead and a small crescent-shaped parking area are on the east (right) side of the road.

Activities: Hiking.

Trail distance and configuration: Kephart Prong Trail; 2 miles one-way, to Charlies Bunion, 6.2 miles one-way.

Degree of difficulty: Easy on Kephart Prong Trail, grows strenuous beyond.

Fees: None.

Closest town: Cherokee, 9.5 miles.

Elevation: From 2,750 feet at Newfound Gap Road to 5,400 feet at Charlies Bunion.

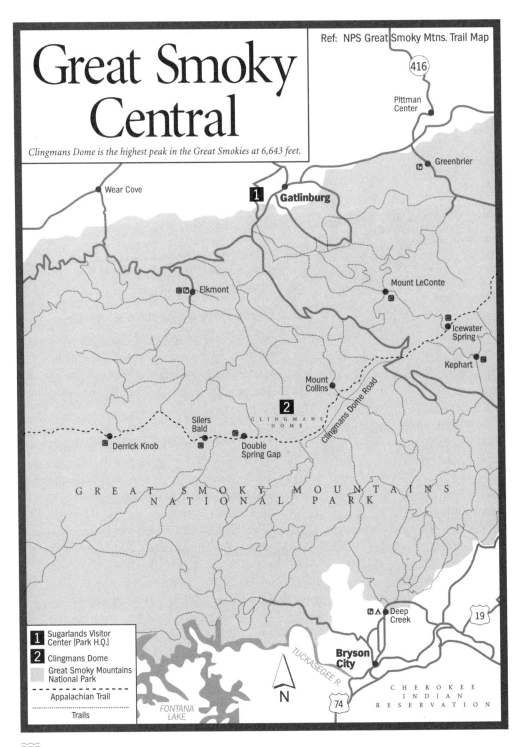

Great Smoky Central

Clingmans Dome is the highest peak in the Great Smokies at 6,643 feet.

Ref: NPS Great Smoky Mtns. Trail Map

416

Pittman Center

Greenbrier

Wear Cove

1 Gatlinburg

Mount LeConte

Elkmont

Icewater Spring

Kephart

Mount Collins

2

C L I N G M A N S
D O M E

Clingmans Dome Road

Silers Bald

Derrick Knob

Double Spring Gap

G R E A T   S M O K Y   M O U N T A I N S
N A T I O N A L   P A R K

Deep Creek

19

1 Sugarlands Visitor Center (Park H.Q.)

2 Clingmans Dome

Great Smoky Mountains National Park

- - - - - Appalachian Trail

.... Trails

TUCKASEGEE R.

Bryson City

N

74

C H E R O K E E
I N D I A N
R E S E R V A T I O N

FONTANA LAKE

Clingmans Dome

[Fig. 43(12)] Rising 6,643 feet above sea level, Clingmans Dome is the highest peak in the Great Smokies, outstripping Mount Guyot by some 40 feet. Standing on the deck of its observation tower, visitors have the park laid out at their feet, with views stretching into seven states on a clear day.

For its ringside seat to the heavens, Clingmans Dome bears the brunt of what they have to offer. It wrings from the skies nearly 27 more inches of precipitation per year than Gatlinburg, located just 22 miles away. Its annual precipitation rate of 83 inches makes it one of the wettest spots in the continental United States. Temperatures regularly dip 10 to 15 degrees Fahrenheit lower than the temperatures in the valleys, and gale-force winds can make a jacket necessary even in summer.

As its cool climes make it a home to one of the Smokies' rare spruce-fir forests, Clingmans Dome has become a focal point of the National Park Service's efforts to battle the balsam woolly aphid and save the Fraser fir from extinction. Originally from Europe, the aphid was introduced on nursery stock into New England around 1900. First detected in the eastern part of the Smokies in 1963, the aphids had spread as far west as Clingmans Dome by the late 1970s. Over the last 20 years, more than 95 percent of the mature fir in the park have been killed by the aphid.

An aphid is a mere millimeter long—a white fleck of snow. But its mouthparts stretch to 2 millimeters. Blown onto a tree by winds or on the wings of a bird, the aphid inserts these strawlike mouthparts into the bark of its new home to suck out sap; as it does so, it releases a toxin that eventually cuts off the tree's internal flow of nutrients. Once stuck, an aphid will not prize itself loose again. Instead, through asexual reproduction, it produces eggs. In southern Appalachia, as many as three generations of aphids may be born a year. Although mere "flecks," they can cover the trunk of a tree so densely it appears washed in white.

In the mid-1980s the National Park Service began to fight back with a spraying program at Clingmans Dome and Balsam Mountain Road. Each year in June foresters comb the woods in these areas to count the number of aphids. Of the 95 mature firs inspected (aphids only attack older trees with thicker bark), some may have more than 100 aphids, others may have none. Trees that will not be sprayed are also studied to establish a control to monitor the success of the program.

In July when the aphids are out in their greatest numbers and are more vulnerable, the actual spraying begins. Using modified fire pumper trucks with high-pressure sprayers, a mild insecticidal soap is sprayed onto trees along both sides of Clingmans Dome Road from Mount Collin's Gap to the Forney Ridge parking area, a distance of about 3.5 miles. On top of the dome, teams of workers range into the forest as far as long, high-pressure hoses will reach. A fine mist of the solution is sprayed onto the base of the tree, so as not to disturb the lichens and mosses that grow there, but the solution gets stronger as the spray moves up the trunk. About 9 acres of forest on Clingmans Dome are treated. In a few weeks, the foresters return to take another count of the aphids. If necessary, reinfested trees are retreated at that time.

Of course, this is at best a defensive effort. Not every fir can be reached by the hoses for treatment, nor can every aphid in the park be tracked. It is also not certain that funding will be appropriated every year for the program. Yet long-term hope remains. Some mature Fraser firs have survived infestation. These trees developed odd scars of toughened bark, like fish scales, where attacked. It is hoped that the next generation of trees will inherit this genetic resistance. Working in conjunction with the University of Tennessee, the Park Service has also collected seeds from surviving trees. A "genetic bank" of Fraser fir now grows adjacent to the park, on property that will soon be donated and included within the park's boundaries.

The secret to resistance cannot be found too quickly. Eight species of mosses and liverworts unique to Fraser fir communities have been affected by the infestation. Among animals, the spruce-fir moss spider has already had its numbers reduced. Classified as a type of tarantula, the spider lives in mats of moist mosses at the trees' bottoms. When the fir dies, sunlight comes through the branches and dries out the spider's habitat. No tree is an island—especially, it seems, in the Smokies.

Directions: From Sugarlands Visitor Center, follow Newfound Gap Road (US 441) into the park for 13 miles. Turn right (west) onto Clingmans Dome Road and drive 7 miles to the parking area.

Activities: Hiking.

Facilities: Displays and signs, restrooms.

Fees: None.

Closest town: Gatlinburg, 22 miles; Cherokee, 26 miles.

Trail distance and configuration: 1 mile round-trip from parking area to observation tower.

Degree of difficulty: Moderate, paved but steep.

Elevation: 6,311 feet at the parking area; 6,643 feet at the observation tower.

Surface: Paved.

ALUM CAVE BLUFFS

[Fig. 43(8)] It is said that, as a boy, the great Cherokee Chief Yanugunski discovered the bluffs of Alum Cave when he tracked a bear to its den there. This is no small feat because the bluffs are situated well up the southern flank of Mount LeConte at an elevation of 5,000 feet.

Alum Cave is not actually a cave. Rather, it is a 100-foot-tall recess beneath a ledge of rock that juts out some 30 feet from the mountainside, an awning built on the grand scale of nature. The elements eroded this outcropping of the slate-based Anakeesta Formation to form this tremendous overhang.

The smell of sulfur wafts off the bluff's inside walls, which are salty and bitter to the taste. What the senses report is proven by further study: Alum Cave is rich in mineral deposits. This fact was not lost on the visitors who followed Yanugunski to the cave. In the 1830's, a manufacturing company was formed to mine epsom salts from the bluff (although records indicate that if mining was done it was not overly successful). During the Civil War, a Confederate colonel ordered another mine built here to extract saltpeter and sulfides for gunpowder. The bluff is named for the potassium aluminum sulfate that can be seen, with saltpeter, encrusted in the walls at the back of the cave.

In modern years, the lode of minerals at Alum Cave has attracted the attention of geologists. Increasingly rare deposits are being discovered. A few of the minerals have never been cataloged before and are believed to be unique to the outcropping.

A trail leading to Alum Cave first passes over a rocky spur known as Inspiration Point. The view from here encompasses the valley below as well as Little Duck Hawk Ridge, a sheer cliff (also of the Anakeesta Formation) that lies across the valley to the west. Historically a nesting place for peregrine falcons (*Falco peregrinus*)—called "duck hawks" by settlers—it may well become one again. Nesting peregrines were reported in the area in the spring of 1997, the first pair to nest in the park since 1946.

The climb up Mount LeConte has garnered a reputation as an important benchmark in any hiker's career in the Smokies. Alum Cave Trail is the shortest but steepest of the five trails to the summit and travels along scenery considered by many to be the best in the park. Overnight accommodations are available at LeConte Lodge, which is a welcomed view a few hundred yards beyond the trail's end. Reservations, however, should be made well in advance as the 50-person lodge is often booked as far as a year in advance.

Directions: From Sugarlands Visitor Center, travel south on Newfound Gap Road (US 441) for 8.6 miles. Parking and trailhead are well marked on east (left) side of road.

Activities: Hiking.

Trail distance and configuration: 4.9 miles one-way (2.5 miles to Alum Cave).

Degree of difficulty: Strenuous.

Fees: None.

Closest town: Gatlinburg, 10.6 miles; Cherokee, 22 miles.

Elevation: From 3,850 feet at Newfound Gap Road to 6,350 feet at junction with Rainbow Falls Trail on summit of Mount LeConte.

For more information: LeConte Lodge, 250 Apple Valley Road, Sevierville, TN 37862, Phone (423) 429-5704.

EASTERN REDCEDAR
(Juniperus virginiana)
Cedar chests are made from the fragrant wood of this tree.

The Chimney Tops

[Fig. 43(4)] The rocky spires of the Chimney Tops rise 50 feet above the summit of Sugarland Mountain. Climbing well above the tops of the surrounding trees, they offer a rare assertion in the forest-blanketed Smokies of the power and might of stone. To settlers, the twin pinnacles must have been a reassuring sight, a landmark as orientating as the top of a neighbor's chimney spied above the tree line. The resemblance of the rocky spires to a chimney holds true close up as well: each pinnacle has a shaft, or a chimney hole, winnowed into its left side.

The Chimneys are an outcropping of the Anakeesta Formation, the Precambrian rock layer that forms much of the crest of the Smokies. Composed of metamorphic slates, schists, and phyllites, Anakeesta is the dark gray color of clay and, in exposures like the Chimneys, is burnished with a rust color that results from oxidation of the iron sulfide in the rock. Pyrite, commonly called "fool's gold," often adds flecks of metallic tint to Anakeesta as well, another indication of the high sulfide content that has earned the formation the nickname "acid rock." The slate layers of Anakeesta break apart relatively easily, and it is this characteristic that has created so many of the steep-sided ridges of the Smokies as well as such rakish outcroppings as the Chimneys and Charlies Bunion (*see* Charlies Bunion, page 265).

Typical of the Smokies, the Anakeesta of the Chimney Tops lies atop a layer of rocks known as the Thunderhead Formation. Exposures of Thunderhead can be seen from the bridges that cross over the West Prong and Road Prong of the Little Pigeon River near the bottom of the trail to the Chimneys. A gritty, light-gray sandstone, Thunderhead is extremely resistant to weathering, and in the creek beds, its uplifted strata makes the water crash around it.

The 2-mile uphill hike to the Chimneys is steep and strewn with small boulders, but it's well worth the panoramic view from the top. It's also not without its rewards along the way. In addition to great tangles of rhododendron, the creek area hosts shadbush (*Amelanchier laevis*) and trilliums in spring, and in summer, bee-balm (*Monarda didyma*), jewelweed (*Impatiens capensis*), and joe-pye weed (*Eupatorium maculatum*). As it climbs, the trail passes through two beech gaps resplendent in spring with such wildflowers as fringed phacelia (*Phacelia fimbriata*), Dutchman's breeches (*Dicentra cucularia*), spring beauty (*Claytonia caroliniana*), trout lily (*Erythronium americanum*), and squirrel corn. Coves of yellow buckeye and yellow birch (*Betula lutea*)—both known for autumn foliage in their signature color—gradually give way to hemlock, red spruce, mountain laurel, and more rhododendron near the trail's end.

Late-spring and summer birds in this area of the park include ruffed grouse (*Bonasa umbellus*), pileated and downy woodpeckers (*Bonasa umbellus* and *Dendrocopos pubsecens*), white-breasted nuthatch (*Sitta carolinensis*), wood thrush (*Hylocichla mustelina*), solitary and red-eyed vireos (*Vireo solitarius* and *Vireo flavoviridis*), black-throated green warbler (*Dendroica virens*), black-and-white warbler (*Mniotilta varia*), black-throated blue warbler (*Dendroica caerulescens*), and scarlet tanager (*Piranga olivacea*).

(Note: Extreme caution should be used when climbing on the rock exposures, especially near the chimney holes and in inclement weather. Injuries have occurred when people attempted to climb beyond the trail to the second, northerly pinnacle.)

Directions: From Sugarlands Visitor Center, follow Newfound Gap Road (US 441) south for 6.7 miles. Parking area and trailhead is on the west (right) side of the road.

Activities: Hiking.

Fees: None.

Closest town: Gatlinburg, 8.7 miles; Cherokee, 24 miles.

Trail distance: 4 mile round-trip.

Elevation: From 3,450 feet at Newfound Gap Road to 4,750 feet at the Chimney Tops.

Degree of difficulty: Moderate to strenuous.

Surface and blaze: Forest floor.

Sugarlands Visitor Center and Gatlinburg Trail

[Fig. 43(2), Fig. 44(1), 46(1)] Hosting more than 800,000 visitors each year, this center is by far the busiest of the gateways to the Smokies, a reflection not only of the popularity of nearby trails but of the crowds drawn to other local attractions. As the sheer sales volume of its T-shirt shops attests, the bustling tourist town of Gatlinburg owes a large part of its thriving economy to dollars brought in by tourism. Sevierville and Pigeon Forge, home of Dollywood, are also within an easy drive.

The center is nestled in the Sugarlands Valley, home in pioneer times to a few scattered cabins and cornfields and reachable only by mule. The name of this once-remote valley comes from the abundance of maples that grow there, known to pioneers as "sugartrees" for their sap. The name that North Carolina settlers used for the valley, however, offers an interesting alternate perspective on its history: they called it "Moonshiner's Paradise."

Two short and easy trails lead off from Sugarlands. The 1-mile Sugarlands Self-guiding Nature Loop [Fig. 43(3)] serves as a good introduction to the wonders of the Smokies, especially after viewing the exhibits and orientation films inside the center. The 2-mile Gatlinburg Trail [Fig. 43(1)] winds past Park Headquarters to follow the West Prong of the Little Pigeon River into Gatlinburg. Hemlock, rhododendron, and mountain laurel grow along the banks, as well as American hornbeam (*Carpinus caroliniana*), sweetgum (*Liquidambar styraciflua*), and the spectacularly flowering Stewartia, or silky camellia (*Stewartia malacondendron*). The loud call of the belted kingfishers (*Megaceryle alcyon*) dipping above the waters has startled more than one of the local joggers and bikers who frequent this path. Swainson's warblers (*Limnoth-lypis swainsonii*) are sometimes summer residents of the rhododendron thickets near the visitor center.

Directions: From downtown Gatlinburg, follow US 441 south 2 miles to intersection with Little River Road. Visitor center is on right.

Activities: Hiking.

Facilities: Visitor center with exhibits and information, filmed orientation, sales area, restrooms, backcountry permits.

Fees: None.

Closest town: Gatlinburg, 2 miles.

Roaring Fork Motor Nature Trail

[Fig. 43(5)] The literature of the movement to create the Great Smoky Mountains National Park is steeped in the enthusiasm of early advocates for whom the mountains represented a heady mystery to be both investigated and shared. Page after page of these booklets declare the wonders of the Smokies. Interestingly, a relatively new invention in the 1920s, the automobile, is also touted in these pages. Horace Kephart, one of the Smokies' most outspoken proponents and one of the great preservers of its ways and lore, even predicted a time when "a skyline highway" would run along the crest of the Smokies to connect its peaks.

Happily, this did not come to pass. Yet such roads as Roaring Fork Motor Nature Trail and Cades Cove Loop Road are in keeping with the spirit of those bygone days, allowing visitors to tour highlights of the park by car, with plenty of places to pull over and enjoy its still-mysterious beauty.

Beginning and ending within miles of downtown Gatlinburg, Roaring Fork Motor Nature Trail is a one-lane, one-way road that for 5.5 miles winds along and across the creek from which it takes its name. As it spills down one of the steepest water gradients in the eastern United States, the rowdy, aptly named Roaring Fork seems to be rushing forward at a greater speed than traffic, which is limited to 15 miles per hour.

The drive passes through an old-growth forest of Eastern hemlocks. The spires of the tall, straight evergreens sometimes reach more than 100 feet, the diameter of the sturdy trunks below stretching as much as 5 feet across. Hardwoods such as sweet birch and black locust (*Robinia pseudoacacia*) grow in these damp woodlands, as does silverbell (*Halesia tetraptera*), a primarily southern Appalachian tree whose white, bell-shaped flowers emerge in spring. Below these trees thrives an understory of rhododendron, mountain laurel, flame azalea, and dog-hobble.

The area along the creek is home to an abundance of birds and other wildlife, such as black-capped and Carolina chickadees (*Parus atricapillus* and *P. carolinensis*), tufted titmice (*Parus bicolor*), and pileated woodpeckers, as well as the barred owl (*Strix varia*), which can easily be identified by its loud call of "Who cooks for you?" The retreating flanks of a black bear are frequently seen hustling out of sight of an oncoming car.

A portion of the drive travels along an old roadbed constructed in about 1850 by local men who used picks, shovels, dynamite, and sweat to clear a level path through the rock. Roaring Fork was then a community of 25 families who all shopped at the same single store and attended the same church and school. Two of their old homesteads, a small tub mill, and a barn are some of the historic buildings preserved along the trail.

Cherokee Orchard lies at the outset of the Roaring Fork Motor Nature Trail. Before it became park property in 1942, a commercial orchard and nursery raised neat ranks of apple trees on this acreage, but the fruit trees have since been shaded out by rapidly growing tuliptrees, silverbells, locusts, and red maples. Rainbow Falls Trail and Trillium Gap Trail leave from here to course up the side of Mount LeConte to its summit, the second highest in the park (*see* Alum Cave Bluffs, page 270).

These trails lead to two of the park's most dramatic waterfalls: Rainbow Falls and Grotto Falls. LeConte Creek flows over a wide lip of Thunderhead sandstone in a 75-foot freefall to form Rainbow Falls. Afternoon sun catches in the mist thrown up by the water in the bottom pool, producing the rainbow effect that gives the falls its name. Located on Trillium Gap Trail, Grotto Falls is a much smaller waterfall of 25 feet. Yet it still manages to drum out all surrounding noise, befitting of the noisy reputation of Roaring Fork which rushes over from its source near the top of Mount LeConte. Here the resistant Thunderhead sandstone is underlain by a softer and siltier layer of Elkmont Sandstone. Salamander sightings are frequent in the pools below these two falls, the zigzag (golden brown and dark green) and dusky (charcoal gray) varieties being most common.

The lower slopes of these two trails are blanketed in a cove hardwood forest of silverbell, hemlock, yellow-poplar, basswood, and scattered white pine. Both red and sugar maples flourish here. Winter wren (*Troglodytes troglodytes*), Kentucky warbler (*Oporornis formosus*), red-eyed vireo, indigo bunting (*Passerina cyanea*), and American goldfinches (*Carduelis tristis*) flit and sing in the branches along the trails. On the higher slopes, a mixed forest of hardwoods and hemlock gives way to red spruce and Fraser fir, many of the latter dead as a result of the exotic aphids that infested the park in the 1960s (*see* Clingmans Dome, page 269).

Wildflowers abound along both trails. Rainbow Falls is noted for its rosebay rhododendron, shiny galax, and trailing arbutus (*Epigaea repens*). In summer, beebalm, sweet pepperbush (*Clethra alnifolia*), and pink turtlehead (*Chelone lyoni*) all come into flower. Not surprisingly, Trillium Gap is known for its namesake flower. Three species grow there, erect painted trillium (*Trillium undulatum*), large-flowered trillium (*Trillium grandiflorum*), and yellow Vasey (*Trillium viride* var. *luteum*). At

Trillium Gap, about 5 miles along the trail, stands a beech gap with attendant spring flowers of fringed phacelia, trout lily, and Dutchman's breeches.

Directions: From US 441 in Gatlinburg, turn onto Airport Road (traffic light number 8), which becomes Cherokee Orchard Road. Roaring Fork Motor Nature Trail begins 3 miles into Cherokee Orchard Road.

Activities: Hiking.

Trail distance and configuration: Rainbow Falls Trail, 6.6 miles one-way (2.6 miles to Rainbow Falls); Trillium Gap Trail, 8.7 miles one-way (1.5 miles to Grotto Falls).

Degree of difficulty: Moderate to strenuous.

Elevation: From 2,550 feet in Rainbow Falls parking area to 6,593 feet at Mount LeConte summit.

Fees: None.

Closest town: Gatlinburg, 3 miles.

For more information: A good companion for the drive is the Roaring Fork brochure available in Sugarlands Visitor Center which describes key points of the trail in great detail.

▓ LAUREL FALLS TRAIL

[Fig. 43(7)] While abundant thickets of mountain laurel justify the first half of this trail's name, the word "falls" is actually a misnomer. As Laurel Branch flows downward from Cove Mountain, it crosses over massive ledges of sandstone that act as stairsteps for the creek on its journey toward the Little River. Because the water steps downs from ledge to ledge and never clears the rock in a free fall, this spot is more properly called a cascade.

Misnaming, however, has not marred the loveliness of the display, which features a spectacular 85-foot drop. Nor has it kept visitors from flocking here. The walk to the falls is paved and only 1.3 miles long, making this well-shaded watering hole a popular and crowded destination on weekends and sunny afternoons.

The same sandstone that forms Laurel Falls also can be seen in the steep rock faces that rise along the trail. This tough and coarse-grained metasandstone, interbedded with thin layers of slate and phyllite, is part of the Thunderhead formation, whose resistance to weathering has helped to create so many of the park's waterfalls (*see* Rainbow Falls, page 275). A crew from the CCC blasted through the rock to cut this wide trail into the hillside.

When it reaches Laurel Falls, the trail cuts between two of the ledges that form the cascade on a concrete bridge. Beyond the falls, the trail gets both rougher and, as a result, quieter. The height must have discouraged loggers because the trail climbs through a venerable old-growth forest of cove hardwoods (one of the park's research plots on old-growth oaks is located just a mile above the falls). Visitors to the Smokies are often amazed by the size of its tuliptrees and yellow buckeyes, and it becomes clear why when viewing fine specimens along this ascent. Fraser magnolia (*Magnolia fraseri*) come into flower with their huge white blossoms in early May.

Directions: From Sugarlands Visitor Center, travel west on Little River Road for 3.8

miles. Parking on both sides of the road, trailhead on the north side.

Activities: Hiking.

Facilities: None.

Fees: None.

Closest town: Gatlinburg, 5.8 miles.

Trail distance and configuration: 2.6 miles round-trip to Laurel Falls, 8 miles round-trip for entire trail.

Elevation: 2,300 feet at junction with Little River Road; 4,050 feet at trail's end.

Degree of difficulty: Moderate to Laurel Falls, more strenuous beyond.

Surface and blaze: Forest floor.

RAMSAY CASCADES

[Fig. 43(6)] This beautiful trail along the Middle and Ramsay prongs of the Little Pigeon River courses through several interesting features, including some of the largest trees found in the park. Tulip poplar (up to 5-foot diameter), silverbell (2.5-foot diameter), sweet birch (3.5-foot diameter), and black cherry (3-foot diameter) thrive here. Unusual-looking yellow birch trees grow along the trail, their roots rising noticeably above the forest floor. These trees grew from seedlings sprouted on downed trees that have since rotted away, leaving the birch roots exposed in midair.

The trail follows an old roadbed through block fields of Thunderhead Sandstone boulders measuring 30 to 40 feet in diameter. These fields are thought to have formed during the Pleistocene era, falling from the cliffs of sandstone on the mountain slopes above. Today, 10,000 years later, the block fields have been altered and obscured by years of weathering and the growth of thick vegetation.

After 1.5 miles the trail leads to the confluence of the Ramsay Prong and Middle Prong with a more strenuous climb through the hardwood and hemlock forest to the sandstone bluff over which picturesque Ramsay Cascades flows, crashing against the sandstone boulders 60 feet below. Ramsay Cascades is the highest falls in the park that can be accessed by trail. To return to the parking area, backtrack on the trail.

Directions: Heading east from Gatlinburg on US 321/TN 73, travel 5.9 miles to the Greenbrier entrance to the park on the right. Travel on the park road for slightly more than 3 miles. When the road splits, turn left, and continue approximately 1.5 miles to the parking area.

Activities: Hiking.

Facilities: On Greenbrier entrance road, picnic area and ranger station.

Closest town: Gatlinburg, 10 miles.

Trail distance and configuration: 8 miles round-trip.

Elevation: 4,300 feet at the Ramsay Cascades.

Degree of difficulty: Moderate to strenuous.

Surface and blaze: Roadbed, forest floor.

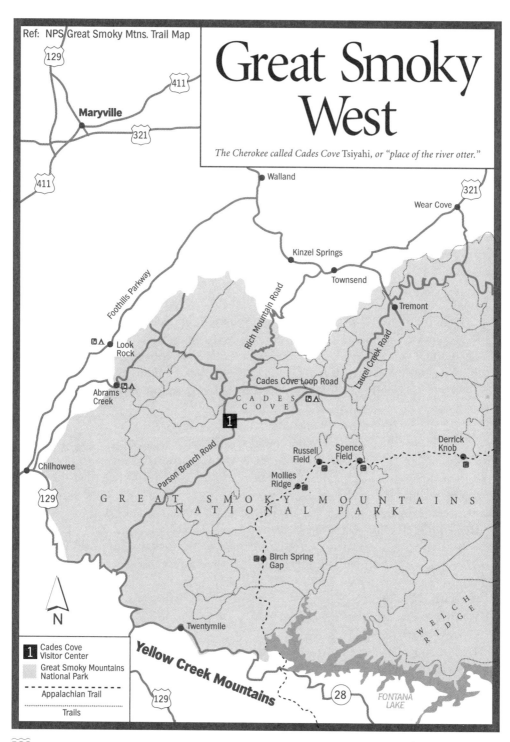

Ref: NPS Great Smoky Mtns. Trail Map

129

411

Maryville

321

411

Great Smoky West

The Cherokee called Cades Cove Tsiyahi, or "place of the river otter."

Walland

Wear Cove   321

Kinzel Springs

Townsend

Foothills Parkway

Rich Mountain Road

Tremont

Laurel Creek Road

Look Rock

Cades Cove Loop Road

Abrams Creek

C A D E S
C O V E

1

Russell Field

Spence Field

Derrick Knob

Chilhowee

Parson Branch Road

Mollies Ridge

129

G R E A T   S M O K Y   M O U N T A I N S
N A T I O N A L   P A R K

Birch Spring Gap

W E L C H
R I D G E

N

Twentymile

1 Cades Cove Visitor Center

Great Smoky Mountains National Park

- - - Appalachian Trail

.... Trails

Yellow Creek Mountains

129

28

FONTANA LAKE

Cades Cove

[Fig. 43(10), Fig. 44(2), Fig. 47(1)] For thousands of years, Cades Cove was a hunting and gathering territory for the Cherokee. They called it *Tsiyahi*, or "place of the river otter." Around 1818 the first European settlers migrated to the 20-square-mile valley. Six generations made their homes here, many in log cabins constructed with the abundant tulip poplar. The Paleozoic limestone of the cove is several million years younger than the rock in the surrounding mountains, and the weathering of this limestone yielded fertile, deep soils ideal for farming.

In 1934, Cades Cove became part of the Great Smoky Mountains National Park. Like the Cherokee before them, cove residents were forced to move. Though just a few log houses, outbuildings, and churches remain of the Cades Cove community, the black walnut trees (*Juglans nigra*) that settlers planted in their front yards still hold their ground. The diverse habitat of the cove, including 4,500 acres of open meadow, forested slopes, caves, and underground springs, supports abundant wildlife. At sunup, on a drive around the 11-mile loop road, it is possible to see as many as 200 white-tailed deer. The nocturnal bobcat (*Felis rufus*), though seldom seen, is still common in the cove, as is the native gray fox (*Urocyon cinereoargenteus*).

The black cherry tree is the favorite fruit of another cove dweller, the American black bear. Other animals include the endangered red wolf (*Canis rufus*) (*see* Red Wolf, page 255), striped skunk (*Mephitis mephitis*), and a wide variety of shrews, moles, and mice. There are several different species of snakes in the cove, and many bats can be found in the abundant caves, which have controlled public access.

As the seasons progress, abundant native flora brighten the meadows and woods. Some species in the cove are rare elsewhere in the park. Among them are swamp dewberry (*Rubus hispidus*) and the buttonbush (*Cephalanthus occidentalis*).

Birds are plentiful in Cades Cove, and the area is well known for its wild turkeys (*Meleagris gallopavo*). Late-spring and summer birds range from the downy and pileated woodpecker, ruby-throated hummingbird (*Archilochus colubris*), common yellowthroat (*Geothlypis trichas*), and blue grosbeak (*Guiraca caerulea*) to Eastern meadowlark (*Sturnella magna*), Acadian flycatcher (*Empidonax virescens*), Eastern wood pewee (*ontopus virens*), and blue-gray gnatcatcher (*Polioptila caerulea*). The sounds of the barred owl (*Strix varia*), screech owl (*Otus asio*), and whip-poor-will (*Caprimulgus vociferus*) can be heard in the night.

Directions: From Gatlinburg, travel south on US 441. Turn right on Little River Road (east) at Sugarlands Visitor Center. From Townsend on US 321, continue south on Scenic 73. Turn right at Laurel Creek Road.

Activities: Hiking, camping, fishing, horseback riding, bicycling, hay rides.

Facilities: Restrooms, camp store, visitor center. Campground is located just before the entrance of the loop road. No hookups. Water available in restrooms throughout the area.

Fees: There is a charge for campground.

Closest town: Townsend, TN, 8 miles.

Trails: Several trails lead from Cades Cove area.

CADES COVE NATURE TRAIL. Easy, self-guiding trail located 1 mile past the Abrams Falls turnoff around the loop road. Brochures available at the head of the trail.

GREGORY BALD. A more challenging trail beginning at the end of Forge Creek Road (a side road next to the Cades Cove Visitor Center). Traverses several acres of old-growth forest and climbs 5,000 feet to a 10-acre grassy bald. Trail is 10 miles round-trip with a 3,000-foot elevation gain.

SPENCE FIELD. Trail starts at the back of the Cades Cove picnic area. This difficult hike is 11 miles round-trip and climbs to about 3,000 feet. At the top of the trail, a left turn onto the Appalachian Trail leads to Thunderhead Mountain.

ABRAMS FALLS

[Fig. 43(9)] Located in the Cades Cove area of the park, Abrams Falls Trail offers access to the beautiful falls and a walk through the Cades Cove geologic window. Throughout the Cades Cove valley, layers of younger, Paleozoic limestone underlie older metamorphosed rock, a result of ancient upheavals and collisions that thrust older rock over younger rock. Over millions of years, the older rock that forms the area's rugged landscape has been worn away by erosion, opening up "windows" into the layers of younger rock.

Abrams Falls Trail follows Abrams Creek, which flows with a strong volume of water. Approximately 2.5 miles into the trail, a short spur trail leads to Abrams Falls, where the stream is broad and robust as it plummets 20 feet over massive beds of Cades sandstone to a 100-foot-wide plunge pool below. Along the route, Arbutus Ridge, named for the abundant trailing arbutus here, provides scenic vistas and a look at the sandstone bedrock riddled with vertical cracks, or joints, as geologists call them. The thin or nonexistent soil that results from the flow of groundwater through these joints supports little plant life.

Not far away, though, rhododendron and mountain laurel begin to get a foothold, forming thick tunnels in some places. These magnificent evergreens, abundant in the mountains and best noted for their extravagant blossoms in late spring, serve a valuable role in maintaining thin soil cover. While their root systems help hold the soil, their thick, waxy leaves protect it from damaging winds and heavy rains.

The creek and falls are named after the Cherokee chief, Old Abram, who lived near the mouth of the creek. He and other chiefs were killed by a young soldier who was avenging the massacre of his family, though it was the Creeks and not the Cherokee who were to blame.

Sadly, there are other stories of man's inhumanity connected to the Abrams area. As recently as 1957 it was determined that "trash" fish, i.e., those that man cannot fish recreationally, should be poisoned to make room for the prized, nonnative rainbow trout. The poison Rotenone was dumped in a 15-mile section of Abrams Creek, killing 31 species of fish. A recovery effort began in 1980, especially of a unique species of catfish called madtoms, and today there is some cause for optimism.

River otters (*Lutra canadensis*) were also the victims of man's overtrapping and logging, which destroyed their habitats and extirpated these graceful creatures from the region. For 50 years the streams were void of otters, until 1986 when 11 otters were reintroduced to Abrams Creek; additional otters were later introduced into the Little River and other streams in North Carolina as well. As reintroductions show slow but steady success, river otter populations are growing once again.

Bird-watching in the Cades Cove Area is particularly rewarding (*see* Cades Cove, page 279). In addition to the birds found generally in the cove, Abrams Falls is a good site for northern parula (*Parula americana*), Swainson's warbler, and yellow-throated warbler (*Dendroica dominica*).

For a longer hike, Abrams Falls Trail continues past the falls for almost 2 more miles to connect with the Hannah Mountain and Hatcher Mountain trails.

Directions: Trail begins at the Abrams Falls parking area on the west end of Cades Cove (5 miles into the 11-mile, one-way loop road) between sign posts #10 and #11.

Activities: Hiking, fishing, horseback riding.

Facilities: None.

Fees: None.

Closest town: Townsend, TN, 13 miles.

Trail distance and configuration: 6 miles round-trip (to the falls and back).

Elevation: 1,710 feet at the parking lot; 1,460 feet at the plunge pool.

Degree of difficulty: Moderate.

Surface and blaze: Forest floor, rocky in sections.

GARTER SNAKE
(Thamnophis sirtalis)
Garter snakes have three stripes, one on back and one on each side. They're often found near water.

Long Trails in North Carolina

There are many opportunities to hike on the long trails in North Carolina.

FIGURE NUMBERS

49 Bartram Trail
50 Appalachian Trail

The Long Trails of
Western North Carolina

Three primary long trails are found in Western North Carolina: The Appalachian Trail, the Bartram Trail, and the Mountains-to-Sea Trail. The Appalachian Trail is probably the most famous long trail in the world, stretching approximately 2,100 miles from Georgia to Maine. The Bartram Trail traces the footsteps of famous naturalist William Bartram, who studied the flora and fauna of the Southeastern United States in the 1700s with his equally famous father John. When completed, the ambitious North Carolina Mountains-to-Sea Trail will extend from Western Carolina to the Atlantic Ocean. Each of these is well worth a hike, whether you do a small portion in a day hike or the entire length over many months.

[*Above:* Hikers enjoy Linville Gorge]

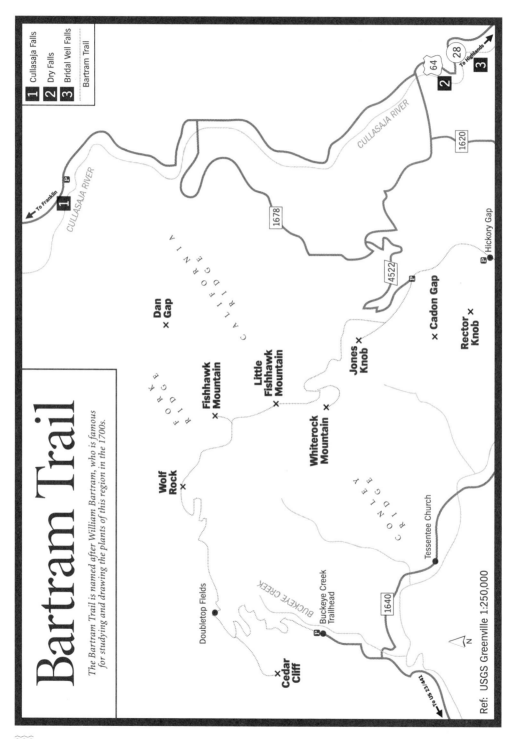

Bartram Trail

The Bartram Trail is named after William Bartram, who is famous for studying and drawing the plants of this region in the 1700s.

1	Cullasaja Falls
2	Dry Falls
3	Bridal Veil Falls
	Bartram Trail

CULLASAJA RIVER

To Franklin

CALIFORNIA

FORK

RIDGE

Dan Gap ×

Fishhawk Mountain ×

Little Fishhawk Mountain ×

Whiterock Mountain ×

Jones Knob ×

Cadon Gap ×

Rector Knob ×

Wolf Rock ×

CONLEY RIDGE

Doubletop Fields

Cedar Cliff ×

BUCKEYE CREEK

Buckeye Creek Trailhead

Tessentee Church

Hickory Gap

CULLASAJA RIVER

1620

1678

4522

1640

64

28

To Highlands

To US 23/441

N

Ref: USGS Greenville 1:250,000

The Bartram Trail in North Carolina

[Fig. 48, Fig. 49] The North Carolina Bartram Trail serves as a living legacy of the work of William Bartram, a native of Philadelphia who spent much time exploring the southern wilderness. Together with his father, John Bartram, he roamed Florida and the coast of Georgia before venturing off on his own through the Carolinas, Georgia, Alabama, Mississippi, Louisiana, and Florida from 1773 to 1778 (*see* Naturalists, page 230).

An avid writer and illustrator, Bartram kept voluminous journals of his travels and botanical research along the way. In 1791, he published these writings as *Travels Through North and South Carolina, Georgia, East and West Florida*, capturing his impressions and exacting descriptions of the flora, fauna, and Native Americans encountered. (The Creeks called him *Puc Puggy*, which translates from the Muskogean language as "the flower hunter.") More than 200 years later, *The Travels*, which earned him an international reputation, is still in print and offers rich accounts and passionate passages from a gentle man in love with his work in the natural world.

Following and in places paralleling the route that Bartram took into the southern Appalachian Mountains in 1775, members of the North Carolina Bartram Trail Society, together with the staff of the U.S. Forest Service, have constructed a memorial trail in the Nantahala National Forest. Based on his journals and other accounts, the 75-mile North Carolina Bartram Trail is divided into seven sections, which separately make excellent day hikes or together, a lengthy through-hike. The Bartram Trail also travels into parts of north Georgia and upstate South Carolina.

Members of the North Carolina Bartram Trail Society are active, hard-working volunteers who have spent two decades mapping, building, and regularly maintaining the trail. Walter G. McKelvey of Brevard led the way in the 1970s by securing government approval and support, researching the trail route, encouraging public interest, and directing trail flagging and clearing until his death in 1977. His dream finally came to fruition with the completion of the last segment of the trail in the summer of 1997. In October 1997, the entire trail was designated a National Recreation Trail.

The North Carolina Bartram Trail, which begins on the Georgia/North Carolina border near Georgia's Rabun Bald (4,696 feet), rises steadily as it passes through the forested rim of the Blue Valley and rocky overlooks, through mature oak forests and understory of rhododendron (*Rhododendron catawbiense* and *maximum*), mountain laurel (*Kalmia latifolia*), flame azalea (*Rhododendron calendulaceum*), and numerous wildflowers on its way across the crest of the Fishhawk Mountains.

Near Otto, the trail drops into the Little Tennessee River Valley, where travelers have a choice of canoeing or hiking an interesting 11-mile trail toward Franklin. From there, a strenuous 12-mile trail segment climbs Trimont Ridge to the highest point on the trail, Wayah Bald, elevation 5,341 feet. Here the yellow rectangular blazes of the Bartram Trail merge for 1.5 miles with the white blazes of the Appalachian Trail (*see* Wayah Bald, page 219). In this more remote section, white-tailed deer (*Odocoileus virginia*), wild turkey (*Meleagris gallopavo*), and black bear (*Ursus americanus*) may be spotted, though the wolves for which the bald is named (*Wayah* is a Cherokee word for "wolf") have been extirpated. Late-spring and summer birds in this area include the ruffed grouse (*Bonasa umbellus*), hairy woodpecker (*Dendrocopos villosus*), veery (*Hylocichla fuscenscens*), rose-breasted grosbeak (*Pheucticus ludovicianus*), ovenbird (*Seiurus aurocapillus*), golden-crowned kinglet (*Regulus satrapa*), a variety of warblers, and sometimes the yellow-bellied sapsucker (*Sphyrapicus varius*).

The Bartram Trail works its way down to Nantahala Lake and continues toward Appletree Campground in the Nantahala Gorge. It then ascends and crosses over Rattlesnake Knob where oaks, white pine (*Pinus strobus*), butternut (*Juglans cinerea*), and basswood (*Tilia americana*) form a canopy over wildflowers such as meadow rue (*Thalictrum revolutum*), Clinton's lily or speckled wood lily (*Clintonia umbellulata*), Indian pipes (*Monotropa uniflora*), and shiny patches of galax (*Galax aphylla*). Eventually the trail reaches the Nantahala River Launch Area before heading up Ledbetter Creek to the mile-high western terminus, Cheoah Bald (5,062 feet). At this point hikers can backtrack or continue north or south on the Appalachian Trail.

Some books still refer to a route that heads into the Snowbird region near Porterfield Gap. This route is now called the "Western Extension" of the North Carolina Bartram Trail, but it is not actively maintained by the society.

Like Bartram himself, the Bartram Trail Society traveled uncharted territory. Armed first with compasses and topographic maps, later with fire rakes, brush axes, and Pulaskis (the ingenious chopping and digging tool invented by U.S. Forest Ranger Edward Pulaski at the turn of the century), volunteers determined the course of the trail. The last section was particularly trying when they ran up against the western wall of the Nantahala Gorge, a near-vertical climb of 1,000 feet. Several scouting trips in 1993 and 1994 ruled out certain routes. According to scouts, the routes would have required nothing less than dynamite, bulldozers, and the state Department of Transportation! In February 1994, however, the dedicated corps bushwhacked, forged, and crawled its way through tangled undergrowth and discovered an old trail that appeared to be the best—and maybe only—way out of the Nantahala Gorge (a trail estimated to have been unwalked for 40 years). It is this kind of dedication, by hundreds of volunteers along dozens of trails in Western North Carolina, that makes it possible for so many to access and appreciate the beauty of the region. In the style of Bartram, these people in love with the natural world document their findings on maps and along trails for all to enjoy.

For more information: The Bartram Trail Society, c/o Dean Zuch, treasurer, PO Box 144, Scaly Mountain, NC 28775. Phone (704) 526-4904. Topographic maps of all seven sections are available for a fee. Or refer to Allen de Hart's book, *North Carolina Hiking Trails*, third edition.

Mountains-to-Sea Trail

The vision for a hiking trail stretching from the peaks of Western North Carolina to the Atlantic Ocean flowed as naturally as a leaf that washes downstream from the mountains to the sea. The foundation for such a vision was laid in 1973 when the North Carolina General Assembly passed the Trails System Act, both evidence of and a rallying point for the state's energetic trail community. A period of excitement and brainstorming followed, with individuals and groups exploring possibilities such as community greenways, canoe trails, and trail connections across the state. Not surprising, then, was the immediate and enthusiastic response in 1977 when Howard Lee, then-secretary of the North Carolina Department of Natural Resources and Community Development, challenged the participants at the Fourth National Trails Symposium at Lake Junaluska to undertake the establishment of a trail that would traverse and showcase the natural beauty of the entire state.

The idea took off, and the Mountains-to-Sea Trail (MST), as it came to be known, was under way, though the first trail segment was not dedicated until 1982. Currently, approximately 365.4 miles are completed, primarily in the mountains and on the Outer Banks. When completed, the MST will course 700 to 800 miles of footpaths, bike trails, horse trails, riverways, and backcountry roads on federal, state, and privately owned lands.

Like many national trails in the United States, the MST is constructed and maintained primarily by a cadre of dedicated volunteers made up of local, national, and even international trail enthusiasts. Project Raleigh, for example, brought 40 young volunteers from 13 countries for a summer of work on the trail in 1988. Made kin by a love of the outdoors, warm correspondences extolling the beauties of Western North Carolina continue today.

Twelve segments of the MST lie within Western North Carolina; nine of these segments are completed and another is well under way. They traverse virtually every habitat in the region, one of the most diverse in a temperate zone where robust plant and animal life thrives. Trails range in elevation from lofty Clingmans Dome, at 6,643 feet the highest peak in the Great Smokies, and Mount Mitchell, at 6,684 feet the highest point east of the Mississippi, down to Linville Gorge, considered to be the deepest gorge in the eastern United States. Blazes on the MST are 3-inch white circles; alternate routes are blazed with 3-inch blue circles. For detailed accounts of each segment, connecting trails, and natural features and attractions, refer to Allen de Hart's book, *North Carolina Hiking Trails*, third edition.

Before planning to hike any segment discussed here, please call ahead to learn if the trail is completed and officially open. For updates on trail development, contact the Mountain Region Trails Specialist, Division of Parks & Recreation, Department of Environment, Health and Natural Resources Regional Office, 59 Woodfin Street, Asheville, NC 28802. Phone (704) 251-6208.

GREAT SMOKY MOUNTAINS SEGMENT

Approximately 25 miles long, this segment in the Great Smoky Mountains National Park is still in the planning stages, but nearly 75 percent is already available for hiking because it will use many existing trails. The observation tower at the Clingmans Dome trailhead affords majestic views of the Smokies. The forest is lush in places, including virgin groves of spruce and American beech (*Fagus grandifolia*) that host birds such as the black-capped chickadee (*Parus atricapillus*), northern saw-whet owl (*Aegolius acadicus*), red-breasted nuthatch (*Sitta canadensis*), and a variety of warblers. White-tailed deer and wild hogs are also evident.

WATEROCK KNOB SEGMENT

Still in the planning stages, this segment will cross the Cherokee Reservation, paralleling the Blue Ridge Parkway.

BALSAM GAP SEGMENT

[Fig. 27(14)] This portion of the trail runs for approximately 35 miles from Blue Ridge Parkway (BRP) Balsam Gap Ranger Station (milepost 442.9) to the intersection of the BRP with NC 215 (BRP milepost 423.2). Abundant wildflowers and shrubs such as rhododendron and azalea and a number of wild berry patches—blueberry (*Vaccinium*), strawberry (*Fragaria virginiana*), and blackberry (*Rubus argutus*)—grow along this scenic section. It harbors northern hardwood and spruce-fir forest bird species including black-billed cuckoo (*Coccyzus erythropthalmus*), brown creeper (*Certhia familiaris*), wild turkey, yellow-bellied sapsucker, and black-capped chickadee. Grassy Ridge mine, an old mica mine, is visible off Grassy Ridge Overlook at BRP milepost 436.8. Spectacular views of the Great Balsam Mountains and the Tuckasegee River Valley are visible from Double Top Mountain Overlook (BRP milepost 435.3). This segment also offers excellent vantage points for watching the monarch butterfly (*Danaus plexippus)* migration.

MOUNT PISGAH SEGMENT

[Fig. 28(11)] Running from NC 215 (BRP milepost 423.2) to the BRP French Broad River Bridge (milepost 393.5) for approximately 39 miles (66 miles if following the alternative Art Loeb Trail, the only loop on the MST at this time), this high-elevation segment follows the Pisgah Ledge through the upper reaches of the Pigeon River watershed to spectacular vistas including views of Devil's Courthouse. The alternative route, Art Loeb Trail, drops down to the Davidson River before climbing back to Mount Pisgah through the Pink Beds (*see* Mount Pisgah, page 147, and Pink Beds, page 153). The trail courses past cascades and waterfalls, conifer groves, thickets of mountain laurel, and tunnels of rhododendrons that are breathtakingly beautiful when their blossoms open in May and June. Wild turkeys and northern bobwhites (*Colinus virginianus*) roam below as common yellowthroats (*Geothlypis* trichas), white-breasted nuthatches (*Sitta carolinensis*), cedar waxwings (*Bombycilla cedrorum*), several species of warblers, and even a few ruby-throated hummingbirds (*Archilochus colubris*) and golden eagles (*Aquila chrysaetos*) fly above.

ASHEVILLE SEGMENT

From the French Broad River Bridge (BRP milepost 393.5) to the Folk Art Center (BRP milepost 382.1), approximately 14 miles, this segment follows rolling terrain through forests of pine and hardwood. The understory includes ferns, orchids, wild ginger (*Asarum canadense*), trailing arbutus (*Epigaea repens*), as well as the ubiquitous rhododendron and mountain laurel. Along the river's edge, it is not uncommon to find great blue heron (*Ardea herodias*), green heron (*Butorides virescens*), and belted kingfisher (*Megaceryle alcyon*). This is also a good site for watching the spring migration of orioles and warblers, generally in April and May.

CRAGGY MOUNTAINS SEGMENT

Approximately 24 miles long and beginning at the Folk Art Center (BRP milepost 282.1), this section parallels the BRP most of the way to Balsam Gap (milepost 359.8) and offers excellent bird-watching opportunities for species such as yellow-bellied sapsucker, golden-winged warbler (*Vermivora chrysoptera*), scarlet tanager (*Piranga olivacea*), indigo bunting (*Passerina cyanea*), black-billed cuckoo, and brown creeper. At one point, the trail follows an old carriage trail to the remains of Rattlesnake Lodge, the former summer home of Asheville physician and outdoor activist Dr. C. P. Ambler. Farther north, The Craggies are considered by many to be the richest botanical area along the Parkway. The forest floor is thick with mosses and ferns, flame azalea, wild geranium (*Geranium maculatum*), and dwarf iris (*Iris verna*), and the late-spring Catawba rhododendron displays near Craggy Gardens are spectacular.

MOUNT MITCHELL SEGMENT

High-country hiking is excellent along this stretch which runs approximately 14.5 miles from Balsam Gap Parking Overlook (BRP milepost 359.8) to U.S. Forest Service Black Mountain Campground. In these spruce-fir forests chances are good for sighting the northern saw-whet owl, pine siskin (*Spinus pinus*), red crossbill (*Loxia curvirostra*), veery (*Hylocichla fuscenscens*), downy woodpecker (*Dendrocopos pubsecens*), golden-crowned kinglet, and a number of warblers. Small mammals and white-tailed deer, black bears, bobcats (*Felis rufus*), and gray foxes (*Urocyon cinereoargenteus*) roam this area. Some of the most spectacular scenery east of the Mississippi includes views of the Asheville Watershed, Potato Knob and Mount Mitchell in the Black Mountain range, and the nearby Great Craggy Mountains. This trail segment also includes a short side trail to the summit of Mount Mitchell, at 6,684 feet the highest point east of the Mississippi River.

WOODS MOUNTAIN SEGMENT

This is a particularly scenic segment running from U.S. Forest Service Black Mountain Campground to US 221 near Woodlawn, North Carolina, approximately 28 miles. This portion of the trail is under construction. Stunning vistas of Grandfather Mountain, Table Rock, Mount Mitchell, Green Knob, and Lake Tahoma surround. White-tailed deer, wild turkeys, and black bears live in the forests, where a thick understory of blueberry, galax, rhododendron, mountain laurel, and trailing arbutus thrives.

DOBSONS KNOB SEGMENT

Still in the planning stages, this segment will follow the established Overmountain Victory Trail for part of its route.

TABLE ROCK SEGMENT

Beginning at Kistler Memorial Highway (old NC 105), this section courses approximately 27 miles to NC 181. Breathtaking and rigorous, it travels from the western rim of Linville Gorge, descending to and fording (no bridge) the Linville River below (elevation 1,280 feet). The trail then ascends to the eastern rim (elevation 3,800 feet) as it heads up Shortoff Mountain and past a geological formation locally known as the Chimneys. This is an excellent area for viewing peregrine falcons (*Falco peregrinus*) and watching the autumn hawk migrations. Monarch butterflies also head through here in September on their annual migration to Mexico. Forests typical of the area feature Eastern hemlock (*Tsuga canadensis*), oaks, white pine, American sycamore (*Platanus occidentalis*), red maple (*Acer rubrum*), yellow-poplar (*Liriodendron tulipifera*), and black locust (*Robinia pseudoacacia*) over an understory of dog-hobble (*Viburnum alnifolium*), chinquapin (*Castanea pumila*), Allegheny sand myrtle (*Leiophyllum buxifolium prostatum*), and blueberry.

BEACON HEIGHTS SEGMENT

Along this segment from NC 181 to Beacon Heights (BRP milepost 305.2), approximately 18 miles, there are many cascades and gorgeous waterfalls, especially along South Harper Creek and North Harper Creek and the Hunt-Fish Falls trails. Though views are limited where the trail ascends the back side of Beacon Heights, the sections near Harper Creek, Lost Cove Creek, and Gragg Prong are picturesque. North Harper Creek is noted for its excellent trout fishing and displays of wildflowers.

GRANDFATHER MOUNTAIN SEGMENT

This biologically diverse segment runs its entire length along the BRP from Beacon Heights (BRP milepost 305.2) to Blowing Rock (BRP milepost 291.9), approximately 26 miles. It utilizes many trails such as the Rich Mountain Trail in the Moses Cone Estate, Boone Fork Trail, and the Tanawha Trail, where views of migrating hawks are excellent. (*Tanawha* is Cherokee for "fabulous hawk.") The Tanawha Trail also showcases the Linn Cove Viaduct and Grandfather Mountain.

Birds along this segment include the winter wren (*Troglodytes troglodytes*), peregrine falcon, black-capped chickadee, northern saw-whet owl, and numerous warblers. Migratory loons, grebes, and mergansers have been spotted near Julian Price Lake and Bass Lake at Cone Memorial Park. This area is also noted for its abundance of salamanders—at least 16 species.

The Appalachian Trail in North Carolina

[Figs. 50, 51] Benton MacKaye, a forester, conservationist, and regional planner, first envisioned a footpath through the Appalachian Mountains as a getaway from the stresses of urban culture. Since his proposal in 1921, the Appalachian National Scenic Trail (affectionately known as the AT) has not only become a reality but, for many, a way of life.

Often referred to as the world's most famous hiking trail, the AT runs along the crest of the Appalachian Mountains from Georgia to Maine, marked with white blazes throughout. The trail traverses 14 eastern states and crosses eight national forests, six national parks, and more than 75 public land areas. Lying within a day's drive of two-thirds of the nation's population, the AT receives several million visitors per year. Inspired by Benton MacKaye's dream, the Appalachian Trail was designed, constructed, and marked throughout the 1920s and 1930s by volunteer hiking clubs joined together by the Appalachian Trail Conference (ATC). In 1968, President Lyndon Johnson signed the National Trails System Act, making the Appalachian Trail the first National Scenic Trail, and the National Park Service was delegated overall responsibility for the trail. Federal agencies began purchasing land in order to protect the trailway from urban development; currently, only 36 miles of the trail remain unprotected.

Although the AT most recently measured 2,160 miles, relocations and other improvements to the route cause the trail's distance to change almost yearly. For example, the Blue Ridge Parkway in North Carolina and Skyline Drive in Virginia displaced more than 120 miles of the trail when they were constructed.

Designed to delight hikers, backpackers, and nature lovers of all sorts, the AT also serves the specific purpose of preserving the natural, scenic, historical, and cultural resources of the region. Hikes on the AT range from scenic walks to strenuous scrambles up spiring peaks, and many guidebooks are dedicated to exploring the AT's finest details. More than 4,000 people have hiked the entire distance of the Appalachian Trail, including section hikers, who complete the journey in segments, and through-hikers, who walk the entire length of the trail in one continuous trip. Most through-hikers begin their three-to-six month journey in March at the southernmost terminus of the trail—Springer Mountain, Georgia. Hikers begin in the South where the weather is already warm and

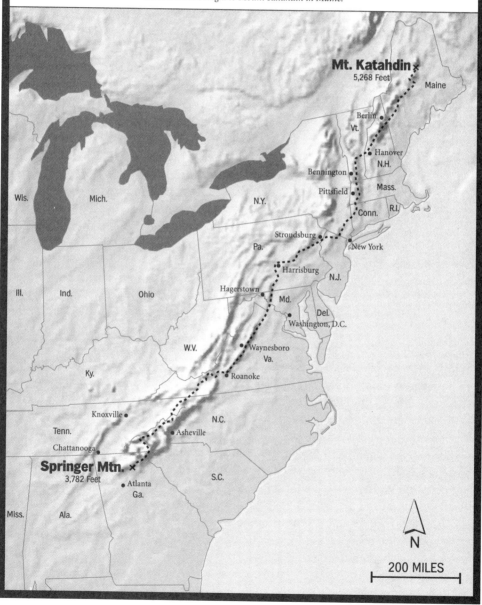

Appalachian Trail

The Appalachian Trail is over 2,100 miles long and stretches from Springer Mountain in Georgia to Mount Katahdin in Maine.

Mt. Katahdin ×
5,268 Feet
Maine

Berlin
Vt.

Hanover
N.H.

Bennington
Pittsfield
Mass.

Conn.
R.I.

Wis.
Mich.
N.Y.

Stroudsburg
New York

Pa.
Harrisburg
N.J.

Hagerstown
Ill.
Ind.
Ohio
Md.

Del.
Washington, D.C.

W.V.
Waynesboro
Va.

Ky.
Roanoke

Knoxville
N.C.

Tenn.
Asheville

Chattanooga

Springer Mtn. ×
3,782 Feet
Atlanta
Ga.
S.C.

Miss.
Ala.

N

200 MILES

enjoy the beautiful unveiling of spring as they move northward. Others, however, begin their trek in Maine at Mount Katadin and hike southward, braving late-season snows and the dreaded bites of blackflies in the summer.

Most forests along the AT have been harvested at least two or three times since colonial days. By doubling the height and tripling the girth of the trees along the trail, one can imagine what the forest may have looked like to the first Europeans exploring the region. Treeline is said to be 7,200 feet in the South, and most of the AT traverses through deciduous hardwood forests composed of hickory, oak, and poplar. As altitude is gained, the evergreen line becomes more apparent, with the forest changing from deciduous, to mixed, to evergreen by 5,800 feet.

Mid-April through mid-May is the peak wildflower season, and trilliums, blood-root (*Sanguinaria canadensis*), mayapple (*Podophyllum peltatum*), bluets (*Houstonia caerulea*), wild azalea, and pink and yellow lady slippers (*Cypripendium acaule* and *C. calceolus*) are common. Heavy rains bring lush vegetation during the summer months, and brightly colored rhododendron and mountain laurel begin coloring the higher elevations in June. The best time to view the fall foliage depends largely on temperature and location. Mother Nature's autumn show begins in late September in the higher elevations and creeps down into the lower elevations throughout October and early November.

The popularity of the AT has added a new common creature to the forest—humans. As many people leave the city to get away from the rat race, they are usually surprised at the number of people they encounter on the trail, especially in the spring and summer months. To really get away, hikers are encouraged to bypass the main areas of busy state and national parks and to venture out on longer trails and to backcountry campsites, where silence still prevails and the moon and stars are the brightest thing in the midnight sky. Campers are also encouraged to use a "minimum impact" camping philosophy—packing out all trash, digging latrines, and camping away from the water sources.

Other common creatures in the southern Appalachian Mountains include white-tailed deer, shrews, spotted skunks (*Spilogale putorius*), timber rattlesnakes (*Crotalus horridus*), copperheads (*Agkistrodon contortrix*), bobcats, and ever-curious deer mice (*Peromyscus maniculatus*). Wild boars, introduced from Europe in the 1930s by hunting clubs, thrive in the forest environment but also consume more than their fair share of the food required by many native species. Hikers often report soil by the AT that looks farm-plowed—a telltale sign of boars rooting near the trail. These animals are very unpredictable, and hikers are advised to keep their distance.

Also common are black bears, which over the years become increasingly less afraid of humans. While human attacks by these animals are rare, hikers should be on the lookout for protective mother bears with cubs. Feeding these animals is highly discouraged since it trains them to snoop around campsites and even challenge hikers for food. Also, since most human foods are not natural to a bear's diet, they

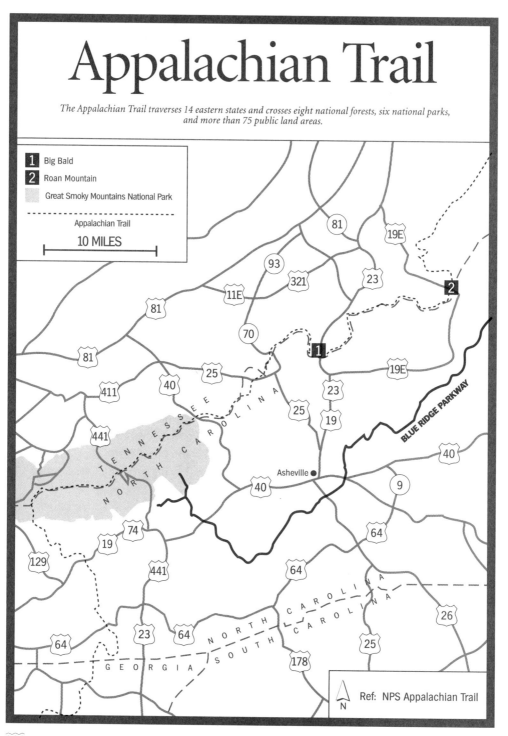

Appalachian Trail

The Appalachian Trail traverses 14 eastern states and crosses eight national forests, six national parks, and more than 75 public land areas.

1 Big Bald

2 Roan Mountain

Great Smoky Mountains National Park

- - - - - - - - - Appalachian Trail

10 MILES

Asheville

BLUE RIDGE PARKWAY

TENNESSEE

NORTH CAROLINA

NORTH CAROLINA

SOUTH CAROLINA

GEORGIA

Ref: NPS Appalachian Trail

N

often cause the animal to have unfavorable reactions including aggressive behavior and sickness. The house mouse (*Mus musculus*), an import from Asia, wins the award from most backpackers as both the cutest and most annoying forest creature. These little rascals inhabit most of the shelters along the trail. Their nocturnal nature keeps them scurrying throughout the night, and they love eating their way into hikers' food bags. Hikers and campers are advised to hang their food bags when leaving them unattended.

Most trail guides cover North Carolina and Tennessee together since many miles of the Appalachian Trail meander back and forth across the land where the two states meet. Combined, the two states offer more than 376 miles of trail. Hikers interested in extended hikes are encouraged to read the *North Carolina–Georgia Appalachian Trail Guide* and the *Tennessee–North Carolina Appalachian Trail Guide*, published by the ATC. Similar detailed guides are available for each of the 14 states covered by the AT. If not available at the bookstore, the guidebooks can be ordered from the Appalachian Trail Conference, PO Box 807, Harpers Ferry, WV 25425. Phone (304) 535-6331.

Suggested Day Hikes

▨ ROAN MOUNTAIN

[Fig. 51(2)] This trail is popular with hikers because of its thick forests, historical settings, thickets, and beautiful vistas. Famous for the Cloudland Rhododendron Gardens and unusual growth of Scotch heather, this part of the AT is heavily hiked in the last two weeks of June when these plants are in bloom. The rock from Carvers Gap to Roan High Knob is reported to be the oldest rock of the Appalachian Trail at 1.8 billion years old. This light-colored rock is composed of coarse-grained gneiss with feldspar.

From the parking area at Carvers Gap, follow the AT south. The trail follows the paved Cloudland Rhododendron Garden Road for awhile, and then curves out into the forest. At mile .25, the trail connects with an old road. Follow the road along switchbacks to its junction with a blue-blazed trail at mile 1.3. Here, a side trail goes left .1 mile to the summit of Roan High Knob. Continue past the picnic area and at the fork, turn left, crossing over an old trail. At the 1.9 mile mark, there is an old cabin site. Turn left, enter the woods, and begin climbing. A grassy area follows, and a small parking lot should be visible ahead. Beyond the parking lot are the Cloudland Rhododendron Gardens which bloom in middle to late summer. Return to the parking area at Carvers Gap by backtracking and taking the AT north (*see* Roan Mountain, page 75).

Directions: The Carvers Gap parking area is at the TN/NC state line, 14 miles south of the town of Roan Mountain. From Bakersville, NC, take NC 261 north for 14 miles.

Trail distance and configuration: 3.8 miles round-trip.

Degree of difficulty: Moderate.

▨ BIG BALD

[Fig. 51(1)] Big Bald is a great example of a southern Appalachian bald mountain. At 5,516 feet, the summit offers brilliant 360-degree views of the Black, Great Smoky, Nantahala, and Unaka mountains, including an excellent view of Mount Mitchell only 20 miles away. Along this stretch of the AT, the rock dates back more than 1 billion years. Big Bald has also been used as a site for raising and successfully releasing peregrine falcon fledglings.

Follow the AT northeast from the dirt road at Street Gap. Look for the trail to run to the right, forking from the road. The trail will pass three junctions with blue-blazed trails. (Blue blazes along the AT indicate spurs that lead to water, views, or shelters and often, though not necessarily, reconnect with the trail farther along.) The last .5 mile is through open meadows to the summit of Big Bald. Continue through an open meadow to a climb up Big Bald. To return, backtrack south on the AT.

Directions: From Sams Gap on the TN/NC state line, drive south 1.5 miles on US 23 to Smith Creek Road. Go east on Smith Creek Road 2 miles to Puncheon Fork Road. Turn left and drive about 1.5 miles to ridge crest and the AT trailhead at Street Gap. Some people get on from Sam's Gap which makes it a 10.4-mile trail.

Trail distance and configuration: 7.8 miles round-trip.

Degree of difficulty: Moderate.

Other recommended AT day hikes with references elsewhere in this book: Wayah Bald, page 219; Standing Indian, page 221; Clingmans Dome, page 269; Chunky Gal Trail, page 247; Lover's Leap, page 103.

Resources: The ATC in Harpers Ferry, West Virginia, publishes guidebooks, maps, educational brochures, newsletters, and a general magazine on the AT. The ATC also provides more than 60 other publications on hiking and backpacking subjects.

For more information: Appalachian Trail Conference, PO Box 807, Harpers Ferry, WV 25425-0807 phone (304) 535-6331. Web site: http://www.atconf.org. For North Carolina–specific AT information, contact the regional ATC office in Asheville at (704) 254-3708.

Trail regulations: Motor vehicles and bicycles are illegal on all off-road sections of the AT. Dogs are permitted everywhere along the trail except Great Smoky Mountains National Park and Baxter State Park, and dogs must be leashed in Shenandoah National Park. Horses are allowed only in designated sections of Great Smoky Mountains National Park. Permits are not needed for day hikes, but overnight campers should obtain permits when in Great Smoky Mountains and Shenandoah national parks, Baxter State Park, as well as parts of White Mountain National Forest.

Appendixes

A. Books and References

Amphibians and Reptiles of the Carolinas and Virginia by Bernard S. Martof et al., University of North Carolina Press, Chapel Hill, NC, 1980.

Best of the Appalachian Trail Day Hikes by Victoria and Frank Logue, Manasha Ridge Press, Birmingham, AL, 1994.

Birds of the Blue Ridge Mountains by Marcus B. Simpson Jr., University of North Carolina Press, Chapel Hill, NC, 1992.

Blue Ridge Parkway Guides by William G. Lord, Manasha Ridge Press, Birmingham, AL, 1992.

A Field Guide to the Birds East of the Rockies by Roger Tory Peterson, Houghton Mifflin, Boston, MA, 1980.

50 Hikes in the Mountains by Robert and Elizabeth Williams, The Countryman Press, Woodstock, VT, 1996.

Freshwater Fishes of the Carolinas, Virginia, Maryland, and Delaware by Fred C. Rohde et al., University of North Carolina Press, Chapel Hill, NC, 1994.

Great Smoky Mountains National Park: A Natural History Guide by Rose Houk, Houghton Mifflin Co., Boston, MA, 1993.

Hiking Trails of Joyce Kilmer–Slickrock and Citico Creek Wilderness Areas by Tim Homan, Peachtree Publishers, Atlanta, GA, 1990.

Horseback Riding Trail Guide to North Carolina by Martha Branon Holden, Bandit Books, Winston-Salem, NC, 1994.

The Insiders' Guide to North Carolina's Mountains, second edition, by Sara Pacher and Lynda McDaniel, Knight Publishing Co., Inc., Charlotte, NC, 1996.

Mammals of the Carolinas, Virginia, and Maryland by W. David Webster et al., University of North Carolina Press, Chapel Hill, NC, 1985.

Manual of the Vascular Flora of the Carolinas by Albert E. Radford et al., University of North Carolina Press, Chapel Hill, NC, 1987.

Mountain Biking the Appalachians by Lori Finley, John F. Blair, Publisher, Winston-Salem, NC, 1993.

A Naturalist's Blue Ridge Parkway by David T. Catlin, University of Tennessee Press, Knoxville, TN, 1992.

Newcomb's Wildflower Guide by Lawrence Newcomb, Little Brown and Company, Boston, MA, 1977.

North Carolina: A Guide to Backcountry Travel and Adventure by James Bannon, Out There Press, Asheville, NC, 1996.

North Carolina Hiking Trails by Allen de Hart, Appalachian Mountain Club Books, Boston, MA, 1996.

North Carolina Waterfalls: Where to Find Them, How to Photograph Them by Kevin Adams, John F. Blair, Publisher, Winston-Salem, NC, 1994.

Touring the Western North Carolina Backroads by Carolyn Sakowski, John F. Blair, Publisher, Winston-Salem, NC, 1990.

Walking the Blue Ridge: A Guide to the Trails of the Blue Ridge Parkway by Leonard Atkins, University of North Carolina Press, Chapel Hill, NC, 1991.

Waterfall Walks and Drives in the Western North Carolinas by Mark Morrison, H.F. Publishing, Douglasville, GA, 1994.

B. Special Events

Throughout the year North Carolina offers festivals and fairs that appeal to a wide range of residents and visitors. The following is a list of some events that occur annually in North Carolina arranged by month. Call the numbers provided to confirm dates and times.

Old Christmas Hickory Ridge Homestead, Boone. A traditional Christmas Celebration during which the community builds a huge bonfire, fueled by their holiday trees, to ensure good luck for the coming year. The event is free and usually takes place on January 6. Phone (704) 264-2120.

Biltmore Estate's Festival of Flowers, Asheville. Take a stroll through the gardens of the Biltmore. April through May. Phone (800) 543-2961.

Hickory Nut Gorge Dogwood Festival, Lake Lure. Celebrate the beauty of the dogwood flower and the return of spring in charming Lake Lure. April. Phone (704) 625-0204.

Pioneer Living Day, Weaverville. Experience the life of early mountaineers. Great food, crafts, and demonstrations. April and September. Phone (704) 645-6706.

Earth Day Celebration, Chimney Rock Park. Environmental awareness programs include demonstrations on composting and recycling, creative uses for kudzu, and guided wildflower walks. April. Phone (800) 277-9611.

Revolutionary War Encampment at FENCE, Tryon. Authentic crafts and foods, musket shooting demonstrations, and traditional campsite. April. Phone (704) 859-9021.

Ramp Convention, Waynesville. Celebrate ramps by eating dishes including the wild, onionlike ramp and by listening to country and bluegrass music. May. Phone (800) 334-9036.

Great Smoky Mountains Trout Festival, Waynesville. Crafts, food, contests, exhibitions, and entertainment. May. Phone (800) 334-9036.

Carl Sandburg Folk Music Festival, Flat Rock. Visit poet Carl Sandburg's farm, Connemara, for a day of folk music. Free. May. Phone (704) 693-4178.

Riverfest, Bryson City. Raft rides, races, great food, and live entertainment. Last Sunday in May. Phone (704) 488-6159.

Folk Art Center Clay Day, Asheville. Demonstrations by professional potters and sculptors. Opportunities for children and adults to make their own clay creations. June. Phone (704) 298-7928.

North Carolina Rhododendron Festival, Bakersville. Includes a 10K road race, golf tournament, pageants, and street dance. Celebrate the beauty of the rhododendron at this three-day festival. June. Phone (800) 227-3912.

Singing on the Mountain at Grandfather Mountain, Linville. Live gospel music and entertainment. Preaching by well-known pastors. July. Phone (704) 733-1333.

Dillsboro Heritage Festival, Dillsboro. Food, crafts, arts, and demonstrations. Second Saturday in June. Phone (704) 586-3943.

Firefly Festival Arts and Crafts Fair, Boone. Arts, music, and food. July. Phone (800) 852-9506.

Shindig-on-the-Green, Asheville. Free music events starting the first Saturday in July and continuing every Saturday night throughout the summer. Downtown Asheville. Phone (800) 257-1300.

Fourth of July Gala, Asheville. Fireworks, music, food, and fun! Phone (704) 259-5800.

Mountain Dance and Folk Festival, Asheville. One of the biggest folk music events of its kind. Fourth of July. Phone (704) 259-5800.

Old-Fashioned July Fourth Celebration on the Square, Burnsville. Wagon-train parade, crafts, and food. Old-time music. Phone (800) 948-1632.

Grandfather Mountain Highland Games and Gathering of the Scottish Clan, Linville. In their fifth decade, these renowned games feature Scottish athletic events, Highland dancing competitions, sheep herding exhibitions, bagpipe and drumming competitions, Celtic music, and traditional Scottish foods. Second weekend in July. Phone (704) 733-1333.

Craft Fair of the Southern Highlands, Asheville. This annual craft fair takes place at the downtown civic center in Asheville and includes exhibitions, demonstrations, and traditional music. Third weekend in July and third weekend October. Phone (704) 298-7928.

Banner Elk Art Festival, Banner Elk. This juried fine arts exhibition features 50 of the nation's best artists working in sculpture, blown glass, and painting (with an emphasis on watercolors). Third weekend in July. Phone (800) 972-2183.

Bele Chere, Asheville. A three-day festival offering excellent entertainment, crafts, and food. Many activities for children and adults. One of North Carolina's most popular festivals. Downtown Asheville, last weekend in July. Phone (704) 251-9973.

Coon Dog Day, Saluda. The second Saturday in July is set aside for the celebration of the Coon Dog. You don't have to be a hunter to enjoy the festivities—music, food, contests, dancing, and more! Phone (704) 749-2581.

Annual Gemboree, Franklin. Shop for gems and jewelry on the second weekend in July. Phone (800) 336-7829.

Folkmoot USA, Waynesville and other locations. Dancers and musicians from around the world meet in the mountains for a muticultural celebration. July. Phone (800) 334-9036.

Mineral and Gem Festival, Spruce Pine. More than 50 dealers from across the country exhibit the earth's bounty, ranging from rocks and minerals to finished products such as jewelry and sculpture. July/August. Phone (800) 227-3912.

Sourwood Festival, Black Mountain. Music, food, arts, crafts, and a carnival for children. Battle of the Bands. Third weekend in August. Phone (800) 669-2301.

Village Art & Craft Fair, Asheville. More than 150 artisans and crafters show their wares at the Historic Biltmore Village and on the grounds of the All Souls Cathedral in Asheville. First weekend in August. Phone (704) 274-2831.

Bluegrass Festival, Cherokee. From noon to night, the best of bluegrass is performed by famous artists over the three-day weekend. More than 16 groups sing and play fiddle, guitar, and banjo. Happy Holiday Campground. August. Phone (800) 438-1601.

Overmountain Victory Trail Celebration, Spruce Pine. Delve into North Carolina history by experiencing this reenactment of the "overmountain boys." September. Phone (800) 227-3912.

Mountain Heritage Festival, Sparta. Celebration of early mountain life. Great crafts and food. Last weekend in September. Phone (800) 372-5473.

Wooly Worm Festival, Banner Elk. Honor the wooly worm with the folks of Banner Elk while enjoying crafts, food, and entertainment. October. Phone (800) 972-2183.

Apple Festival, Boone. Crafts, entertainment, and lots of apples. October. Phone (800) 852-9506.

New River Festival, Todd. Storytelling, checker competitions, and fishing tournaments are just a few of the things that Todd's festival has to offer. Second Saturday in October. Phone (910) 877-1128.

Valle Country Fair, Valle Crucis. Mountain music, fine arts, and crafts. All proceeds from the fair benefit local charities. Mid-October. Phone (800) 852-9506.

Madison County Heritage Festival, Mars Hill. Traditional mountain crafts and food, storytelling, dancing, and much, much more. First Saturday in October. Phone (704) 689-1424.

Annual Forest Festival Day, Pisgah Forest. Relive the past by attending weaving, spinning, trail-building, and whittling demonstrations and more. October. Phone (704) 877-3130.

Pumpkin Fest, Franklin. Costumes, crafts, and pumpkin decorating. Last Saturday in October. Phone (800) 336-3704.

Choose and Cut Weekend. Make choosing and cutting this year's tree a family event. December. Sparta/Alleghany County: Phone (800) 372-5473. Ashe County: Phone (910) 246-9550. Watauga County: Phone (800) 852-9506.

Christmas at Connemara, Flat Rock. Visit the Carl Sandburg home for an old-fashioned Christmas. December. Phone (704) 693-4178.

Festival of Trees, Brevard. Gifts, cookies, treats, and beautifully decorated trees. December. Phone (704) 883-3692.

C. Outfitters

The following outfitters are listed alphabetically by city.

Rolling Thunder River Company. Canoe rentals and rafting trips. PO Box 88, Almond 28702. Phone (704) 488-2030.

Zippy Boat Works. Sales of canoes, kayaks, and paddling equipment. Clinics and rentals. US 25-A, Asheville 28803. Phone (704) 684-5107.

Black Dome Mountain Sports. Sales of backpacking, hiking, and snowboarding gear. Professional guide service. 140 Tunnel Road., Asheville 28805. Phone (800) 678-BDMS, (704) 251-2001.

The Compleat Naturalist. Hiking trips and field classes. Nature/wildlife art gallery. 2 Biltmore Plaza, Asheville 28803. Phone (704) 274-5430.

Hearn's Cycling and Fitness. Sales and repair. 34 Broadway, Asheville 28801. Phone (704) 253-4800.

Blue Spruce Outfitters. Sales of outdoor clothing, camping, and hiking gear. 117-C Cherry Street, Black Mountain 28711. Phone (704) 669-6965.

High Mountain Expeditions. Overnight hiking and rafting trips. Whitewater rafting on the Nolichucky and Watuga rivers. PO Box 1299, Blowing Rock 28605. Phone (800) 262-9036.

Boone Bike and Touring. Full-service bike shop. Repairs and rentals. 899 Blowing Rock Road, Boone 28607. Phone (704) 262-5750.

Footsloggers. Sales of hiking, rock-climbing, and camping equipment and accessories. 553 W. King Street, Boone 28607. Phone (704) 262-5111.

Rock and Roll Sports. Sales of bike, rock-climbing, and ice-climbing equipment. Bike and shoe rentals. 280 E. King Street, Boone 28607. Phone (800) 977-ROCK, (704) 264-0765.

Wahoo's Whitewater Rafting and Canoe Outfitters. Rafting down the Nolichucky, Watuga, and Pigeon rivers. PO Box 1915, Boone 28607. Phone (800) 444-RAFT, (704) 262-5774.

Nantahala Outdoor Center. Equipment sales. Guided tours: bicycling, canoeing, kayaking, rafting. Rentals. 13077 Highway 19 West, Bryson City 28713. Phone (800) 232-7238, (704) 488-2175.

Brookings. Sales of fly-fishing and canoeing equipment. Fly-fishing trips. Route 70, Box 191, Cashiers 28717. Phone (704) 743-3768.

Highland Hiker. Sales of camping, canoeing, fly-fishing, and mountain biking equipment. Canoe rentals and mountain-biking trips. US 64E and NC 107S, Cashiers 28717. Phone (704) 743-1732.

Queen's Trading Post and Outfitters. Mountain bike rentals. Sales of camping and mountain-biking equipment. Hiking and biking trips available. US 441N, Cherokee 28719. Phone (704) 497-HIKE.

Slickrock Expeditions, Inc. Backpacking, camping, and canoeing trips to Joyce Kilmer–Slickrock Wilderness, Snowbird Wilderness, Bonas Defeat Gorge, and Panthertown Valley. PO Box 1214, Cullowhee NC 28723. Phone (704) 293-3999. Call for a brochure.

Berndt's. Sales of camping, canoeing, skiing, and backpacking equipment. 117 Government Avenue SW, Hickory 28602. Phone (704) 322-1222.

Outdoor Supply Company. Sales of camping, rock-climbing, and paddling equipment. Camping and canoe rentals. 3006 N. Center Street, Hickory 28601. Phone (704) 322-2297.

Highland Hiker. Sales of camping, mountain-biking, fly-fishing, and canoeing equipment. Canoe rentals. Fly-fishing trips available. 100 E. Main Street, Highlands 28741. Phone (704) 526-5298.

French Broad Rafting Company. As the name implies, the river is the focus of this whitewater rafting company, but the company also features guided hiking trips for landlubbers and nonwhitewater canoe funyak rentals. 376 Walnut Drive, Marshall 28753. Phone (704) 649-3574.

Backcountry Outdoors. Guides available for mountain biking and rock climbing. 18 Pisgah Highway, Pisgah Forest 28768. Phone (704) 883-WILD.

Headwaters Outfitters, Inc. Sales of paddling and fly-fishing equipment. Topo maps available. Canoe and kayak rentals and sales. Canoe trips and vehicle shuttles. US 64 and NC 215, Rosman 28772. Phone (704) 877-3106.

D. National Forest Service Ranger Stations and Information Centers

Blue Ridge Parkway General Information Line, phone (704) 298-0398. Emergencies, phone (800) 729-5928.

Great Smoky Mountains National Park, National Park Service, 107 Park Headquarters Road, Gatlinburg, TN 37738. Phone (423) 436-1200. Web site: http://www.nps.gov/grsm/homepage.htm.

NANTAHALA NATIONAL FOREST

Cheoah District Ranger Station, Route 1 Box 16A, Robbinsville, NC 28771. Phone (704) 479-6431.

Highlands District Ranger Station, Route 1, Box 247, Highlands, NC 28741. Phone (704) 526-3765.

Tusquitee District Ranger Station, 201 Woodland Drive, Murphy, NC 28906. Phone (704) 837-5152.

Wayah District Ranger Station, 8 Sloan Road, Franklin, NC 28734. Phone (704) 524-6441.

PISGAH NATIONAL FOREST

French Broad District Ranger Station, PO Box 128, Hot Springs, NC 28743. Phone (704) 622-3202.

Grandfather District Ranger Station, Route 1, Box 110-A, Nebo, NC 28761. Phone (704) 652-2144

Pisgah District Ranger Station, 1001 Pisgah Highway, Pisgah Forest, NC 28768. Phone (704) 877-3350.

Toecane District Ranger Station, PO Box 128, Burnsville, NC 28714. Phone (704) 682-6146.

Forest Supervisor, North Carolina Section, PO Box 2750, Asheville, NC 28802. Phone (704) 257-4200.

E. Environmental & Outdoor Organizations

STATE ORGANIZATIONS

Friends of the Blue Ridge Parkway, PO Box 341, Arden, NC 28704. Phone (704) 687-8722.

NC Environmental Defense Fund, 2500 Blue Ridge Road, Suite 330, Raleigh, NC 27607-6454. Phone (919) 821-7793.

NC Wildlife Federation, PO Box 10626, Raleigh, NC 27605. Phone (919) 833-1923.

Pamlico–Tar River Foundation, PO Box 1854, Washington, NC 27889. Phone (919) 946-7211.

Piedmont Land Conservancy, PO Box 4025, Greensboro, NC 27404. Phone (910) 691-0088.

Save Our Rivers, Inc., PO Box 122, Franklin, NC 28744. Phone (704) 369-7877.

The Southern Appalachian Highlands Conservancy, 34 Wall Street, Suite 802, Asheville, NC 28801-2710. Phone (704) 253-0095.

NATIONAL AND GLOBAL ORGANIZATIONS

American Whitewater Affiliation, PO Box 636, Margaretville, NY 12455. Phone (914) 586-2355.

Appalachian Trail Conference, PO Box 807, Harpers Ferry, WV 25425. Phone (304) 535-6331.

Environmental Defense Fund, 259 Park Avenue S., New York, NY 10010. Phone (212) 505-2100.

The Nature Conservancy, 1815 N. Lynn Street, Arlington, VA 22209. Phone (703) 841-5300.

National Audubon Society, 700 Broadway, New York, NY 10003. Phone (212) 979-3000.

Rails-to-Trails Conservancy, 1100 17th Street, NW, 10th Floor, Washington, DC 20036. Phone (202) 331-9696.

Trout Unlimited, 1500 Wilson Boulevard, Suite 310, Arlington, VA 22209. Phone (703) 522-0200.

The Wilderness Society, 900 17th Street, NW, Washington, DC 20006. Phone (202) 833-2300.

OUTINGS CLUBS

Carolina Mountain Club, PO Box 68, Asheville, NC 28802.
Nantahala Hiking Club, 173 Carl Slagle Road, Franklin, NC 28734.
North Carolina Bartram Trail Society, PO Box 144, Scaly Mountain, NC 28775.
Western Carolina Paddlers, PO Box 8541, Asheville, NC 28814.

F. Selected Attractions

GEM MINES

Crystal Mountain Gems, PO Box 275, US 276, Cedar Mountain, NC 28718. Phone (704) 884-5499. Website: http://www.crystalmountaingems.com.
Emerald Village, PO Box 98, McKinney Mine and Crab Creek roads, Little Switzerland, NC 28749. Phone (704) 765-6463.
Gold City, 9410 Sylva Road, Franklin, NC 28734. Phone (704) 369-3905.
Nantahala Gorge Ruby Mine, PO Box 159, US 19 W, Almond, NC 28702. Phone (704) 488-3854 or (800) 245-4811.
Old Pressley Sapphire Mine, 240 Pressley Mine Road, Canton, NC 28716. Phone (704) 648-6320.
Smoky Mountain Gold and Ruby Mine, Route 1 Box 134A, US 441 N, Cherokee, NC 28719. Phone (704) 497-6574.

GEM MUSEUMS

Franklin Gem and Mineral Museum, 25 Phillips Street, Franklin, NC 28734. Phone (704) 369-7831.
Museum of North Carolina Minerals, Blue Ridge Parkway at Gillespie Gap, Milepost 331, Spruce Pine, NC 28777. Phone (704) 765-2761.
Ruby City Gems and Minerals, 44 E. Main Street, Franklin, NC 28734. Phone (704) 524-3967.

SKI AREAS IN NORTH CAROLINA

Appalachian Ski Mountain, PO Box 106, Blowing Rock, NC 28605. Phone (704) 295-7828 or (800) 322-2373.
Cataloochee Ski Area, Route 1, Box 502, Fie Top Road, Maggie Valley, NC 28751. Phone (800) 768-0285 or (704) 926-0285.
Ski Beech, 1007 Beech Mountain Parkway, Beech Mountain, NC 28604. Phone (800) 438-2093 or (704) 387-2011.
Ski Hawknest, 1800 Skyline Drive, Seven Devils, NC 28604. Phone (800) 822-HAWK or (704) 963-6561.
Ski Scaly, NC 106 S, Scaly Mountain, NC 28775. Phone (704) 526-3737.
Sugar Mountain, PO Box 369, Banner Elk, NC 28604. Phone (800) SUGAR-MT or (704) 898-4521.
Wolf Laurel Ski Area, Route 3, Box 129, Mars Hill, NC 28754. Phone (704) 689-4111 or (800) 817-4111. Website: http://www.ioa.com/home/wolflaurel.

G. Glossary

Anticline—Arching rock fold that is closed at the top and open at bottom. Oldest formation occurs in the center of an anticline.

Basement—Complex of igneous and metamorphic rock that underlies the sedimentary rocks of a region.

Biotic—Pertaining to plants and animals.

Boreal—Relating to the northern biotic area characterized by the dominance of coniferous forests.

Carbonate rock—Collective term including limestone and dolomite.

Coniferous—Describing the cone-bearing trees of the pine family; usually evergreen.

Continental drift—Theory that the continental land masses drift across the earth as the earth's plates move and interact in a process called plate tectonics.

Deciduous—Plants that shed their leaves seasonally and are leafless for part of the year.

Endemic—Having originated in and being restricted to one particular environment.

Escarpment—Cliff or steep rock face formed by faulting that separates two comparatively level land surfaces.

Extinct—No longer existing.

Extirpated—Extinct in a particular area.

Feldspar—Complex of silicates that make up bulk of the earth's crust.

Fold—Warped rock including synclines and anticlines.

Gneiss—Metamorphic granitelike rock showing layers.

Granite—Igneous rock composed predominantly of visible grains of feldspar and quartz. Used in building.

Igneous—Rock formed by cooled and hardened magma within the crust or lava on the surface.

Karst—Area of land lying over limestone and characterized by sinkholes, caves, and sinking streams.

Lava—Magma that reaches the surface of the earth.

Magma—Molten rock within the earth's crust.

Metamorphic—Rock that has been changed into present state after being subjected to heat and pressure from the crust, or chemical alteration.

Monadnock—Land that contains more erosion-resistant rock than surrounding area and therefore is higher.

Orogeny—A geologic process that results in the formation of mountain belts.

Outcrop—Exposed bedrock.

Overthrust belt—An area where older rock has been thrust over younger rock.

Rapids—Fast-moving water that flows around rocks and boulders in rivers; classified from I to VI according to degree of difficulty navigating.

Schist—Flaky, metamorphic rock containing parallel layers of minerals such as mica.

Sedimentary—Rocks formed by the accumulation of sediments (sandstone, shale) or the remains of products of animals or plants (limestone, coal).

Shale—Sedimentary rock composed of clay, mud, and silt grains that easily splits into layers.

Syncline—A rock fold shaped like a U that is closed at the bottom and open at the top. The youngest rock is at the center of a syncline.

Talus—Rock debris and boulders that accumulate at the base of a cliff.

Watershed—The area drained by a river and all its tributaries.

Index